U0735011

大学翻译学研究型系列教材

总主编　张柏然

英汉口译理论研究导引

An Introduction to Theories of Interpretation between English and Chinese

仇蓓玲　杨　焱　编　著

南京大学出版社

图书在版编目(CIP)数据

英汉口译理论研究导引 / 仇蓓玲，杨焱编著. — 南京：南京大学出版社，2012.6
大学翻译学研究型系列教材 / 张柏然总主编
ISBN 978-7-305-09833-8

Ⅰ. ①英… Ⅱ. ①仇… ②杨… Ⅲ. ①英语－口译－高等学校－教材 Ⅳ. ①H315.9

中国版本图书馆 CIP 数据核字(2012)第 068717 号

出版发行　南京大学出版社
社　　址　南京市汉口路 22 号　　　　邮　编　210093
网　　址　http://www.NjupCo.com
出 版 人　左　健
丛 书 名　大学翻译学研究型系列教材
总 主 编　张柏然
书　　名　**英汉口译理论研究导引**
编　　著　仇蓓玲　杨　焱
责任编辑　冯培培　　　　　　　　编辑热线　025-83621456
照　　排　南京南琳图文制作有限公司
印　　刷　南京市溧水秦源印务有限公司
开　　本　787×1092　1/16　印张 14.75　字数 368 千
版　　次　2012 年 6 月第 1 版　2012 年 6 月第 1 次印刷
ISBN 978-7-305-09833-8
定　　价　35.00 元
发行热线　025-83594756　83686452
电子邮箱　Press@NjupCo.com
　　　　　Sales@NjupCo.com(市场部)

大学本科翻译研究型系列读本
大学翻译学研究型系列教材

顾 问（按首字母排序）

黄国文　中山大学

廖七一　四川外国语学院

潘文国　华东师范大学

王宏印　南开大学

王克非　北京外国语大学

谢天振　上海外国语大学

许　钧　南京大学

仲伟合　广东外语外贸大学

总　序

张柏然

　　到了该为翻译学研究型系列教材说几句话的时候了。两年前的炎炎夏日,南京大学出版社责成笔者总揽主编分别针对高等院校翻译学本科生和研究生学习与研究需求的研究型系列读本和导引。俗话说,独木难撑大厦。于是,笔者便千里相邀"招旧部",网罗昔日在南大攻读翻译学博士学位的"十八罗汉"各主其事。寒来暑往,光阴荏苒,转眼两年过去了。期间,大家意气奋发,不辞辛劳,借助网络"上天",躲进书馆"入地",上下求索,查阅浩瀚的文献经典,进而调动自己的学术积累,披沙拣金,辨正证伪,博采众长,字斟句酌,终于成就了这一本本呈现在读者面前的教材。

　　众所周知,教材乃教学之本和知识之源,亦即体现课程教学理念、教学内容、教学要求,甚至教学模式的知识载体,在教学过程中起着引导教学方向、保证教学质量的作用。改革开放以来,我国各类高校组编、出版的翻译教材逐年递增。我们在中国国家图书馆网站上检索主题名含有"翻译"字段的图书,检索结果显示,1980 至 2009 年间,我国引进、出版相关著作 1800 余种,其中,翻译教材占有很大的比重。近些年来,翻译教材更是突飞猛进。根据有关学者的不完全统计,目前,我国正式出版的翻译教材共有 1000 多种。[*] 这一变化结束了我国相当长一段时间内翻译教材"一枝独秀"的境地,迎来了"百花齐放"的局面,由此也反映了我国高校翻译教学改革的深化。

　　但是,毋庸讳言,虽然教材的品种繁多,但是真正合手称便的、富有特色的教材仍属凤毛麟角。教材数量增多并不足以表明教学理念的深刻转变。其中大多都具有包打翻译学天下的纯体系冲动,并没有打破我国既往翻译教材编写从某一理论预设出发的本质主义思维模式和几大板块的框架结构。从教材建设看,我国翻译理论教材在概念陈设、模式架构、内容安排上存在着比较严重的雷同化现象。这表明,教材建设需要从根本上加以改进,而如何改则取决于我们有什么样的教学理念。

　　有鉴于此,我们组编了"大学翻译学研究型系列教材"和"大学本科翻译研究型系列读本"这两套系列教材。前者系研究生用书,它包括《中国翻译理论研究导引》、《当代西方翻译理论研究导引》、《当代西方文论与翻译研究导引》、《翻译学方法论研究导引》、《语言学与翻译研究导引》、《文学翻译研究导引》、《汉语典籍英译研究导引》、《英汉口译理论研究导引》、《语料库与翻译研究导引》和《术语翻译研究导引》等 10 册;后者则以本科生为主要读者对象,它包括《翻译概论读本》、《文化翻译读本》、《文学翻译读本》、《商务英语翻译读本》、《法律英语翻译读本》、《传媒英语翻译读本》、《科技英语翻译读本》、《英汉口译读本》、《英汉比较与翻译读本》和《翻译资源与工具读本》等 10 册。这两套教材力图综合中西译论、相关学科(如哲学、美学、文学、语

---

[*] 转引自曾剑平、林敏华:《论翻译教材的问题及编写体系》,《中国科技翻译》,2011 年 11 月。

言学、社会学、文化学、心理学、语料库翻译学等)的吸融性研究以及方法论的多层次研究,结合目前高校翻译教学和研究实践的现状进行创造性整合,编写突出问题型结构和理路的读本和导引,以满足翻译学科本科生和研究生教学与研究的需求。这是深化中国翻译学研究型教材编写与研究的一个重要课题,至今尚未引起翻译理论研究界和教材编写界的足够重视。摆在我们面前的这一课题,基本上还是一片多少有些生荒的地带。因此,我们对这一课题的研究,也就多少带有拓荒性质。这样,不仅大量纷繁的文献经典需要我们去发掘、辨别与整理,中西翻译美学思想发展演变的特点与规律需要我们去探讨,而且研究的对象、范畴和方法等问题,都需要我们进行独立的思考与确定。研究这一课题的困难也就可以想见了。然而,这一课题本身的价值和意义却又变为克服困难的巨大动力,策励着我们不揣浅陋,迎难而上,试图在翻译学研究型教材编写这块土地上,作一些力所能及的垦殖。

这两套研究型系列教材的编纂目的和编纂特色主要体现为:不以知识传授为主要目的,而是培养学生发问、好奇、探索、兴趣,即学习的主动性,逐步实现思维方式和学习方式的转变,引导学生及早进入科学研究阶段;不追求知识的完整性、系统性,突破讲授通史、通论知识的教学模式,引入探究学术问题的教学模式;引进国外教材编写理念,填补国内大学翻译学研究型教材的欠缺;所选论著具有权威性、文献性、可读性与引导性。具体而言,和传统的通史通论教材不同,这两套系列教材是以问题结构章节,这个"问题"既可以是这门课(专业方向)的主要问题,也可以是这门课某个章节的主要问题。在每个章节的安排上,则是先由"导论"说明本章的核心问题,指明获得相关知识的途径;接着,通过选文的导言,直接指向"选文"——涉及的知识面很广的范文,这样对学生的论文写作更有示范性;"选文"之后安排"延伸阅读",以拓展和深化知识;最后,通过"研究实践"或"问题与思考",提供实践方案,进行专业训练,希冀用"问题"牵引学生主动学习。这样的结构方式,突出了教材本身的问题型结构和理路,旨在建构以探索和研究为基础的教与学的人才培养模式,让年轻学子有机会接触最新成就、前沿学术和科学方法;强调通识教育、人文教育与科学教育交融,知识传授与能力培养并重,注重培养学生掌握方法,未来能够应对千变万化的翻译教学与研究的发展和需要。

笔者虽说长期从事翻译教学与研究,但对编写教材尤其是研究型教材还是个新手。这两套翻译学研究型教材之所以能够顺利出版,全有赖各册主编的精诚合作和鼎力相助,全有仗一群尽责敬业的编写和校核人员。特别值得一提的是,在这两套系列教材的最后编辑工作中,南京大学出版社外语编辑室主任董颖和责任编辑裴维维两位女士全力以赴,认真校核,一丝不苟,对保证教材的质量起了尤为重要的作用。在此谨向他(她)们致以衷心的感谢!

总而言之,编写大学翻译学研究型教材还是一项尝试性的研究工程。诚如上面所述,我们在进行这项"多少带有拓荒性质"的尝试时,犹如蹒跚学步的孩童,在这过程中留下些许尴尬,亦属在所难免。作为教材的编撰者,我们衷心希望能听到来自各方的意见和建议,以便日后再版修订,进而发展出更好更多翻译学研究型教材来。

是之为序。

二〇一二年三月二十七日
撰于沪上滴水湖畔临港别屋

前　　言

自 1972 年"翻译学科的创建宣言"——美籍荷兰学者詹姆斯·霍姆斯(James S. Holmes)的论文《翻译研究的名与实》("The Name and Nature of Translation Studies")发表至今,翻译研究无论是在西方还是在中国都逐渐发展成为一门独立的学科。作为翻译研究内部一个重要的分支,口译研究也随着口译工作的普及和繁盛逐步发展起来。在当前全球化、信息化的时代环境下,各国之间的交往日益频繁,口译工作几乎遍及了所有的社会生活领域。时代的这一特征决定了社会对口译人才的大量需求和更高要求,也给口译教学带来更严峻的挑战。研究生阶段的口译教学的基本教学目标是培养社会发展所需要的职业口译员,同时应力求提高学生的口译理论水平和研究能力,为社会输送具备一定口译理论基础的高级口译实践工作者和研究型口译人才。这一目标更直接显示研究生阶段口译理论教学的必要性和重要性。虽然口译研究本身已经从早期的零星的口译效果分析式的研究发展成为今天多学科复合性的一门学科,但是,口译理论教学中将口译视为一门独立的复合性学科的概念意识依然相当薄弱。另外,根据对相关课题的调研发现,在目前国内外市场上的口译理论教材数量相对欠缺的同时,大部分教材介绍口译理论的方式都是综述式的、点评式的,很少有启发式的、导读式的,国内更鲜有适合研究生阶段的口译理论选读教材。相比较近年来口译研究本身的跨学科蓬勃发展来说,口译理论教材和教学的发展仍处于滞后的状态。

我们知道,翻译总与所处的时代背景密不可分。翻译的观念、方法、标准、风格等,无不与时俱进。口译理论教学和教材编写理应突显翻译的这一与时俱进的特点,转变观念以适应新形势的需要。《英汉口译理论研究导引》一书正是在这样的新形势下,为进一步推动口译研究作为一门独立学科的发展,为适应目前高校研究生口译理论教学的需要而编撰。作为"大学翻译学研究型系列教材"中的一本,本教材秉承整套系列教材的编写理念,即:注重学生思维方式的训练和研究能力的培养,突出研究范例性;同时,突出口译理论研究中多元化、跨学科的相互借鉴、交流、交锋、渗透的研究模式,以口译理论的专题研究模式构造全书,介绍和吸收国内外口译研究的新成果,为学生提供具有代表性的选文作为学习范本,让学生在掌握第一手口译研究成果的同时,培养运用这些成果和理论去发现和解决口译学习以及口译实践过程中遇到的新问题的研究习惯,动态化地知晓理论、挑战理论、运用理论,而不是记忆式地了解一些口译理论名词。

本教材按照口译理论的专题研究模式共分为十一章。前两章是对口译本体论和口译史论研究的探讨。在介绍关于口译本质以及中西方口译历史研究成果的同时,更多地启发和引导读者注重口译研究的跨学科多维化视角,避免单一化地看待口译的"名与实"以及口译的发展史,为全书所遵循的多元化研究模式打下基调。第三章开始分别从语言学派、认知学派、文化学派、释意学派、心理学派、功能学派、口译语料库、口译质量评估、口译教学与培训等九个主要学科和领域对口译理论进行了专题研究。选取这九个专题的理由主要在于它们都是目前口译理论研究领域发展比较成熟的研究学派(比如释意学派口译理论研究)或者极具发展前景的新兴研究方向(比如基于口译语料库的口译理论研究)。

本教材各章均由导论、选文、延伸阅读、问题与思考四大部分构成。导论主要负责对各个专题中的口译理论研究系统地梳理,概述该专题在整个口译学科中的发展状态、贡献及前景。选文是教材中最重要的组成部分,给读者提供各专题研究中的第一手理论成果,尤其注重介绍国内外最新口译研究成果。教材中的选文均选自 20 世纪 90 年代以来有代表性、有影响的当代口译理论流派的中英文论文或理论著作,每章两篇,共计 22 篇。为更好地引导读者进入选文,每一篇选文之前都设有选文导读,或简明扼要地介绍选文的研究主题,或提出与选文主题相关的问题以启发读者边读边思考。延伸阅读则弥补了选文数量和话题上的不足,针对各个专题列出更多的文献,建议读者可以结合自己对各专题的兴趣找到相关著述作进一步研读,开拓视野。每一章最后还附有问题与思考,引导读者运用各专题理论对相关问题进行更多的思考和探索,有助于读者自身口译研究能力的培养。

本教材适于大学英语专业、翻译专业本科高年级及研究生口译课程使用,也可供广大口译工作者或口译研究者使用。本教材对于口译理论研究、口译教学和培训具有较强的基础理论意义,对于口译课程的教师、学生,以及口译从业者具有实践指导意义。

本教材在编写过程中得到了南京大学张柏然教授和南京大学出版社的大力支持,在此深表感谢。同时本教材中所引文献大部分已获得原作者的使用授权,对于因种种原因无法与原作者取得联系并获得使用授权的,我们也在此对原作者表示歉意与感谢。

由于编者水平所限,本教材错误之处在所难免,敬请广大读者和专家同仁批评指正。

仇蓓玲

2012 年 4 月于美国伊利诺伊大学香槟分校

目　　录

第一章　口译本体论研究

导　论

　　在对一切学科进行认识论研究之前,研究者都应该首先做好关于该学科的本体论研究。口译研究也同样如此。所谓本体论,广义上讲就是指"一切实在的最终本质",本体论研究就是对事物"本原"或"基质"的研究。因此,口译本体论研究就是对口译本质的研究。口译本体论研究在帮助我们更好地认识口译活动的内在规律性和特殊性的同时,更能够向人们展示和论证口译作为一门独立学科的不容忽视的地位。

　　口译本体论研究是紧随口译这项职业在国际上正式得到认可而真正开展起来的,而且近年来,随着各类交叉学科的引入,口译本体论研究的视角已经从单一化向多元化、综合性方向发展。口译本体论研究主要包括对口译概念、口译特点、口译分类、口译过程和口译标准等口译本质问题的探讨。

　　关于口译的概念,根据不同的研究视角可以有不同的界定。比较简单的定义如:口译是指"对口头表达的信息及文本进行的口头翻译"(Shuttleworth & Cowie, 1997: 82)。一般从语言学角度认为,口译(Interpreting,也称 Interpretation)是一种翻译形式,又称传译,指的是译员以口头的形式将一种语言所表达的内容忠实地用另一种语言表达出来。从交际学角度对口译进行界定比较有代表性的包括:胡庚申(2000)对口译的定义——口译是将口头表达的信息等价地从一种语言转换为另一种语言的过程,根本目的在于使交际双方或各方能即席地相互理解;以及梅德明(1996)给出的定义——口译是一种通过听取和解析原语(source language)所表达的信息,随即将其转译为目标语(target language)语言符号,进而达到传递信息之目的的言语交际活动,是人类在跨文化、跨民族交往活动中所依赖的一种基本的语言交际工具。钟述孔(1999)则从文化角度出发界定口译的概念:口译不是单纯意义上的言语行为,而是一种涉及诸多知识层面的跨文化的交际行为。释意学派则从会议口译的原理出发,认为翻译即释意,遵循三角程序,即:从讲话的有声符号出发,经过语义和认知知识融合的非语言过程,构成篇章的片断意义从而开始重新表达(Lederer, 1994)。除此之外,也有从认知角度和心理学角度对口译进行界定的,认为口译是一项高智能的思维科学形式和艺术再创造的活动,口译思维从主体上说属于抽象思维,更注重逻辑推理和分析;如果说翻译是艺术,那它离不开形象思维,离不开感知(刘和平,2001:10)。

　　关于口译的特点,国内外学者的研究内容大同小异,重点都强调口译有别于笔译,突出"准、顺、快"三大特点。有的将口译的特点归纳为即时性、动态性、达意性。有的认为口译是及时地、独立地进行的一次性(口头)翻译。相比较笔译而言,口译的突出特点包括时间上的封闭性与空间上的开放性,即席性强(Extemporaneousness)、工作压力大(Stressfulness)、独立性强(Independence)、综合性强(Comprehensiveness)、涉及的知识面宽(Miscellaneousness)。口译自身有别于笔译的特点说明口译应该享有独立学科的地位,已经有越来越多的学者通过口译本体论研究认识到这一点,他们侧重从口译的思维特点和语言特点等入手,论证口译在翻译学科中的重要地位(参见刘和平《口译理论与教学》一书)。

口译的分类按照不同的标准可以产生不同的分类情况。按其操作形式,口译可分为以下五类。(1) 交替口译(Alternating interpretation),指口译员同时以两种语言为操不同语言的交际双方进行轮回交替式口译。交替口译是最常用的一种口译形式,口译人员的业务训练一般都是从交替口译开始的。(2) 接续口译(Consecutive interpretation),指一种以句子或段落为单位为演讲者传递信息的口译方式。(3) 同声传译(Simultaneous interpretation),指口译员在说话人讲话的同时边听边译的口译方式。在这种情况下,口译员不会打断讲话者,翻译和讲话几乎是同时进行的。同声传译是一种高效率、高难度的口译形式,一般是在熟练掌握交替翻译技巧的基础上经过特殊强化训练后才能达到的境界。(4) 耳语口译(Whispering interpretation),简称耳译,指口译员把听到的讲话内容连续不断地小声传译给身边听众的翻译方式。耳译与一般同声传译的区别在于,一般意义上的同声传译主要用于国际会议和国际学术会议的大会发言,而耳译则往往只针对一两名听众,多用于小组讨论、观看文艺演出等场合。(5) 视阅口译(Sight interpretation),简称视译,指口译员以阅读的方式接收原语信息,用另一种语言直接连续不断地把所阅读的原语信息译给听众的口译方式。

按其传译方向,口译可分两种。(1) 单向口译(One-way interpretation),指口译的原语和目的语固定不变的口译,口译员通常只需将某一种语言译成另一种语言即可。(2) 双向口译(Two-way interpretation),指两种不同的语言交替成为口译原语和目的语的口译。这两种语言既是原语,又是目的语,译员在感知、解码、编码、表达时必须熟练而又快捷地转换语言。在前面所讲的五种口译操作形式中,交替口译属于双向口译的范畴;接续口译因场合不同可以表现为单向口译或双向口译;同声传译、耳语口译和视阅口译这三种形式则通常表现为单向口译。

口译按其内容和文体大致也可分为以下几种。(1) 谈判口译(Negotiation interpretation),包括商务谈判、外交谈判等口译。(2) 礼仪口译(Ceremony interpretation),包括礼宾迎送、欢迎词、告别词、宴会祝酒词、开幕词等口译。(3) 宣传口译(Information interpretation),包括观光、导游、演讲等口译。(4) 会议口译(Conference interpretation),包括各种国际会议、学术交流会等口译。

口译过程一般包括三大部分:理解、转换、表达。在整个口译过程中,第一步理解显得尤为重要,因为理解是口译员对接收的语言信息进行分析、解意、综合等加工处理而后做出正确判断的前提。理解包括语言的理解、知识的理解和逻辑的理解。口译过程的三大部分可具体再分解为信息的接收、解码、记录、编码和表达这五个阶段。口译员必须在有限的时间里同时完成听、分析、记忆和表达的任务(陈菁,2005)。具体来说,口译的基本过程表现为:输入—解译—输出;口译过程的形式表现为:原语输入—语码转换—译语输出;口译过程的内容表现为:信息感知—信息处理—信息表达。

近些年来跨学科的发展也促进了口译本体论研究者运用口译理解阶段与表达阶段中所涉及的各种跨学科理论来揭示口译活动的内在规律性和特殊性,由此带出对口译技巧和口译标准的探讨。比较有代表性的包括翻译目的论、跨文化交际学、认知心理学、心理语言学、释意学派等相关理论。

目的论(Skopos Theory)认为,口译是一项具有明确目的的跨文化交际活动,可以根据不同的文本,不同的读者对象,客户的不同要求、目的调整翻译标准,采取为达到目的的所有可能手段。在口译中,目的只有一个,即实现跨文化交际。口译的即时性、动态性的特点决定了口译的标准比笔译的标准要宽松,因此只要保持"准确"和"流利"即可。其次,口译员在口译活动中可以突显很强的主体性。目的论认为,口译员以翻译要求(Translation brief)为指导,从特殊的翻译任务中总结出目的语的交际目的,交际目的则驱使口译员决定以何种方式完成口译任务。在整个口译过程中,口译员起着积极的主导作用,掌握使用何种翻译手段达到翻译的目的。原语只是任由口译员使用的"原材料",决定目的语(面貌)的是翻译目的(Vermeer, 1996:12-15)。因此,口译员不必拘泥于原语的字词结构,而应重在达到口译的沟通传意目的。当然口译员也要负责任,在许可的范围内尽量明确自己的权限,遵守职业道德规范。口译员的主体性要受到"忠诚原则"的制约,口译员不能胡译、乱译、随意篡改原语、歪曲说话人的意图。因此,目的论认为虽然翻译目的决定了口译的手段,但口译的首要标准依然是"准确",即不能脱离说话人的宗旨。目的论还坚持语内连贯和语际连贯。也就是说,口译员译出的内容本身应该是有逻辑性的,言之成理的,能表达完整的意思,而不是支离破碎的语句;同时,口译的内容与原语应紧密相关,不可以任意发挥。

跨文化交际学(Intercultural Communication)则认为口译的一个基本特点表现为它是口头上的双语交际,"恰恰是口译的双语交际特点可以解释真正意义上的翻译交际行为"(刘和平,2005:13)。口译的交际特点决定了口译活动中要运用一定的交际策略,同时,口译活动也可以多方位地加强口译员的交际能力。交际能力是一个人运用各种可能的语言和非语言手段实现某种交际目的的能力,涉及一个人的语言知识、认知能力、文化知识、文体知识、情感因素等多种因素。在口译实践中,口译员要在瞬间独立地完成一次性翻译,没有足够的时间反复推敲,也不大可能在现场求助于他人、查阅词典或其他资料,这就要求口译员要有敏捷聪颖的头脑、扎实的语言功底、较好的汉语和英语表达能力、良好的记忆存储能力、逻辑思维能力和辨析解意能力,能够根据需要使用适当的文体和语体,还要有较广的知识面和抓重点、记笔记的能力(梅德明,1996:13)。因此,口译员不仅要把握好口译现场的交际时机,在平时的口译训练中就要不时的掌握一些可预见的场合的常用语言,同时还要具备一定的文化素养和较强的应变反应能力,以保证随时解决口译中可能出现的各类障碍。所以说,口译活动不仅表现出较强的交际特点,同时能够多方位地促进口译员交际能力的提高。

认知心理学和心理语言学理论则认为,口译是一个信息处理的过程,是一种即席性很强的语言符号转码活动,也是大脑理智地认识事物和获取知识的思维活动。口译过程是由语言信号输入—转码—表达三大环节构成的。口译第一环节中,口译员"听"的能力非常重要。听,不仅是听懂语音,更重要的是听出说话人的意图,因此,口译"思维理解"的技术是口译的一大基本功(鲍刚,1998)。口译中对说话人意图的理解就是对原语信息进行解码的过程。解码后的信息需要在很短的时间内重新编码,所以需要口译员发挥其在脱离原语语言外壳(Deverbalization)时记忆阶段中的作用。

释意学派口译理论认为(Lederer, 1994):口译不仅是听懂词语,而且是通过词语听懂说话人所说的话,然后立即用易懂的话把它表达出来。因此,口译并不是把一种语言译成另一种语言,而是理解言语,然后再用人们能够理解的方式表达出来传达给别人。口译的最终目的和任务在于它的意义传递,因此,口译员不必拘泥于原语的词语和句子结构,不应当把它们逐一译出,因为它们只是指路的信号,而不是道路本身。口译的任务是传达话语所含的信息意义,而不是把表达意义的语言转换成其他语言。在话语所传达的意义与意义借以形成的语言之间存在着根本的差别,这些差别说明言语功能并非语言功能,说明口译是一种交际行为,并非语言行为。释意理论的核心思想是,翻译的主要目的是译意,而不是原语语言外壳,翻译的对象是信息的内容,而不是语言,其主要思想是提倡在翻译中进行"文化转换"(王东风,1999:59)。释意学派学者认为,交际中人们不是对语言本身感兴趣,而是想了解对方试图表达的思想和信息,这才是交流的根本目的之所在。翻译不是简单的代码转换,翻译的目的应为传递意思,亦即交际意义;口译员所译的东西应为篇章所传达的信息内容,是言语(亦即语言的使用),而不是语言本身。口译并非基于对原语说话人语言的记忆,而是基于口译员对原语说话人所传递的交际意义的把握以及随后用译语对该交际意义进行的重组,是通过释意来传递意义,是精神代码的传递。因此,根据释意学派的理论,"是否传意"应该作为评判口译成功与否的标准,口译活动的目的应该重在把语言的潜在性变成语言的现实性,使作者所欲之言与读者揭示的意义尽量吻合,以便达到其传意的目的。

跨学科理论的广泛介入极大地丰富了人们对口译本质的认识,使得口译本体论研究越来越趋向整体化、多维化,也为口译理论研究的跨学科发展创造和拓展了空间。

选 文

选文一　口译特点决定其在翻译学中的地位
——节选自《口译理论与教学》
刘和平

导 言

任何学科的研究首先都离不开对该学科的本体论认识,口译研究同样如此。只有在对口译本质进行充分全面了解的基础上,口译研究者才可能做好这门重在实践的学问。长久以来,口译研究被视为一种实证研究,大量的研究都着眼于口译实践和口译培训本身,但事实上,随着近年来口译目的论、口译交际理论、口译认知学理论、口译信息处理理论、释意学派口译理论等跨学科理论视角的不断涌现,人们对口译本体的研究越来越关注,越来越深入,引发了对一系列相关热点问题的探讨,如口译的意义理论、认知模式、信息处理、母语译入外语等。这反映了人们不再满足于单纯的口译教学和培训,开始将目光转向口译的本质性研究,也表明了口译研究正在走向成熟。刘和平所著《口译理论与教学》首先对口译本质特征进行了论述。该书采用梳理与归纳相结合的方法,阐述和分析了口译的特点和要求,分析不同类型口译的异同,并由此引出口译理论与口译教学法的关系,同时在论述口译研究特点和回顾总结口译研究现状的基础上,融入作者对口译本体认识、口译理论的地位和口译教学领域等一些重要问题的思考。选文节选于该书中关于口译特点论述的章节,侧重于从口译的交际特点、口译的逻辑思维、形象思维、灵感思维及记忆特点、口译的语言特点等方面论述口译在翻译大学科中不可或缺的重要地位。口译区别于笔译的明显特点充分说明对口译的本体论研究可以更完整并客观地再现双语交际的本来面目,为翻译的宏观研究提供更有说服力、符合人类认知能力和水平的成果。因此,对口译的本体论研究和认识论研究,都是翻译学中不可忽视的重要组成部分。

　　按照杨自俭的划分,口译研究属于微观工程技术研究范畴,可以对其进行描述性研究。如何在翻译学的宏观框架下研究口译和口译教学,这是首先应该回答的问题。就笔译和口译实践而言,口译更具有特殊性,而这些特殊性恰恰可以帮助我们正确认识人类的翻译活动,为上一层研究提供有力和必要的证据,科学地解释和说明翻译学要解决的根本问题,即人类翻译的本质、对象和任务及其内在规律。

　　早期的口译研究处于口译实践和教学实践的经验论阶段,讨论集中在口译的口语特点、口译原则、译员应具备的条件和教学内容等层面,研究局限于思辨性和归约性。很长一段时间内,国际、国内的翻译学研究几乎都停滞在对翻译活动的静态层面描述上,对翻译的性质、对象、原则和可译性等争论不休,忽视了翻译活动的客观现实和自身规律。之所以在翻译学研究的基本问题上众说纷纭,主要原因是翻译研究大都以笔译为对象,以翻译的结果为分析素材,以语言分析为手段,强调用“语言进行思考的活动过程”,似乎翻译仅仅是把一种语言的话语转换为另一种语言的话语。有些研究人员虽然从生理和心理因素角度研究翻译,但他们仍然强调翻译的语言转换过程,忽视了翻译过程中逻辑思维活动是促使语际转换的重要因素,忽视了翻译中呈现出的复杂文化和社会现象。这类研究仍无法准确回答翻译的性质、对象和任务,因为翻译成功与否的关键是人,其智机能始终处于动态的转换过程是应该关注的核心问题。

1.2.1　口译的交际特点

　　勒代雷(Lederer)教授认为,翻译是由交际双方和两种不同语言组成的交际活动,这种交际同使用同一种语言的交际有相同之处,但也存在着诸多不同因素。另外,口译和笔译虽然都是双语交际行为,但分析和研究两者之间存在的差异可以揭示口译的特殊性,恰恰是这种特殊性会带给我们不同的思考和启示。

　　笔译和口译两种翻译形式的相同之处是:译前准备内容及方法相近,翻译的理解、抓住信息意义和表达程序相似。但两种翻译活动之间的差异也十分鲜明:笔译中译者可以随时停下来查找资料或咨询专家,可以反复斟酌语言表达的含义,并在时间和条件允许的情况下对翻译结果进行“无休止”的修改和润色。这种“马拉松”式的翻译在口译中是无法想象,也根本办不到的。口译中有声语链瞬间即逝,听不懂记不住就无法完成语言表述。笔译的结果鉴定可以文字为证,为与原文进行比较提供了便利,但读者的信息反馈相对匮乏。然而,口译结果除译员本身的自评外,还可以询问会议组织者和翻译需求者,也可以依赖录音/录像进行比较和分析。除此之外,对译文效果进行分析和研究是口译拥有的得天独厚的优势,听众的反应是即刻的,因为他们是所涉及领域的专家,如果译文出现含混不清或者出现错误,听众会立即有所表示,例如用目光询问、紧缩眉头,或示意或提问。会议组织者对每一场翻译也可以做出即时评判,因为不同语言社团双方的交际完全依赖口译。笔译则不同,作者和译者都很难了解和准确掌握读者的反应,为保证译文的准确性,译者尽可能调动自己的认知知识和语言知识,反复斟酌推敲,以保证对原文的忠实,但他对读者的反应是不可得知的,况且他的译文无需等待或根据读者的反应进行调整。由此可以说,恰恰是口译的双语交际特点可以解释真正意义上的翻译交际行为。

1.2.1.1　口译交际双方在场

笔译工作者面对的可能是几个世纪前的作品,也可以是现代作品,但完成作品的人不在场。译者和作品的关系相对稳定,换句话说,作品一经问世将不再变化,译者在翻译时根据自己的语言知识、主题知识和认知知识对一成不变的作品进行不同的阐释。然而,这种分析和阐释过程同口译过程有很大差别。口译是双语的自然交际,译员不仅直接参与交际,还同原语听众一样借助各种渠道和方式试图理解讲话人的交际意图,当场接受交际信息。译员同普通听众的差别在于,他听讲使用的是一种语言,表达使用的是另一种语言,他在听讲时不能筛选,不能分心,必须全部听懂,并借助笔记全部记忆,否则便无法用译入语重现信息内容。这种直接的、面对面的交流更具有活力,更方便信息的传递。一段讲话结束,听懂了就听懂了,听不懂就无法翻译;同声传译中,如果没有听懂或遗漏了就很难弥补。在条件允许的情况下,交替传译员可以求助于讲话人,询问或确认应该翻译的信息。通常在会议上,这种可能性不大,除非是交际双方小规模的交流。

听众双方在场对信息的理解和表达会有很大帮助,不懂可问,根据听众反应可以随时校正。在交替口译[①]实践中可以遇到这样的情况:译员翻译一段讲话后,译入语听众流露出茫然的目光。这说明传达的信息有可能不够清晰或有误,译员可以根据他们的反应或要求立即重新翻译;同声传译中也有类似的现象:下面的听众戴着耳机回头找译厢中的译员,有的时而用手指着耳朵想表达什么,通常情况下可能是翻译使用的译语传输通道发生错误⋯⋯这种双语交流同使用同一语言的交流没有本质的差别,唯一不同的是译员必须参加交际双方的交流,双方的即时反应对译员的翻译有重要作用。

1.2.1.2　交际环境和背景相对理想

口译同笔译一样,是跨语言跨文化的交际活动,而且是不同语言社团现代生活重要的交流形式,是两种思维的转换过程。在这种转换中,翻译思维会受到"客观世界(自然、社会、思维三领域)、原文作者、原文、原文读者、译者、翻译过程、译文、译文读者"(杨自俭,2000:4-7)等因素

---

① 为保证读者对文中一些关键术语理解的一致性并参照方梦之主编的《译学辞典》,文中统一使用"交替口译"(交传)代替"即席翻译"或"连续传译"。

的影响。按照认知学理论,"意义的构成不是词汇的简单叠加。因此,应该考虑人类的各种表达方式。其方式通常为三种:手势、声音和词汇"。(K. Martel,J. vivier,2003:研讨会论文待发表)交际者在交际中使用的语言、手势及音调都属于交际因素,这在交际中对信息的理解和表达有重要的作用。口译中,讲话人在场,他的表情、手势、声调、眼神等都可以成为阐释信息的必要参数,从而做到较好地理解讲话人的意思。此外,由于讲话速度非常快,译者根本没有时间一步一步分析构成篇章的语言成分,他只能借助对主题的了解及先前或刚刚获得的认识知识快速分析篇章表达的信息,对信息意义做出判断,然后用译语听众能够接受的方式合乎逻辑地、贴切地表达理解了的篇章意义。笔译则不同,同样的一段表述,有可能出现多种理解,如何确定意义的正确性成为关键。口笔译中语言上下文固然重要,但信息发出的时间、地点、环境和在场人员的情况是理解不可缺少的重要成分。由此可以看出,口译同笔译相比更具有得天独厚的交际环境。口译实践反复证明,同样的话语在不同场合可以出现截然不同的话语意义。"门!",可以指"开门!",也可以指"关门!",在只翻译能指"门",却不能实现交际目的的情况下,原语中的暗喻应该在译语中变为明喻。在国际会议上,讲话人通常使用投影仪展示要讲的内容,这对译员的理解和翻译也有帮助。有时,讲话人列举一连串数字,同传译员可以根据图片显示的内容讲其"翻译"成数字1、2、3,而不必重复这些数字。这类实例举不胜举。

同样,交际背景知识对理解也很重要。笔译中,译者可以通过翻阅资料查找完成作品的历史背景,然后通过注释对相关信息做出补充。口译则不同,无论是广义的背景,还是狭义的背景都相对完整。

President Chirac,when he was Mayor of Paris,paid same air tickets in cash.
(Lederer 教授在一次讲座中使用的例子)
……

译员可以根据现场听众的知识水平和场合将其翻译成:

……

希拉克总统在当巴黎市长时曾用现金支付机票款。
法国总统希拉克在当巴黎市长的时候曾用现金购买机票。
法兰西共和国总统希拉克任巴黎市长时曾用现金支付机票款。

当然,如果是中国的普通听众,如果他们对法国的情况不是十分了解,译员还可以在适当时机解释为什么总统用现金付款会引起媒体的关注。

同样,可以将
Children have forgotten how to eat, completely forgotten how to eat. 译成:
孩子们忘记了怎么吃饭,完全忘记怎么吃饭了。
孩子们身体十分虚弱,几乎忘记了怎么吃饭。
孩子们虚弱得连饭都不会吃了。

在口译中,上下文和主题十分清楚,交际双方和译员都在交际现场,译员会根据这些条件立即准确翻译,歧义几乎不存在。有些时候还可以通过一定的声调把握并解决信息的准确性问题。这样的操作和处理方法在笔译中有一定困难,需要不同的解决方案。

1.2.1.3 交际效果立竿见影

翻译的对象不是语言,而是语言表达的内容。这一论题看似简单,但长期以来始终是翻译研究争论的焦点之一。笔译中,由于缺乏口译具备的语境和交际环境,加上时间充裕,译者的目光可以停滞在某一个词上,一个句子可以反复阅读,甚至由于查找资料频繁停顿出现思维不同程度的中断,每一次查找完资料都要重新阅读已经阅读过的段落,有时甚至会出现每次阅读后理解都不一样的现象。口译截然相反,在特定的单元时间内要完成听辨、分析、推理、思维判断、理解和记忆等任务,认知过程和逻辑思维的结果会通过表达立刻显现出来。如果停留在语言层次,根本不可能完成理解,译员必须也只能借助所有相关知识并启动认知功能在有限的时间内完成智能机能转换的全部过程,即从用译出语听到用译入语表达,因为听众需要对话,需要立即了解讲话人的意图,讲话人也需要立即了解听众的反应,并根据交流的结果简化或深入解释要表述的内容。

应该承认,笔译中出现理解错误不易被发现,因为读者对原文"一无所知",同原文"距离"甚远,如果出现某些表达方面的错误,读者自己还可以通过反复阅读进行纠正。口译却不同,倘若理解出现偏差,表达不到位,双语交际便无法继续进行。交际中经常可以遇到以下情形:原语听众听完一段讲话后"喜"形于色,欣然点头,或"怒"形于色,表示愤慨;然而,当译员翻译结束时,译语听众如果没有出现类似的反应,讲话人会立刻对此做出如下判断:翻译出现了偏差或问题。他或是重新讲解,或是根据需要改变演讲方式,以便实现双方的沟通,达到交际的目的。1995 年一次 200 多人参加的中法商贸洽谈会上,记者就中国政府对中国经济过热采取的紧缩政策向中国代表团的领导提出问题:"您认为中国政府的紧缩政策是否会对贵市的投资开放政策带来很大影响?"这位领导的回答是:"我走访参观过欧洲的许多国家,我注意到这样一个事实,那就是去教堂参加洗礼的孩子有刚刚出生的,父母将他们抱在怀里,但也有两三岁的,甚至还有六七岁的。这是事实……"译员的逻辑思维让她很快明白了其"言外之意",为表达清楚,她在翻译最后一句话时,将陈述句翻译成反问句:"事实不是这样吗?(=木已成舟)"。翻译的话语刚落,会场上响起十分热烈的掌声。讲话的领导听到掌声后露出满意的微笑,记者的提问也转向了其他话题。这样的处理方式在笔译中似乎很难让人接受,译者可以预测读者的反应,但很难按照口译的处理方式形成文字。

对成功口译的研究可以帮助我们认识到,翻译的对象不是语言,而是语言所表达的信息。一位资深翻译说,在某些技术交流场合,你不会技术词汇都没关系,你把意思准确翻译过去,对方肯定能懂,这比你乱用技术词语反而更有效(例如,把"核反应堆堆芯"说成了"反应堆心脏")。这样讲并不是给译员的"知识漏洞"寻找借口,而是想说明,在特定时间内,信息内容比其语言形式更重要。

最近,作者同一位刚刚读完语言学博士学位的教师就翻译问题进行交谈,她的观点是:语言学已经能够解释句子与句子之间的连接问题,只要把语言段落连接解决了,篇章意义就清楚了。因此,只要把语言搞明白了,就可以进行翻译了。她的分析有一定道理,但问题是,人理解语言靠什么?靠语法?靠词汇?还是靠已获得的认知知识理解语言?我们讲母语时有多少人

是先分析语法然后才明白语言表达的意义的？由于长期以来人们对翻译的偏见,不少人在做
"翻译"时采用的都是语言分析,例如,面对一段文字,特别是面对不认识的词汇,干脆停下来查
词典,一个个单独的词查完了,再阅读文字,而字典提供的多种含义使人无所适从,可能是这个
意思,也可能是另一个意思,似乎一段文字真的会有多种意思。恰恰是这种语言层次的多义性
和个人知识的局限性使人产生错觉,认为语言一定是多义的。然而,成功的口译实践证明,连
贯地听和读能避免多义性的出现。在查找一些不认识的词之前应该首先知道作者是谁,主题
是什么,在什么情况下完成的作品,他的目标读者是谁等,然后阅读全文,至少是相关段落,接
下来才是查找词典,将语言含义限制在交际背景和上下文规定的情形中,从而减少"多义性",降
低笔译由于交际环境不明确带来的可能的歧义。总而言之,笔译的交际效果远不如口译明显。

　　当然,经过反复推敲泼墨于纸上的文字水平和译文质量某种意义上讲应该比口译高,但翻
译质量的评定标准是需要讨论的另一问题。根据何种标准评判口译质量,这涉及口译质量评
估这个十分复杂的问题,本书的 2.2.2.5 将对此进行介绍和分析。

1.2.2　口译的思维特点

　　由于前面已经陈述的原因,传统的翻译研究由于将注意的中心放在静态结果上,很少关注
翻译的动态过程,因此无法合理地解释人类双语思维活动的本来面目。应该说,人类对大脑的
研究已经取得了丰硕成果,但对双语思维转换机制还缺乏了解和实验,这给认知科学提出了新
课题。

1.2.2.1　对口译的动态过程研究

　　口译是借助认知知识听辨语言、分析、综合、推断、理解、意义产生、记忆和表达的过程。无
论是安德逊的(Anderson)程序性知识发展模式,还是他把知识的习得划分为知识编译和协调
程序,以及认知学习和能力发展模式,或是吉尔(D. Gile)的精力分配模式,都从不同角度分析
了口译过程的各个活动环节,指出认知知识自动化处理的可能性和范围。综合几类不同的模
式,根据口译的特点,蔡小红提出了交替口译过程模式(2001:26-29)。该模式有三大块组成:
左边是原语,右边是译语,中间最高处连接左右两边的是信息概念的转换。交替口译全过程
包括:
　　A. 信息源的输入;
　　B. 处理环节包括理解阶段的辨认有声的输入、分析及综合机制,产出阶段的形式合成机
制和发声机制;
　　C. 记忆部分主要由概念形成机制组成,其任务一是把发言人的话语变为自己的交际意
图,二是据此拟定话语计划,综合机制也部分承担记忆任务;
　　D. 储存部分主要指长期记忆,包括与输入、输出、内部监控相联结的心理词。
　　这些模式表明,口译过程始终处于动态中,借助认知知识和主题知识对语言进行阐释和理
解实际上是进行逻辑推理和分析,这种推理和分析绝对不是对语言的简单辨识,而是了解语言
承载的信息意义。边听边分析,边分析边记忆,记忆后是表述,同声传译为记忆的同时开始表
述。在这个过程中,译员的注意力是分散的。有些理论家认为,人类具有在不受干扰的情况下
可以同时顺利完成两种复杂任务的能力。这些理论家支持多种特异性加工资源的观点,认为

如果两个任务分别利用不同的加工资源,那么任务之间应该不存在干扰(M. W. 艾森克,M. T. 基恩著,2002:199)。因此,译员理解过程中的信息加工并没有超出人的正常能力。但必须指出的是,译员在理解后存储的内容不是语言,而是信息意义。实际上,意义的形成过程也是表述动机生成的过程,没有表述动机,表达将是不可能的,这是语言交际的客观规律。"意在笔先"讲的正是这样的道理。

法国巴黎高等翻译学校创建的释意理论是最早对口译的动态过程进行研究的学派。20世纪60年代当语言学占绝对地位的时候,该派创始人塞莱斯科维奇(Seleskovitch)便发出了不同的声音,引起了许多语言学家的质疑。由于该派理论在口译研究中有举足轻重的地位,我们将在后面作专门介绍。

1.2.2.2 口译的逻辑思维、形象思维、灵感思维及记忆特点

对口译过程的研究将传统的对翻译的静态研究带入了动态研究,它对我们更好地认识人类翻译活动并推动翻译研究向跨学科和科学化道路的发展很有帮助。但如果想科学地解释口译的智机能转换过程,恐怕还需要神经学、认知学及信息学专家的参与。目前世界上已有认知心理学专家对口译的认知行为感兴趣,例如法国卡昂大学认知研究中心主任魏威(J. Vivier)和他的美国博士生马尔泰(K. Martel)。他们的研究领域是国际会议翻译,研究课题是讲话人的手势在译员理解和表达中的作用。他们对数场翻译进行录像,剪接所有出现手势的片段,对照相关的原语和译文进行分析。初步研究结果证明,国际会议译员在听讲话人的信息时处于"全方位"接受和分析信息状态,手势是语言外直接影响信息意义的重要因素之一,对译员的思维和分析有重要意义。

如果想解释译员的思维特点,首先要定义什么是思维。思维指在表象、概念的基础上进行分析、综合、判断、推理等认识活动的过程。思维活动在翻译过程的心理机制中占有中心的、主导的位置。思维活动的规律及其内容制约着翻译活动的全过程。思维内容指思维主体在思维活动中加工、处理的一切信息和知识。思维内容决定于思维主体在社会实践中所接触的思维对象(《译学辞典》,2004:256-257,267)。口译交际行为不同于单一语言的口语交际。首先,参与交际的译者既是信息的被动接收人,也是信息的主动发布者。具有双重作用的译者在听辨信息时不允许任何懈怠或带有偏见,他必须听懂全部内容,绝不能凭个人的好恶取舍信息;在表达时更不能掺杂任何个人的观点,他必须忠实地将信息用另一语言加以表达。用一种语言接受信息,用不同的语言表达同一信息是翻译交际行为的突出特点。研究口译的信息接收和发布可以发现,口译中抽象思维和形象思维有其明显特点。"尽管'人为什么能够理解'在相当长的时间内仍会是秘密,但'人如何理解'或理解的逻辑——其法则或规律背景——则可以被揭示。""语言研究显示,一个人思维的形式受制于他没有意识的固定的模式规律。"(本杰明·李·沃尔夫,2001:241,255)

● 口译逻辑思维的重要性

逻辑思维也称抽象思维,即运用逻辑工具对思维内容进行抽象和推演的思维活动。逻辑思维的特点是:对象纯粹化、映像清晰化、涵义一般化,三点的综合被称为对象抽象化(《译学词典》,267)。学外语的人可以有这样的体会,听完一段话后,脑子里剩下的是断断续续的单词,每句话似乎都听了,但是意义没有产生,一片空白,似是而非。其主要原因在于:A. 语言水平不足(这不在此文讨论的范畴);B. 没有启动相关知识理解语言表达的内容;C. 缺乏逻辑分析

和推理,过于被动地听;D. 即使听懂了,没有将信息真正记忆储存在大脑中。在翻译讲话或文章的时候,首先应该清楚讲话者是谁,主题是什么,讲话特点是什么,其内在的逻辑关系是什么,要在听的时候有意识地记忆。在正常交往中,讲话人总要实现某种目的,不了解这些因素,便有可能出现分析及推断等方面的逻辑思维混乱。在翻译论述性讲话时,译者的逻辑思维能力尤为重要,抓不住讲话者的思路,翻译出来的东西必然支离破碎,很难实现交际目的。论述类讲话由若干部分组成,每一部分可能又由几个部分构成,论点和论据、顺序和逻辑关系、结论等都应该是记忆的内容。在 2004 年暑期《中国翻译》编辑部组织的口译教学法培训中,一位教师听完一段讲话后自认为理解了,也记住了,但重新表达的时候却全忘了。她反复对老师说:"我真的记了,但就是说的时候不知道怎么全忘了。"对这种问题的初步诊断应该是:听的同时没有对听的内容进行逻辑分析,由于听到的"声音"几乎都是词汇,译员没有从"声音"中提炼出彼此间存在的内在信息逻辑关系,更没有有意识地记忆信息的内容,最终造成在翻译的时候只能说听到了某些词,脑子里一片"空白"。

译员对有声语链是如何进行逻辑分析的? 有这样一段讲话,主题是"环保关系到经济的可持续发展,更关系到子孙后代的未来"。从题目看,讲话的逻辑关系是:环保与经济的关系,目前经济的发展与可持续发展的关系,可持续发展与未来的关系,未来生活和工作环境对子孙后代生存的重要性。对于译员来说,翻译前抓住讲话的这种逻辑关系对跟踪讲话的内容和顺序很重要,即使讲话人在演讲过程中有这样或那样的"插曲",但讲话会"万变不离其宗"。

在交替传译中,译员的逻辑分析还可以透过口译笔记体现。下面的笔记是一家公司总经理在年会讲话开头部分的记录,讲话大约 2 分钟:

好!

代表……感谢

讲四点

现状
文体
措施
计划

依靠笔记的提示,译员便能非常有逻辑地回忆起讲话的每一个具体内容,最终完成完整的口译。这是因为,译员记忆的信息与先前的知识有联系,信息线索与信息一起被贮存在大脑中。译员拥有超常记忆是很多人的看法,这种看法有一定的道理,但也有偏见,后面我们还会专门讨论口译记忆问题。

● **口译形象思维的重要性**

以形象为主要手段的思维活动为形象思维。形象思维包括以下方面:A. 把握对象的形象特征来识别对象,不仅识别对象的表层,而且识别对象的本质;B. 把握对象的形象联系来理解、推断对象;C. 把握对象形象的景貌、神情来描述对象,包括艺术文学的描述和科学技术的描述;D. 把握对象形象的构图来控制人对对象的操作活动,包括已有形象的复制操作和未有形象的创造。形象思维是人的基本思维活动之一。(《译学词典》,264)

无论是文学翻译,还是一般性讲话的翻译,译者的形象思维能力是不可缺少的。"十指如葱"在汉语中可以用来描述窈窕淑女纤细美丽的手指,产生美学效果,但在有些西方语言中却不能产生类似的效果,甚至效果大相径庭,理由是他们食用的常常是我们所说的"鸡腿葱"。同样,描述西方的山村或乡下生活,也需要译者具备与本土人相同的文化背景知识,脑海中呈现必要的形象,否则翻译出来的内容会出现偏差。中国人现在谈到山村时恐怕还有不少人将其与"落后"和"贫穷"联系在一起,还没有西方人"享受或回归大自然"的那种感受。况且,无论是逻辑思维还是形象思维在口译中都有助于译者的概念化和记忆存储,大大提高表述的质量。例如厂家在介绍产品特性时通常是先从外形特征谈起,然后谈其技术和使用特点,最后是价格问题。如果能在听讲时将听到的信息或情景形象化,会有助于讲话的翻译。中国人由于汉语象形文字特点,形象记忆能力相对较强,开发使用好这一特点对口译非常有益。口译人员接触描述性讲话的机会很多,可以描述一个人的特征,一个产品的特征和特性,一个地方的特征等。这些描述性讲话也常常需要形象思维能力的发挥。

● 口译灵感思维的重要性

灵感思维是人类已发现的三种基本思维类型之一。灵感是借助直觉和潜意识活动而实现的认知和创造。灵感思维过程是有意识发动的被意识到的思维活动,亦即显思维活动。灵感思维过程是思维活动转化为显思维活动的过程。潜思维内容被意识到并转化为显思维内容的过程,就是灵感的出现。灵感是三维的,它与抽象思维、形象思维有不同的特征:突发性、偶然性、独创性和模糊性(《译学词典》,265)。如果文学翻译需要译者的灵感,口译也不例外。由于时间的限制,译者听完讲话必须立刻表述听懂的内容,这种即刻表述很大程度上是对译者灵感的考验,没有灵感,翻译出来的内容有可能显得僵硬、死板,或者拘泥于语言形式;相反,灵感会使译文生辉。口译中灵感的产生还依赖其他因素,如果译员事先所做的主题准备非常充分,休息充足,灵感的产生便有可能。要说明的是,口译中的灵感不是灵机一动,它受到许多交际因素的限制和影响,换句话说,大量的练习和实践是"灵机一动"的前提条件和保证之一。尤其是遇到诗句、固定词组、比喻、文化差异等问题时,灵感是灵活处理的前提条件之一。如果用中文说一个人"瘦得像钉子",虽然中国人能接受,但不是常见说法,不如用"瘦得像猴子",这里不单单是固定词组的翻译问题,因为在笔译中译者有相对充足的时间思考,从而选择更恰当的译文;口译中可以根据自己的水平和当时的情况将其翻译成"瘦瘦的","很瘦","瘦得像钉子","苗条"或者"纤细"。中文讲一个人由于病重"卧床不起",法语中可以用"钉"在床上。这里只是一个简单的比喻,在职业翻译中遇到的需要灵感的情况远比这些要复杂得多。

● 口译记忆的特点

我们说,不应该排除译员中有记忆超常的人,但绝大部分人并非具有超人的记忆力。他们的记忆,或者说记忆技能满足了艾利逊(Ericsson, 1988)提出的以下三个条件:

> "——意义编码(meaning encoding):信息应该在意义层次上加工,把信息与贮存的知识联系起来;这与加工水平理论类似。
> ——提取结构(retrieval structure):线索应该与信息一起贮存以利于其后的提取;这与编码特异性原则类似。
> ——加速(speed up):广泛练习以使编码和提取所涉及的加工过程越来越快;这就可以导致自动化。"

有些人认为有译员有超常记忆,那么学者对记忆的研究结果又是什么?是否存在超常记忆?看似记忆超常的人的记忆方式如何?艾利逊和肯舒(Kintsch)(1995:216)认为,特殊记忆能力依赖于所贮存的知识而不是一个加大的工作记忆容量。根据他们的观点,拥有特殊记忆才能的关键要素是："被试者必须把编码信息与恰当的提取线索联系起来。这种联系允许被试者以后能激活某一特定的提取线索,从而部分恢复了编码时的条件以便从长时记忆中提取合乎要求的信息。"(《认知心理学》,349)艾利逊和肯舒发展的关于以上三个超常记忆的模式说明,意义编码是译员具有"超常记忆能力"的基础,特殊的提取结构和提取速度是意义"超常"记忆的保证。职业译员听的是信息,储存的是经过大脑加工的意义线索,且这些意义相互联系,相互依赖,笔记对他们来讲只是帮助激活线索的手段之一。由于他们通常接受过专门的训练,信息提取的速度是非常快的,换句话说,他们的反应速度比一般的听众要快,况且,对信息的"特殊关注"(注意力的高度集中)让他们能提高对信息的加工速度,从而保证在短时间内将以一种语言理解的信息用另一语言加以表达。应该说,译员的逻辑思维、形象思维和灵感思维能力是记忆的基础和保证。很显然,对记忆的分析不仅进一步否认了翻译是单纯语言转换的说法,而且对口译教学中的记忆训练提出了明确的要求。

1.2.2.3 语言与篇章

为什么在分析口译的时候要讨论语言和篇章问题呢?上面介绍的口译的特殊性可以帮助我们认识语言与篇章的真正关系。如何解释语言的多义性和篇章意义的单一性?语言同由语言构成的篇章有何区别?为何译者对主题的认识了解有利于对篇章意义的理解?为何讲话的频率对理解信息意义十分重要?表达使用的词汇和作者意图有何差别?塞莱斯科维奇和勒代雷教授在《口译推理教学法》(Pédagogie raisonnée de l'interpétation)第七章中提出了以上语言学没有能够回答的问题。近些年,许多翻译研究人员坚持不懈地探索,利用"它山之石"攻翻译学之"玉",采用科学方法论对以上问题分别做出了自己的回答。

这里,应该首先回答的一个问题是:篇章与构成篇章的语言有何差别?语言的社会属性确定了同一语言集团的人对该语言的能指、所指和所指对象有基本一致的理解;然而,篇章具有个性特点,会由于讲话人的社会地位、受教育程度、修养等因素千差万别。在交替口译中,当译者听到一连串的有声语链后,他要立即启动相关的语言知识、主题知识和认知知识,努力捕捉原语表达的信息,并记忆下来,然后用符合译入语规则的方法表达这一信息。时间不允许译者切分句子,也不允许他反复斟酌和思考,他必须当机立断,抓住语链表达的意义。同声传译更是如此,一句话没有听懂,或停留在个别数字、单词的反应上,下面的话语就会悄然溜走,造成意义的短路或遗漏。当然,口译中交流者双方均在场,交流环境对译员的理解更有利。笔译中,眼睛停留在文字上的时间稍长,字词便有可能出现多义性,况且译者拥有相对充裕的时间作语言分析(语法、句法、词汇等),他还可以反复阅读,或查找资料,或询问专家,甚至可以在没有完全理解篇章意义的时候借助词典翻译理解单词和句子。正是在这种条件下,语言翻译的可能性加大,意义翻译退居二线。相比较而言,口译的时间限制为摆脱语言多义性提供了良好的客观条件,无论译员的理解对与错,篇章意义通常是单一的,同一时间内一句话不可能出现多种含义,即使由于种种原因偶尔出现,译员也不可能将几种可能性都翻译给听众,因为他既无时间仔细斟酌,也不可能把意义的选择权留给不懂译出语的听众,在场听众只能根据译员的翻译寻找自己能够理解的逻辑性。如前所述,篇章意义绝对不是单词含义的叠加结果,而是由语言加译者的语言外知识构成的,意义的形成和重新表达完全依赖译者的智机能转换。

口译研究成果表明,翻译不是语言的简单转换,翻译也是交际行为,是使用两种不同语言进行的交际活动。翻译的对象是信息意义,语言只是信息意义的一个载体,交际环境、交际背景、交际人等都会影响信息的意义。更重要的是,用一种语言表述的信息必须通过译员大脑的复杂思维活动才能传输给译入语听众,整个交际过程始终处于动态中。

综上所述,职业口译同笔译相比具有明显的特殊性,因此,对口译的研究可更完整并客观地再现双语交际的本来面目,为翻译的宏观研究提供更有说服力、符合人类认知能力和水平的成果。无论是对口译的微观技术工程研究,还是宏观描述,或是随着科学技术的发展对口译的跨学科实证研究,都是翻译学不可忽视的重要组成部分,换句话说,对口译研究的客观性、深入程度和科学性都会大大推动翻译学宏观研究的发展和进步。

选文二 打开口译理论的大门
——评介刘宓庆的《口笔译理论研究》

夏伟兰 文 军

导 言

相对于笔译研究而言,我国的口译研究一度处于落后的状态,甚至有些研究者还鼓吹"口译无理论"。这种状况在很大程度上是因对口译本体缺乏全面多元化的认识所造成的。刘宓庆所著的《口笔译理论研究》一书为口译研究者打开了一扇通往口译本体认识的大门。该书侧重对口译进行了整体化、多维化的研究,主要借助于维根斯坦的语言观(即"语言游戏"论)和理论思想,同时运用语用学、传播学、符号学和认知科学的理论,按照"特征描写—机制描写—实施描写—效果描写"的程序模式展开对口译理论的探讨,着眼于强化口译跨语言文化的社会传播功能,集中探讨了话语结构、话语意义、话语效果和话语机制四个核心问题。该书有助于提高口译研究者对口译的本体认识,为口译本体论研究开拓了一个全新的多元化的格局。正如该书作者所述:"20世纪的科技发展使人们看到了前所未有广阔视野。研究的跨学科性日益为人们所认识,尤其是翻译学这类综合性极强的学科,我们必须十分关注以整体观来对它加以关照,不放过任何一个学科视角对它的审视。开放性应是21世纪翻译研究的重要特色。"因此,该书给口译研究者最大的启示就在于对口译的本体论研究应打破传统的一元化束缚,采用多维的、跨学科的视角。选文对该书进行了较为全面和中肯的评介。

如今翻译已经步入了前所未有的高潮。翻译实践、翻译理论的研究逐渐增多,各种翻译理论的书籍开始丰富翻译领域。近几年来口译市场也急剧扩大,口译人员与日俱增。而我国对于口译的研究,一直远远落后于对笔译的研究。1996年以前中国当代发表的翻译研究文章约2 500篇,据统计,其中研究口译的不足50篇,即不足2‰(黎难秋,2002)。这与口译发展的态势不相符合。2004年1月由中国对外翻译出版公司出版的刘宓庆编著的《口笔译理论研究》

从口译理论依据、认识论、对策论和方法论等各方面出发,回顾并展望了口译的发展,为口译理论的研究和发展提供了很好的范本。该书作为"翻译理论与实务丛书"之一,把口译纳入了翻译学不可或缺的一部分,使口译研究和发展又前进了一步。

全书除去引论部分共六章,大致可分为三部分,第一、二章讨论了口译理论与一般翻译理论比较存在的特殊性;第三章到第五章具体介绍了口译的认识论、对策论和方法论;第六章回顾、展望了口译的发展。不难看出,该书介绍的重点是口译理论,虽然书名为《口笔译理论研究》,笔译只是与口译进行对比。

引论提出了口译的基本概念,并指出口译与其他学科之间的密切关系:如语言学中的语言结构、功能和语言心理;符号学中语言符号的意指;传播学中的效果论、价值论、表现论和方法论;认知科学中的言语生成、语言转换等机制问题。这四门学科构成了口译理论的四个维度:结构、意义、效果和认知机制。本书各章就是围绕口译与这四门学科之间的关系集中探讨话语结构、话语意义、话语效果和话语机制四个核心问题的。

该书结构清晰,每章都遵循相同的编排模式。每章采用总—分—总的形式,先概论本章所讲内容,引导读者,使他们对本章内容有一大概印象,然后一一展开,深入浅出地进行详细叙述,最后结语总结全章,让读者加深印象。这种编排方式有利于读者理清思路,从而宏观把握全书。

首章开篇论述了维根斯坦的语言观与翻译。维根斯坦认为翻译是一种"语言游戏",在语言游戏中,游戏规则至关重要,运用到口译中也是如此。维根斯坦还认为意义在于使用,所谓"意义即使用"(meaning is use),而"生活形式"(forms of life)是意义"使用"的基本依据,也是语言游戏最高最基本的规则。因此在口译中,有一条最基本的法则——重视语境。维根斯坦的理论奠定了全书的基础,为以后的论述作了铺垫,这种思想贯穿在全书中。第二章总述了口译作为一种特殊形式的翻译传播行为,与传播学、认知心理学、认知语言学的密切关系以后,对口译特征问题进行了具体的探讨:1. 操控权的转移。口译员作为媒介,是互相不通语言的A、B两方交流得以进行的工具。口译员处在A、B之间,既需要与A合作,又需要与B合作,是A、B合作得以实现的实际操控者。因此口译最重要的特征是交流操控权的转移(shift of manipulative power)。2. 口译"语言游戏"的"在场"和"不在场"。在口译"游戏"中,口译员必须既要把握A和B的在场性,还要了解A、B所处的历史语境和现实语境,从而把握他们的不在场性。3. 当下性。口译的一个重要特征是当下性,即要求译者在当场进行语言转换交流,不容延宕,这给口译员提出了很高的要求。根据认知心理学家威克尔格伦(W. A. Wickelgren)的Speed-Accuracy Trade-off实验图,作者得出要求口译员2～3秒的当下性是合适的。4. 口译传播中的语境化特征。口译是特定语境下特定的翻译传播行为,特定语境赋予了特定的意义。维根斯坦说过,意义取决于使用,"使用"意味着语境;意义具有"不确定性"和"游移性",只有语境才能将特定的意义固定下来;语境使语言的意向性更加明确。5. 听觉意义解码功能的前沿化。在口译中,听觉处于前沿地位,译者首先通过听觉来进行翻译。所以听力好的译者在口译工作中具有优势。

第二部分论述口译中的认识论、对策论和方法论。

第三章,"口译传播的认知论证"。口译不是简单的"刺激—反应"过程,和大脑语言功能区域的发挥作用是密切一致的,因此认知科学的发展为解开口译的秘密提供了依据:1. 在口译中,听觉处于前沿地位,听觉感知接收到语音符码,进入理解过程。认知心理学家A. W. 艾利斯和A. W.杨(A. W. Ellis and A. W. Young)通过实验提出了听觉认知模式。根据此模式，"听"的理解—表达过程也就是"口译"的理解—表达过程。2. 口译反应论为口译要求的"当下性"提供了参考依据。反应时间受个人差异及外界因素的影响较大，又往往与表达式选择成正比。习惯性反应是在认知过程中积累的"经验的成果"。皮尔士的反应论的本能—经验—习惯的过程，以及延展、归纳和演绎的认知程序论是习惯性反应的理论依据。3. 口译中非言语意义解码的认知论证。口译中非言语形态的存在使口译变得更复杂，而认知系统可以整合暗含意义、语音变式、面部表情和体态表情这些听觉和视觉中的意义。4. 同声传译的认知剖析。同声传译的基本"游戏规则"有：后起跟踪、化整为零和一心三用。在同声传译中，认知系统运作使"一心三用"成为可能，口译员边听边想边说。5. 口译理解理论的认知论证。作者提出了口译中的三个能力，即感应能力、关联能力和推理-判断能力并详细论述了关联能力，其中包括符号与意义的关联、符号与语境的关联和文化关联。6. 口译中记忆的认知分析。认知科学家认为记忆有三个系统，即感觉贮存、短时贮存和长时贮存。在口译记忆中，注意是前提，理解是条件，"记忆保持"不是恒久不变的。记忆还受制于心理压力，压力越大记忆效果越差。认知学使翻译摆脱传统的形式主义、机械主义、经验主义和虚无主义，走上学科建设的科学化道路，开拓了翻译学研究的新领域。

第四章是"口译的对策论"。1. 口译的基本策略：解释。对专名、缩略词、专用词组或搭配，隐语、成语、典故和俚俗语、文化词语等，口译员必须做出解释，在解释时，口译员有充分的酌情权和自由度，主要从语源、意义、形式、文化、效果和审美六个维度来审视。2. "对应"是一个范畴。维根斯坦提出"家族相似"，而不是对等、等同、等值和等效，因为人类使用的语言是"范畴化了的语言"，所以在口译中，可以只要求"对应"，而且可以是扩大了幅度和容限的对应。3. 形式的功能观。形式是内容的外壳，我们要通过形式来把握意义。形式具有双重意义，即认识论和本体论意义。认识论意义产生于形式结构分析，其中包括形式分析、形态分析和形式逻辑分析。另外，形式本身也具有意义。4. 口译中的"原语效应"(SL effect)问题。在语言转换时，语言之间必定存在相似性，原语必定会影响目标语翻译的进行。因此在特定时空限制下，原语的积极作用不可忽视。5. 口译中的文化翻译对策。口译行为是一种跨语言的解释行为，而文化翻译是关于文化的跨语言解释行为。由于深层的语言文化心理、语言文化历史背景和文化传统，操不同语言的人对同一事件、在同一场合、为同一目的所说的话千差万别。面对差异，口译员只有顺应，因势利导地将原语顺顺畅畅地解释到译语中。6. 口译中的推理策略。为准确地理解话语，我们需要对SL进行合理推理。翻译的推理集中于准确把握意义和意向，主要为跨文化性和语言性。7. 口译心理调控对策。心理压力会干扰注意的稳定性，因此需要减压。从本章中我们可以从认知的角度知道必须提高口译员的能力和加强各方面的学习。

第五章谈论方法论，即"表现论"。清晰、简要和实事求是是口译表现法的基本原则，为达到这些原则，口译时有以下方法可供使用：1. 阐释或疏解；2. 同步或伴随VS分切或拆译；3. 明说与暗说VS直接与间接；4. 增与删VS繁与简；5. 融合与提炼。

全书的最后一章对翻译进行了回顾与展望。翻译研究的全部理论包括五个范畴：本体论、认识论、应用理论研究、效果论和价值论。在五个范畴下，还包括许多学科，翻译与其他学科的交叉发展使翻译获得了全新的生命。为打造多维化、整体化的研究格局，作者提出要革新观念、革新方式和突破窠臼，同时要求改革翻译学的研究方法，从单一的论证手段过渡到多方法论证，向传播学和现代科技方法借鉴学习，走跨学科的道路。为发展翻译事业，作者还提出要建立翻译研究"孵化中心"和统筹中心,最后,作者展望了翻译的发展前景,指出翻译是永远不会消失的。

内容环环相扣,前呼后应。全书内容以维根斯坦的理论为基础,并以话语结构、话语意义、话语效果和话语机制为核心问题展开论述。作者在第一章中提到口译与笔译一个突出的"非相似性"是口译与传播学密切相关(P24),口译作为一种特殊形式的翻译传播行为,与传播学密切相关,这就涉及了第二章中传播学的内容。作者在概述中讨论、比较了拉斯威尔(H. D. Lasswell)的传播程序和笔译传播程序,得出口译的运作流程与传播程序相似的结论,从而把传播学和口译结合起来,将传播理论应用到口译理论领域。Anderson 则把语言生成的三段式认知程序模式应用到翻译中,使口译的语言生成程序有了认知依据。维根斯坦认为的相似性(resemblance)使认知语言学家提出了"范畴与原型理论"(Prototypes and Categories),并引证了拉波夫(W. Labov)的"器皿系列实验",从而把认知语言学与口译联系起来,使口译理论的发展进入了新的领域。

第二章"口译是一种特殊形式的翻译传播行为"中谈到在特定的语境中,语言有特定的意向性,如何做到"意向翻译"(P70)以及口译中谈话含义模糊度的弱化和信息含量的强化涉及口译的技巧问题(P80),这些都涉及第四章的"对策论"。口译中,我们可以只要求"对应",而且可以是扩大了幅度和容限的对应。这个扩大了的幅度和容限的对应绝不是随意的,第一层级是基本对应,把概念看做一个范畴;第二层级是关联对应,语境可以帮助我们选择一个最适境的词;第三个层级是类属对应;第四个层级是功能对应,意向翻译使双语中的功能得到同样的发挥;最后一个层级是"零对应",主要通过音译来达到契合。隐喻翻译的对策论思考。隐喻是从概念思维切入形象思维的一种认知思维方式,在翻译中不存在无法翻译的"零对应"现象。

第三章"口译传播的认知论证"中谈到语用学和传播学中意义和意向的整合问题(P142),口译怎么对待文化问题时(P160),以及口译中判断和推理对策的使用(P161)都涉及了下面几章的对策论和表现论。诸如此类,本书俯拾皆是,在此不一一枚举。

作者还驳斥了"口译无理论",使口译理论研究又向前迈出了一步。自从不同民族不同国家之间发生交往开始,就发生了口译活动,而笔译活动只是在人类发明文字以后相互交往的产物,因而口译的历史远比笔译的历史悠久。然而对口译的研究却一直远远落后于对笔译的研究,而且以口译实践、口译技巧为重,对口译理论的研究更少。从 1952 年瑞士赫贝尔第一本口译手册的出版,到 1968 年法国塞莱斯科维奇第一本口译专著的问世,从 1958 年北京大学东语系日本语教研室编辑出版《中日口译手册》,到 1998 年鲍刚第一本口译理论专著的出版,口译理论和研究经历了半个多世纪的漫长艰难岁月,也取得了令人欣慰的初步成果,为下一步的发展奠定了良好的基础(鲍刚,2005)。我国翻译研究中翻译研究的理论意识已经觉醒(谢天振,2001),《口笔译理论研究》的出版,意味着口译理论的研究又向前迈出一步。

本书难免有瑕疵,存在一些不足之处:

1. 本书貌似口笔译理论研究,但此书通篇讲的都是如何口译,很少论及笔译,提到时也是为口译服务,与口译进行对比,并没有笔译理论研究。

2. 该书在印刷和编辑过程中有不少小错。如把影响口译当下性的四项因素说成五种(P64)。"口译的对策论"应为第四章,而在第二章中却误写成"第三章"(P74);在吉尔福特(J. P. Guilford)的智力(资质)三维结构形态图中,思考结果应有 6 项,而在图中只有 5 项,与下面的解释不符(P106);而在回顾和展望翻译史时,作者指出了要打造多维化、整体化研究格局的四个方面,在实际中却只提出了三个方面。我们希望以上这些印刷错误在将来再版时能得到订正。

　　总而言之,本书分析透彻,逻辑严密,对口译理论进行了有益的探索,对研究口译理论具有很大的启发意义。对有志于本领域的学者,这是一本不可多得的好书。

【延伸阅读】

1. Cranefield, Jocelyn & Yoong, Pak. The role of the translator/interpreter in knowledge transfer environments. *Knowledge and Process Management*. 2007,14（2）:95-103.

2. Pöchhacker, F. *Introducing interpreting studies*. London:Routledge,2004.

3. Shuttleworth, Mark & Cowie, M. *Dictionary of Translation Studies*. Michigan:St. Jerome. Pub,1997.

4. 白枚. 口译的特点及标准. 大连民族学院学报.2005(1):14-18.

5. 鲍刚. 口译理论概述. 北京:旅游教育出版社,1998.

6. 蒋凤霞,吴湛. 口译的跨学科理论概述. 外国语文.2011,27(2):79-84.

7. 刘和平. 口译理论与教学. 北京:中国对外翻译出版公司,2005.

8. 刘宓庆. 口笔译理论研究. 北京:中国对外翻译出版公司,2006.

9. 王东风. 中国译学研究:世纪末的思考. 中国翻译.1999(2):7-11.

10. 王永秋. 论口译的特点. 长春大学学报.1996(1):47-49.

11. 钟述孔. 实用口译手册. 北京:中国对外翻译出版公司,1999.

【问题与思考】

1. 口译的思维特点主要体现在哪几个层面?

2. 应该如何看待口译和笔译的关系?

3. 口译的跨学科性决定了口译本体论研究应采用多维的视角,那么口译的本体论研究究竟应如何体现口译的跨学科性特点? 试从口译目的论、口译交际理论、口译认知学理论、口译信息处理理论、释意学派口译理论等几方面分别加以阐述。

4. 为什么说口译的特点决定了其在翻译学科中的地位?

5. 你同意"口译无理论"的观点吗? 为什么?

第二章　口译史论研究

导　论

　　口译活动伴随着人类各民族相互交流的需要而产生和发展起来,其最远历史可以上溯到人类各种语言逐渐形成后的时期。从这个意义上讲,口译的历史比笔译的历史久远得多,但是口译活动在历史上的记载其少,而口译作为一门学科被加以专门研究也起步较晚。哥伦布发现新大陆后曾将大量印第安人运到西班牙学习西班牙语,并将他们培养成口译员。明清时期中国的一些小说中对口译员有了正式的称呼——"通事"。第一次世界大战之后,各个国家之间的交往日益频繁,口译员的需求急剧增加,而口译作为一项在国际上被认可的职业就始于第一次世界大战之后的"巴黎和会"。1919 年的"巴黎和会"首次打破了法语在国际会议和外交谈判中的垄断地位,借助英法两种语言的口译进行谈判。当时的口译方式主要是发言人讲一段,口译员翻译一段,即"交替传译",也可称"连续口译"或"接续口译"。从此,职业口译正式登上历史舞台。之后,在第二次世界大战后的纽伦堡战犯审判中,"同声传译"的口译方式得以正式启用。"同声传译"也由此很快在大多数国家普及,并且代表着口译工作的一种发展方向。一批专门为国际会议培养高级译员的翻译学院在德国、瑞士、法国和美国应运而生。1953 年"国际会议译员协会"的成立,标志着口译人员社会地位的确立。口译开始成为一项欣欣向荣的高尚职业。

　　然而,口译作为一门学科受到学者们的关注和研究,起步却相对较晚。西方的口译研究基本始于第二次世界大战之后,而在中国直到 20 世纪 70 年代末 80 年代初才开始有一些分析口译特点和口译技巧的文章,90 年代后期才得以迅猛发展,出现了一批系统性的研究。

　　具体来讲,西方口译的研究始于第二次世界大战后。随着当时各种国际组织的大量兴起,口译需求剧增,各种口译训练项目相继建立,口译研究开始起步。按照口译研究界代表人物法国里昂第二大学的吉尔(Daniel Gile)教授的梳理,一般认为西方口译研究经历了以下四个发展阶段:经验总结为主的初级阶段(Pre-research Period)、实验心理学研究阶段(Experimental Psychology Period)、从业人员研究阶段(Practitioners' Period)和 20 世纪 80 年代后半期开始的蓬勃发展阶段(Renewal Period)。

　　第一阶段是 20 世纪 50 年代的起始阶段。这一时期主要以口译从业人员谈论个人经验、对口译行为及译员的工作环境进行观察和思考为主,探讨的问题包括对口译员语言和知识方面的要求、口译员工作中遇到的困难、与客户之间的关系等因素对口译产出结果的影响等。在这一阶段,日内瓦译员艾赫贝尔(Herbert,1952)和罗赞(Rozan,1956)分别以自身的口译实践经验为基础发表了两本经典的"手册式"的著作。其中罗赞一书阐述的交替口译笔记的基本原则和方法，至今仍得到广泛的认可。但这一阶段真正意义上的理论研究不多，基本上是经验总结，理论性不强。

第二阶段是 20 世纪 60 年代末至 70 年代初的实验心理学研究阶段。主要是一些心理学家和心理语言学家利用心理学和心理语言学的理论框架研究口译的认知问题，对口译过程提出了一些假想，并分析原语、噪音、发言速度等变量对口译的影响及口译员采用的对策等。这个时期心理学家的参与给口译研究打开了认知科学的大门，为研究口译程序、口译思维提供了新的思路，但是对于这一阶段的研究是否能真正有助于更好地了解口译过程，有部分学者持怀疑态度。

第三阶段是 20 世纪 70 年代至 80 年代中期的从业人员研究阶段。主要以从业人员投身到口译研究中为特点，其代表是法国巴黎释意学派理论，其研究特点是以内省式和经验式的理论推演为主。该理论强调口译以意义为中心，而不是字词和语言结构的对译。到上世纪末，该派正式出版论著十余部，至今在口译界有一定影响。但这段时间内，翻译理论研究与其他学科的沟通甚少，研究相对孤立，也鲜有科学化的实证研究。

第四阶段以 1986 年在意大利特里斯特(Trieste)大学举办的一次重要的口译会议为转折点，实证研究受到重视，各学派之间开始广泛深入地交流，口译研究进入更具跨学科性的研究阶段，也进入了一个比较兴旺的发展阶段。

西方口译研究走过了五十多年的发展历程，形成了相对成熟的理论体系，产生了不同的研究范式，比如：释意理论范式主要考查口译的语言重构过程，认知处理范式及神经语言学范式主要研究口译过程中的认知处理模式并探究其神经生理基础等。西方口译研究表现出几个突出的特点——以会议口译研究为主，研究视角多样化等，但同时也面临着许多诸如缺乏科研方法的培训、缺乏实验研究对象、缺乏相关学科的支持等问题。

中国的口译研究比西方要晚，起步于 20 世纪 70 年代末 80 年代初。但是 90 年代末以来，随着中国经济的发展，中外交往也日益频繁，我国口译事业取得了长足进步，也促进了口译研究工作的发展。从 1996 年到 2002 年分别在厦大、广外、北外等地召开的口译理论与教学研讨大会把中国的口译研究带出了初级研究阶段，并日益走向成熟。综观国内的口译研究成果，我们大致可以将其分为三大类：理论性研究、技巧性研究和教学与培训研究。

口译理论性研究方面包括对口译的定义、特点、程序、心理和质量评估等的研究，此类研究一直都占相当大的比例。在口译定义方面具有代表性的研究有：胡庚申(2000)认为，口译是将口头表达的信息等价地从一种语言转换为另一种语言的过程，根本目的在于使交际双方或各方能即席地相互理解；梅德明(1996)认为，口译是人类在跨文化、跨民族交往活动中所依赖的一种基本的语言交际工具。对口译特点的研究，内容大同小异，重点都强调口译的"准、顺、快"，基本将口译的特点概括为现场性、现时性、即席性、限时性和交互性等。关于口译的程序则有一些不同的说法，比如陈菁(1997)认为口译人员必须在有限的时间里同时完成听、分析、记忆和表达四个环节，而胡庚申(2000)则认为口译是双语转换的过程，这一过程的运行有其内在的规律。在口译心理研究方面，国内学者都认为良好的心理素质是口译员做好口译的重要保证。一般对口译员心理的研究着眼于内外两个因素。内因包括口译员的临场随机应变能力、心理和体力等非智力因素等；外因则包括口译员所处的不同语言环境、口译机器设备好坏以及正确使用与否等。在口译质量评估方面，近些年来研究逐渐增多，主要分为理论研究和实证研究。理论角度主要是提出理论假设，探讨各种有效进行口译质量评估的方法和模式；实证研究则主要针对口译质量的评估进行问卷调查，以获得实际的评估效果。

口译技巧性研究主要包括综合性口译技巧、同声传译技巧、应用口译技巧等。其中应用口译技巧涉及的领域很多，包括科技口译技巧、商务口译技巧、导游口译技巧等。对各项口译技巧的研究实际上是对口译工作者的实践经验的总结。近年来技巧性研究颇多，反映了人们对总结实践经验以及对口译质量的重视。

口译教学与培训研究涉及口译教学与培训的各个方面。近年来与教学和培训相关的口译研究层出不穷，但主要是从理论上对其进行探讨，基于实地调查、取样的实证研究仍然很少。

总的来说，我国口译研究历时较短，但近年来我国口译理论研究进步非常快。如刘和平所述，我国口译研究"从早期的口译经验谈和问题陈述逐步走向深层次理论研究，从对口译本身的封闭性研究逐步扩展到开放性的跨学科的多领域研究，而且成为构建中国翻译学框架研究不可缺少的一部分"（2005：40）。尤其是近十年，我国口译研究呈现出一些鲜明的特点。一是口译研究的范围趋向更广，比如口译宏观理论研究、术语研究、量化分析等。二是口译的理论性研究由过去的粗放、宽泛转向具体，比如对口译质量评估、口译标准、口译员主体身份定位等具体领域的研究。三是研究方法日趋科学，从单纯介绍一些翻译技巧，发展到定量、定性等研究手段的运用。四是口译教学和培训方面的研究越来越深入，涉及认知模式、信息处理、非智力因素的考查等。五是跨学科、跨国界的口译研究趋势越来越明显，产生了口译研究与心理学、系统功能语言学、认知语言学、功能学派翻译理论等交叉学科的研究，而且无论是中国口译研究成果的对外介绍，还是国外口译研究成果在国内的广泛传播，其数量都在不断增多。这些无不反映了国内的口译研究跨学科特征越来越明显，研究水平也在努力朝着国际水平发展。

当然，我国的口译研究目前也存在普遍的不足，主要表现在：研究的深度和广度仍然不够，对问题的研究未能触及问题的根源，解释也不够充分；缺乏大量实证性研究，鲜用数据进行分析，导致结果令人难以信服，而以客观口译材料对相关理论或思想进行实证性的验证、修正或革新则更是罕见；重规定、轻描写的研究现象仍然存在；相当一部分研究还只是停留在经验层面上，跨学科理论借鉴研究的比例偏低，跨学科借鉴的层次也较低，多是简单地套用其他学科的概念和理论来解释口译现象，很少结合具体口译实践对口译活动进行深层次的分析和说明，理论借鉴做得不够；研究方法单一重复，大部分都是对口译进行经验总结性和归纳思辨性研究，科学性不强。

总体来说，无论是西方还是我国国内的口译研究，在数十年的发展历程中，已经先后形成了一些较为成熟的口译研究范式，包括释意理论的研究范式、认知处理的研究范式及心理语言学的研究范式等。口译研究的主要课题也包罗万象，包括口译中的语言问题、口译中的认知问题、口译的质量问题、口译教学与培训等。中西方的口译研究的总体发展路径正在向跨学科的多元式研究扩展。

选 文

选文一　西方口译研究：历史与现状

肖晓燕

导　言

西方口译研究因为起步较早，系统性相对较强，有很多值得中国口译研究者加以探讨和借鉴的地方。选文系统梳理了西方口译研究的历史背景和特点，并指出了西方口译研究目前面临的问题以及未来的发展趋势。西方口译研究以会议口译的研究最为系统，其发展过程呈现出四个明显的阶段性，即初级研究阶段、实验心理学研究阶段、从业人员研究阶段以及跨学科的蓬勃发展阶段，主要围绕口译训练、语言、认知、问题和从业这五大研究主题，产生了信息处理范式、释意派理论、神经生理学研究和跨学科实证研究这四个极具影响力的研究视角以及多个口译研究中心。选文虽然着眼于西方的口译研究，但其更为深远的意义在于通过对西方口译研究的历史与现状的评介，为中国译学构架中起步较晚、一直处于薄弱环节、急需大力发展的口译研究提供一定的参考与借鉴。

引　言

随着中国加入世贸组织和北京申办 2008 年奥运会的成功成为现实，中国的国际化程度正不断提高，这种趋势必将带来对口译这种即时、高效的语言服务的巨大需求。正是为了顺应时代的要求，高等教育外语专业教学指导委员会于 2000 年 5 月将口译课列为中国高校英语专业必修课，有些学校早已开始在研究生阶段培养专业口译人才以满足社会对高质量口译人员的需求。口译理论和教学研究正面临新的机遇与挑战。中国的口译研究起步晚，发展水平低，在中国的译学构架中一直是个被忽视的薄弱环节。虽然 20 世纪 70 年代末中国的主要翻译和外语刊物有零星几篇关于口译的文章发表，中国学者对口译研究的初步认识和探索基本上从 20 世纪 80 年代初开始，发表的文章主要围绕口译的特点及技巧进行论述，属于经验谈和问题陈述阶段。进入 90 年代后口译研究发展迅速，开始呈现开放型跨学科研究的态势，但是发展水平仍大大滞后于起步较早、发展较为成熟的西方（包括欧洲、美洲和澳洲）。本文旨在通过对西方口译研究的历史与现状的评介，为中国口译研究的发展提供借鉴与参考，希望口译研究能引起翻译界及相关学科的足够重视，获得更大更快的发展，早日成为中国译学的一个不可忽视的分支。

1. 西方口译研究的历史背景

口译作为一种现象或活动，它的历史可以追溯很远。自从有了语言，不同语言群体之间有了交流的需要，就有了口译。但是口译作为一种在国际上得到认可的职业，却始于第一次世界大战末期，1919 年的巴黎和会首次打破了法语在国际会议和外交谈判中的垄断地位而借助英、法两种语言的翻译进行谈判，从此职业口译正式登上了国际舞台。第二次世界大战后的 50 年代随着各种国际组织的大量兴起，对快速有效的语言转换产生了巨大的需求，于是各种口笔译训练项目如雨后春笋般首先在欧洲建立起来，口译研究也开始起步。

西方口译研究至今为止经历了近 50 年的发展，形成了较为成熟的理论体系，表现出几个突出的特点，当然也面临着不少问题。

2. 西方口译研究的特点

2.1 以会议口译的研究为主

口译有多种分类，按照传送方式的不同，可分为同声传译（simultaneous interpreting）、交替传译（consecutive interpreting）和耳语式传译（whispered interpreting）；按照场合和口译内容的不同，则可分为会议口译（conference interpreting）、陪同口译（escort interpreting）、法庭口译（court interpreting）、媒体口译（media interpreting）、商务口译（business interpreting）和社区口译（community interpreting）等。会议口译，顾名思义，是指在多语言环境的国际会议上借助口译员这一媒介使与会者能自如正常地交流，而几乎不察觉他们之间存在的语言障碍。会议口译包括各种国际会议、高层官方访问、科技研讨等。目前的国际会议基本上以同声传译为主要形式，以至于有些作者将同声传译与会议口译等同起来，这样说并不正确。虽然交替传译在西方国际会议上使用的比例越来越小，同声传译并没有完全替代交替传译。

西方最早的口译研究开始于对会议口译的研究，至今这方面的研究进行得最多也最为系统，发展水平相对于其他类型的口译研究（如法庭口译、社区口译等）更为成熟。

2.2 呈现四个发展阶段

西方口译研究的发展有四个阶段：

2.2.1 20 世纪 50 年代至 60 年代初的初级研究阶段（Pre-research Period），主要以口译从业人员谈论个人经验、对口译行为及译员的工作环境进行观察和思考为主，探讨的问题包括对译员的语言和知识方面的要求、译员工作中遇到的困难、和客户的关系或疲劳等因素对译语产出的影响等。这一阶段的研究理论性不强，不过这期间出版的 Rozen（1956）和 Herbert（1952）[①]两本手册堪称经典，其中 Rozen 一书阐述的交替传译笔记的基本原则和方法，至今仍

---

① Rozen, J. , 1956, La prise de notes en interprétation consécutive《交替传译中的笔记》. Genéve: George. ; Herbert, J. , 1952, Le manuel de l'interprète. Genéve: George. 此书在中国大陆有两个中文译本：孙慧双（1982）《口译须知》，北京：外语教学与研究出版社；张晨君（1984）《高级口译手册》，北京出版社。

得到广泛认同。

2.2.2 20世纪60年代到70年代初期的实验心理学研究阶段(Experimental Psychology Period),主要是一些心理学家和心理语言学家利用心理学和心理语言学的理论框架研究口译的认知问题,对口译过程提出了一些假想,并分析了原语、噪音、发言速度、EVS(Ear-Voice Span,即原语和译语两股语流的时间差)等变量对口译的影响及译员常采用的对策等。然而对这一阶段的研究是否真正能帮助人们更好地了解口译过程,有些学者持怀疑态度。

2.2.3 20世纪70年代初到80年代中期的从业人员研究阶段(Practitioners' Period),以口译从业人员(其中大多为兼职口译教师)进行理论研究为主。最有代表性的理论为巴黎高等翻译学校(ESIT)创立的释意派理论(théorie dusens),强调口译以意义为中心,而不是字词和语言结构的对译。释意论曾一度成为口译界的主导性理论,在口译训练中至今仍有着积极的影响。然而这一阶段的研究相对孤立,学派之间缺乏交流,实证研究的意义几乎被完全忽视。

2.2.4 20世纪80年代后半期开始的蓬勃发展阶段(Renewal Period),以1986年在意大利的Trieste大学举办的一次重要的口译会议为转折点,口译研究从此进入新的历史时期。第三阶段占主导地位的观点和理论受到公开质疑和挑战,口译界结束了多年来的封闭孤立状态,各学派之间开始广泛深入地交流,实证研究受到重视,口译研究进入更具科学性和跨学科性的研究阶段。

2.3 研究视角多样化

在口译研究的各个发展阶段,人们从不同的视角对口译问题进行了研究,最有影响的口译研究视角有四种:

(1) 第二阶段开始盛行至今仍很有影响的信息处理范式(information-processing paradigm),指借用认知心理学的概念和模式,注重研究原语和译语间的信息传递,将原语的语法结构视为造成处理困难的重要因素。同声传译被视为一个多阶段的系列过程,包括听(或解码)、分析(或转换复述)、储存及译文输出(编码、翻译)等不同阶段过程,其中有些过程之间允许有重叠,各过程共享人脑有限的总体处理能力。代表人物有Gerver和Lambert,其中Gerver提出了最早的同声传译全过程模式。

(2) 在第三阶段占主导地位的以巴黎高等翻译学校和Seleskovitch为代表的释意派理论,提倡口译以意义单位为基础,将口译视为三个阶段:(a) 听力理解;(b) 脱离原语语言外壳获得其表达内容;(c) 译语表达。正是由于第二阶段的存在,口译中的语言与口译过程无关,因为译员在接收到原语信息后必须抛开原语的表层结构而在脑中形成其表达的思想内容或概念,然后再将该内容或概念用译语表达出来。释意论被应用在口译训练中,要求学生在参加训练前就完全掌握工作语言,训练中强调对内容的理解和翻译,排除语言因素的干扰,因此这一理论对口译训练有着积极的影响。

(3) 20世纪90年代上半期以意大利的Trieste大学为主进行的口译神经生理学研究(neurophysiological approach),由于Trieste大学目前在口译界的地位和多产而产生了较大的影响。代表人物是神经生理学家Fabbro和会议口译员兼口译教师Gran,主要研究口译时译员脑神经的反映,以及译员脑组织的偏侧性(lateralization)。

(4) 当今最流行的研究视角是对口译进行跨学科实证研究(the general empirical

interpreting research with interdisciplinary input①），指并不遵循单一的某种范式，而是结合其他学科，如认知心理学、语言学、社会学等对口译进行实证研究。法国的 Daniel Gile 教授是跨学科实证研究最著名的代言人，是口译界目前最为多产的作者，从事大量的实证研究。他最受瞩目的成就之一在于他借用认知科学概念创立的口译认知负荷模型（Effort Models，前译"多任务处理模式"）。另外，从描写翻译研究（Descriptive Translation Studies）视角研究口译以及从语言学和语篇语言学（text-linguistic）视角研究口译也引起越来越多的关注。

2.4 围绕五大研究主题

在口译研究的四个发展阶段，研究人员从不同视角对口译的相关问题进行了较为广泛的研究，归纳起来主要有以下五个研究主题：

2.4.1 口译训练

从第一阶段开始口译训练就一直是最热门的口译研究题材，文献大多围绕训练原则和训练方法进行讨论并对不同地区的训练项目进行介绍。口译训练之所以成为长盛不衰的研究主题，一是由于口译文献的作者大多是从业人员兼口译教师，训练是他们最熟悉的领域，另外，口译理论研究的主要应用价值在于两个方面，即口译训练和机器翻译。

2.4.2 语言问题

口译是一项高度复杂的双语活动，语言是口译训练的重要内容之一，因此语言问题也一直是研究热点。围绕语言能力的培养、不同语言组合的对比及对口译产生的影响等问题，同一阶段和不同阶段的学者都提出了不同的看法。例如第三阶段的主流观点是口译与所牵涉的语言无关，只要充分掌握了两种语言，译员就能驾轻就熟，毫不费力地进行口译。许多职业口译员并不赞同这一观点，最早的反对之声来自德语国家的学者，如 Wilss 认为，当两种语言的句法结构差异大时（如英语和德语），口译中需要进行较多的句型转换，相对于句法结构相似的语言组合（如英语和法语）来说，口译难度更大。中文口译员也提出，由于中文关键词右置，译员需要记忆更多的内容才能输出译文，短期记忆负担容易超重。除语言特殊性（language specificity）问题外，口译中的语言方向（language direction）、原语转换成译语后其准确性（correctness）、韵律（prosody）、语体（linguistic style）、连贯性（cohesion）、语用（pragmatics）等方面发生了什么变化等问题也引起了不少研究人员的兴趣。

2.4.3 认知问题

认知问题曾是第二阶段实验心理学研究的热点，认知科学家们对口译时译员的心理活动、错译漏译现象、同声传译的时间变量、原语和译语两股语流的比较、高语速及噪音情况的处理等问题进行了研究。从 20 世纪 70 年代中期开始，认知心理学家和口译员利用认知心理学概念发展同声传译模式，心理学家还研究用一只耳朵听和用两只耳朵的听力效果的不同。进入90 年代，从认知心理学的视角研究口译仍不断吸引众多的研究人员。

2.4.4 质量问题

口译质量曾成为第三阶段的研究主题之一，多为规约性文章。从 20 世纪 80 年代中期开始，质量问题成为实证研究关注的热点，目前口译界对质量问题的热衷也日趋升温。如 Gile（5：31）提出，口译是一种交际行为，口译质量的判定取决于参与交际的各方包括讲者、听者

---

① D. Gile 教授与本文作者通信中提出。

和雇主(如会议组织者等)认定的交际效果。Shlesinger 探讨了不同用户对质量提出的不同要求,有的用户对直译的要求超出对语体及流利程度的要求,有的则将连贯性和清晰度放在首位,也有的用户对完整性格外敏感等。

2.4.5 从业问题

由于口译文献作者大部分是口译从业人员,因此如何成为合格的口译员(如对语言能力、百科知识、心理素质等的要求)、口译员的工作环境(设备、资料、与客户的关系等)以及译员的社会地位等从业问题也一直是口译界热衷的研究题材。

除了围绕上述研究主题外,交替传译中的记忆、笔记、从笔记到译文产出的过程等引起了认知心理学研究者的关注;近期以意大利的 Fabbro 和 Gran 为代表的口译神经生理学研究也在口译界产生了较大的影响。另外随着 IT 技术的快速发展和国际交往的日益密切,电话口译、可视会议口译及媒体口译等也渐渐发展成为业内关注的研究题材。

2.5 形成多个有影响的口译研究中心

西方有几个地区在出版的文献数量和对口译研究产生的影响方面成绩显著,堪称口译研究中心。

巴黎(Paris)

法国巴黎曾经是且至今仍是欧洲最重要的口译研究中心之一。以巴黎高等翻译学校和 Seleskovitch 为代表的巴黎学派创立的释意论是中国口译界最熟悉的口译学派,也曾一度成为口译界最有影响的口译理论。不过巴黎高等翻译学校在口译界的代表地位目前已经大大削弱,有影响的作品也不多。而来自巴黎的目前在口译界最有影响的学者是执教于法国里昂第二大学(Université Lumiére Lyon 2)的 Gile 教授,他创办并主编《国际口译研究信息网公报》(*The IRN Bulletin*),每年的 6 月和 12 月两次发布口译研究和理论的最新信息,包括近期的相关活动,出版情况及硕、博士论文等。Gile 教授极为多产,所发表的论文数量及被引用次数都遥遥领先于其他作者,是口译跨学科实证研究的代言人,他的专著《口笔译训练的基本概念与模式》(*Basic Concepts and Models of Interpreter and Translator Training*,1995)在口笔译界产生了较大影响,也是中国口译界可以参考的不可多得的口译专著之一。

特里斯特(Trieste)

意大利 Trieste 大学翻译学院(SSLM)近年来发展成为非常有影响的口译研究中心。SSLM 于 1986 年主办的一个大型口译训练研讨会标志着口译研究进入一个新的历史时期(参见 2.2)。该学院以用科学实验方法研究口译而著称,其主办刊物《口译通讯》(*Interpreters' Newsletter*)是口译界第一本学术研究刊物。该学院最著名的代表人物 Gran 和 Fabbro 进行了跨学科合作,从神经科学(神经生理学、神经心理学和神经语言学)角度研究口译。

维也纳(Vienna)

奥地利维也纳大学的翻译系(Department of Translator and Interpreter Training, University of Vienna)由于 Ingrid Kurz 的多产而成为研究中心之一。Kurz 是西方口译研究的开拓者和领导者之一,是职业口译员(AIIC[①] 会员)及心理学家,并成为世界上第一个获得

---

① AIIC, Association Internationale des Interpretes de Conferences,国际会议口译员协会,1953 年于瑞士日内瓦成立。

口译博士学位的人(1969)。她的研究涉及题材广泛,包括口译的历史、口译技术和从业问题、不同的客户对质量的不同要求、心理口译时人脑活动的神经生理测试等。

乔治敦(Georgetown)

美国乔治敦大学翻译学院(Interpretation and Translation School of Georgetown University)以 David & Margareta Bowen 为代表,所从事的研究主要围绕口译训练中的口译语言能力测试以及口译历史研究。

除上述几个有影响的口译研究中心外,加拿大是美洲最活跃的口笔译活动和研究中心,蒙特利尔大学(University of Montreal)出版的 Meta 可能是口笔译界拥有最大读者群的学术刊物。澳大利亚则是社区口译的一大中心,口译研究以社区口译为主。在欧洲,芬兰各大学、布拉格的查尔斯大学(University of Charles of Prague)的口译研究也成果显著。西班牙则是不容忽视的新兴力量。

3. 存在问题及趋势展望

口译研究经过近 50 年的发展,取得了令人瞩目的成绩,然而也面临许多亟待解决的问题。其中最突出的有:

3.1 缺乏科研方法的培训

口译文献的作者绝大多数是口译从业人员,他们大多没有接受过科学研究方法的培训,因此发表的文章有的存在严重的方法论错误。在借用相关学科的理论和概念研究口译时,则表现出跨学科发展的不平衡性,例如结合认知科学研究口译的成果迄今为止并不理想,大部分研究仅仅局限于对相关概念、理论和范式的借用,而在实证研究中却游离于认知科学的范畴之外。另一种跨学科研究的不平衡发展体现在身陷其他学科而认识不到口译本身的实质问题,如 Trieste 大学的口译神经生理学研究虽产生了一定的影响,但研究的是译员的大脑,而不是口译本身,而且实验均在实验室里进行,与真实口译情景有较大的差异。

3.2 缺乏实验研究对象

口译研究要真正具有科学性,取得突破性的发现与进展,势必离不开实证研究。然而注册的职业口译员(如 AIIC 会员)数量极其有限,加上社会和心理原因,大部分译员不愿意作为被试对象,因此可供使用的被试者大多为口译训练班学员,这给口译实证研究数据的真实性带来了一定的困难。

3.3 缺乏相关学科的理解和支持

口译研究尚属于新鲜事物,无论是作为一门独立学科还是作为翻译学的分支,都没有在学术界完全确立自己的地位,发展水平也相对落后,因此难免受到其他发展更为成熟、学术地位较高的学科的轻视,认为口译没有理论可言,研究也不具科学性。有些专职研究人员即使有兴趣研究口译,在研究中也常常看不到口译本身的实质问题。

3.4 缺乏作研究的动力

西方口译文献的作者绝大多数是口译从业人员,他们拥有第一手口译资料,然而做口译的经济回报远远高于口译研究,加上西方不少口译员的从教单位对这些口译教师并没有科研要求,因此口译员大多忙于做口译,而没有时间从事研究工作。然而,西方口译研究正朝着更具科学性和跨学科性的方向发展。要使跨学科科学研究不至于成为一句空洞的口号,真正地进行学科交融,口译界不仅需要提高自身的科研能力,还应该尽量吸引其他相关学科(如认知科学、心理学、语言学、社会学等)的研究人员加入到口译研究的行列中来。

4. 结束语

中文是联合国的六种官方语言之一,然而西方口译界对中文作为国际会议语言的了解少得可怜,能找到的与中文有关的口译研究资料微乎其微,应该说这不仅是中国口译的遗憾,也是世界口译的一大缺憾。我们的邻国日本由于日本同行不懈的努力和 Daniel Gile 的推动,在西方口译界已经引起重视并产生了一定反响。笔者呼吁,国内同行能够一方面立足本国,加大加快口译研究步伐,另一方面及时有效地借鉴和共享西方口译研究成果,避免不必要的弯路,推动中国口译研究的更大发展,使它能进入一个真正的"蓬勃发展"阶段。

选文二 我国口译研究的现状和发展趋势
——第六届口译大会综述

王东志

导 言

全国口译大会作为我国国内口译界规模最大、影响力最广的学术活动,其会议本身呈现的特点以及反映出来的问题向来是我国口译研究现状的一面镜子。选文通过对第六届口译大会的综述,对当下我国口译研究的现状进行了归纳总结。第六届全国口译大会突显了当前我国口译研究的特点,比如:口译研究的问题由宽泛转向具体,研究手段更加科学;承袭了国外当前几个主要口译理论学派的研究取向;质量标准化趋势明显;对口译本体研究的兴趣明显增强。同时透过口译大会,我们也可以发现当前我国口译研究领域存在的一些问题,比如:研究问题不够深入、研究不够规范、理论借鉴做得不够等。对于未来我国口译研究的发展趋势,选文在最后做出了预期,指出我国的口译研究将朝着精细化、专业化的方向发展,实践—研究型人才将不断涌现,口译研究方法将是实证与实验、定量与定性的综合,并且将大量借鉴认知科学、人工智能、心理学、社会学、语言学、笔译研究的理论和科研方法等诸多学科的知识,以此推动我国口译研究的跨学科发展。

第六届全国口译大会暨国际研讨会于 2006 年 10 月 20～21 日在对外经济贸易大学召开。参会代表达 210 余人,他们来自不同行业,有来自各大外语院校从事笔译教学和研究的教师,有政府、组织和机构代表,如 AIIC、欧盟口译总司(DG SCIC)和翻译工作者协会、外交部和商务部的代表等,这反映出这一新兴学科强大的吸引力和人们对口译事业的关注。按照日程安排,19 日下午举行了专家专题讲座,容纳 200 人的会议厅里座无虚席。释意派创始人之一勒代雷(Lederer)首先介绍了释意派理论,接着日内瓦大学的 Robin Setton 介绍了口译研究的起源、范围与方法,最后维也纳大学教授 Franz Pöchhacker 介绍了口译研究的最新动态。讲座之后,专家与听众进行了广泛深入的交流,气氛热烈。20 日上午大会正式开幕,来自欧盟口译司、商务部外事司、AIIC、中国译协、外交部翻译室培训处的代表从不同的角度谈了对口译与口译员的认识,其间美国蒙特雷翻译学院院长鲍川运介绍了口译的准则与教学大纲革新。下午和第二天上午进行分组会议,与会者围绕口译质量与评估、口译研究、口译教学及教材、从母语译入外语四个主题进行了热烈的讨论。21 日下午是大会发言。勒代雷谈如何提高译入外语的质量,Robin Setton 从语言、文化与技能角度比较了东西方译员培训模式,北外高翻院院长王立弟分析了翻译培训如何提高翻译质量,广外副校长仲伟合教授阐述了专业口译教学原则与方法,上外高翻院柴明颖院长介绍了翻译学科口译方向博士生的培养,北京语言大学刘和平教授论述了口译培训的目标与教学,最后是经贸大学王恩冕教授对比了中日韩三国由母语译入外语的经验。本次大会共提交 112 篇论文摘要,超过了历次大会的规模。

一、现状

全国口译大会是国内口译界规模最大、影响力最广的学术活动,因此会议本身呈现的特点以及反映出来的问题集中体现了当前我国口译研究的现状。

1. 本次会议的特点。自 2004 年上外高翻院召开第五届口译大会以来,口译界又出现了许多新的变化:两年来又有许多院校和机构都开展了口译培训课程;大量经过专门培训的口译员进入社会,译员的整体素质提高,口译市场出现前所未有的繁荣局面;开始出现从事口译方向的博士研究生;关于口译研究的专著、教材、文章数量明显增多;出现联合办学的新趋势。正是由于这些新的变化使得此次口译大会呈现出不同于以往的新特点,分述如下。

(1)研究的问题由宽泛转向具体,研究手段更加科学。

以前大家多是介绍一些翻译技巧或个人的经验之谈,很少就某一具体问题展开研究。而在这次大会上我们不仅看到研究的问题具体了,如开始研究口译员的角色、信息的处理、口译的质量、口译的认知过程,以及评估模式和方法等,而且研究的水平也不再停留在个人认识的基础上,能够运用定量、定性等应用语言学的研究手段进行研究。事实上,语言学经过多年的发展,已经比较成熟,而且也积累了很多行之有效的科研方法,而这正是口译研究所欠缺的。很多外国学者早就将语言学的研究方法借入到口译研究中来,取得了不小的成就。口译大会上出现的这种新的研究取向确实是一个鼓舞人心的好消息,同时这也反映出国内的研究水平在努力朝着国际水平发展。

(2)承袭了国外当前几个主要口译理论学派的研究取向。目前影响较大的口译理论有三派:释意学派(Interpretive Theory)、信息处理学派(Information Processing)和认知-语用学派(Cognitive-Pragmatic Analysis)。这三大派系的领军人物分别是 Seleskovitch 与 Lederer、

Daniel Gile 和 Robin Setton。Seleskovitch 是巴黎高翻院创办者也是释意派的开山鼻祖和 AIIC 的创始人,Lederer 是前巴黎高翻院院长,她们提出的释意理论虽不如几年前影响那么大,但仍然在理论界占有一席之地,其地位不可撼动。信息处理学派更加关注口译的认知过程,它强调信息处理的模式和过程。Daniel Gile 提出的 Effort Model 就是这一理论的代表,工作记忆(working memory)是其中一个非常重要的概念。近年来 IP 理论吸引了越来越多人的主意。Robin Setton 是语言学出身,因此他对语言学理论如数家珍,1999 年他将 Sperber & Wilson 提出的关联理论(Relevance Theory)引入口译研究领域,撰写了 *Simultaneous Interpreting: A Cognitive-Pragmatic Analysis* 一书,这标志着认知—语用学派的诞生。Robin 试图从语用的角度去解释口译的过程。会上我们看到一些国内研究人员正在介绍、引用、探索、发展这些理论,试图将它们与自己的研究紧密结合起来。

(3) 质量标准化趋势明显。国外在口译质量标准方面的研究已相当普遍,但目前这一问题尚未引起国内理论界的足够重视,这方面的研究还不多。会上来自维也纳大学的 Pöchhacker 介绍了口译的行业标准和西方对质量标准的研究,引起了与会者的极大兴趣。他介绍了 AIIC、欧盟、ASTM 以及奥地利的口译质量标准;接着阐述了在学术上主要从两个角度来研究质量问题,一个是对译员质量要素的调查,另一个是对用户预期的调查。最后指出需要通过理论研究来推动行业服务的标准化。如今,翻译工作者协会正在制定的口译质量标准,以及各种口译资格的认证,都反映了质量标准化的趋势。这次大会提醒人们质量标准化趋势是一个不容置疑的客观事实。

(4) 人们对口译本体研究的兴趣明显增强。大会所涉及的内容大体上可分为两类:与教学相关的口译研究和对口译本体的研究,前者包括培训模式、培训教材、评估手段等,后者包括母语译入外语的研究和对口译认知过程的研究。本次会议的一个亮点就是人们对口译本体研究的空前关注,两天时间里这一专题的听众人数是最多的。除此以外,这方面的论文不仅比以前要多很多,而且研究得也比较深入,所涉及的都是这一领域的热点问题,如意义理论、认知模式、信息处理、母语译入外语等。这反映了人们不再满足于单纯的教学和培训,开始将目光转向口译的本质性研究,表明了我国的研究工作者正在走向成熟。

2. 发现的问题。当我们看到口译研究出现这些新特点的同时,也看到了一些明显的、带有普遍性的不足,主要表现在以下几个方面。

(1) 研究问题不够深入。虽然研究的问题越来越具体,但研究的深度不够。这体现在:第一,对问题浅尝辄止,没有触及问题的根源,或是解释不够充分;第二,缺乏实证性研究,没有用数据说话,或是缺乏对数据的科学分析,给人空中楼阁的感觉,导致结果令人难以信服。

(2) 研究不够规范。这里是指研究方法,国内的口译研究尚在起步阶段,而且这方面的理论也比较少,很多口译教师学术训练不够,缺少很明确的研究方法,暴露了研究粗糙的弱点。相对来说,台湾学者在这方面就比我们做得好,他们的研究一丝不苟、中规中矩。比如说来自国立台北大学应用外语学系的廖伯森教授在其论文《台湾口译研究回顾:记台湾翻译学学会十年有成》中,他对十年来台湾的口译文献进行了检索、分类、分析,检索详尽,分类明确,分析透彻,显示出受过正规的学术训练。

(3) 理论借鉴做得不够。虽然人们承袭了口译理论的不同学派,但在相关学科的借鉴上做得还很不够。我们知道做研究不能缺少理论的支持。口译研究历时短、发展快,还没有形成自身完备的理论体系,必须要多借鉴其他学科,才能实现理论突破。在这次会议上,我们看到很多研究还是停留在经验的层面上,即使借鉴也只是最为热门的认知科学,而像其他学科如心理学、社会学、语言学、人工智能、笔译理论涉及得不多。实际上,这些学科的理论发展已相当成熟,在口译研究中都可以发挥很大的作用。另外一个问题就是对理论的生吞活剥,有的时候为说明一个问题强行拉上一个理论,而本身对这个理论就一知半解,或者这个理论与研究的问题相关不大,因此很多时候解释起来显得力不从心,漏洞百出,结论也不能自圆其说。

当然这些问题在理论发展的道路上是不可避免的,我们不能因此否定最近几年特别是2000年之后口译事业蒸蒸日上,口译研究取得了长足发展这样一个事实。同时我们也看到,口译研究方兴未艾,有着广阔的发展空间。

二、口译研究未来发展的趋势

在大会召开的前一天,Pöchhacker 教授作了题为 Interpreting Studies：Evolution and Recent Trends 的专题讲座,介绍了西方在口译研究领域的发展历程和最新动态。结合本次大会的特点,我们可以看到未来我国的口译研究将表现出如下的趋势。

1. 口译研究将朝着精细化、专业化的方向发展。从这次大会来看,绝大部分的论文都把口译作为一个整体进行研究,但也有为数不多的几篇是关于法庭口译、电视口译、旅游口译等。在口译理论中这些都被统称为社区口译(community interpreting)。口译在中国的发展也就是二十几年的时间,还没有得到充分的发展和完善,细分不明显。对我们来说口译分为同传和交传,实际上这只是口译的不同工作方式而已。在西方,口译发展得比较成熟,已被应用到社会生活中的方方面面,如用于会议、司法、医疗、教育、手势语交流、移民和难民事务等方面。这种以工作方式进行的简单划分已不能满足需要,因此,西方往往把口译分为会议口译(conference interpreting)、社区口译(包括司法、社会、医疗口译)和其他形式的口译。随着未来口译行业的进一步细分,口译研究也将呈现出多样化、精细化的趋势。

2. 口译研究方法将是实证与实验、定量与定性的综合。在专题讲座时,几位外国专家也提到了研究方法的问题,他们都认为现在人们盲目崇拜实验的方法,而实际上有很多实验与研究的内容不相关,因此无法充分地解释所研究的问题。同时也无可否认,实验是一种比较科学、客观的研究方法,如果能与实证性研究找到最佳结合点,就能发挥很大作用。对于口译研究来说,应以定量研究为主定性研究为辅。定量研究包括问卷调查、个案研究、语料观测、数据分析等,这些都是定性分析的基础材料。

3. 口译研究将大量借鉴其他学科的知识,从中汲取营养。特别是认知科学、人工智能、心理学、社会学、语言学、笔译研究的理论和科研方法将为口译研究做出突出贡献。有很多研究人员已经做过了成功的尝试,比如说刘敏华借助认知科学和心理学研究口译中工作记忆(working memory)的问题;R. B. W. Anderson 从社会角度研究口译员的角色;Robin Setton 借助语言学理论工具研究口译问题等。

4. 未来实践-研究型人才将不断涌现。随着翻译博士点的设立,越来越多的研究人员将接受正规的学术训练,专业研究队伍将不断壮大。这些人当中绝大部分都是口译从业者,他们兼有研究者和实践者双重身份,能够做口译、教口译、研究口译。这种情况在国外极为普遍。实践能够丰富研究,给他们提供更多的素材,也能使他们在实践中发现很多问题;反过来,他们所做的研究也不是纸上谈兵,更具实用、指导和推广价值。

综上所述,尽管存在着不少的问题,但近年来我国的口译理论进步非常快。刘和平教授曾撰文指出"中国口译理论与教学研究虽然起步较晚,但发展迅速,从早期的口译经验谈和问题陈述逐步走向深层次理论研究,从对口译本身的封闭性研究逐步扩展到开放性的跨学科的多领域研究,而且成为构建中国翻译学框架研究不可缺少的一部分"。21世纪将是我国口译事业的成熟期和发展的繁荣时期。随着专业研究队伍的不断壮大,相信到2008年广外召开第七届口译大会的时候,中国的口译研究水平会再次实现大的跨越。

【延伸阅读】

1. 胡庚申,盛茜. 中国口译研究又十年. 中国科技翻译. 2000(2):39-43.
2. 蒋凤霞,吴湛. 口译的跨学科理论概述. 外国语文. 2011,27(2):79-84.
3. 李金泽. 国内口译研究的历史与现状. 边疆经济与文化. 2010,74(2):101-102.
4. 刘绍龙,王柳琪. 对近十年中国口译研究现状的调查与分析. 广东外语外贸大学学报. 2007(1):37-40.
5. 帅林. 跨学科口译理论研究在中国. 中国科技翻译. 2007(3):50-52.

【问题与思考】

1. 西方口译研究经历了哪四个阶段? 每一个阶段分别体现出什么样的研究特点?
2. 西方口译研究的视角有哪些? 请对其代表人物和口译研究理念分别加以简单论述。
3. 西方口译研究面临的问题有哪些? 对于中国的口译研究有何借鉴意义?
4. 如何理解"口译研究方法应将实证与实验、定量与定性相综合"这一观点?
5. 中国的口译研究当前存在哪些特点和问题?

第三章　语言学派口译理论研究

导　论

　　口译首先也始终是一项语言活动,任何口译活动的基础部分都必定包含着一系列隶属于语言学的分析和活动内容。同时,口译的本质是一种跨语言和跨文化的交际活动,其最终目的是将讲话者的真正意图传达给目的语的听众。口译研究涉及的问题是如何根据讲话者的意图、讲话者与目的语听众的关系以及由此而产生的交际情境和语言情境来诠释意义。因此语言学派理论对口译理论产生指导作用的前提是要将"交际"确定为一个重要的组成部分,其对口译研究的启发性不应该仅仅局限于语言本身。从理论研究的视角来看,我们也不应该把对口译这一语言问题的探讨局限于纯语言学的视野之内,而应把它置于更广阔的跨学科视域中来进行研究。所以说,语言学派口译理论的一个鲜明特点就是其跨学科的独特视角,研究者们从语言学派理论中发掘出各式各样适用于口译研究的学说,比如:语义学理论、语用学理论、语言交际理论、系统功能语言学理论、认知语言学理论、心理语言学理论等。

　　语义学理论认为,人类的语言使用一些基本语义类别,如事物、状态、事件、动作等,以及因果关系、时间关系、从属关系等来组织构建话语"含义"(signification)。这些语义类别构成认知主体的"认知常量",这些"认知常量"是人类认知系统用来感知、表征外部世界的基本概念类别。这些语义类别具备个体性且由个体的认知特点来决定。相对于"逻辑分句"而言,这些"认知常量"是高层次的认知类别。在话语理解过程中,话语映像的构建是从话语理解的基本单位"逻辑分句"开始,一层层来实现的。在"逻辑分句"的基础上,认知主体构建事件、状态、动作等基本语义类别,并通过时间关系、空间关系、因果关系、从属关系等联系将这些基本语义类别进一步组织起来,形成宏观事件、宏观状态和宏观动作等更高层的语义单位(Denhiére & Baudet, 1992)。而口译过程正是这样的一种语言交际和转换过程,因此,语义学中的"认知常量"和"语义单位"的概念可以帮助深入研究口译中的"意义转换过程"和"意义单位"。

　　美国结构主义语言学代表人物弗里斯(Charles C. Fries)提出的语言交际理论则认为:语言是交际的工具,在语言交际中有三个重要概念,即言语行为(speech acts)、意义(meaning)和语言(language)。根据这一理论,言语行为是连接对话双方——A 与 B——的一种物理手段,是由 A 发出、B 接受到的声音序列,一个社区的言语行为总和并不构成其语言;意义是 A 试图传递给 B 的信息内容;语言既不是言语行为,也不是意义,而是一套抽象的信息代码。只有当言语行为符合这套代码所重现的模式并为人们所掌握和认识时,它才获得意义。口译在本质上是一种复杂的交际行为。口译员作为一个为交际双方提供交际服务的中介,承担的任务是解码一种语言所代表的意义,然后用另一种语言将其表达出来,从而促使交际顺利完成。用语言交际理论来细化这一交际行为过程，我们可以发现，口译员实际充当的是一个"意义处理器"的作用，为了获取 A 的意义，口译员必须能够解读 A 声音序列中所指示的信息代码。同时为将该意义传递给 B，口译员发出的声音序列必须符合 B 所熟悉的信息代码。根据这一模式，口译的三个重要组成部分中：接受和输出声音序列是前提，解析信息代码（语言）是手段，获得和传递意义是目的。语言交际理论帮助细化了口译的过程，让我们看到，一个口译单位的完成需要口译员首先能够听懂原语，完整接受用原语发出的声音信息，然后越过语言的表面意义去获取深层意义，即诠释意义，最后用目的语将这一深层意义表达出来。

以韩礼德（Halliday）为代表的系统功能语言学家们则更加关注语言的社会属性以及如何实现语言的社会功能。系统功能语言学认为语言是"做事"的一种方式（a form of "doing"），而不是一种"认识"或"知识"（a form "knowing"），在此基础上，语言就不再是人的一种知识能力，而是"文化和社会所允许的选择范围"，也就是"在语言行为上所能够做的事情的范围"，其更多的关注在于语言与环境的关系。以系统功能语言学观建立起来的系统功能语法体系使人们摆脱单独分析语言内部结构的片面性，对语言多层次的内容结构和多种外在因素进行静态分析和动态分析。系统功能语言学理论带给口译研究的启示在于：在口译中，口译员不仅要有"语义意识"，还应注重考查口译发生的语境和背景，将口译活动视为社会大系统中的一部分，要保持"语言的社会功能意识"，力争做到译语与原语不仅意义等值，且发挥的社会功能——亦即语用功能——相同，这样才能确保译语的准确性，发挥口译的最佳社会功能。

在众多语言学派口译理论当中，司徒·罗斌（Robin Setton）教授创建的同声传译认知语用理论（Cognitive-Pragmatic Theory of Simultaneous Interpretation）被认为是近十年同声传译研究领域的最大突破之一，而用认知语言学理论来研究口译也成为语言学派口译研究的一大特色。司徒教授认为，社会个体要完成不同的语言任务，需要具备并且调动不同的语言处理能力。他提出的"口译基本能力和子过程框架图"模型中指出，口译员在口译过程中至少需要具备三种能力（Setton，2002：17）：感知表述能力、语言处理能力（包括语法和词汇）和高级认知活动能力。其中，第三种能力被划分为推测推理能力（deduction-inference）和元表征能力（meta-representation）这两种关键能力。在口译活动过程中，口译员根据映像的抽象程度、持续时间和可重建性将它们标签、标记并分类（同前：16）。认知语言学派口译理论研究的关注点在于"口译的过程"。一般认为口译要经过听（感知信息）、理解（解码）、记忆（重新编码与储存）和表达（信息输出）等四个过程。"听"，亦即信息的输入过程，就是口译员感知语音信息并把它转化为语言的深层含义（交际信息）的过程。以言语作为外部信息作用于大脑而言，"听"是接受性的，但这并不等于说口译员就应该被动地感知信息而没有任何分析、归纳等思维活动。恰恰相反，在"听"的时候，口译员的大脑是异常活跃的，要全神贯注于语言的内部结构即音、词、句以及语言的外部结构即情景及文化语境，通过发话者使用的各种衔接手段找出句与句之间的关系，并联系语言及文化语境理解整个语篇。此时的"听"已经自然过渡到了"理解"阶段。所谓"理解"并不是说口译员可以一字不差地重复演说者的话语，而是指口译员通过对信息的解码，抓住它的内在含义后能用自己的语言将其准确地再现出来。连续口译的理解是发生在语篇层面上的。理解的方式有两种：自下而上（bottom-up）和自上而下（top-down）。"自下而上"是指口译员从具体感知到的信息材料，如语音、单词、句子以至语篇，逐层上升达到理解的手段。由于这种方式是通过声音的识别、单词形象的建构、命题的编制等层层激活口译员大脑中的语言知识而达到理解的，所以它被称为"数据驱动式"（data-driven）。在这一过程中，口译员的任务就是主动快速地检索大脑中的知识并与感知到的信息相匹配,从而合成意义。"自上而下"的方式则相反,它是从宏观的角度利用口译员对感知材料的社会与文化语境、中心议题及对话参与者的了解而对理解起主导作用的一种方式。此时,口译员的知识加上推理的参与会帮助他将预期与新输入的信息加以吻合,从而理解语篇。由于这种方法是"高层次的普通常识,决定了对低层次的语言材料的知觉"(桂诗春,1991),故称"概念驱动式"(concept-driven)。当然,这一过程同样要求口译员积极主动地参与,而不是被动等待两者的吻合。不难发现,用人类认知的原理来分析口译的语言工作机制,以认知语言学的研究成果来解释口译中的语言现象在口译理论研究中大有可为。

选　文

选文一　The Glossy Ganoderm:
Systemic Functional Linguistics and Translation

M. A. K. Halliday

导　言

　　系统功能语言学的创始人韩礼德认为语言的性质决定人们对语言的要求,即语言所必须完成的社会功能。相比较传统的语言学家们而言,系统功能语言学家更加关注语言的社会属性以及如何实现语言的社会功能,所以系统功能语言学家集中力量去发现和描写由于社会情境和说话人的情况不同而产生的各种语言变体,以及这些变体与社会功能之间的关系。系统功能语言学认为语言是"做事"的一种方式(a form of "doing"),而不是一种"认识"或"知识"(a form "knowing"),并且在可能的语言行为和实际的语言行为之间进行区分。在此基础上,语言就不再是人的一种知识能力,而是"文化和社会所允许的选择范围",也就是"在语言行为上所能够做的事情的范围",其更多的关注在于语言与环境的关系。系统功能语言学非常重视对个别语言、个别语言变体的分析,并用"连续体"的概念来解释语言的不同表现形式,引进了"阶"(scale)和"精密阶"(scale of delicacy)两个概念(例如:不符合语法—不符合习惯—有点不符合习惯—比较符合习惯—合乎语法)。系统功能语言学的核心是以"系统"作为基本范畴,把语言看做是一套"系统"。每一个"系统"就是语言行为中的一套可供选择的可能性,即在特定环境中可以选用的一组语言形式。以系统功能语言学观建立起来的系统功能语法体系使人们摆脱单独分析语言内部结构的片面性,对语言多层次的内容结构和多种外在因素进行静态分析和动态分析。该系统功能语言学理论应用到翻译理论研究中,为翻译理论研究提供了一个新的视角,同时也给翻译实践活动,包括口译实践,带来如下启示:在翻译中,译者不仅要有"语义意识",还要保持"语言的社会功能意识",力争做到译文与原文不仅意义等值,且发挥的社会功能——亦即语用功能——相同,这样才能确保译文的准确性,从而使翻译活动能更有效地进行下去。因此,口译活动过程中,口译员也应注重考查口译发生的语境和背景,将口译活动视为社会大系统中的一部分,进行"得体"的口译,发挥口译的最佳社会功能。

When we investigate translation from the standpoint of linguistic science, we are applying our understanding of language as a "semogenic," or meaning-making, system in two stages. On the one hand, translation theory is a domain of research (along with, for example, literary studies) in descriptive and comparative linguistics. On the other hand, translation practice is an activity that has a high value in our social and cultural life; it requires the training of translators, the production of dictionaries and other multilingual materials, and even the setting up of special institutions for professional translators to work in. So we start by "unpacking" the concept of translation, seeing it as a relation between languages, and as a process of moving from one language into another. In either of these two perspectives, translation is an extraordinarily complex achievement of the human brain. The translator may be "invisible," in Venuti's term (Venuti, 1995); but the translation process has to be illuminated, so that we can see it. This means that we have to direct light on it from many angles, such as are determined by the nature of language itself.

In his book *Towards a General Comparative Linguistics*, written over 40 years ago (1996), Jeffrey Ellis located translation as a domain within comparative descriptive linguistics. It can be seen as a fairly specialized domain, in the sense that relatively few linguists working in either functional or formal linguistics have paid explicit attention to translation; but it has been recognized as a kind of testing ground, since if your theory cannot account for the phenomenon of translation it is clearly shown up as inadequate. Here my first point of reference for systemic functional work on translation is another book written over 40 years ago by Ian Catford (1965); Catford used an early systemic model of language to analyse translation and the notion of translation equivalence, in a remarkably rich and insightful way.

More recently others, such as Christopher Taylor (1998) and Carol Taylor-Torsello (1996), have brought translation into the compass of a functional linguistic theory; and Erich Steiner has further enriched the field in focusing on context and on register (e. g. 1998, 2004). My main source of reference for the present paper is the book *Exploring Translation and Multilingual Text Production: Beyond Content* edited by Erich Steiner and Colin Yallop (2001). This is a major work all parts of which—including papers by Michael Gregory, Juliane House, Erich Steiner, Elke Teich and Colin Yallop—are central to my discussion; but first and foremost I am drawing on one particular chapter, that by Christian Matthiessen entitled "The environments of translation" (pp. 41-124). It is a long chapter;

but then, Matthiessen is treating a long topic—or rather a whole range of topics which he has had to organize into a continuous progression unfolding as the text proceeds.

Matthiessen takes as one cornerstone of his analysis the reciprocal notions of translation equivalence and translation shift—terms that were used by Catford in the course of his own discussion. Matthiessen writes "I shall assume that translation equivalence and translation shift are two opposite poles on a cline of difference between languages"—from "maximal congruence" to "maximal incongruence" (p. 78). He adds, "The general principle is that the wider the environment of translation, the higher the degree of translation equivalence; and the narrower the environment, The higher the degree of translation shift." This is the principle of contextualization: The "widest" environment is that in which the translation is "maximally contextualized" (pp. 74-75), and therefore, by the same token, is likely to be "maximally effective."

So what are the "environments" that Matthiessen is referring to here? They are, or rather are defined by, the various dimensions along which language is organized: stratification, instantiation, rank, metafunction, delicacy and axis (see Figures 11 and 12, pp. 77 and 81, in Matthiessen's paper). Taken together, these are what give a language its inexhaustible power of making meaning, opening up all the different vectors—of abstraction, of combination, of depth in detail, of functional specialization and so on. Let me say a little about each of these in their own terms, and then go on to relate them to translation, where they define the various kinds of translation equivalence. All translators know from their own experience that there are different kinds of equivalence whose demands very often conflict; but beyond very general labels like "literal" and "free" we seldom come across a clear typology of equivalences which can put them into a coherent frame (cf. Koller, 1995).

Stratification refers to the way a language is organized as a hierarchy of strata, or levels of realization: phonetic, phonological, lexicogrammatical and semantic. These are usefully grouped into two pairs, those of expression (phonetic, phonological) and those of content (lexicogrammatical, semantic), because it is at the juncture between these two "planes" that translation is traditionally (and prototypically) located. "Same content, different expression" is the prototype from which basic translation strategies are derived. Then, above the semantic, we may add a further stratum of "context;" this is outside language—it is the non-linguistic environment in which texts come into being—but it can be modeled as the "upper" stratum in the realizational hierarchy. In Matthiessen's terms the context is the widest of the environments defined along this dimension.

Instantiation is the scale linking the instance—the text, the usual object of the translation process—to the system of the language that lies behind it. The text is meaningful because it is an instance of the total systemic potential; those who understand the text do so because they control that meaning-making resource. It is along this scale that we can recognize the various sub-systems, or registers, that are so critical to the effectiveness of a translation—often known in machine translation as "sub-languages." The translator, of course, is moving up and down this scale all the time, retrieving from the resources of the system (perhaps with the aid of a guide to these resources such as a dictionary) some instance that satisfies the requirement of an equivalent text.

My third heading was rank, sometimes referred to in structuralist terms as "size level." This is again a hierarchy, most clearly defined at the inner strata of lexicogrammar and phonology; there is some apparent variation here among different languages, but within grammar, at least, the familiar hierarchy or rank scale, of clause, phrase/group, word and morpheme, together with "complex" extensions of each—clause complex, phrase complex and so on—is valid for many of the languages we come to deal with, including Chinese and English. The questions of a rank scale on the semantic stratum is often debated, in particular the question whether one such can be generalized across all registers (see Hasan et al., 2007); since a text is itself defined as a semantic unit, this is an issue that needs to be explored very thoroughly in the context of translation theory and translation practice.

The fourth heading was metafunction, which is a dimension that, as Matthiessen points out, has long been recognized (or, at least, one aspect of it has) in translation studies but has seldom been addressed systematically. As the name proclaims, metafunction has something to do with function; but (here is the "meta" part) not the function or functions of the text—that is built in to the notion of context—but the functional order that is fundamental property of every language system, as the basis for the organization of meaning. Any instance of language—any text—is a complex of three orders of meaning, which we call ideational, interpersonal and textual; these can be analysed out at the semantic stratum, but in the lexicogrammar they are fused into an integrated progression of wording. The ideational is the representational aspect of meaning: meaning as the construal of experience, as narrative of the things and the qualities and the happenings of the world around us. The interpersonal is the active component of meaning, meaning as our way of interacting with other people, working on them so to speak, and introducing our own judgments and desires and our own angle on the situation. Interlacing these two strands of meaning in the text has always been seen as a problem for the translator, since this is one place where the demands of "equivalence" are most likely to conflict—priority is usually given to the ideational ("denotative") meaning, partly because it is felt to be more important and partly, perhaps, because it is easier to decide whether the translation is right or wrong. There is however a third component of meaning which is largely neglected in translation work, both theory and practice; this is the textual aspect, the organization of the meaning as a flow of discourse, with its balance between the old, or "given," and the new, and its ongoing fabric of connections with itself and with the context surrounding it (see Ventola, 1994; Zhu, 1996).

Delicacy, the fifth heading, refers to the depth of detail, in a scale running from most gross to most fine or "delicate." It seems to have been relatively little explored in translation theory, though it turned up in machine translation studies under the name "granularity." Delicacy has been a familiar concept in systemic functional theory for well over 40 years, in reference to what we might call "metadelicacy"—the degree of differentiation that is built in to the categories of the description; it is the basic concept behind our system networks, which represent progressively finer distinctions in, for example, the grammar of a language (e. g. clause—dependent clause—dependent clause of expansion—dependent clause of expansion by cause or condition ...); but we are able to set up this scale in the description because variable delicacy is a property of language itself (not just of our metalanguage). Translators often face the problem of matching the degree of specificity found in the source language text; in other words, of maintaining equivalence in delicacy. The question becomes most obvious in taxonomies of things, such as animal: reptile—snake—python—water python ...); but it arises throughout the lexicogrammar of every language.

Matthiessen's final heading is that of axis, which refers to the two dimensions of the semiotic space occupied by every element of the text at every stratum: the paradigmatic and the syntagmatic. We can think of this as the address of the element in the linguistic landscape. The syntagmatic environment is modeled as structure: what comes before and after—what combines, or can combine, with the element as parts in some organic whole. The paradigmatic environment is modeled as system: what could have come instead—what contrasts the element is entering into, what are the other alternatives that might have occurred (but did not). Taken together, the two axes of system and structure define the space in which the text is unfolding—at the lexicogrammatical stratum, the structures and grammatical classes, the collocations and lexical sets, which make up the context within which the translator is operating. The meaning of any element is the product of relations on both the axes; but the paradigmatic axis is what defines the "translation potential," since it involves relations with things that are not present in the particular instance, but are as it were lurking behind the text. (This is why the same term system enters into both oppositions: that of axis—system and structure—and that of instantiation—system and text.)

These six dimensions—stratification, instantiation, rank, metafunction, delicacy and axis—are critical to any comparison of two or more different languages; and hence to the process of translation, because they are the parameters that define equivalence (and therefore also non-equivalence, or shift). We need to illustrate these at work; but first, a note about the important concept of functional variation, or register. This is not a separate dimension; it is a property, and a product, of the regular association between meaning and context; between the culturally recognized situations in which language is used and the semantic (and therefore also the lexicogrammatical) features that are "at risk"—that are typically encountered in those situations. Since we assume, in translation, that the context remains the same, we can talk of equivalence in register—that is, equivalence in the linguistic strategies that are deployed, in the selection of features (typically features of the content, but also perhaps of the expression) that the situation demands. We recognize, of course, that such equivalence may be impossible if the cultural distance is such that no equivalent situation type is readily available. [①]These registers, or "sub-languages" as they are known in machine translation circles, are not some special feature or outgrowth on a language. Every text has its registerial "profile;" registers are the varieties of discourse that have evolved within a language, characterized by the tendency to select some options rather than, or more frequently than, others. Following J. R. Martin's work we have come to refer to culturally recognized, more or less institutionalized "macroregisters" by the rhetorical term genres; these have become a defining feature of educational applications of the theory, and writers on translation, who have long been familiar with the term in its literary and rhetorical connotations, often use it also to designate recognizable text types; see Shore (in Steiner & Yallop, 2001, p. 256), "... texts representing vastly different genres, e. g. an EU directive, a pop song, a highly valued literary text, a television commercial." (see Martin & Rose, 2007)

For illustration and discussion I have chosen two passages of translation between English and Chinese. Text A is from p. (v) of the *Times Chinese-English Dictionary*, published in 1980 jointly by Federal Publications in Singapore and by The Commercial Press in Hong Kong; A. 1 is the Chinese version; A. 2 is the English version; and A. 3 is my own translation of the Chinese version into English. Text B is a description of the "Tortoise and Crane" motif, printed on a card inserted in the box in which the metal reproduction was packaged; again, B. 1 is the Chinese version, B. 2 is the English version, and B. 3 is my own rendering of the Chinese version into English. In Text B, it is clear that the Chinese version is the original. In Text A we cannot be certain, but it is likely that here too the Chinese version was composed first.

I will examine some of the comparative features of these two pairs of texts, referring in particular to cases of translation shift, where the English and the Chinese are in some respect non-equivalent (since it is non-equivalence that needs to be explained). Text A will be considered first. I will start with the hierarchies of stratification and rank, taking them up together so as to save space; and I will begin at the highest level, where as Matthiessen says the relationship between the texts is maximally contextualized and there is the greatest potential for congruence between the two languages.

In Text A, the immediate contexts for the two texts are totally equivalent; they are in fact identical, since the texts appear one above the other on the same page of the same book. Interestingly, however, the titles of the two are different, not just in wording (lexicogrammatical stratum) but also in meaning (semantic stratum)—although it would have been quite acceptable for the Chinese to say 前言 "Foreword," or even 序 "Preface," or

---

① This is always a matter of "more or less;" there is no absolute equivalence or absolute non-equivalence. In the translation of the Bible, for example, the text may play a large part in bringing about the context of its use; cf. the role of translated texts in developing new registers (of science, administration and so on) in languages that had not previously operated in these functional contexts. (Steiner & Yallop, 2001)

for the English to say "Publishers' Note." There is a shift in the contextual function which the two texts are having assigned to them.

At the semantic stratum, we notice quite a lot of different ordering—much more than is required by the lexicogrammar. The flow of information in the two texts is quite different, particularly in the first half of the text. For example, in para. 2:

English:
This edition, which is a joint effort ..., aims to meet ...
This is the first medium-sized dictionary to be published locally
Chinese:
"In order to meet ..., Federal Press and Commercial Press combined"
"... revised the original to become a medium-sized dictionary, called ..."

Compare also para. 1, the location of "published in1979;" and, in para. 3b:

The adaptation ... provides a book ... new ... and ... practical
It will be ... indispensable ... for ... It will also be useful for foreigners learning ... Chinese ...
"After revision, the book will be ... a resource indispensable to ..."
"Its contents are new and ... practical and it will provide a reference for foreigners ... studying ... Chinese"

Apart from these shifts in the ordering of the material, there are other cases of non-equivalence in the translation:

para. 1:
lexicographical work of unprecedented dimensions
"task of compilation and revision"
para. 2:
different needs of a wider range of dictionary users
first ... to be published locally
"needs of a wide readership"(or "wide needs of the readers")
——

para. 3a:
——
"Other than this ... still ..."
Para. 4:
over 40 000 ... and over 40 000
"over 40 000 ... total ... over 80 000"

Para. 5：

—

"translations ... reflect the ... characteristics of the Chinese language"
Para. 6：

for the convenience of the user

All these are shifts at the semantic stratum; they are of course realized in the lexicogrammar, but not determined by it. Other than these, there are of course shifts in the grammar that arise from differences between Chinese and English; we can note three that are familiar.

(1) At clause rank, where there are qualities that are informationally "New." Chinese prefers to predicate these, while English tends to make them Epithets or Qualifiers: English "(provide with) a book new in content," Chinese "its contents are (relatively) new;" English "over 50 took part," Chinese "(those) taking part were more than 50." (The prototype for this is a pair such as English "she has long hair," Chinese "her hair is long," or "her, the hair is long.")

(2) At group rank, in Chinese all Modifiers precede what they modify, whereas in English the ordering depends on the rank: words premodify, phrases and clauses postmodify. I haven't mimicked the Chinese in my translation, but of course "the stylistic characteristics of the Chinese language" in Chinese is "the Chinese language's stylistic characteristics." But the shifts in ordering, already referred to, mean that there are fewer instances of this difference than would otherwise be expected; e.g. "the first dictionary to be published locally" would come out in Chinese as "the first locally published dictionary," but in fact this item of information is left out.

(3) At the ranks of clause and group: there may be a shift between the two. In Text A there is slightly more nominalization in the English than in the Chinese, but not very much—although sometimes the Chinese neutralizes the distinction. In para. 1, English "is an adaptation of" corresponds to Chinese "is adapted from;" but in para. 3b, where English has "the adaptation is an attempt to provide," the Chinese has 经过改编后 "having gone through adaptation" or perhaps "after having been adapted."

Lexically there is a high degree of equivalence, but with some shifts; for example, 精华 in para. 3a is not equivalent to "approach" but rather to "essence" or "essentials;" and in the same paragraph 词条 is not equivalent to "allusions," but to "(dictionary) entries." There are one or two shifts in delicacy: English "this edition," "this dictionary," where the Chinese spells out the full title; English "asterisked," Chinese 标出 "marks out." Other lexical shifts are the omissions already referred to, where an item occurs in one version but not in the other.

So let me turn to our fourth heading, that of metafunction. Ideationally, apart from shifts already mentioned, there is a high degree of equivalence. Textually, there were the shifts in the ordering of information, and also one or two shifts in clausal Theme, for example (para. 5), English "Emphasis was placed on using modern Chinese … " Chinese "In the compilation of this dictionary … modern Chinese is given priority." But the most striking metafunctional shift is in the interpersonal, where English has (para. 1) "work of unprecedented dimensions," (para. 2) "the first mediumsized comprehensive … dictionary," (para. 6) "for the convenience of the user," none of which figures in the Chinese. This gives the English a noticeably more boastful quality; even something like "Over 50 specialists, both Chinese and non-Chinese … " sounds more hyped up than the Chinese equivalent. This presumably reflects the fact that the intended market, those who are being targeted to buy the book, are anglophones rather than sinophones. And there is one reversal: the Chinese has "… (translations) reflect the stylistic characteristics of the Chinese language." This is not in the English, which leads one to wonder why not.

But perhaps we can suggest why not. Let me remark here that I selected this passage just to show the linguistic theory at work; but (as so often happens when you are dealing with texts!) once you analyse, you find unexpected matters of interest. Consider the first point we noticed, namely the title: "Foreword" in English, but "Publisher's Note" (or, more exactly, "Publisher Explanation") in Chinese. Now, under this Chinese heading we expect to read a factual account of the work, and its origins, written by the publisher to introduce it. But under the heading of "Foreword" we expect some evaluation, telling us that "this is a great work;" and the Foreword is always written by someone else. So here, despite an identical context of situation, the two texts have different functions with respect to that particular context.

This explains the special features in the English, which we noted: it has features of positive appraisal, or "plugs," encouraging you to buy the book. What the Chinese has, and the English has not, is the clause just cited, about the English translations reflecting the stylistic characteristics of the Chinese language 汉语的语体特点. Now tè diǎn 特点 contains the morpheme tè 特, which means "special." But the anglophone customer doesn't care about reflecting the stylistic particularities of the Chinese, and may even be put off by the idea; so that bit is left out. And now we can account for some of the differences in the information flow; for example, the Chinese "to suit the needs of a broad readership, these two publishers combined," in contrast to English "this book (a collaborative work) aims to meet the needs of a broader readership," which is a significantly different message to put to the reader.

Now let me look briefly at another example, "Crane on Tortoise's Back" (Text B). Contextually the Chinese and the English are equivalent, not only systemically but also instantially—that is to say, not only could they function in the same context, in fact they did: They were on the two sides of the same card, inserted in a box together with the object being described. It might be questioned whether they have the same function within that context; the Chinese might be designed more as sales promotion ("give this as a gift to your foreign friends"—that is how we got it), and this would be reflected in the shifts that we observe when we consider the Stratum of semantics.

Semantically, at the rank of the text the two versions are largely equivalent, except for the title and the blurb at the end, both of which occur only in the Chinese version. The organization of the rhetorical units, however, shows some shifts which we could summarize as follows (for "rhetorical unit" see Cloran, 1994):

English:

description maker Ⅱ *source meanings*$_{1,2}$

Chinese:

description 《*source*》*meaning* $_{general}$, *meaning*$_1$ *meaning*$_2$

The Chinese omits the height of the ornament; and also, curiously, the maker's name (though that may have been printed on the outside of the box). The English omits much more: It leaves out much of the descriptive detail, the reference to the folk tradition, the fact that the piece is "rich in meaning," and much of what that meaning is—notably the reference to the interpretation of crane as female and tortoise as male.

In the lexicogrammar there are some striking differences. The Chinese text is made of clauses; many of them are relational, with processes realized by verbs, such yì yù 意喻 "symbolize," dài biǎo 代表 "represents," wéi 为 "is," yǐ … zhī yì 以……之意 "has the meaning of," rú tóng … bān 如同……般 "is like," but some are material: gēn jù … ér chéng 根据……而成 "is produced according to," lì yú … shàng 立于……上 "stands on," kǒu xián 口衔 "holds in the mouth." In the English, the whole of the first paragraph is presented as a nominal group complex (in that respect being more like the title in the Chinese). The second paragraph is presented as three written sentences; the grammar is clausal, all five clauses being relational—the only material process is the rank shifted (embedded) clause beginning at "displayed." The English is thus much more static: "proposed" and "made by" are non-finite, while the material processes equivalent to "standing" and "holding" are realized not by verbs but by prepositions ("on," "in"). By contrast, the Chinese text creates a history, unfolding in the course of time.

Here the Chinese text is obviously the original; the shifts take place in the translation into English. The English is clearly intended to be equivalent in register, and it largely is. The words "proposed" and "imitation" are probably translation shifts; they have no equivalent in the Chinese, but I take it that "proposed" is an ideational error for "designed," while "imitation" is interpersonally wrong because it is negatively loaded—it should have been "reproduction." But the one item that is strikingly out of place is the "gloosy ganoderma."

This leads us to consider the limits, or rather perhaps the fringes, of the translation process; the gloosy ganederma will serve as the way in. Of course it's a misprint; "gloosy" should have been "gloosy." And "glossy ganoderma" is what the translator would have found in the dictionary as the English equivalent of líng zhī 灵芝. Its Latin name is

Ganederma lucidum. But here it is quite out of register: There is a violent shift, with the meaning of lingzhi being realized in the lexicon of a different sub-system. In this respect a closer equivalent would be "wonder iris" or "miracle iris."①

This matches the registerial mode of the rest of the text, as in the words "crane," "tortoise," "youth," "elixir" and so on.

We could perhaps retain the word "glossy;" but the text doesn't have "glossy," it has "gloosy," with a shift at the strata of expression, both orthographic and phonological. Now, most translation does not provide for equivalence in phonology, though it may need to be taken into account. One of my earliest published works was an English translation of the well-known Chinese song jiào wǒ rú hé bù xiǎng tā?《叫我如何不想她》; my translation was done for performance at a recital by a singer, so it had to fit the music—I t had to match the rhythm of the Chinese. I rendered the title line as "How should I not think of her?" Even here, however, it would not be thought necessary to consider the articulation—the vowels and consonants; they are usually regarded as neutral, just automatized realizations of the wording. But perhaps we should explore this a little further.

The word "gloosy" doesn't exist in English. But it could exist, and we can have a good idea of what it would mean if it did. Note the initial consonant cluster /gl-/. Words beginning with /gl-/ often have to do with light, typically momentary and bright, like "gleam," "glint," "glimmer," "glitter." These have a front vowel; with a back vowel, the light is faint, as in "gloom" and "gloomy;" and perhaps "gloaming," though with a more open vowel the light seems to be more diffuse, like in "glow" and "gloss" and "glare." But what about the -ossy /-uːzɪ/? This is fuzzier; note "woozy" meaning "half asleep," "snoozy" meaning "sleepy", "boozy" meaning "fuddled with drink," and also "oozy" meaning "muddy and slow moving." When we put /gl-/ and /-uːzɪ/ together, this suggests wandering around sleepily with only a very dim light.

This kind of pattern is known as phonaesthesia, or sound symbolism. It is not onomatopoeia; there is no imitation involved, because these meanings have no sound to imitate. There is just a direct line from phonology to a lexicalized semantic field. I think there is something similar in Cantonese, where nasal initial /n-/, /m-/ or /n-/ plus high front vowel often means squeezing or pinched tight, as in the following words:

niù	杽	"slender"	nín	撚	"squeeze"
nit	𪘁	"grasp"	mì	寐	"close(eyes)"
nip	捻	"pinch"	ngit	齧	"nibble"
nip	錜	"pincers"	nì	闑	"hide"
nip	吅	"press flat"	nìm	拈	"carry in fingers"

① I think it is a kind of iris, though dictionaries have different views: One dictionary told me that it was a "fungus," and another gave "lotus." Whatever it is, the translator needs to find a word from the general, not the learned vocabulary.

(I first noticed these when learning Cantonese many years ago. The characters and English translations given here are taken from the dictionary I was using at the time, *The Student's Cantonese-English Dictionary* published by the Field Afar Press, New York, in 1947.)

Sound symbolism figures prominently in the phonology of English. There is a website listing a large number of phonaesthetic series; not all of them are convincing, to me at least, but that still leaves a considerable number that are. They tend, naturally, to carry more semiotic force in spoken language—but also in those varieties of written language that are designed to be read aloud, particularly books written for young children. They might seem to be only of marginal interest in the present context—except that such books are in great demand as texts for translation. As the humorous writer Paul Jennings said many years ago, "Paradoxically, the more a work expresses some special national genius, the more it attracts translatore" (1963, p. 32). Jennings' "special national genius" was not defined; but he gave examples from Beatrix Potter's stories for children which contain many instances phonaesthesia. An example is the "Tale of the Flopsy Bunnies. " With the name "flopsy," it was clear that these bunnies were laid-back, easy-going and rather idle (compare "flat," "flabby," "flaccid," "floppy," "flighty"); they took neither themselves nor anything else very seriously. The German translation was "die Geschichte der Hasenfamilie Plumps" (the story of the rabbit family Plumps). If they had been "Plumps" in English, the effect would have been very different; they would have been rather pompous, taking themselves very seriously (think of "plummy," "plushy," "plume" as in "plume oneself;" also "plumped up," and many words ending in -ump). This would have had a different effect on the whole story.

The question is, what is "equivalence" in this situation? Do we simply say that it is verbal humour, a form of punning and therefore untranslatable? With a pun there can be no equivalence, in another language, in the meanings that share the same sound, except by the occasional "happy coincidence. " For the same reason it is impossible to translate cryptic crossword puzzles, which depend entirely on verbal play. Not all verbal humour involves punning, of course; there are other kinds without word play, such as the mixed cliché like "(I had to do) the lion's share of the donkey work" or "(I suspect you're) skating on the thin end of an icy wedge. " But they all make problems for the translator, for a combination of two reasons: One, there are seldom any equivalent forms of wording; the other, different cultures have different ideas about what's funny.

This is in principle no different from the problem that arises at the other extreme—at the upper end of the traditional scale of textual value, in the translation of literature. In translating poetry, the translator may choose to produce what is simply a gloss on the meaning of the original. But some translators seek to create a text of equivalent value, matching (say) lyric poetry with lyric poetry, if there appears to be an equivalence between the genres. But where, in terms of our model, is the equivalence established? For many decades now there has been a tradition of translating Japanese haiku and tanka into English while retaining the syllable count: Seventeen syllables in the haiku, 31 in the tanka. But the syllable in English is a very different matter from the syllable, or "mora," in Japanese; the equivalence here is quite illusory. Meanwhile, however, both these forms are now being written as original works in English; this has become a recognized genre in its own right (my daughter-in-law has won many prizes for hers). But evaluated according to what ae perceived as the essential semantic motifs of the original Japanese model. Translators of Chinese lyric poetry, the shī 诗 of the Tang dynasty, have never (as far as I know) tried to preserve the syllable count of the original Chinese, though one could—the Chinese syllabic rhythm is much more like that of English (cf. Huang, 2002). Here is a version of one of the best known Tang lyric poems, which is a quatrain with five syllables per line, rhyming AABA, and with each syllable realizing one simple (monomorphemic) word:

> *Bed foot, bright moon's shine—*
> *Ground seems decked with rime.*
> *Head raised, watch bright moon;*
> *Head bowed, home thoughts chime.*

The problem here, for translation theory, is that while there is near equivalence on the dimensions of strata and rank, even down to the monosyllabic construction of the verse lines, there is in the English a kind of built-in exoticism, which is not present in the Chinese. There is not enough grammar in the English, which needs pronouns and determiners and prepositions—of course, there is grammar (it is quite clear what it means), but not the outward signs of it, which are needed for comfort in English, but not in an East Asian language such as Chinese. Translators of Chinese poetry sometimes use imperfective non-finite clauses, which sound a little less exotic because they are used by English poets; they avoid the need for subjects, and for choosing a particular tense. Here is an alternative rendering in this manner:

> *Before bed, bright moon shining—*
> *Ground beneath frost reclining?*
> *Head raised, watching bright moon;*
> *Head bowed, for old home pining.*

But this still remains a marked option by contrast with the finite, whereas there is no such markedness in the Chinese—in fact no system of finiteness. So here there is shift on the paradigmatic axis: Either the systems are not equivalent, or, if they are, there is shift in the pattern of marking.

I have considered two texts, Text A and Text B, each in two versions, one Chinese and one English; together with a third version which is my rendering of the Chinese into English. Text A provided illustration of some fairly straightforward patterns of equivalence and shift; Text B, on the other hand, led us out towards the fringes of translatability. This has been a very brief exercise in comparative discourse analysis, whereby it is possible to be reasonably precise in locating the patterns of equivalence and shift between the two related versions. It does not matter how such texts have been produced—whether by translation one from the other, human or mechanical, or by separate composition given the same contextual specifications; the analytic method is the same. Such a linguistic analysis has, I think, a value in the teaching of translation, and thus in the training of translators, because it enables teacher and learner to direct attention to all the relevant issues, knowing exactly what it is they are talking about. This is not as easy as it sounds, and it makes the analytic effort worth while.

What about the evaluation of the product? Does the linguistic analysis help us to say whether, and why, a translation is effective, or one translation better than another? One way to explore this is to take two or more translated versions of the same text where you feel that one is clearly better than another, and observe what emerges from the analysis. Your judgment will have something to do with the degree of equivalence; but there can be no exact correlation—it is impossible to give an overall measure of equivalence because, as we have seen, equivalence is of so many different kinds. But that itself suggests a further step: That different kinds of equivalence have differential value, and that the value accorded to different kinds of equivalence will vary according to the context, both the context of situation and the context of culture.

Matthiessen postulated the general principle that on the hierarchical scales of stratification and rank, the "higher" levels tend to carry the higher value. One the other dimensions, we may assign value to particular instances or classes of translation: We might say, for example, that in translating lyric poetry equivalence in the interpersonal metafunction takes precedence, or that equivalent delicacy is essential in a medical treatise but only secondary in a tourist guide. Juliane House, in her paper "How do we know when a translation is good?" (Stener & Yallop, eds. 2001) makes a key distinction between "overt" and "covert" translation, and sets a different scale of values for the two. An "overt" translation is one that proclaims itself clearly as a translation, and makes no attempt to operate, and no claim to operating, in the same functional context as the original; it needs to be equivalent in register, and also in what House calls the "language/text level" (semantics and some lexico-grammar), but not necessary in "individual textual function." With a "covert" translation, which pretends not to be a translation at all, "individual textual function" must be held equivalent, if necessary with the insertion of a "contextual filter," but equivalence in "language/text" can be dispensed with. Interestingly, she then uses the overt/covert distinciton as itself the bearer of value, and criticizes a particular translation of a children's story from English into German because it was covert, where in her view an overt translation would have been more appropriate.

It is important, as Juliane House says (ibid., p. 156), to maintain the distinction between linguistic analysis and value judgment, however much the two are interdependent. The analysis in systemic functional terms is a resource for interrogating the text—in this case, for interrogating a pair of related texts, by comparing the one with the other. Only certain parts of the analysis are likely to be relevant to evaluation. But we shall not know which parts these are until we have looked into them all—or at least gained some idea of where there is equivalence and where there is shift, and related these findings to our overall impression of the texts in their respective functional contexts.

I chose the gloosy ganoderm as an eye-catching (and ear-catching) instance which would open up several of the dimensions of our analysis, in a way that was rather different from, and perhaps complementary to, the features of the *Times Dictionary* text. Between them they provided illustrations of a general theory of language as a resource for translation studies. Translators are all the time exploring the potential that is defined by all these parameters of a language; when we make them explicit, our discussion of the issues and problems involved in the translation process becomes very much more focused and effective. As linguists, we are always concerned to distinguish between the indicative and the imperative stance—between describing what is and evaluating, and perhaps prescribing, what ought to be. Traditionally, the linguist's theory of translation has been descriptive, the translator's has been evaluative. But in real life, texts carry value, and we need to explain that value in terms of what we know about semiosis—about meaning and how meaning is made. This is true of all analysis of discourse; but in translation studies it is the central issue. A linguistic theory of translation cannot avoid the challenge of becoming—or at least supporting—a theory of good translation.

选文二　维根斯坦的语言观与翻译
——节选自《口笔译理论研究》

刘宓庆

导　言

　　刘宓庆在其《口笔译理论研究》一书的开篇集中论述了语言哲学的奠基人维根斯坦的语言观对翻译——特别是口译——的启示。维根斯坦认为人与人之间的对话都是游戏，但是不同的语言游戏有不同的游戏规则。翻译也是一种"语言游戏"，在这个语言游戏中，游戏规则至关重要,运用到口译中也是如此。维根斯坦还认为"意义在于使用",所谓"意义即使用"(meaning is use),而意义"使用"的基本依据就是"生活形式"(forms of life),这是任何语言游戏的最高规则,也是最基本的规则。口译是特定语境下特定的翻译传播行为,口译语言行为具有很强的当下性,根据维根斯坦"意义取决于使用"的语言哲学观,这里的"使用"意味着"语言环境",即"语境"。意义具有"不确定性"和"游移性",只有语境才能将特定的意义固定下来,语境使语言的意向性更加明确。因此在口译中,一条最基本的法则就是"重视口译的语境"。维根斯坦的语言观奠定了该书对口译中话语结构、话语意义、话语效果和话语机制四个核心问题进行探讨的基础。选文节选于该书中论述维根斯坦语言哲学观与翻译关系的章节。

1.0 概述

"语言游戏"(language games)论是维根斯坦对自己的语言观所作的一个既感性、又极富启发性的简约表述,据说他是在看一场足球赛的时候突然悟出来的。[①] "语言游戏"论也是他对自己在前期提出的语言观——"语言图像"说的一种否定。[②] 维根斯坦在他的后期著作《哲学研究》(*Philosophical Investigations*)中曾经多次提到翻译,并明确指出翻译属于"语言游戏"。他写道:

> Here the term "language-game" is meant to bring into prominence the fact that the speaking of language is part of an activity, or of a form life.
> Review the multiplicity of language-games in the following examples, and in

---

① 以下一段论述,供参考。

根据维根斯坦的描述,语言游戏具有如下明显特征:(1) 它具有自主性,不依赖于任何外在的对象,而在于使用的对错与否;(2) 它不需要用其他的目的或标准来证明,也不是任何推论的结果,而只是我们生活的一部分、无需对它加以反思;(3) 它具有多样性和复杂性,不能把它们归结为某种单一的本质;(4) 它必须遵守规则,不同的规则带来了不同的游戏,也决定了不同语言的用法。这些特征集中反映了维根斯坦后期思想的主要内容。

引自《新编现代西方哲学》,刘放桐等编,北京,人民出版社,2000 年,第 276 页。

② 前期的维根斯坦语言观集中表现于"语言图像论"。"图像论"认为:语言与"经验世界"(也就是现实世界)的关系可以用客体与图像的关系来描述。20 世纪二三十年代之交,维根斯坦以严谨的科学态度否定了自己提出的"图像论"。他在《哲学研究》序言中说:

……自从 16 年前我重新开始哲学活动以来,我不得不承认在我的第一本书(指《逻辑哲学论丛》)里犯有严重的错误。我是在拉姆塞(Frank Ramsey)的批评帮助下认识到这些错误的。从某种程度上讲,我本人无法判断这些错误。在拉姆塞生命最后两年里,我与他进行了无数次的讨论。在与我的思想交锋中,他常常是明确而且有力地批评了我。除此之外,我还得感谢剑桥大学的教师斯拉法(P. Sraffa)先生,许多年来,他都在不懈地对我的思想进行批评。这激发了本书坚持的许多重要见解。对此,我非常感激。……

我带着疑惑之情发表此书。在这贫困和黑暗的时代,要使这本书确能照亮人们的头脑,虽非妄想——但的确是不太可能的。

我不应奢望我的著作能使人摆脱思想混乱。但是,如果可能,我确实希望它能激励人们独立思考。

后世有人批评维根斯坦,认为不必根本否定"图像论",因为语言确实在一定程度上"显映出世界的面貌";有人认为"图像论"可以与"游戏说"互为补充。

others：

Giving orders, and obeying them—

Describing the appearance of an object, or giving its measurements—

Constructing an object from a description (a drawing)—

Reporting an event—

Speculating about an event—

Forming and testing a hypothesis—

Presenting the results of an experiment in tables and diagrams—

Making up a story; and reading it—

Play-acting—

Singing catches—

Guessing riddles—

Making a joke; telling it—

Solving a problem in practical arithmetic—

Translating from one language into another—

Asking, thanking, cursing, greeting, praying.

—It is interesting to compare the multiplicity of the tools in language and of the ways they are used, the multiplicity of kinds of word and sentence, with what logicians have said about the structure of language. (Including the author of the *Tractatus Logico-Philosophicus*.)

(Prt Ⅰ, §23, 11e)

[这里提出的"语言游戏"这一术语意在强调下面的事实：说某一种语言就是从事某种活动的组成部分，或是生活的某种形式。

下面的例子(还有其他例子)使我们看到语言游戏的多样性：

发出命令和服从命令——

描述一个对象的外表或对它进行测量——

通过描述(一幅图画)来构建一个对象——

报告某一事件——

思考某一事件——

形成和检验某一假说——

将实验结果绘成图表——

编写并朗读一个故事——

演戏——

唱歌——

猜谜——

编笑话、讲笑话——

解应用算术题——

将一种语言译成另一种语言——

发问、感谢、诅咒、问候、祈祷。

——将语言中各式各样的工具和使用这些工具的方法以及语词和语句种类的多样性与逻辑学家关于语言结构所说的话，包括《逻辑哲学论》的作者——即维根斯坦本人——作一番比较，是很有意思的。]

维根斯坦为什么将各式各样的语言交流比做"语言游戏"呢？

当代西方语言哲学界的一个基本的看法是维根斯坦在倡导哲学和语言向自然回归，这也是他自己对前期哲学研究取向（即用人工语言学来批判日常语言学，以引文中提到的《逻辑哲学论》的出版为标志）的反思。这个自我批判的态度可以从引文的最后一句话看出来。

后期的维根斯坦认为日常语言最自然，它是我们的一种"生活的形式"。维根斯坦说"想象一种语言意味着想象一种生活形式"（"to imagine a language means to imagine a form of life", Prt Ⅰ, §19, 8e）。翻译就像日常生活中的下棋。A 走一步，接着 B 走一步，如此轮流；口译也一样。A 说一句或一段，接着 B 说一句或一段，如此轮流，直至结束。我们看看下面将两者相比的例子就明白（I＝interpreter 译员）：

↓A 走第一步棋：

A：I'm not a doctor, but I play one when I'm talking about TV. And the American Medical Association and I agree：Television is bad for kids.

I：我不是医生，但我可以权当医生来谈论电视。美国医师协会和我都同意：电视对孩子有害。

轮到 B 走下一步了：

↓B：Could you specify?

I：您可以解释一下吗？

↓轮到 A 走下一步了：

A：Young people not only would kill to watch TV; they do kill from staring goggle-eyed at the box, a truly internal machine that delivers 200 000 acts of violence to the typical youngster's brain pan before he's old enough to drive.

I：年轻人不仅可能从看电视中学会杀人，而且他们确实真枪真刀地干了，是他们瞪着双眼从电视里学的。可恨的电视机在一个孩子达到驾车年龄以前就将 200 000 个暴力行为塞进他的脑袋里。

↓轮到 B 走下一步了：

B：Could you further specify?

I：您能不能再谈具体一点呢？

↓又轮到 A 了：

A：Every kid in America, on average, witnesses 16 000 murders on TV before reaching the ripe old age of 18. And you wonder why they throw candy wrappers on the side walk or refuse to give an old lady a seat on a crowded bus?

I：在美国，在孩子到达成熟年龄即 18 岁以前，要在电视中目睹 16 000 起谋杀案。这就足以解释他们为什么会将包糖果的纸扔向人行道，足以解释为什么他们在拥挤的公共汽车中不给年老的妇女让座了！

↓谈话可能继续下去

这样一来一往地交流不确实与下棋等游戏一样吗？

笔译也是一种语言交流。笔译中的篇章（text）只不过是口译中的一句、一段的延长、扩展罢了，它们之间都有"家族相似"。

但翻译与下棋或一般的语内交流（intralingual communication）之间除了基本相似以外，有一个突出的"非相似性"（non-resemblance），那就是不论口译或笔译语言游戏，参与者之间必须有一位（或几位）翻译作媒介（medium）。这个问题与传播学密切相关，我们在下一章再议。

维根斯坦之所以将翻译归到语言游戏家族中还有一些其他的根据。我们可以再回头看看他列出的 15 项游戏例子。归纳起来，有以下几点，对语言游戏至关紧要，对口译也至关紧要。

1.1　遵守规则与驾驭规则

所有的"游戏"都有规则，翻译"语言游戏"（包括口译）也不例外。在这里，维根斯坦提出了三点：(1) 对所有的游戏参与者来说，遵守规则都是强制性的，除非他不愿参与这项游戏（Prt Ⅰ，§ 219，85e）。这时他确实是"盲目的"；(2) 我们是在参与游戏的过程中学会遵守规则（Prt Ⅰ，§ 54，27e）；(3) 如果想要游戏成功地进行下去，就要实现关于"遵守规则"的一条辩证法：从"遵守规则"跃进到"驾驭规则"（skillfully handle the rules and laws）。维根斯坦写道，如果你细心观看游戏，你就会发现，"在游戏参与者的行为中存在着具有特征的符号"（"There are characteristic signs of it in the players behavior", Prt Ⅰ，§ 54，27e），符号之别常常表明不同的游戏参加者如何在"遵守规则"中各自一步一步从熟悉规则做到自如地"驾驭规则"。

维根斯坦说：

...

And is there not also the case where we play and—make up the rules as we go along? And there is even one where we alter them—as we go along. (Prt Ⅰ，§ 83，39e)

（难道不也存在这样一种情况：我们玩游戏并在玩的过程中制定规则？——甚至还存在这样的情况：我们一边玩游戏，一边修改规则。）

不仅如此，维根斯坦还指出了"游戏规则"的辩证性质：

"But then the use of the word is unregulated，the 'game' we play with it is unregulated."—It is not everywhere circumscribed by rules; but no more are there any rules for how high one throws the ball in tennis, or how hard; yet tennis is a game for all that and has rules too. (Prt Ⅰ，§ 68，33e)

"可是这样一来，'游戏'这个词的用法就没有什么规则了，我们玩的游戏也就没有规则了。"——游戏并不是处处都要受到规则的约束，没有什么规则规定网球应当打多高或打多重；但网球仍是一种游戏，并且也是有规则的。

这中间的辩证法维根斯坦称之为"规管游戏的自然法则"（"a natural law governing the play"，Prt Ⅰ，§54，27e）。他认为规则用以指引取向，认定取向要达到目的地，这一切要靠游戏参与者在参加游戏的过程中富集自己的经验，不为规则所累而能驾驭规则，原因是"语言中并没有什么充分至极的规律性"（"There is not enough regularity for us to call it 'language'"，Prt Ⅰ，§207，82e）。维根斯坦说：

A rule stands there like a sign-post. Does the sigh-post leave no doubt open about the way I have to go? Does it show which direction I am to take then I have passed it；whether along the road or the footpath or cross-country? But where is it said which way I am to follow it；whether in the direction of its finger or（e. g.）in the opposite one? —And if there were，not a single sign-post，but a chain of adjacent ones or of chalk marks on the ground—is there only one way of interpreting them? —So I can say，the sign-post does after all leave no room for doubt. Or rather：it sometimes leaves room for doubt and sometimes not. And now this is no longer a philosophical proposition，but an empirical one.（Prt Ⅰ，§85，40e）

（一条规则就像一杆路标。路标难道不是确切地、公开地告诉我要去的路吗？当我走过路标时，它难道不是表明了我将要去的方向，是沿着大路走去，还是沿小道或穿过田野？可是它在哪里指出我该走的路呢？它又在哪里指出我是沿着它所指的方向还是——比如在相反的方向——走去呢？还有，如果不是一块路标，而是一排毗连的路标或是在路面上画的许多粉笔标记，那么，难道只有一种诠释它们的方式吗？——因此，我可以说，路标毕竟没有留下什么怀疑的余地。或者可以说，它有时留下了怀疑的余地，有时没有。既然如此，那么就不再是哲学命题，而是经验命题了。）

毫无疑问，维根斯坦这些见解对我们研究口译是至关紧要的。不论口译还是笔译，我们都不可能找到可以规管一切翻译现象和行为的规则。关键在于：首先要遵守规则，并让我们通过实践做到驾轻就熟，即"驾驭规则"。我们将在本书中结合口译实际逐步展开对如何辩证地理解"遵守规则"这一课题的探讨。

1.2　意义取决于使用（"Meaning is use"）

口译员怎样从话语中获得准确的意义？这是翻译理论首要的问题。

维根斯坦认为"意义即使用"（"use"，也可以是"application"，G. Anscombe），"意义寓于使用"。维氏论证说，儿童学习语言、把握意义就是始于"使用"（Prt Ⅰ，§9，6e），"只有根据语言的各种初始运用来研究语言现象"，才能"驱散（语言的）迷雾"。正是在语言的初始应用中，人们可以清晰地看到词语的目的和功能（Prt Ⅰ，§5，4e）。维氏认为词语的意义是由它的用法（use）决定的（Prt Ⅰ，§139，54e）。某一特定的意义适合于某一特定的用法（"the meaning fits the use")；维根斯坦也简明扼要地说"meaning is the use"(Prt Ⅰ，§138，53e)。[①] 维根斯坦的论断是：

For a large class of cases—though not for all—in which we employ the word "meaning" it can be defined thus：the meaning of a word is its use in the language. And the meaning of a name is sometimes explained by pointing to its bearer.

（就我们使用"意义"一词的大多数情况——虽然不是全部情况——而言,可以这样为"意义"下一个定义：一个语词的意义就是它在语言里的用法。同时,一个名称的意义有时也可以凭借它指向的载体来加以解释。）

维根斯坦进而考察说,意义其所以取决于用法,是因为意义"肯定必须属于某一语言的某一语境"("... they must surely belong to a language and to a context"，Prt Ⅱ，§xi，217e)，语境使意指(to mean；to signify)确定化、具体化为此情此景的"对象"(the object，Prt Ⅰ，§6，4e)，而不再是游移不定的东西。这样,"语境—用法—意义"之间就有了互为条件的联系,这实在是极其重要的翻译规律,是"翻译语言游戏"最基本的法则。维根斯坦说：

If you were unable to say that the word "till" could be both a verb and a conjunction，or to construct sentences in which it was now the one and now the other，you would not be able to manage simple schoolroom exercises. But a schoolboy is not asked to conceive the word in one way or another out of any context，or the report how he has conceived it.

...

We take a sentence and tell someone the meaning of each of its words；this tells him how to apply them and so how to apply the sentence too. If we had chosen a senseless sequence of words instead of the sentence，he would not learn how to apply the sequence.

---

① 以下引文取自苟志效著《意义与符号》(广东人民出版社,1996年,第42页),作者批评维根斯坦说：

正如美国学者 M. K. 穆尼茨所指出的那样："维特根斯坦的《逻辑哲学论》是一部公认的现代哲学的经典著作。这本书和他后期的主要著作《哲学研究》一起,确保他在哲学史上享有一个持久的地位。"其实,维特根斯坦的功用论意义定义同样存在着严重的缺陷。首先,维特根斯坦把语词当成表达意义的既成工具,显然不能自圆其说。维特根斯坦指出："想一下工具箱中的各种工具吧。有锤子、钳子、锯子、螺丝起子、尺子、熬胶锅、胶、钉子和螺钉。——词的功用就和这些东西的功用一样是各种各样的。"然而,锤子、钳等工具是人造的,词又从何而来? 事实证明,词也是人造的。但是,词是有意义的"工具",也即是说,词的出现在于意义的支持,离开了内在的意义,无论人的语音还是书写符号,都不会成为词。这样一来,维特根斯坦就陷入了意义在于词的用法,而语词是意义外化的产物这样一个怪圈中。用语词说明意义,又用意义解释语词,这是维特根斯坦无法摆脱的逻辑矛盾。其次,维特根斯坦一方面认为,语词的意义就是它在语言中的使用,而语言的使用不过是一种游戏。

其实上述"逻辑矛盾"并不存在。首先,维根斯坦并不是在为意义下定义。维氏的"意义即使用"一语旨在答复"意义在哪里呢?"的提问,这可以从他的前后文及全书主旨看得很清楚。维根斯坦自始至终在强调意义对语境、对用法的敏感性以及语境、用法对意义的制约作用,而不是在作意义生成机制的探讨。很明显,"使用"本身不是"意义","使用"制约,规管"意义","意义取决于使用"(或"意义寓于使用",Prt Ⅰ，§197，80e)是较妥的表述式。这对翻译是至关紧要的,也是我们关注的中心。

（如果你无法说出"till"一词既是动词又是连词，或者不能用这个词造句，其中它时而是动词，时而是连词，那么你就无法指导简单的课堂练习。但是，没有人会要求学童用这种或那种脱离语境的方式来构想词语，或者要他说说他是怎样构想出来的。

……

我们说出一个语句，并把这个句子中的每个词语的意义都告诉了某人；这就等于把如何使用这些词语以及如何使用这个语句告诉了他。假如我们选择的是一个无意义的词语序列而不是语句，那么他就不能学会如何运用这个序列。）

可见，维根斯坦非常重视语境。他认为不仅意义受制于语境，意向（intention）也含蕴于并受制于语境，"意向依附于情景中"（"An intention is embedded in situation", Prt I, §337, 108e）。维根斯坦认为意向的自然表达无不伴随与该意向相吻合的情景，"境中有情，情为意表"（情境中表现意向），因此我们可以从把握情境来分析出大体的意向，并将它表现在语言中。维氏将这个道理密切联系到现实情景（"生活的形式"）中，并解释说：

What is the natural expression of an intention? —Look at a cat when it stalks a bird; or a beast when it wants to escape.

(Connexion with propositions about sensations.) (165e)

（意向的自然表达是怎样的呢？——看一只猫潜行捕鸟或一只野兽想要逃走时的情状就清楚了。）

（与关于感觉的命题有联系。）

在翻译中我们如何凭借"使用"来把握意义和意向并赋形（外化）为表达式呢？这里的关键是要运用感性为原语的意义和意向寻求符合情景的译语"自然表达式"（犹如"痛楚"而发出"喊声"——这"喊声"就是自然表达式，§§665，666，667）。这时，意向就被整合在意义中而外化表现为译语词句了。[①] 维根斯坦举了下面一个例子来表示"经验—意义—意向—表达式"的内在关系：

I look at an animal and am asked, "What do you see?" I answer, "A rabbit."—I see a landscape; suddenly a rabbit runs past. I exclaim, "A rabbit!"

Both things, both the report and the exclamation, are expressions of perception and of visual experience. But the exclamation is so in a different sense from the report: It is forced from us. —It is related to the experience as a cry is to pain. (Prt II, §xi, 197e)

（我看着一只动物，有人问我："你看见什么？"我答道："一只兔子。"我看见一片风景；忽然一只兔于跑过去，我惊叫道："一只兔子！"

两件事情，报道和惊叫都表达了知觉和视觉经验。但是，惊叫的表达式在意义上不同于报道：它是我们见景而喊出来的。——它与视觉经验的关系有如叫喊与疼痛的关系。）

---

① 在维根斯坦看来，"意向"永远被整合在意义中并体现为某种"自然表达式"，也就是说"意指"中永远含蕴"意向"。这正是语言游戏的一部分。维根斯坦举了下文中的一个例子来表示"经验—意义—意向—表达式"的关系。

1.3 "生活形式":意义"使用"的基本依据

维根斯坦认为意义取决于"使用"（"use"，指适应某种目的或功能的"用"；也可以是"应用"，指凭借某种工具的"用"；"运用"，指强调行为操控的"用"）。"使用"必然要体现在某一基于实际情景的语境中，"没有语境"（"free from any context"）的意义应用，无确定的意义可言。维根斯坦为什么要将"生活的形式"引人他的语言观中呢？

以 20 世纪二三十年代之交为起点，维根斯坦从人工语言（也就是理想语言）研究转而致力于对日常语言的悉心观察和哲学阐释。生活感受和哲学思考使他领悟到脱离了语言现实的实证逻辑分析的片面性和日常语言的无限生机。他在第一次提出"语言游戏"论的后期著作《蓝皮书和褐皮书》（*Blue Book and Brown Book*，Frankfurt，Suhrhamp，1922）中写道：

> 有人说我们在哲学上认定理想语言与日常语言相对立。这种看法是错误的。因为这使人觉得，我们似乎能够改造日常语言。事实上，日常语言完全正确，用不着我们去改造。同时，当我们试图构建"理想语言"时，目的不是为了用它来取代我们的日常语言，而仅仅是为了排除人们的错觉：以为他们已经掌握了日常语词的精确用法。正因为如此，我们的方法是不仅列举语词的实际用法，而且旨在提出新的用法。（根据德文译出，德文版，p. 34）

维根斯坦的语言观到后期明显倾向于日常语言，最终扬弃了对理想语言的追求。他用隐喻的手法写道：

> The more narrowly we examine actual language, the sharper becomes the conflict between it and our requirement. (For the crystalline purity of logic was, of course, not a result of investigation: it was a requirement.) The conflict becomes intolerable; the requirement is now in danger of becoming empty. —We have got on to slippery ice where there is no friction and so in a certain sense the conditions are ideal, but also, just because of that, we are unable to walk. We want to walk: so we need friciton. Back to the rough ground! (Prt I, §107, 46e)
>
> （我们越是精益求精地考查实际语言，它与我们的要求之不相容便越是尖锐——因为，毫无疑问，那水晶般的逻辑的纯净不是研究的结果，它只是我们的一种要求——现在，这二者成了水火不相容了！眼下这一要求也有落空的危险——我们已经濒临那没有摩擦的光溜溜的冰面。因此，在某种意义上说，这种情况是再好不过的，但正因为如此，我们便不能行走了。人要行走，就需要摩擦。回到粗糙的地面上来吧！）

维根斯坦的寓意很深刻。理想语言固定"没有摩擦"，犹如"光溜溜的冰面"，日常语言固然芜杂粗糙，但是，哲学家像语言学家还是不能不回到"粗糙的地面"。这是什么缘故呢？

维根斯坦的回答看似非常简单："don't think, but look!"（不要想，但要看！Prt I，§66，31e），但却是一个真理；"看"什么呢？维根斯坦说，"看"实际生活中的游戏，看"生活的实际"就会明白一切了：

> Consider for example the proceedings that we call "games." I mean board-games, card-games, ball-games, Olympic games, and so on. What is common to them all? —Don't say: "There must be something common." Or they would not be called 'games'—but look and see whether there is anything common to all. —For if you look at them you will not see something that is common to all, but similarities, relationships, and a whole series of them at that. To repeat: Don't think, but look! —Look for example at board-games, with their multifarious relationships.
> [看看我们称之为"游戏"的活动吧。我意指的是下棋、玩牌、赛球、奥林匹克运动会等。它们的共同点究竟是什么？不要说："应该有某种共同点"，否则它们就不会被称做"游戏"了。但重要的是要看，并看出所有游戏活动中是否有着共同点——因为，如果你（认真）看它们，那么你并看不出所有游戏活动中有什么共同点，而只有相似、关系，以及一系列的相似和关系。再说一遍：不要想，而要看！例如，看一看下棋以及它们各式各样的关系。]

只有付诸对实际生活形式的观察，"看"才能评判、判断、定夺语言陈述和意义把握的曲直是非。而且，维根斯坦指出，更重要的是，人们在"看"、"观察"、"评判"、"判断"以后，有了各自的意见、看法，并取得了一致或造成了不一致。一致也好，不一致也罢，究竟由什么来定夺？维根斯坦说得很明白——由"生活形式"：

> "So you are saying that human agreement decides what is true and what is false?"—It is what human beings say that is true and false; and they agree in the language they use. That is not agreement in opinions but in form of life. (Prt I, § 241, 88e)
> （"那么你认为真假取决于人类的约定吗？"——正是人类说出的东西才有真假；他们在语言的使用上做出约定。这不是见解上的一致，而是生活形式上的意见一致。）

维根斯坦认为生活形式是人类认知的基础和依据，它是不容忽视的。人们要参与游戏就要遵守游戏的规则，而"生活形式"（包括行为方式、生活方式、思维方式，以及人与自然的关系、人与人的关系、人与社会的关系）则是所有的语言游戏最高也是最基本的规则：要符合"生活形式"，回归到"生活形式"，回归到自然！

这一点对口译（也是对整个翻译实务和理论）的启示是：

第一，"生活形式"是语言游戏的本体论基本规则

所谓"本体论性质"就是指某一事物的本源、实质、本质或最基本的性质。维根斯坦虽然不提倡"本质论"，他只提出"相似性"，但他并不否认相似性中的本质基因。譬如一个人类（H）的家族（h）。其 n 个成员固然具有相似性，但同时又都具有其本质特征"人类（H）"。而每一个家族成员的相似性都必然要依附在他的本质特征中，正如本质特征必然要体现在成员的相似性中一样。于是人类（H）的家族（h）就形成了如下的特征序列，这个序列可以有无穷个替代式，

鸟类、酒类等等也一样：

人类（H）的家族（h）：Hh_1，Hh_2，Hh_3，$\cdots Hh_n$

鸟类（B）的家族（b）：Bb_1，Bb_2，Bb_3，$\cdots Bb_n$

酒类（W）的家族（w）：Ww_1，$W\ w_2$，Ww_3，$\cdots Ww_n$

$$\vdots \qquad\qquad \vdots$$

X 类（X）的家族（x）：Xx_1，Xx_2，Xx_3，$\cdots Xx_n$

这个序列的意旨其实就是"从一滴水看海洋"。不同的水可能具有不同的颜色或微量成分，但它的基本相似性都是 H_2O。它是现实世界的一种"形式"，维根斯坦将它称做"生活的某种形式"。这一思想对我们解释（口译）、阐释（笔译，根据 hermeneuties 的主张）意义的重大意义是不言而喻的。

据此，翻译学有理由扩大意义转换的对应幅度。这中间的道理恰如认知语言学所说的，人类是按范畴来表达自己。（F. Ungerer et al，1996：1-3）以下的解释或阐释（尤其是在当下性要求很高的口译中）都应视为合理：

● 五加皮酒→a Chinese medicinal wine（liquor，spirit）；*严格对应词是*"a liquor with acanthopanaxian flavour"

● 药典→a book describing all sorts of drugs；*严格对应词是*"pharmacopeia"

● claustrophorbia→*一种闭门不想见人的病*；*严格对应词是*"幽闭症"

● cooking forte→*最擅长的一道菜*；*严格对应词是*"烹调绝招"

学海无涯。没有人可以说自己精通一切，尤其是涉及三百六十行的口译——更由于要在两三秒钟内翻出来让人听到！这个问题我们还将在本书第五章"表现论"中加以阐述。

第二，"生活形式"是语言游戏的价值论基本规则

在维根斯坦看来，语言游戏是我们生活中的一部分。语言游戏的规则反映人类的生活行为的基本方式：普天之下的人的"普遍的参与"。人们参加游戏可能扮演不同的角色，但就"参与"而言，没有人必须排除在外，也没有人比别外的人高出一等，人人都平等参与。

"普遍参与"带来的是全体参与者的全程互动（interaction）、合作与默契（tacit understanding），这是任何游戏包括语言游戏的普遍特点，口译当然也不例外。

"生活形式"作为翻译的价值标准还有以下意义：

（1）翻译的意指（signifying）应该不悖于"生活形式"，一般指现实事实。所谓意指错误就是"张冠李戴"或"此帽无头可戴"。

以下例子都取自口译实例：（→表示"被误译为"）

（a）国家海洋局→（误）National Sea and Ocean Bureau

（正）State Oceanographic Administration

（b）甲壳类动物→（误）beatles（此词只指英国"披头士"乐队，The Beatles 1959—1969）

（正）shellfish

(c) 紧缩银根→(误)monetary shrinks

                (正)squeeze (on)

(d) 基本建设→(误)fundamental construction

                (正)infrastructure

(e) Jardine's Representative of Affairs→(误)"渣丁公司的代表处"

                      (正)怡和洋行代表处(旧)

(f) a crossed cheque→(误)作废的支票

                (正)画线支票

(g) FPA covering partial loss→(误)包括 FPA 的局部损失

                (正)包括单项损害的平安险(FPA:Free from Particular Average)

(h) DKNY's annual collection→(误)DKNY 的每年意见收集

                (正)DKNY 的年度时装发布(会)

    口译中的意指错误是大量的。荒唐的意指错误常使在场的听众莫明其妙,难免影响整体效果。因此我们要尽量避免。

    (2)翻译的理解应该不悖于"生活形式",一般指现实事实。理解错误常常不是由于语句太难,而是另有原因:

    (a) A: ... in order to close the relationship with the Bank's clients, our department deals with all kinds of consultant services to assist them in finding cooperation partner.

(误)I:为结束本行与客户的联系,我部门可向他们提供各种咨询服务,以便他们找寻合作伙伴。(误将 close"加深"理解为 close"结束"。其实,按上下文,口译员应运用推理意识到此译不对)

(正)I:为加深银行与客户的联系……

    (b) A:We'd like to propose shipping you a small initial consignment on trial. Then we'll be guided for future shipments by your reports on the different grades which may suit your market best.

(误)I:建议先装运少量试销产品。然后我们会指引你们对不同等级分类产品提出报告,这样做比较适合贵公司的市场所需。(对原句子结构理解错误)

(正)I:我们建议先装运少量试销产品。然后我们将根据贵公司的报告指引,按不同等级,选择最适合贵方市场的产品供货。

    (c) A:香港警方披露说,每年都有许多流浪狗被私家车和货运车辗死。

(误)I:According to HK police, many dogs are killed each year by automates and trucks roaming unleashed. (香港有"流浪卡车",不是很可笑吗? 将"roaming unleashed"放在"dogs"之后即可)

    (d) A:国税局很难做到对所有的人实施缴税监管。国税稽查员对很多逃漏税者根本碰都不碰。

（误）I：The IRB cannot hardly audit all tax returns. *None* of its audits *never* touch many cheaters.

（正）I：The IRB cannot audit all tax returns. Its audits *never* touch many cheaters.

第三，"生活形式"是语言游戏的表现论基本规则

翻译的表现论是翻译语言游戏的重要部分。表现论研究的目的是要让一切意义运筹落到实处，否则功亏一篑，等于前功尽弃。

口译的表现论在自己的特色，包括以下三个方面的标准：一、话语表意的明晰性（clarity）；二、语句意涵的连贯性（coherence）；三、语体的适境（adaptability）。以上三个方面涉及很多问题，我们将在第五章专论。

语言中的相似性问题也是维根斯坦的语言观的重要组成部分，我们已在前面论述过，此处从略。

维根斯坦的语言观强调语言应用必须符合生活的形式，他的名言是"想象一种语言就意味着想象一种生活形式"（"And to imagine a language means to imagine a form of life"，Prt I，§19，8e）；强调相似性是语言中的普遍现象，是生活形式在语言中的反映。这样，维根斯坦就赋予了语言以最高的人文性，也为他的语言观赋予了最高的人文性。

1.4　结语

综上所述，我们可以将维根斯坦的语言观（其实也体现了他的翻译观，另见表现论）以图示表述如下：

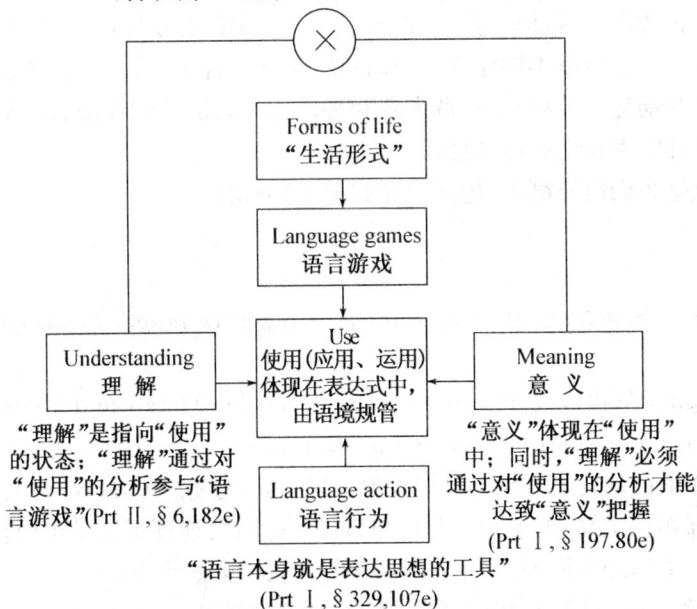

"理解"与"意义"之间无直接通道，必须通过"使用"（或"应用"、"运用"."用法"，Prt I，§138,53e）

Forms of life
"生活形式"

Language games
语言游戏

Understanding
理　解

Use
使用（应用、运用）
体现在表达式中，
由语境规管

Meaning
意　义

Language action
语言行为

"理解"是指向"使用"的状态；"理解"通过对"使用"的分析参与"语言游戏"（Prt II，§6,182e）

"意义"体现在"使用"中；同时，"理解"必须通过对"使用"的分析才能达致"意义"把握（Prt I，§197.80e）

"语言本身就是表达思想的工具"（Prt I，§329,107e）

图1.1　维根斯坦的语言观示意图

如图所示,维根斯坦的意义理论以"use"(应用、使用、运用或用法)为核心,他的语言观也是以语言应用为核心。这中间突出的是人类现实的语言行为中的"用"。这个传统,后来自哲学家 G. 赖尔(Gilbert Ryle,1900—1976),奥斯汀(J. L. Austin,1911—1960),斯特劳逊(P. F. Strawson,1911—)和奎因(Willard Van Ormam Quine,1908—)继承了下来,并由语用学和当代认知语言学家发扬光大,为语言学研究和译学研究发展开拓了疆域。维根斯坦的语言观及其继承者的研究对翻译学的启示如下。

第一,翻译是一种语际语言游戏。任何游戏都重在自主参与,重视身历其境的亲身参与。这就是说,对翻译而言,直接经验永远是最重要的。在翻译中,不存在不必亲身参与、不"身经百战"即可"神而明之"的"虚拟世界"的奥秘。

第二,任何游戏都有规则,翻译也一样。在语际转换的各个平面——语义平面、句法平面、话语结构平面、审美平面、文化表现平面、逻辑思维平面——都有相关的规则(规范、理论):翻译者是在一边玩游戏,一边学会规则。不仅如此,游戏参与者还在一边玩游戏,一边制定规则;一边在玩游戏中遵守规则,一边渐入佳境而能运用自如、驾轻就熟地驾驭规则。

第三,意义即使用(应用、运用)。"用"必然具有时空条件,也就是语境。语境使意义的游移性相对固定。因此,要把握意义就要把握语境。翻译者不要脱离语境去"想"词语、句子的意义,而要"看"它们是怎么用在特定的话语语境中。

第四,语言中处处存在着"家庭相似",语际转换也一样。"本质"存在于"个别"中,"实质"存在于"非实质"中。因此,等值、等同、对等、等效都是虚拟的、表征的。语际转换的普遍事实是"对应",而对应则是一个家族的"相似性范畴"。人类正是按"相似性范畴"来表达自己的概念和思维并相互交流。翻译当然也不例外。

第五,"生活形式"是判断语言真值的最终依据。翻译者在"看"(审视)以上诸平面的双语转换运作中都要看看自己的操控("用")是不是符合生活的形式:翻译就是翻译,不要将主体的虚拟世界当做客体的真实世界来呈现。

第六,每一位游戏参与者都享有同等的权利和义务,游戏参与者一律平等:翻译者既不是原创的"附属品",也不是可以不顾原文的"独行侠"。从功能上说,翻译者还要看到自身的独特作用:他是游戏的互动运动的启动者、调节者和翻译的有效活动的保证者。翻译者用自己的才情使原创再生。因此,翻译也有原创性。

以上六点,就是我们研究翻译(包括口译和笔译)的指针。

【延伸阅读】

1. Setton, R.. *Simultaneous interpretation: A cognitive-pragmatic analysis*. Amsterdam: Benjamins,1999.

2. Vandeweghe, Willy, Vandepitte, Sonia & Velde, Marc van de (eds.). The study of language and translation. *Belgian Journal of Linguistics*. 2007(21):1-200.

3. 陈菁. 弗里斯的语言学理论与口译原则. 厦门大学学报. 2005,167(1):125-128.

4. 胡开宝,郭鸿杰主编. 英汉语言对比与口译. 大连:大连理工大学出版社,2007.

5. 刘宓庆. 口笔译理论研究. 北京:中国对外翻译出版公司,2006.

6. 罗选民主编. 语言认知与翻译研究. 北京:外文出版社,2005.

7. 唐姿. 语言·文本·翻译——论翻译研究的语言学派与独立的翻译学科的建立. 山东

外语教学.2003(5):109-112.

【问题与思考】

1. 系统功能语言学理论对"语言"的认识与传统语言学有何不同？对于口译有何借鉴意义？

2. 口译员在口译中经常会发生"死译"、"乱译"以及遭遇"干扰"等现象,试从语言学派的口译研究视角出发,解释这些现象并给出解决方案。

3. 根据语言学派的观点,理解的方式分为两种:"自上而下"和"自下而上",试论这两种方式在口译理解过程中的作用。

4. 试用弗里斯的语言交际理论对口译的过程进行分析。

5. 试从维根斯坦的语言哲学观角度论述口译作为一种"语言游戏"的特点及其基本"游戏规则"。

第四章 认知学派口译理论研究

导 论

和其他很多领域一样,随着研究工作的不断深入,口译研究中也相继引入了一些相关学科的研究成果,认知学就是其中之一。

口译是一个认知过程,是语言和文化认知过程的整合,是话语"所指"的映现和重构。口译中,口译者经历了"语言—思想—语言"的三段式的认知过程,完成了从"能指"到"所指"的双重映现。具体来说,口译就是借助认知知识,对听辨语言进行分析、综合、推理、理解,意义产生、记忆和表达的过程。而这个过程中的各个环节,事实上不是单一存在或罗列顺序逐一进行的,而是交织在一起的一个复杂的认知过程。了解口译的认知过程,对口译理论和口译实践不无裨益。

作为多学科口译理论相结合的典范,认知学派口译理论研究在促进口译研究跨学科发展的同时,其自身的发展也得到了其他学科的帮助和促动。认知学派的口译研究与其他很多学派的口译研究之间存在着交叉性,比如符号学、语言学、释意学、心理学等,这其中最具代表性的有塞莱斯科维奇和勒代雷的释意理论、吉尔的精力分配模式等。

按照方法来研究口译过程就是把口译当做一种能力来研究,按照目的来研究口译则是把口译作为一种活动来考查。从 Jean Herbert 开始的早期口译研究,主要讨论了语言转换和口译技能问题,并未触及在这些操作活动之下的译者心理活动问题。但在实际的口译过程中,口译员为了更好地理解讲话人的意思,讲话人的表情、手势、声调、眼神等都可以成为阐释和解读信息的必要参数。因为在特定单元时间内,口译员要完成听辨、分析、推理、思维判断、理解和记忆等多项任务,所以如果仅停留在语言层次,根本不可能完成理解,口译员必须也只能借助所有相关知识并启动认知功能在有限的时间内完成从用译出语听到用译入语表达的过程(刘和平,2005:16)。这就是口译过程中理解到表达阶段的认知机制。在认知系统的参与下,译员对原语讲话进行解码,并将理解到的意义与原语讲话的语言符号和结构分离,以一种非语言的意识状态留存在大脑之中。据此,塞莱斯科维奇大胆摒弃了早期研究重"客体"(原语)轻"主体"(译者)的传统,从人的认知思维入手研究口译过程。释意学派提出的口译过程"三角模型"在显示了其学术创新精神的同时也加速了国际口译研究的认知心理学转向,使口译研究有了浓厚的认知心理学色彩烙印,具有了更为明显的跨学科特征。

法国口译研究者吉尔则针对口译工作方式提出了精力分配模式,由此展开了对大脑认知资源的最佳利用模式的探讨。吉尔认为可供译员使用的大脑注意力总量是有限的,如果译员在口译中所需要的注意力总量超过可供使用的认知资源总量,那么口译的质量就得不到保证。

人的脑力(即认知资源)总量是相对稳定而有限的,同时,注意力的分配需要占用和消耗口译员的认知资源。所以,如果口译员在口译过程的某个步骤上投注太多的注意力,其他几个步骤能够得到的注意力自然就会减少。而且,在实际的口译过程中,这些步骤是环环相扣、互为因果的,彼此之间紧密配合,其中任何一个环节出了问题,都必然影响整个口译过程的输出质量。

我国口译理论研究界也相继有学者对认知学的研究视角给予肯定和重视,比如刘和平就从认知的角度论述了思维科学和口译程序的关系。她指出,无论对口译怎样定论,口译都具有开发性特点,对口译进行多层次描述,必须采用跨学科研究方法,特别是从认知心理学对其进行研究,这对科学说明人类翻译的性质、任务和对象以及翻译培训尤为重要,也为口译研究打开了认知科学的大门,给口译程序、口译思维研究提供了新的思路与方法(2005:10)。

通过认知学派的口译理论研究,我们可以发现口译理论的形成与发展与认知研究的发展密不可分,后者为前者所蕴含的认知因素提供了理论基础和科学依据。认知学领域的研究成果也不断地被应用到口译实践和口译教学中,比如,关于认知与记忆的研究结果就已经被用于开发口译员的最佳长短期记忆能力等。认知学派理论的跨学科应用,不但丰富了口译理论研究,也使得口译研究越来越具有科学性和说服力。

选　文

选文一　巴比塔隐蔽的一面
——通过同声传译揭开认知、智力和感知的面纱

仲伟合

导　言

　　语言是人类独有的认知和交际手段。语言不仅可以成为交际的桥梁,同时也构成了人类对现实世界认知的本身,但语言有时也会阻碍交际,因此,语言成为研究人类认知的一个绝妙对象。口译员所从事的是语言的转换工作,他们转换的不仅是不同的表达方式,同时还有不同的认知视角。口译研究的认知语言学范式不仅可以透过口译现象揭示人类语言的认知运作模式,同时也可以整合语言学、心理学、语义学、认知科学等诸多领域的知识,用以解释口译的工作机制和译员口译的内在机制,从而帮助口译员解决口译过程中的诸多认知和语言障碍。Laura Bertone 于 2006 年出版的《巴比塔隐蔽的一面——通过同声传译揭开认知、智力和感知的面纱》一书正是为口译认知研究的跨学科路径做出新探索的杰作。该书从五个部分——信息与内容:译员所言;译员发挥的作用:译员之行;同声传译的工作机制:借用跨学科

成果的解释;内部探索:译员工作的内在机制;巴比塔的重建:综述及结论——对同声传译中的隐蔽机制(亦称"巴比塔隐蔽的一面"),即口译员的感知、认知及智力的机制,尤其是口译的外在工作特点和译员认知的内在机制,进行了深刻的揭示。选文对该书进行了非常全面精准的评述。

　　跨学科研究目前已成为人文学科研究的一种趋势。跨学科研究通常会经历三个阶段:第一阶段可称为简单借鉴,即某学科借用其他相关学科的术语或概念作为本学科的学术话语,这种情况往往出现在新兴学科;第二阶段可称为深度借鉴,即某学科借鉴其他相关学科的理论并在其基础上有所发展;第三阶段可称为相互借鉴,到这个阶段,不再是单方向的借鉴,而是双方的相互借鉴,即某学科借鉴相关学科理论后,促进相关学科的发展。

　　对人类认知进行研究的成果主要体现在认知科学(尤其是认知心理学)领域。虽然从认知角度进行的跨学科路径的口译研究自 1986 年意大利 Trieste 口译研究大会后开始成为口译研究的一个主要方面,但对于口译研究这门新兴(子)学科来说,这种研究主要着眼于探索口译过程及译员的认知运作,目前尚处在跨学科研究的第一阶段,正向第二阶段迈进。Laura Bertone 于 2006 年出版的《巴比塔隐蔽的一面——通过同声传译揭开认知、智力和感知的面纱》(*The Hidden Side of Babel—Unveiling Cognition*, *Intelligence and Sense through Simultaneous Interpretation*)为口译认知研究的跨学科路径做出了新的探索。

　　Laura Bertone 是巴黎大学的语言学博士,从事跨文化研究及普通语义学(general semantics)研究,并拥有 20 余年国际会议传译的经验。在这部著作中,作者以其独特的视角,从国际会议口译的实践中撷取典型例子,试图探索并解释人类的感知、认知及智力的机制,尤其是人类语言交际的外在特点和内在机制,即"巴比塔隐蔽的一面"。

　　全书分五个部分。第一部分,"信息与内容:译员所言";第二部分,"译员发挥的作用:译员之行";第三部分,"同声传译的工作机制:借用跨学科成果的解释";第四部分,"内部探索:译员工作的内在机制";第五部分,"巴比塔的重建:综述及结论"。

　　作者开宗明义地指出,本书的目的有四:一是通过对同声传译的研究,揭示人类语言的认知运作;二是启发研究者发现新的研究视角,指出认知研究往往忽视的一些方面;三是希望读者读完本书后,会觉得不仅知道得多了,而且知道了一些与众不同的观点;四是探索人类语言认知现象,进行多角度、多层面的跨学科研究的方式,在目前看来,如要包容与语言相关的感知、感觉、感情、思想、表征、思维等现象的研究,仅仅靠语言学是不够的,而应该综合各种与认知相关的学科。

　　语言不仅是交际的"桥梁",而且构成了人类对现实世界认知的本身。然而,语言不一定时时都起着"桥梁"作用,有时也会对交际沟通起阻碍作用;语言不一定时时都对人类的认知起建构作用,有时也会起解构作用。正因为语言如此复杂、如此丰富、如此神秘,它可以成为我们研究人类认知的一个绝妙对象。

　　本书的研究起点与一般的语言研究著作不同。本书通过探索现场会议口译的语言互动和交流是如何达成或者失败的,尤其是同声传译译员如何"实时地"传译他人的话语。作为会议口译员,几乎每天都在做着语言转换的事情,而且,实际上,他们转换的不仅仅是不同的表达方式,更是不同的认知世界的视角。因此,他们往往会对语言现象有着更深的认识。

在日常的语言交际中,由于交际方式的透明性和普遍性,人们对于其中所隐蔽的认知机制往往浑然不觉;然而,对于同传译员来说,由于他们的语言转换和表达面临着时间及空间的压力,透视他们的工作过程,我们能够比较清楚地发现其语言交际的认知运作过程。作者所采用的研究方法是:通过对同传译员的口译话语与发言人的原语的偏离、不同和有差距的片段的采集、比较、分析,进而发现背后起作用的认知机制。这些"异常"现象正如一面放大镜,对其认知机制的研究恰恰能够揭示常态的语言交际背后隐蔽的认知机制。

为达成其研究目标,作者充分借鉴了跨学科的成果,包括语言哲学、语言学、认知科学、心理语言学和实验心理学、翻译研究和口译研究、普通语义学等诸多领域的研究成果。

本书第一部分"信息与内容:译员所言",包括第 1～7 章,内容有:语言如游戏;话语意义——从一面到另一面;话语的隐含义;话语动机;自相矛盾的信号;认知过程的两轴;认知运作的同时性。

语言如游戏。语言的意义往往是变动不居的,意义往往是相对的。即使是很简单的句子如"我买了报纸"在不同的场合中也可能具有诸多不同的意义,尤其是不同的隐含义。以语言哲学的代表人物奥斯汀(Austin)及塞尔(Searle)的言语行为视角来看,同样一个直接言语行为,在不同的场合中往往可能蕴含诸多不同的间接言语行为。通过比较常态的语言行为和口译中的语言行为,作者得出以下结论:1. 不同的言说方式可能产生不同的意义;在口译中不仅应考虑发言人所言,还应注意其言说的方式;2. 同样的言说在不同的场合中可能具有不同的意义;在口译中,译员所了解的场合知识越多,口译往往越到位;3. 言说的风格不一样,意义也可能不一样;在口译中,译员要注意传达原语的言说风格,以便产生相同的言说效果。

译员在口译过程中是如何把握本来变动不居的意义呢? 译员主要参照以下参数:发言人是谁,听众是谁,在何时,在何地,为什么如此言说。(即五个 W)在口译过程中,译员首先要做的事情往往是推定其尚未把握的参数,从而把握发言人言说的意义。由此可见,译员在口译现场的"在场"(presence)亦是决定口译成败的重要因素。然而,译员的在场及译员角色的"凸现"(intrusion)应把握好适当的度。

即使是在日常语言交际中,我们也能体会到,话语的含义往往不只是在字面。在翻译中亦是如此,双语之间语词的对等不等于信息的对等,形式的对等也不等于内容的对等以及效果的对等。译员作为原语与目标语交际的中介,置身于现场异语双方语言交际的中枢位置,更能深切体会到话语意义的隐含层面。话语的隐含义主要有两类:一是逻辑隐含义(logical implicatures),包括语词本身的隐含义和话语行为的隐含义;二是心理隐含义(psychological implicatures),包括心理活动在话语层面不自觉的呈现(如口误)所产生的隐含义、对话语风格的有意识操控(如使用反讽语气)所带来的隐含义、修辞隐含义等。另外,话语所附带的重音、强调、语调等均可能给话语加上新的含义。

如前所述,要翻译发言人 A 刚说出的原语句子 n,译员同时考虑到:A 于时间 t、地点 y 就话题 x 对其听众 B 说出了这个句子,译员根据自己对以上因素的考虑形成假设 h,进而以此为基础理解句子 n 的意义并把该句翻译成目标语句子 n'。在上述诸因素中,发言人的话语动机亦是构成意义的一个重要方面。"译义不译词"(Do not interpret what the speaker says but rather what he means.)是口译中一条众所周知的原则,尤其是对于初学口译的学生来说,教师往往会要求"忘掉语词,想想发言人的意思是什么"。然而,当我们把发言人的话语动机引入意义的视域后,再重新审视这一原则,也许会反思其问题所在:首先,我们如何知道发言人的意思是什么? 用哪些参数来衡量? 其次,这一原则是否意味着译员必须把发言人所隐含的意思明晰地说出来? 另外,从话语风格的角度来看,这一原则似乎也站不住脚,例如,原语发言人极尽迂回曲折、委婉表达之能事说了一段话,其目的就是要拒绝对方提出的要求,译员当然听出了他的意思,可译员是否能把原语简单地译为"某某代表的意思就是要拒绝"呢? 当然不行,因为一旦这样译出,听众肯定会觉得原语发言人的话语风格是直截了当,而这种印象与原语迂回曲折的委婉风格大相径庭。

另外,发言人的话语中有时会出现前后分歧或自相矛盾的信号。对这种情况译员是怎么处理的呢? 作者的发现是:首先,译员的主观愿望是充分理解发言人的意思并希望自己所译出的意思被听众充分理解;其次,译员在翻译表达中会注意追求表达的逻辑一致性;再次,如果出现了把握不准原语的意义及其逻辑线索的情况时,译员一般会选择暂时性的沉默或者省略,而不是以讹传讹;另外,在面临原语信息过于密集、语速过快,或者原语信息中出现明显自相矛盾的情况时,同传译员做出的翻译决策一般基于这样两条原则——一是译出主要信息,压缩和省略次要信息;二是注意保持目标语表达的逻辑性。

实际上,在译员对原语进行理解并译出的过程中,有两条轴线的认知机制在同时发挥作用:一条是共时的认知轴;另一条是历时认知轴。通过共时的认知轴,译员同时对不同性质的多种认知元素进行理解,包括上文所分析的原语的语词片段、发言人的行动和表情、现场的场合信息,以及发言人在讲话的同时展示的幻灯片等。通过历时的认知轴,译员能够把现场的认知信息和其记忆中的相关的认知信息联系起来,从而理解现场的话语意义和发言人的意思。

正是由于两条轴线的认知机制的同时作用,同传译员才能够成功地对原语的显性义和隐含义、对发言人的话语意图和交际目标形成正确的理解假设,并在此基础上做出正确的分析和预测,进而成功地传译。

第二部分,"译员发挥的作用:译员之行",包括第8~14章。第8、9两章对第一部分的内容进行简要的回顾和总结,在此基础上概述已得出的初步结论。第10至14章的内容分别为:口译策略;口译中的期望和预测;会议口译的礼仪形式;会议场景的作用;译员的立场。

口译策略是体现"译员之行"的主要方面。在第10章,作者通过示例和分析,揭示同传译员常用的口译策略,包括:(1)把正在传译的片段与已传译的和即将传译的片段联系起来,把传译的语段与发言人的话语主题和主旨联系起来,把现场刚听到的信息与记忆中的已知信息联系起来,把正在听到的信息与正在看到的信息联系起来;(2)碰上暂时无法理解或明显前后矛盾的原语片断时,往往采用沉默或等待新的信息补充的策略;(3)在上述情况下,如果话已说出一半而无法选择沉默或等待策略时,译员倾向于把话说完,保持目标语表达在形式上完整;(4)当信息负荷过重(如原语的语速太快、内容太难)或精神过于疲劳时,口译往往由具体转向笼统;(5)在同传中需要争取时间时,译员往往会采用把间接表达转译成直接表达的策略;(6)在传译过程中,由于原语的结构和语义并非受译员的掌控,因此,译员在语言表达形式上采取灵活顺应的策略;(7)在个别情况下(如发言人讲一个笑话时),译员可能选择传译言语效果而非言语意义的策略。

在第11章中,作者分析了同传译员是如何在口译过程中进行期望和预测的。首先,如前文所述,译员在口译过程中对以下参数的推定能够为译员的理解和预测奠定初步基础,这些因素包括:发言人是谁,听众是谁,在何时,在何地,为什么如此言说。其次,在对原语初步理解的基础上建立的语义场能帮助译员把握发言人言说的意义并确认预测。当然,虽然同声传译过程中适度的预测是必要的,但要注意避免思维定势的消极影响。

人类交际的规则与各种人群的文化和习俗密切相关,几乎每一种交际行为都有相应的礼仪形式镶嵌于其中。本书的第 12 章讨论了会议口译的礼仪形式。礼仪可被定义为支配正式交际场合的一套规则,礼仪意味着某种行为模式的系统化重复。礼仪形式本身就附带着意义,译员掌握各种口译场合的礼仪形式知识有助于准确地评估发言人言说的主旨含义。另外,正如人类用礼仪形式来组织交际行为一样,人类用于交际的语言也因不同人群的文化背景而表现为不同的语言程式。例如,在某些语言中,某些词语的重复就是一定场合中礼仪形式的体现。

译员的对意义的认知不是单靠听辨和理解发言人的语词得来的,人类在交际中对意义的认知亦同此理。首先,人往往采取的是整体认知的方式,这种方式意味着听的一方不一定要听到/听清说的一方的每个语词才能理解其意义,采用类比、比较和联系的办法,人往往可以通过意义的一个部分推测全部意义。其次,正如译员通过对会议场景各要素及要素之间关系的分析可以就发言人的言说意图和意义做出推断一样,认知场景也能够为语言交际中的各方提供认知"脚本",便于其推断言说的意义。

第 14 章讨论了译员的立场涉及的问题,这些问题也是目前从社会学角度进行的口译研究中的热门问题,因此,作者在本书中没有也不可能得出确切的答案。作者提出的问题包括:译员是否在任何时候都应与发言人的身份认同一致?译员在口译现场的身份是否像联合国官员评论("今天的译员干得不错,我们都没感觉他们的存在")中反映的那样"透明"?译员传译过程中在目标语表达方式的选择上似乎有很大的自由度,但他又必须始终忠实于原语发言人,这是否意味着一个两难选择呢?

第三部分"同声传译的工作机制:借用跨学科成果的解释",包括第 15~20 章。内容分别为:感知整合;联想网络;认知干扰;口译失误。

心理学及心理语言学的研究成果显示,人的听觉和视觉感知均遵循抽象及简化的原则,即对事物的结构性特征进行整合从而认识事物的整体,而不是把事物的所有细节不分主次地累加在一起。译员的口译同样符合这一原则。例如,在发言人原语发布的逻辑关系不够清晰时,译员往往会把逻辑关系加以理清,并有意识地把握其中的主干信息;在同传中由于原语发布语速加快而让译员不得不加快语速甚至压缩目标语表达时,译员会有意识地保留主要信息而去除次要信息。由此可见,感知整合(perpetual integration)是人类语言交际一个典型的认知特征。

人对事物的整体性认知主要是通过建立感知的"联想网络"(networks of associations)来进行的。一方面,人在认知过程中会理清所感知到的各种元素之间的关系(如相同、相似、相邻、对比、相反等),建立整体性的意义网络;同时,又不断根据感知中新涌入的元素对已建立的关系和网络进行修正。同传译员的工作过程亦是如此:一方面以感知整合的方式建立一种"从上往下"的整体性的意义网络;另一方面又始终通过敞开的感知之门不断接纳新的感知元素,以一种"从下往上"的方式对已建立的意义网络进行修正。这样,同传译员就能避免按原语字面"死译"或是完全按自己的臆测"乱译"的发生。

译员在同声传译的过程中面对的一个最大的困难是来自于内部和外部的干扰。对此,相关学科能提供些什么解释呢? 如果干扰产生于两种语言之间,这属于"迁移"(transfers)的情况;如果干扰产生于一种语言之内,这属于"失误或口误"(lapses or slips of the tongue)的情况。产生于两种语言之间的干扰与讲话者母语或其他主导性语言的语音、词汇、句法语义及语用的规则密切相关;产生于一种语言之内的干扰与共时的(感知)或历时的(记忆)多种认知信息元素之间的冲突有关。

同声传译中偶然的失误是难免的。口译失误的原因主要来自两方面:一是外部的压力,如原语信息过于密集、原语发布语速过快、原语的理解难度太大以及同传设备出现问题等,都可能给译员造成认知负荷上的压力而导致口译失误;二是内部的原因,如译员双语能力不够、主题知识欠缺、精神不够集中、身体过于疲累等,都会导致同声传译中的失误。作者的观点是,以理性的头脑来看,失误是人类常态语言交际中一个必然存在的部分,我们必须正视它,口译失误也不例外。就口译来说,这意味着发言人在可能给译员造成认知负荷过大的地方对其原语内容和发布做出适当的调整,也意味着译员不应耻于向发言人确认或请求重复,以免造成交际失败。

第四部分"内部探索:译员工作的内在机制",包括第21~24章,内容为:认知的内在机制;意义的变量与恒量;理解过程;大脑内部。

人类认知的主要方式有:感知、观察、联系、比较、区分、识别等,其中,比较、区分和识别都意味着对模式的认知。在随时进入人的感知的无数元素中,人往往会选择一部分加以注意,并在这些元素之间建立起关系,然后以整合的方式进行认知。在人类的高级认知方式中,人的象征能力(symbolizing capacity)、抽象能力(capacity for abstraction)和综合能力(capacity for synthesis)起着重要作用。人类认知的内在机制在同声传译的工作过程中有显著的反映:首先,如前文所述,译员总要寻找几个基本问题的答案,即,发言人是谁,对谁言说,在何时,在何地,为何言说。其次,译员要注意对口译现场各种信息的感知和观察;然后,在整合上述认知信息的基础上,形成对原语意义的假设;最后,根据即时的新信息,对意义假设进行确认或修正,做出实时的传译。

多元性、多样性和复杂性是人类生活的基本特征之一,正如古希腊哲学家赫拉克利特(Heracleitus)所说,"人无法两次踏进同一条河流"。那么,人类是如何在这纷繁复杂的人类生活中进行感知识别、分门别类等理解和认知活动的呢?神经生物学家霍金斯指出,"自然的进化解决了人类如何认知变动不居的世界这个难题,大脑皮层上自有代表恒量的机制"(Hawkins,2004)。如上节所述,人类的象征能力、抽象能力和综合能力使得人能够在面对纷繁复杂、变动不居的诸多变量(variance)时把握认知的恒量(invariance),进而做到对意义的理解和相互之间的交流。口译过程中的语言交际亦同此理。

理解是人类认知的核心。没有理解,人类之间的意义传递(尤其是语言交际)就无法实现,在口译的实践中,没有理解,译员的口译就会成为机器一样的逐字硬译。理解是一种人类内部认知的动态过程,主要特征是根据即时感知的信息进行联系、比较、区分、综合、抽象和识别,另外,根据记忆中已有的信息和最新感知的信息进行预测和修正也是人类理解的重要特征。那么,是什么在影响译员的理解呢?影响译员理解的主要因素有:感知的信息太少或太多;关于五个W的基本信息不完整;错误地判断发言人的动机和意图;缺乏背景信息;对会议主题有错误的思维定势;外部或内部的干扰;发言人的信息自相矛盾等。

从脑科学的最新研究成果来看,人类认知的内在机制是具有生物学基础的。根据神经生物学家霍金斯于2004年发表的研究结果,目前我们知道的人类大脑皮层至少具有以下四个功能:一是以恒量形式存储认知模式;二是存储认知模式的序列;三是存储认知模式的层级;四是以自动的、联想的方式回忆认知模式。

第五部分"巴比塔的重建:综述及结论",包括第25～26章,内容为:巴比塔的倒塌;语言运用和语言研究的新视域。

人们往往容易注意到不同语言之间交流是存在障碍的,而不太容易注意到同一种语言本身也可能给交际造成障碍。举例来说,墨西哥前总统佛克斯的一次言论曾在国际范围内引起轩然大波,事由是他曾说"即使是非洲裔美国人也不会干美国人提供给墨西哥人的某些工作"。这一言论被普遍认为有歧视非洲裔美国人之嫌,他自己则坚持认为,他的话只是为了维护本国的人民,无意伤害其他种族的人。可事件的后果却使他陷入了"政治不正确"的尴尬处境。如此看来,巴比塔倒塌所象征的变乱不仅存在于不同语言之间,而且存在于同一语言之内。

在本部分,作者在综述本书前文结论的基础上,指出研究人类语言交际及其认知机制的必要性和重要性。她强调,从理论研究的视角来看,我们不应该把对语言问题的探讨局限于纯语言学的视野之内,而应把它置于更广阔的"认知科学"的跨学科视域中来进行研究。从实践的角度来看,人们有必要受到更多的语言认知、语言能力和交际能力的训练。

语言是人类独有的认知和交际手段。语言的认知机制、语言的潜力和局限等"巴比塔隐蔽的一面"尚有诸多问题值得人们去深入探讨。

本书的一个鲜明特点是其跨学科的独特视角:以分析同声传译的工作机制来印证人类认知的原理,以认知科学的研究成果来解释口译现象。具备这一特点,本书不仅能为译员反思其会议口译活动提供指引,而且对于那些对人类认知活动及人类语言机制感兴趣的人来说也是一部视角独特的参考书。

本书的第二个特点是,全书始终在同声传译和日常语言交际及戏剧表演之间进行类比分析。具备这一特点,本书不仅对口译研究者和译员有参考作用,而且能为语言研究者开拓思路,为语言工作者拓宽视野。

本书的第三个特点是,虽为学术研究著作,然全书行文深入浅出,语言表达生动,并配有大量现场的例子及形象的插图。具备这一特点,本书对于语言研究者和口译研究者之外的普通读者来说,也是一本提高语言交际能力的平易而又实用的参考读物。

本书的美中不足之处在于两个方面。一是本书提出了口译研究、语言交际研究和认知研究方面的诸多课题,然而,对于不少课题的探讨尚不够深入。这体现在一个明显的特征上,本书共26章,除去其中4章属总结综述的性质,其他20余章均涉及不同的课题,但不少章节都篇幅过短,让读者有浅尝辄止、不够深入之憾。二是本书虽然探讨了不少课题,但是其论证方法大多属于传统的经验例证分析法,这无论是对于口译研究还是认知研究来说,都有科学性欠缺之嫌。当然,本书探讨分析的诸多问题只是得出了初步的结论和假说,这在一定意义上也为我国有关学界进行实证检验性研究提供了丰富的课题。

选文二　口译认知过程中"deverbalization"的认知诠释

许　明

导　言

翻译不是单纯的语言转换,而是一种特殊形式的翻译传播行为,这种传播行为可以从认知科学的言语生成、双语转换角度来说明翻译的原理和机制。德国学者 Julius Wirl 研究了翻译的心理过程,指出翻译过程的本质就是原语文本意义和语言形式的分离,即"意义脱离原语语言外壳"(Pöchhacker,1992:212)。这是目前已知的最早的"脱离"假说(Deverbalization)。持有"脱离"假说观点的学者们认为语言和思维是可以分离的,意义的理解与储存不需要语言符号的介入。在认知系统的参与下,译员对原语进行解码,并将其理解的意义与原语的语言符号和结构分离,以一种非语言的意识状态留存在大脑之中。这一理论视角在口译研究领域的应用丰富了人们对口译活动的认识,标志着口译研究的认知心理学转向。选文对"Deverbalization"的概念从认知角度进行了系统研究,追其渊源,分析其存在形式和范围,界定其与口译理解的界限、讨论其发生机制,并尝试对这一概念进行了科学定义。选文的研究结果有助于进一步验证"Deverbalization"在口译认知过程中存在的合理性,同时也从跨学科的角度丰富了口译理论研究的内容和方式,以便于揭示完整的口译认知过程,为解释各种口译现象和口译问题提供认知理论支持。此外,选文研究课题的意义还在于可以借鉴其研究结果,用以加强口译理论对口译教学和口译实践的指导作用,开辟符合口译认知规律的口译认知教学法。

Deverbalization 是巴黎"释意理论"学派的核心。根据该理论,在口译过程中,在话语理解和译语再表达之间,"意义"会"脱离"语言的具体表达形式而独立存在。从 deverbalization 的提出到现在,国内外译界还未能对此阶段做出科学解释。本文将从跨学科的角度出发诠释并规范口译认知过程中 deverbalization 的存在形式、界定范围、发生机制和科学定义。

1. Deverbalization 溯源

Deverbalization 的概念源于巴黎高级翻译学院(ESIT)Seleskovitch 和 Lederer(1984)两位翻译学家所创立的"释意理论",是其核心概念之一。"释意理论"创立之初被称为"意义理论"(théorie du sens)(Seleskovitch,1975,1978;Lederer,1981a)。在"意义理论"中,Seleskovitch(1975)首先提出口译过程中存在一个 deverbalization 阶段。在接下来的论著中,Seleskovitch(1978)及 Lederer(1981a)先后提及 deverbalization 的概念。Lederer(1981b)曾试图用 conceptualization 的术语来替代 deverbalization。但最终,在"释意理论"中,Seleskovitch 和 Lederer(1984)还是采用 deverbalization 这一术语来表述口译过程中话语"意义""脱离原语

语言外壳"而独立存在的这一阶段。

"释意理论"认为,口译不是从原语到译语的直接转换,而是"建立在理解基础之上的再表达"(Seleskovitch & Lederer,2001:19)。口译过程类似于在单一语言交际环境下展开的理解和再表达的过程。口译的实质在于感知 X 语言所表述的话语并把握其"意义",然后再用 Y 语言对原语意义进行再表达(ibid:73)。因此,在口译过程中,在原语感知和用译语对"信息"进行再表达之间存在一个 deverbalization 阶段。在此阶段,译员需要完成口译过程中呈现的可感知因素(sensible elements)和认知因素(cognitive elements)的即时归纳整合(immediate synthesis)(ibid:10)。

关于口译过程及 deverbalization 阶段所涉及的认知机制及其运作模式,释意理论稍有触及。该理论认为,口译过程主要涉及瞬时记忆和短期记忆两种记忆。瞬时记忆主要负责处理语音输入(phonological input),其处理能力在 7 至 8 个单词之间,处理后的词汇能在瞬时记忆中持续 2 至 3 秒的时间。短期记忆主要负责存储"脱离语言形式支持"(linguistic formal support)的语义因子(semes),该记忆是语义记忆的基础。在口译过程中,话语信息(通常是包含 7 到 8 个单词的字符串)将首先被输入瞬时记忆,这些瞬间存储的话语信息而后会在认知补充(cognitive compliments)的帮助下被转换成语义单位,这些语义单位接下来会进一步融合而形成更大的语义单位。当整个句子范围内所有的语义单位完成与主题知识、背景知识的融合后,就会形成一条完整的"信息"。这条"整合的信息"所能持续的时间将超出瞬时记忆所允许的范围,而且能在瞬时记忆范围之外的时间被表述出来(Seleskovitch & Lederer,1986:144-145)。

在 2003 版的《口译推理教学法》中,Seleskovitch 与 Lederer 对 deverbalization 的相关表述方式作了改进。她们把口译的理解过程表述为"思想"(ideas)或"意义"(meaning)在大脑里的"感知和升华"过程。她们认为,在口译过程中,话语形式随着话语所表述的"思想"或"意义"的形成而逐渐消失,话语"意义"最终"脱离原语语言外壳"在大脑意识里形成一种存留状态(我们简称为"意义"潜留状态)(Seleskovitch & Lederer,2003:41)。而且,此阶段的"意义"跟记忆有关。在口译过程中,译者需要通过"回忆"才能将其转化为自己"欲表达的内容"(ibid:221)。这些全新的表述形式反映了两位翻译家在 deverbalization 认识上的进一步发展。她们开始注意到 deverbalization 阶段"意义"的形成过程、表现形式及其与记忆的关系,把 deverbalization 的定义提升到了一定的认知高度。

结合这些最新进展,Seleskovitch 与 Lederer 从交际学的研究途径出发,分四步分析了"释意理论"框架下的"口译链"(ibid:220-222)。该"口译链"以口译的整个交际过程及该过程中所涉及的交际角色(包括发言人、译员和话语对象)为基础,阐明了口译交际过程中不同的话语处理情况,表明了 deverbalization 在口译过程中承前启后的关键作用。据此"口译链",我们可以演绎出如下口译交际流程图(参看图1)。

1. X 语言知识 2. 百科及主题知识 3. 共享知识	1. X 和 Y 语言知识 2. 百科及主题知识 3. 理解后的"意义"	1. Y 语言知识 2. 百科知识
欲表达的内容 → 生成音符串 →	脱离语言外壳后"意义"潜留状态 →	"意义"的记忆 = 欲表达内容 → 译入语生成 → 意义的理解 → 脱离语言外壳 → 意义的记忆
发言人	译员	听众

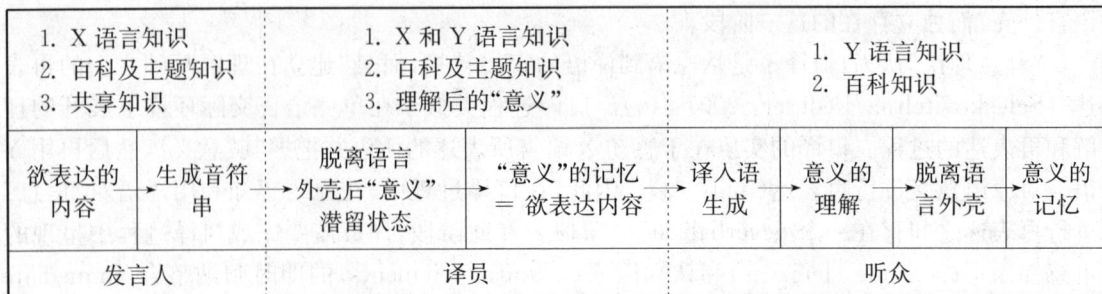

图 1 从 Selescovitch & Lederer (2003)《口译推理教学法》
中演绎来的口译交际流程图 (pp. 220-222)

我们注意到,在此"口译链"中,Seleskovitch 与 Lederer 并没有将听众理解过程中的 deverbalization 与口译译员的 deverbalization 区分开,以至于在听众这一环节又一次使用了这一概念。Deverbalization 作为译学的专业术语应该具有其特定的内涵和所指,而不能将其等同于其他以非翻译为目的的、具有"脱离原语语言外壳"性质的语言理解过程。以翻译为目的的语言理解过程具有特殊的认知含义,它决定口译认知过程中认知机制的调动和运作方式。此外,从认知的角度来看,此"口译链"中 deverbalization 阶段的界定比较模糊,它所涉及的具体心理过程及其"意义"在此阶段的具体表现形式有待进一步发掘。

2. 国内外研究现状

目前,国内译界对口译心理过程和认知过程的研究还处于起步阶段,真正对口译认知过程进行跨学科研究的论著很少。国内译界对"释意理论"中"脱离原语语言外壳"的相关研究还仅局限于探讨该阶段对口译教学实践的指导意义。

在国际译界,Isham(1994)使用心理学实验的方法,通过研究同声传译过后译员对语句形式的记忆效果来验证 deverbalization 阶段是否存在。Isham 的研究发现,相对于从英语到 ASL(American Sign Language for the deaf)的翻译过程而言,译员在完成从法语到英语的口译过程后对话语语句形式的记忆效果较差。Isham 认为,译员在两种翻译过后对话语形式记忆效果的差别侧面验证了 deverbalization 存在的可能性,但是这种差别也有可能是由于同声传译"表述"过程中所产生的"语音干扰"造成的。Isham 的研究结果并不能对 deverbalization 阶段在口译过程中是否存在做出终结性的结论(Ladmiral, 2005)。

Setton 从认知和语用的角度来研究口译过程。他认为,社会个体要完成不同的语言任务需要具备并且调动不同的语言处理能力。在他提出的"口译基本能力和子过程框架图"模型中,译员在口译过程中至少需要具备三种能力(Setton, 2002:17):感知表述能力、语言处理能力(包括语法和词汇)和高级认知活动能力。其中,第三种能力具体包括范畴化(categorization)、形式匹配(pattern matching)、推理、猜测和规划等能力,这些能力又被 Setton 进一步划分为推测推理能力(deductioninference)和元表征能力(metarepresentation)两种关键能力。在 Setton 的口译模型中,没有单独用来表示记忆的模块。Setton 认为,在记忆中所完成的操作,都是依赖于表征和元表征能力来完成的。在此类操作过程中,译员根据映像的抽象程度、持续时间和可重建性将它们标签、标记并分类(ibid: 16)。周期性记忆、语义性记忆和隐性记忆等记忆是以此类标志着不同时间、从属和结构关系标签的映像的形式被调动处理的。Setton 在自己的口译过程模型中虽然没有正面提及 deverbalization 的阶段，但是他对高级认知处理活动能力尤其是对表征和记忆关系的笼统介绍可以看做是对 deverbalization 阶段认知活动的一个初步解释。

Ladmiral 第一个从多学科的角度深入研究了 deverbalization 的相关问题。他指出，翻译的主要特征之一是原语和译语之间的"不连续性"(discontinuity)，而 deverbalization 是从原语到译语的一个跳板(2005：473)。他认为，翻译过程中没有地方来安插 deverbalization 这样一个"独立"的"中间阶段"。他将翻译过程比喻为三个分割点所确立的两个连续的矢量线段(ibid：476)。这三个分割点分别为话语录入的开始，"脱离原语语言外壳"的"意义"和译语表达的结束；两条矢量线段分别表示原语的理解及译语的再表达(ibid：477，478)。Ladmirale 认为，不管口译交际过程是两段的还是三段的，所有的翻译交际活动都涉及一个 deverbalization 的过程(ibid：478)。这个过程实质上是在心理层面或认知层面展开的，是话语信息从话语语言层面到心理认知层面的过渡。Deverbalization 的功能在于完成信息的概念化，同时将信息从瞬时记忆传递到语义记忆。此外，"意义"是不可能没有相关支持而独立存在的，因此"意义"在 deverbalization 阶段的存在形式及其本质需要确定(ibid：473)。

Mouzourakis(2005)认为"释意理论"所倡导的 deverbalization 对于译员培训的教学价值应该是值得肯定的。但是，"释意理论"并没有提出具体的机制来解释 deverbalization 的发生过程。为了解答 deverbalization 在口译实践和口译理论中是否有效，Mouzourakis 从观察"释意理论"提出时的主导语言理论(即将语言视为一种符号系统)入手，结合 Kintsch 和 Van Dijk 提出的语篇理解与话语理解模型及 Wilson 和 Sperber 提出的关联理论，来探讨 deverbalization 的可能性发生机制。Mouzourakis 的研究为 deverbalization 的解释提出了一个可能性的理论框架，但其理论基础比较陈旧，并没有结合口译实践对 deverbalization 进行详细解释。

3. Deverbalization 所面对的实质性问题

从科学发展的角度来讲，deverbalization 是 Selescovith 与 Lederer 两位翻译家在译学方兴未艾的阶段提出的一个具有跨学科性质的超前命题。这个命题的提出大大超越了当时人类对语言及其语言理解过程的认识。

3.1 Deverbalization 在口译过程中的存在状态

在"释意理论"中，deverbalization 起初是作为口译过程中一个与原语理解和再表达并列存在的独立阶段提出来的(Selescovitch & Lederer，1984)。但在 2003 版的《口译推理教学法》中，她们倾向于将 deverbalization 看做是一种"意义"在大脑意识里的存在状态(Seleskovitch & Lederer，2003：41)。"释意理论"在 deverbalization 前后表述上的改进涉及 deverbalization 的界定及其与话语理解的关系问题。这一问题实质上就是 Ladmiral(2005)在自己的研究中提出的口译过程应该是两段论还是三段论的问题。要解决这一问题，我们认为，必须将口译过程中的动态处理过程和静态处理结果区分开，同时将不同处理阶段的处理对象，即将话语信息或"意义"的不同存在形式考虑在内。这是一个方法论的问题。

Deverbalization 到底是一个话语信息或"意义"的动态处理过程还是理解之后形成的"意义"的一种静态存在状态？如果把 deverbalization 看做是一个动态处理过程，就需要阐明此阶段包含哪些话语信息或"意义"处理过程，同时将其与原语理解和译语生成界定开来；如果将 deverbalization 看做是动态处理过程所形成的静态处理结果，只需阐明其"意义"的存在形式即可。而决定这两者取舍的关键在于 deverbalization 在口译过程中实际对应的认知处理活动。只有将口译的整个话语处理活动放在认知的视角下才能最终界定 deverbalization 这一概念。

3.2　Deverbalization 与口译理解过程的界定

在口译过程中，话语理解是实现口译交际目的的首要前提。但是，以翻译为目的话语理解与普通交际环境下的话语理解有着本质上的区别。两者在某些层面是互通的，在有些层面却大不相同。而这些不同的层面在很大程度上决定着认知主体在话语处理过程中的认知去向和认知机制的运作方式。

口译理解过程是受口译交际环境限制的一种特殊的话语理解过程。与普通环境下的话语理解相比，该过程也具备主观性和个体性，也是译者管理调动储备知识、主观构造认知映像、对多渠道、多模式信息进行认知整合和加工处理的心理过程。但是，以口译为目的的话语理解过程，不是为了在长期记忆中建立起连贯的心理映像、储备知识，而是以在有限的交际环境下顺利实现双语转换为首要任务。

Deverbalization 作为口译过程中话语理解之后一个紧密相连的认知过程，无论是作为一个动态的处理阶段还是作为"意义"在某一时刻的一种静态存在状态，都将直接受到话语理解结果的影响。话语理解结果将直接决定 deverbalization 的界定及其"意义"在此阶段的存在形式。因此，作为译学的一个专业术语，deverbalization 的定义不应该仅仅突出"意义""脱离原语语言外壳"的表现形式，还应该强调其在口译交际环境下的特殊性及其对口译认知活动的导向性。

3.3　Deverbalization 阶段"意义"的组织存在形式

"释意理论"是在"意义理论"的基础之上发展而来的，该理论中的"意义"是在口译实践和交际理论的基础上发展而来的。"释意理论"将词汇和句子的所指含义与话语"意义"区分开来。词汇和句子的所指含义是指译者在语音、词形（signifier）与其基本含义（signified）表层对应的基础上建立的词汇和句子的表层含义。而"意义"则是指译者在特殊的、具体的上下文（context）和话语环境（situation）中阐释理解的话语的意思。该"意义"是通过同时在语言层面与超语言层面进行的话语理解活动来完成的。语言符号及它们之间的关系是译者进行解码的基础，但在解码过程中译者需要将理解过程融合到一个完整的交际过程中来，结合话语的生成环境，包括交际环境、话语环境、上下文环境、表述环境、社会文化环境、话语的语用功能等因素，来对话语信息进行全方位的理解、阐释。

"释意理论"从语言学和交际学的角度出发，对"意义"的解释和定义并不能满足话语信息的认知处理需要。话语信息随着口译过程中认知处理活动的展开是在不停地变换着存在形式的。"意义"在不同处理阶段、不同认知机制中的组织表现形式是不同的。我们需要结合认知语义学的相关理论才能对 deverbalization 阶段"意义"的组织存在形式做出解释。

3.4　口译特殊交际环境对 Deverbalization 的限定

现有的口译认知领域的研究已经证明,口译的特殊交际环境及其实际交际过程中出现的各类问题和困难直接影响口译效果,如同声传译共时表述过程中的表述抑制和语音干扰、交替传译过程中译员与讲话人的交际场景对其理解效果的影响等。同声传译过程中多任务的"共时性"和交替传译过程中多任务的"后时性"对诠释 deverbalization 提出了特殊的限定。

在口译过程中,译员需要在有限的时间和认知资源范围内高效地完成口译交际任务。这就涉及一个译员在特殊的口译交际环境中要完成口译交际任务需要进行多深的语义处理的问题。绝大多数情况下,译员的处理须既能满足口译的功能性需要,又不能超越口译特殊交际环境所允许的范围,更不能超过译员可支配的认知资源。要解决该问题,不仅要阐明口译理解过程中不同的语义处理阶段,还需要结合口译的特殊交际环境及译员在口译过程中调动的认知机制和认知处理活动来综合阐述。

4. 诠释 deverbalization 的理论框架

Deverbalization 这一命题的跨学科性质决定了该命题只能从跨学科的角度来进行阐释。近几十年来迅速发展起来的语篇理解理论、认知语义学理论、记忆理论和知识表征理论为 deverbalization 的认知诠释提供了有力的理论支持。

语篇理解理论认为,普通交际环境下的话语理解过程是在话语接收对象与话语本身间展开的一个多层次的动态交互过程。该交互过程的最终目的是在长期记忆中建立一个连贯的心理映像(Kintsch,1998)。在最表层,话语接收对象需要感知语言符号的音、形特征,并在记忆中进行编解码。这些语言符号所形成的记忆痕迹并不稳定,且很快消失。在超越话语表层符号的层面,读者需要在"逻辑分句"(proposition)层面进行解码,同时借助推理在他们之间建立起连贯的局部联系(local coherence)。此步骤之后,更多的信息将会被更长时间地存储在记忆中。但是,在"逻辑分句"层面建立起来的映像并不能保证理解的最终结果。话语接收对象需要利用自己长期记忆中的主题知识和百科知识来补充"逻辑分句"所提供的语义内容,以建立起一个超越话语表层的、整体上连贯(global coherence)的心理映像。这个整体上连贯的话语映像可以储存在长期记忆中,成为情景模型(situation model)(Kintsch & van Dijk,1978;Graesser,Singer & Trabasso,1994)。

认知语义学范围内基于"认知常量"(cognitive invariants)的语义生成和语义组织理论为诠释 deverbalization 过程中"意义"的存在形式提供了全新的理论依据。认知语义学认为,人类的语言使用一些基本语义类别,如事物、状态、事件、动作等,及因果关系、时间关系、从属关系等来组织构建话语"含义"(signification)(Le Ny,1989:163)。这些语义类别构成认知主体的"认知常量",这些"认知常量"是人类认知系统用来感知、表征外部世界的基本概念类别。这些语义类别具备个体性且由个体的认知特点来决定。相对于"逻辑分句"而言,这些"认知常量"是高层次的认知类别。在话语理解过程中,话语映像的构建是从话语理解的基本单位"逻辑分句"开始,一层层来实现的。在"逻辑分句"的基础上,认知主体构建事件、状态、动作等基本语义类别,并通过时间关系、空间关系、因果关系、从属关系等联系将这些基本语义类别进一步组织起来,形成宏观事件、宏观状态和宏观动作等更高层的语义单位。(Denhiere &

Baudet，1992)口译是一个系统的、策略性的话语信息处理过程,该过程涉及的认知机制及其认知运作模式十分复杂。Deverbalization 的认知诠释需要结合认知心理学提出的认知机制的原始理论模型和口译的特殊交际环境来综合解释。该过程所涉及的认知处理机制主要有:视觉、听觉器官接收到听觉或视觉刺激信号后所形成的感知记忆(从理论上讲,只能持续 300 毫秒);信息处理过程中用于短期信息存储和信息加工的工作记忆(包括音位圈、视觉空间板和"周期性缓存"三个子系统)(Baddeley & Hitch，1974；Baddeley，2000)(许明,2008：19);由用来保留处于激活状态的"信息提取线索"(information recuperation cues)的短期工作记忆和用来联系这些"信息提取线索"和长期记忆的"信息提取结构"(information recuperation structure)这两大要件构成的长期工作记忆(Ericsson & Kintsch，1995);主要由语义性记忆(semantic memory)和周期性记忆(periodic memory)构成的、用于存储语言知识、百科知识和主题知识的长期记忆。Deverbalization 的认知诠释需要协调上述各认知机制之间的关系。

口译的理解过程是长期记忆内知识的激活过程。知识在长期记忆中是以语义网的形式存储、通过"激活扩散"的方式来传播的(Collins & Quillian，1969)。语义表征是知识激活的基本形式,"逻辑分句"或"图式"是认知活动中知识在大脑里的两种主要表征方式。"逻辑分句"是话语理解过程中以语言结构为依托所形成的心理映像。图式(schemas)是认知个体主观形成的关于某一局部世界的心理映像,是知识的组织方式之一,同时也是一种理解、推理和记忆方式。话语理解过程中,局部语义网被激活的同时其他相关联的图式也会被激活。话语理解过程中,无论多复杂的话语信息或认知映像,它们最终在长期记忆中都是以被激活的概念和概念与概念之间的关系体现出来的。话语映像的复杂程度实质上取决于长期记忆中概念的激活数量、语义的处理深度及其概念间组织关系的复杂程度。

5. 同声传译及交替传译认知过程中 deverbalization 的认知诠释

为了能从根本上解决 deverbalization 所要面对的四个根本问题并规范 deverbalization 过程,我们须从观察同声传译和交替传译理解过程中的语义表征模式入手。此观察过程主要遵循两条线索:其一,信息(或语义)在不同处理阶段和处理机制内的存在模式;其二,不同认知机制在处理不同信息时的相互作用方式,具体来讲,包括在感知系统、短期缓存系统和长期储存系统内完成的感知、缓存、记忆、存储、激活、提取等认知活动。

5.1 同声传译和交替传译理解过程中的语义表征模式

同声传译的理解过程是从译员对发言人的话语感知开始的。发言人将自己欲表达的内容转换成话语语音流。话语语音流经过译员的听觉系统以听觉刺激信号的形式进入译员的感知记忆,并在感知记忆中形成极为简短的印痕。进入感知记忆的刺激信号,经过选择注意力的筛选被传输到工作记忆。在工作记忆中,译员首先要根据"音位圈"所接收到的听觉刺激信号的语音特征及长期记忆中激活的语言符号系统对语言符号进行认定。待语言符号认定后,译员须结合长期记忆中存储的语言系统对语言符号进行解码,并激活相应的语义特征。语言符号的语义特征激活后,译员须根据语言符号的语义特征,在 7 至 8 个字符范围内,找到相关语言符号间的"述谓关系",完成"逻辑分句"的划分,并结合长期记忆中的百科知识完成这些"逻辑分句"真假命题的判断。经过选择注意力的进一步筛选后,译员将会在工作记忆(或短期工作记忆)内完成对部分"逻辑分句"的最后一步操作,即找到"逻辑分句"间的"主谓关系",生成相应的事件、动作或状态等高层次的语义映像。与此同时,译员会有选择性地同步激活长期记忆内相关的背景知识和图式。在译员需要和同声传译实际交际情景允许的情况下,译员会对这些生成的高层次的语义映像在长期工作记忆中进行"关系组合",即找到这些事件、动作或状态间所维系的结构关系,如时间关系、空间关系、逻辑关系、因果关系等,进一步形成宏观事件、宏观动作和宏观状态。这个(或几个)在7至8个字符基础上形成的宏观语义单位是同声传译交际条件限定下译员认知能力所允许的最大的语义单位。这个(或几个)宏观上的语义单位以关键的概念信息及其特有的组织结构为基本组成部分。这些关键的概念信息及其特有的组织结构在长期记忆中有两种对应方式:一是与译员语义性记忆中处于激活状态的"结点"和"连线"相对应;二是与周期性记忆中激活的图式内容(或概念)和图式结构相对应。

　　除去基于语言层面的直接转换外,同声传译的整个理解过程就是在上述阶段的基础上往复循环来实现的。在每个工作记忆所允许范围内的语义处理循环结束后,译员会在开始另一个循环的同时,开始转换并用译语表述所形成的语义映像。整个口译理解过程可以分为词汇处理、语义处理和知识激活三个组成部分。其中,词汇处理和语义处理构成同声传译理解过程的两个阶段。前者所囊括的范围从话语感知开始一直持续到语言符号的语义激活。后者所囊括的范围从寻找"述谓关系"开始,到形成高层次语义单位或宏观语义单位结束。知识激活是指在上述两个处理阶段中所有在长期记忆内展开的知识激活、调动、组织等认知过程。在理解过程中,知识激活是与其他认知活动协调展开的,所激活的知识类型、知识结构和知识范围受认知活动、交际目的和交际环境的限定。知识激活为词汇处理和语义处理提供语言知识、百科知识、图式框架等认知补充,是词汇解码、语义切入、语义构建的前提,是生成话语映像、构建宏观话语信息的必要组成部分。

　　在循环过程中,译者可以根据话语接收效果、信息密度、信息重要程度、交际需要和可支配的认知资源来动态调整自己的语义处理深度和翻译策略。比如,可以对未听清的话语加大话语接听范围,浓缩表达过程中的语义内容;可以对信息密度大的话语信息进行较浅的语义处理,且尽快传送出去,以避免影响其他同步的认知活动;可以对相对不重要的信息,进行基于语言层面的直接转换等。无论译员的表述基于怎样的语义处理深度,从哪一个语义层面开始,译员除了保证同声传译的正常运转外,还要通过不同的策略需要保证"意义"的连贯性。

　　在交替传译理解过程的各轮认知循环中,从话语信息的感知到事件、动作或状态等高层次语义映像的生成都与上述同声传译的各步骤相对应。不同的地方是,在各轮循环形成了相应的高层次语义映像之后,译员必须继续进行相应的宏观语义单位的构建,而且绝大多数情况下译员会根据需要在这些宏观语义单位的基础上构建更高层次的宏观语义单位。在工作记忆所允许范围内的每一轮循环结束之后,译员会将该轮循环所形成的宏观语义单位与上一轮所形成的宏观语义单位进行整合,按照两者之间的逻辑关系组织起来。交替传译的认知处理活动就是这样依次循环,级级深入,直至在讲话人结束一段讲话后形成一个连贯的多层次的宏观语义网络。

　　从认知机制的角度来看,交替传译过程中同一处理循环内部宏观语义单位的构建和各循环之间更高层次宏观语义单位的构建都应该是在长期工作记忆内来完成的。在用译语表述的过程中,译员从短期工作记忆中处于激活状态的"信息提取索引"入手,按照长期工作记忆中储存的"信息提取结构",即高层次宏观语义单位和宏观语义单位间的结构关系,来完成整段话语信息的激活和提取，并根据话语接收对象及其译语的语言习惯做出适当的调整后，选择恰当的译语表达出来。

5.2 Deverbalization 的存在形式、界定、定义和发生机制

结合上述同声传译和交替传译理解过程中的语义表征模式，我们可以发现，如果采用 Selescovitch 及 Lederer(1984)对 deverbalization 的原始定义，即强调"意义"脱离具体语言表达形式的支持而独立存在的特征，口译过程中的 deverbalization 须看做是一个相对独立的动态处理阶段，该阶段的开始位置应该是按照"主谓关系"和特定结构组织起来的"逻辑分句"，即状态、事件、动作等高层次的语义单位，其截止阶段应该是在 7 至 8 个字符基础上形成的宏观事件、宏观动作及宏观状态等宏观语义单位(同声传译)或者更高层次的宏观语义单位(交替传译)。因此，可以说，除去专有名词、数字等特殊情况外，状态、事件和动作等高层次的语义单位、宏观语义单位(同声传译)和高层次的宏观语义单位(交替传译)是"意义"在口译 deverbalization 阶段的基本存在形式(而非唯一)。"逻辑分句"间的主谓关系，事件、状态和动作间的结构关系和宏观语义单位间的组织关系构成该阶段"意义"的主要存在特征(而非仅有)。但是，遵循此逻辑，我们可以发现，相对于同声传译和交替传译的整个认知理解过程而言，deverbalization 开始之前的认知处理过程不等同于口译的理解过程。如果按照我们对 deverbalization 的阶段划分，该阶段所囊括的语义处理过程只能看做是口译理解过程的高级处理阶段。这时，deverbalization 作为译学的专业术语只能被定义为"口译理解过程中话语信息脱离语言形式支持后，在语义层面和其他话语层面展开的、以满足口译特殊交际条件下的功能性需要为目的的高级认知处理过程"。而此时的口译过程就变成了 Ladmiral(2005)所提出的只有原语理解和译语再表达的两个阶段的两段论，这个定义不吻合口译实践。

但是，如果按照 Selescovitch 及 Lederer(2003)对 deverbalization 的最新表述倾向，即强调 deverbalization 是理解之后所形成的"意义"在大脑意识里的一种存留状态，那 deverbalization 只能看做是"意义"的一种静态存在状态，该状态从译员完成相应的、能满足特殊交际环境下口译的功能性需要的语义处理层开始，到开始根据话语对象和译语环境对"意义"进行转换时结束，中间还有可能掺杂其他话语信息和语用信息的处理过程。该状态下的信息是在长期工作记忆内存储的。"意义"在此状态下的存在形式与译员开始表述前所进行的语义处理深度有关，其对应范围从事件、动作、状态等高层次的语义单位(同声传译)，到宏观语义单位(同声传译)或更高层次的语义单位(交替传译)。在此状态下，如果结合 Selescovitch 及 Lederer(1984)对 deverbalization 的原始定义，我们可以发现，从"脱离原语语言外壳"到"意义"最终在长期工作记忆内形成一种存在状态，中间不仅间隔好几层的语义处理过程，而且还可能掺杂语义信息与其他话语层面，如语调、节奏等所表现出来的话语信息和语用信息的整合过程。也就是说，在 deverbalization 状态下的"意义"具有"脱离原语语言外壳"的性质，但该状态下并不能囊括话语信息"脱离原语语言外壳"后所有的认知处理活动。两者之间的矛盾只能允许我们选择其中的一个。如果坚持"释意理论"对口译过程三段论的假设，我们只能选择 deverbalization 作为"意义"在长期工作记忆中的一种存在状态。此时，既能保持"释意理论"的三段论，又能保持理解过程的完整性。而 deverbalization 只能被定义为"口译过程中，译员为完成特殊交际条件下的功能性需要、在整合语义信息和其他层面的话语信息和语用信息的基础上，在长期工作记忆内形成的、以高层次语义表征或多层次宏观语义网络为基本存在形式

和主要存在特征的意义存在状态"。此定义较吻合口译实践,且与相关口译理论相照应。

6. 研究意义及展望

对口译过程中 deverbalization 进行认知诠释的目的在于:界定 deverbalization 与口译理解的界限,规范其认知特征和含义,验证其在口译认知过程中存在的合理性;同时,从跨学科的角度丰富口译理论研究的内容和方式,揭示完整的口译认知过程,为解释各种口译现象和口译问题提供认知理论支持;此外,加强口译理论对口译教学和口译实践的指导作用,开辟符合口译认知规律的口译认知教学法。

【延伸阅读】

1. Bertone, Laura E. *The hidden side of Babel unveiling cognition*, *intelligence and sense through simultaneous interpretation*. Buenos Aires:Evolucion,2006.

2. Setton, R. *Simultaneous interpretation*:*A cognitive-pragmatic analysis*. Amsterdam:Benjamins,1999.

3. Timarová, Šárka & Salaets, Heidi. Learning styles, motivation and cognitive flexibility in interpreter training:Self-selection and aptitude. *Interpreting*. 2011,13(1):31-52.

4. 李明远. 认知心理学与口译课. 四川外语学院学报. 1998,70(4):79-83.

5. 刘绍龙,夏忠燕. 中国翻译认知研究:问题、反思与展望. 外语研究. 2008,110(4):59-66.

6. 吴莹. 认知心理学在口译记忆中的应用研究. 辽宁教育行政学院学报. 2010,27(4):104-105.

7. 熊毅. 口译认知过程的符号学阐释. 罗选民主编. 语言认知与翻译研究. 北京:外文出版社,2005:340-351.

【问题与思考】

1. 简述认知学派理论与口译研究的关系。

2. 试从认知学角度阐释口译的过程并分析交替传译和同声传译在认知模式构建方面的异同。

3. 你同意"理解是口译认知的核心"这个观点吗? 为什么?

4. 口译是一个认知过程,是语言和文化认知过程的整合,是话语"所指"的映现和重构,试从符号学的角度阐释口译的这一认知过程。

5. 你认为口译过程中存在"deverbalization"吗? 试从认知角度对此进行诠释。

第五章　文化学派口译理论研究

导　论

　　口译是一项以语言为基础的活动。译员的主要任务简单说来就是传达信息,实现双语间的交流。但口译又不是单纯意义上的言语行为,而是一种涉及诸多知识层面的跨文化的交际行为。很多情况下,口译活动最终交流失败或受阻,并不是因为口译员遇到了语音、词汇或语法方面的障碍,而是由于口译员只注意语言形式的对等,忽略了转达语言所承载的文化内涵所造成的。口译不只是把一种语言转换成另一种语言,还是把一种文化转换成另一种文化。随着世界各国交流的增多,口译作为一种独立的职业得到社会的广泛认同和关注,可以说口译工作的认可是和所谓的"地球村"的发展分不开的,也是和口译员的文化素质分不开的,这更突显出口译中实现不同文化交流和理解的重要性。在我国各外语专业的教学大纲中,都或多或少地阐述了文化传达在口译中的重要性,口译的教学目标中都包括有诸如"通过大量的听说实践,训练学生在政治、经济、社会文化等方面的口译能力,同时还应注意提高学生的政策水平和涉外工作的能力"这样的要求。而对口译的教学要求则往往包括"在无预先准备的情况下,能承担生活翻译;经过准备后,能胜任政治、经济、文化等的翻译;忠实原意,语言表达流畅,并能区别各种不同的语感和说话人的心态"等类似的说明。可以看出,在口译过程中,文化传达相当重要。近年来,不少口译研究者就口译与文化的关系问题进行了深入的研究,这些从文化视角切入研究口译中的跨文化交际、跨文化差异、文化缺省、文化转移和文化特征的行为统称为"文化学派口译理论研究"。

　　关于口译中"文化"的定义,从研究文化差异的角度来看,Thomas(1991:192)所作的阐释比较贴切:文化是一种万有的、对一个社会、国家、组织或团体极为典型的定位系统。这一系统由特殊的标记构成,在每一个社会里以口头形式得以世代传承。它影响到全体社会成员的感知、思维、价值判断和行为,并以此对他们的社会属性作了界定。从语言哲学和逻辑学的角度来看,文化也可被阐释为"内涵"和"外延"两部分:文化的"内涵"包括理念和价值观、审美、宗教和社会标准以及法律法规,它们以谚语、歌曲、童话、故事、轶事、笑话等形式被口头流传;"外延"则明显表现为不同文化载体更为丰富的行为活动,"外延"可有过程和结果之分,这一点从建筑物、工业产品和节假日的庆祝场面可以看出。此外,人们还可谈及"狭义文化"(带有"艺术"标志)和"广义文化"(由人所创造的一切)以及"高级文化"和"低等文化",并使之与"文明"建立起一种联系(付天海,刘颖,2006:56)。

　　文化学派口译理论认为口译不仅是语言之间的转换,也是跨文化交际的方式。在口译这样的跨文化交际过程中,交际双方要想达到预期的目的,就必须要有共同的背景知识或语用前提，这样在交流时就可以省去一些对双方来说是不言而喻或不说自明的东西，从而提高交际效率。然而，往往由于讲话人和听众生活在不同的社会文化环境中，所以很可能交际双方并不具备相同的文化背景知识。因此，在这样的跨文化交际活动中，口译员就充当了文化交流的使者。口译员通过自己的理解和阐述，将不同的文化视域融合成一个更大的视界，最终达到实现双方交际的目的。

文化学派口译理论研究的一个非常积极的意义在于其提出了在口译活动中，译员应具备较强的"跨文化意识"。"跨文化意识"是指在跨文化交际中自觉或不自觉地形成的一种认知标准和调节方法，或者是对文化的一种敏感性。跨文化交际本身就是不同文化的交际双方以语言为媒介，通过"信息源—编码—信息传递—解码—反馈"等环节所构成的一个双向信息交换的动态过程。在这个过程中，信息在一种文化背景下进行编码，而在另一种文化背景下进行解码，所以口译员作为跨文化意识的载体在信息传递中起着桥梁作用。口译员之所以不同于翻译机器，就在于口译员对两种语言所涉及的不同文化的了解与掌握，更在于其能从字面意思之外领悟到说话人言语中的语用意义。

在近年的口译理论研究中，国内外学者已经意识到了口译中文化研究的重要性，但口译中的文化视角仍有待更进一步的研究和分析。目前，文化学派口译理论研究的热点已经从以往的关注文化客体因素转向口译员主体因素，着重考察口译过程中口译员的"文化使者"主体身份、不同口译场合的口译员如何在"即时性"的口译环境下有效处理口译中的文化障碍、实现文化交际等，这些都为口译理论研究开辟了一个全新的视角。

选　文

选文一　Book Review of *Crossing Borders in Community Interpreting*: *Definitions and Dilemmas*

Michal Schuster

导　言

口译人员作为语言的中介和桥梁，在商业、聋哑人等社区中扮演着重要的跨文化交流管理者的角色。有些观点认为口译人员应该是中立的或隐形的，但是这样的理论对现实的口译活动和口译工作造成了诸多限制，给口译人员带来很多困惑，因为作为跨文化交流中的积极参与者，口译人员如果对自身"文化主体性"的认识不够充分，必将误导其口译行为。对于社区口译人员而言，"跨文化意识"显得尤为重要，因为他们是在跨文化的背景下为不同的客户提供服务，他们的服务范围很广，包括商业领域、工厂、医院、法庭等，他们的客户可能具有完全不同的背景知识，对同一问题有不同的理解，因此，社区口译人员在不同的口译环境下充当着不同的角色，有时是传声筒，有时是调解现实生活中跨文化交流的管理者，有时是强有力的文化干预者，有时是能深入当地文化社区的人员。从文化角度对社区口译活动和社区口译人员的主体性进行口译研究具有很强的现实指导意义。

A physician in a community clinic in Israel once had this to say about the tasks of the cultural mediator in medical settings: "She has so many different tasks to perform that she is unable to fully concentrate on telling me what the client wants of me, and telling him what I want of him." The complexity of the community interpreter's role, as expressed by this physician, was the core topic of the conference titled "Translation as Mediation or How to Bridge Linguistic and Cultural Gaps," held in April 2005 at the University of Alcalá de Henares, Spain. The book under review is an outcome of that conference, following which researchers from around the globe were called upon to send in empirical papers and others dealing with research projects in the field of community interpreting, its needs and how these are met. The book's central theme—the role of the interpreter—has become a matter of growing interest to researchers in recent years. The book discusses the immense complexity of this role, and the way it is perceived both by the interpreter and by those who rely on him/her, the boundaries of the interpreter's role and any changes that have occurred—or should occur—in these over time. Some of the writers raise the question of whether cultural mediation, or even advocacy, might be regarded as part of the community interpreter's role, or whether a distinction must be made between "pure" language mediation and more active forms thereof.

Some of the most prominent writers in the field of community interpreting of spoken languages (Angelelli, Hale, Mikkelson, Pöchhacker) and signed languages (Swabey, Turner) as well as the editors themselves have contributed to this volume. A refreshing addition to this ever-growing knowledge base are the papers of several lesser known Spanish researchers.

The editors point out that the papers are arranged in loose thematic order: a theoretical paper, codes and standards of spoken-and-signed-language interpreters, interpreting in the legal context and in the police force, medical interpreting and interpreting in the fields of education and welfare. The inclusion of papers dealing with signed languages is relevant, since role perception debates are heard, perhaps even louder, in the deaf community and among signed-language interpreters. A comparison between these two groups, focusing on similarities and differences in the dilemmas they confront, would have been a welcome addition.

Since one cannot describe all of the papers in the space of a short review, I have chosen to report on a few which I found particularly interesting.

The paper by Cynthia Giambruno (Miguélez) on the role of the interpreter in the governance of sixteenth-and-seventeenth-century Spanish colonies offers a detailed review of interpreters in the Spanish crown colonies in the "New World." Articles examining the role of community interpreters from a historical perspective are relatively rare, although interpreters acting as cultural mediators have been around for millennia. The historical preface makes mention of the role of interpreters in early Jewish history: the turgeman, the person who would not only provide a lingual interpreting of the holy script, but would also provide an interpretation of the difficult text to those praying in the synagogue, mediate between the various groups in society and serve as proof that what the learned scholar said must be regarded as a formal regulation for the entire community. The interpreters in the Spanish crown colonies served not only as aides for oral communication, but also as mediators between the two parties (in most cases, the conqueror and the conquered) and sometimes as reconcilers who fostered trust between the two parties. With the expansion of Spain into the New World, the need arose to teach some of the inhabitants how to act as language mediators, who would not only serve the local population but would also assist the Spaniards to become familiar with the ways of life of the native inhabitants. The line of decrees known as "Las Leyes delas Indias," legislated in the sixteenth and seventeenth centuries, deals with different aspects of life in the colonies. Title 29 in the second volume is devoted to the topic of communication between the Spaniards and the native residents, and gives a detailed outline of the rights and obligations of interpreters who work in the legal system. The paper presents key terms from the legal field and the work of the interpreter, analyzes the central clauses of the law (providing the original text and an English translation), and illustrates how the issues mentioned in the clause are relevant to present-day legal interpreting; e. g. the need to ensure that interpreters are proficient and able to carry out the task at hand, and their right to be respected as part of the staff of the legal system. When reading the clauses of the law, one cannot but notice that the same issues that interest researchers of legal interpreting today were already being raised four hundred years ago, and some even reflect the very same ethical codes of legal interpreters. That said, it is quite unfortunate that some of these codes have yet to be implemented—e. g. the stipulation requiring a sufficiently large roster of interpreters and ensuring that interpreting shifts are completely manned on every given work day, or that interpreting is provided without undue delays.

Franz Pöchhacker discusses the dimension of mediation in the concept of community interpreting. He contends that characterizing interpreting as a form of mediation might create misunderstandings and obscurity as far as the interpreting profession goes, and suggests a differentiation between the functions of inter-cultural mediation and interpreting in public institutions. To prove his point, Pöchhacker analyzes concepts from semantic fields related to interpreting, community interpreting and mediation in German and Italian.

Cultural mediation is perceived by public institutions, as well as academia, as a profession detached from the relatively developed field of conference/business interpreting (often intentionally), because, for the most part, it is done by bilingual individuals with little training, if any. It would be interesting to read about the claims voiced in German-and Italian-speaking countries regarding the mediating function of community interpreters. This particular article reminded me of complaints often aimed at those who serve as mediators between immigrants from Ethiopia to Israel in their contacts with caregivers in the fields of education, welfare and health. It is not uncommon to hear such remarks as: "She was too much in favor of the clients. She took their side and disagreed with us [the therapists] and our treatment." Or vice versa, clients belonging to minority groups might remark: "You forget where you came from; you are part of the Establishment already." In short, mediators are usually accused of siding with the other party, so that some role clarification, delivered to both sides before the interpreted interaction begins, may be in order.

Anne Martin and Isabel Abril Martí present a case study of community interpreters in Andalusia, examining their views about role boundaries, information addition and omission, as well as cultural explicitations. Although the paper does not present any earth-shattering discoveries regarding the perception of the interpreter's role, it is well-structured and gives a clear outline of the background, methodology (questionnaires validated in previous studies), target population and results as well as the limitations of the study. The authors give a detailed account of all stages of their research and their reservations about the methods chosen—such as a possible bias because of the setting in which the questionnaires were distributed and the need to adapt their content to the level of the participants' interpreting skills.

The paper by Juan Ortega-Herráez and Ana Foulquié Rubio is devoted to the field of police interpreting, about which not much has been written—inter alia, due to the difficulty of conducting studies in that specific environment. The paper provides a view of possible interpreting solutions in the Spanish police force, followed by the results of a study in which questionnaires were presented to police interpreters and police officers. The authors offer a revealing discussion of the obstacles they faced, including the impossibility of obtaining feedback from the police investigators, who were wary of having external researchers examine police protocols. Perhaps an alternative research method (interviews) should be tried in future, or a study that the police force itself would regard as beneficial (e. g. as part of a training program, or some sort of cooperation between academia and the police force, to prove that efficient interpreting assists in executing the law). Cooperation by the interpreters was very limited as well: Only seven questionnaires were returned. These results cannot provide a conclusive answer to the research questions, but it seems like the researchers did extract all they could from the data in presenting an encompassing analysis of the responses. These questionnaires might be considered for future use, when broader access to police interpreters and other police employees is available.

This collection of papers discusses the role of the interpreter from a number of angles and in a number of occupations, but like other related articles, most of them discuss interpreters' self-perception (e. g. Martin & Abril Martí, Dickinson & Turner), and only a few take the provider's perspective (e. g. Hale, Giambruno), yet they do not present the topic from the point of view of the minority-group consumers (with the exception of one component in Hans Verrept's relatively old study). To my knowledge, there have not been many articles dealing with this issue (with notable exceptions such as Garber & Maufette-Leenders 1997 and Edwards et al. 2005). Despite the methodological difficulties, this angle is very worthy of further research, and might even bring about changes in the interpreters' code of behavior.

Also noteworthy is the fact that about half of the thirteen papers in the collection present empirical studies that may be replicated, while the others are status reports, or are philosophical in nature. True, this collection includes more empirical studies than earlier publications, but in order to enhance research in this field (especially in non-Western countries, which have no research tradition in the field of community interpreting) more empiricism would be welcome. Be that as it may, both the surveys and the practical proposals concerning training for interpreters (e. g. the papers by Mikkelson and by Swabey & Gajewski Mickelson) contribute to the development of the field as far as both training and practicalities are concerned.

To summarize, this collection of papers contributes to the knowledge base in the field of community interpreting in general, and especially so to one of the most discussed topics in recent years, the role of the interpreter and its boundaries, as perceived by interpreters, their clients and their trainers. The fact that the very essence of the community interpreter's role is not carved in stone, but is given to ongoing discussion, shows—more than anything else, perhaps—that the occupation at hand is developing into a professional practice and a discipline of study in its own right.

选文二　口译中的文化特征与思维建构

付天海　刘　颖

导　言

　　翻译中的文化现象向来是翻译研究者倍加关注的层面，但是绝大多数论著都着眼于笔译中的文化现象，重在对语言、文化及翻译三者之间的关系进行审视和探讨。而口译的"即时性"特点决定了口译员在处理口译中的文化现象时必定会有别于笔译工作者，口译员如何在

"瞬间"的过程中对文化现象进行准确的认知和恰当的语言转换,都有赖于其瞬间的思维过程。因此,在对口译中的文化现象进行研究的过程中,有些研究者敏锐地抓住了口译中独特的"瞬间思维"特征,引入了对文化、语言和思维三者之间关系的探讨。可以说,口译员的思维建构在口译中起着至关重要的作用:口译中的分析综合是思维建构的基本特征,口译中的逻辑推理则是思维建构的表现形式。选文正是从这样的视角出发,引入哲学领域的思维建构说,通过分析文化在口译中的表现途径和表现方式,以及不同口译类别中的文化特征,从理论层面上说明了口译思维的基本特征和内在本质,从而揭示出口译过程中文化、语言和思维三者之间的联系。口译视角中的文化几乎涵盖了翻译所涉及的各个领域,并在其中表现出鲜明的文化特征。口译中的文化特征在很大程度上取决于不同的交际范围,因此不同口译类别的文化倾向性也有所不同,比如文化口译(博物馆、朗诵会、电影、戏剧)就比专业口译具有更多的文化内涵。而在"理解(感知、分析)—思维建构—表达"的口译过程中,在口译员的所有思维分析维度中,文化特征都产生了一定的影响。因此,口译过程中,离开瞬间的思维建构,语言和文化的转换就无从谈起。这种瞬间的思维建构时间虽短,承担的文化转换任务却最重。正如选文所述,"口译员在极短时间内完成的思维建构不仅是对原语语言文化的深度理解过程,更是对于原语语言文化的理性加工和二度创造过程,是实现文化在语言转换中得以体现的桥梁和纽带"。

1. 引言

近年来,不少专家学者、科研人员和高校教师就翻译与文化的关系问题进行了研究。他们通过不同的交流平台,进行了大量富有创见的理论性探讨和细致入微的实践性总结,使我国的译学研究得到了极大的丰富。不可否认,笔译和口译无论在表现形式抑或表现手法上都存在着较大的差别。笔译是对文字形式固定的书面语言进行翻译,译者有充裕的时间去反复阅读、理解,从内容到文字进行仔细的分析与推敲,译者可以查阅资料、工具书,甚至求助于他人,在完成初稿后还可以多次修改润色。而口译则完全不同,它的对象不是固定的书面文字,而是无形的口头语言,口译具有时间上的即时性,即译者没有更多的时间进行思考,要迅速地把听到的信息流畅贴切地转换成另一种语言。口译者不能参阅任何工具书,无法向专家求教,在完成信息转换过程后还须当场得到预期的反应。口译和笔译的这种"貌合神离"决定了语言的文化特征和译者的思维建构在口译中的特殊性。

2. 口译视角中的文化

各民族社会生活的道义原则具有同一性,同时这些原则的文化体现又具有很大的差异性,因为所有的文化都深谙乐于助人、热情好客、彬彬有礼、相互馈赠等价值标准,借助于此,人们相信能够最大限度地维护自己的利益,最有效地避免或消除矛盾冲突。但是怎样详细说明这些价值标准,它们在不同文化中的地位如何以及它们通过何种象征化的描写得以表述,各文化之间在这一点上出现了偏差。从在口译中研究文化差异的角度来看,Thomas(1991:192)对文化这一概念所作的阐释比较贴切:文化是一种万有的,对一个社会、国家、组织或团体极为典型的定位系统。这一系统由特殊的标记构成,在每一个社会里以口头形式得以世代传承。它影响到全体社会成员的感知、思维、价值判断和行为,并以此对他们的社会属性作了界定。

各民族文化都会以这样或那样的方式与其他某种文化发生联系,绝对封闭的文化在当今世界是不可想象的。人类学的研究表明,在文化和人种形成过程中会构造出一种特定的行为领域,它包括从被创造和使用的物体到公共机构、理念和价值观。当然在一种文化内部还存在若干亚文化,它们的价值体系和评判标准都不尽相同。尽管如此,一种文化全体成员的行为由共同的文化标准,即一种文化共同体的价值隐含意义特征所决定。从语言哲学和逻辑学的角度来看,文化概念可被阐释为内涵和外延两部分:文化的内涵包括理念和价值观,审美、宗教和社会标准以及法律法规,它们以谚语、歌曲、童话、故事、轶事、笑话等形式被口头流传。相反,外延则明显表现为不同文化载体更为丰富的行为活动。外延可有过程和结果之分,这一点从建筑物、工业产品和节假日的庆祝场面可以看出,此外人们还可谈及"狭义文化"(带有"艺术"标志)和"广义文化"(由人所创造的一切)以及高级文化和低等文化,并使之与"文明"建立起一种联系。

3. 文化借助于语言在口译中的显现

可以确定的是,口译员在翻译活动中面对的虽然是文化的外延,但他对过程更为深入的理解只在考虑内涵因素的情况下才成为可能。而内涵的天然不确定性阻碍了译者正确理解和清晰解释说话者的表达意图,因为内涵随社会团体、智力、年龄、行为、人的心理类型以及上下文语境的不同而发生变化。

不同口译类别的文化倾向性也有所不同。所谓的文化口译(博物馆、朗诵会、电影、戏剧)要比所谓的专业口译具有更多的文化内涵,而后者的口头专业交际无疑也揭示出一定的文化特色。文化特征的载体首先可以是表达内容,然后是语言实现和语言表现。它一方面指论题的选定、问题点之间的关系、论证和表达意义,也就是说怎样公开和透彻地将意图用言语表达出来;另一方面也指庞杂结构中不同元素的逻辑建构。语言的组织可有多种表现形式,如"以玩笑形式开场",开始时使用复杂或极其简单的句子,采用对一种交际行为来说恰如其分的"亲密"度,表述的形象化,以及微笑、幽默等来比照不同功能和形式的严肃等。一篇报告所具有的韵律学结构无疑蕴含着文化特征,伴随报告始末,属于语言表现范畴的准语言(表情、用以表达习惯和情感的手势)也是如此。

口译员通过多种途径来分析原语信息传达:(1)明确的语言途径(表达的语义结构);(2)通过模式知识连带介绍的内涵的构想成分;(3)口译前和口译中考虑到潜在兴趣和意向的语用学途径;(4)谈话的韵律学表现;(5)谈话的准语言表现。在所有这些分析维度中,文化特征也都产生了一定了影响。在此后的再创造即二次加工过程中,口译员须决定怎样使这些意义成分在目的语翻译中被"滞后"地反映出来。原语表达中重要的隐含信息、以韵律学方式传达的信息或准语言信息在目的语中不必通过多种途径表现出来,因为用相同的手段真实地再现某些语言中惯常的表情和手势要求口译员需具有一定的熟巧程度,而且这样做还有可能扭曲听者的印象。

具体的目的语生成需要与口译任务和由此衍生出的口译策略(语义策略或交际策略)相一致,口译策略表现为某种特定的转换方式。比如面对建筑工程师所采取的口译策略首先是一种交际策略:口译应能够提供信息和说明情况,口译内容应以逻辑思维形式连贯地被传达,就像目的语听众所习惯的那样。因此阻碍篇章连贯性的空隙(Tschenlow,1987:29)必须被填补,知识在抽象表达中不能过度凝聚,否则这种语义的不连贯性会引发听者的自发言论。

4. 不同口译类别中的文化特征

上文谈到的文化特征在很大程度上取决于不同的交际范围。

国际会议:会议口译蕴含最低程度的文化特色,因为这种场合的国际性要求与会者严格遵守国际惯例和标准,即形成一种文化适应现象。此外,许多国际会议上主要使用的语言为英语,这样许多发言人并不使用自己的母语,从而渐隐本民族的文化。这种报告式口译在一种相对正式的气氛中进行,发言内容往往并非自发生成(尽管有时听起来会带有自发的痕迹),文化特点也就不甚明显。这种场合不会或很少有直接的沟通,即使在交传口译时也是如此。讲话者的文化水准一般都相对较高,而口译员是否需要掌握文化知识则主要取决于会议或发言的主题。

接下来进行的讨论(事先准备或即兴)就对口译员提出了较高的文化素养方面的要求。讨论者不再像在作报告或发言时那样遵守国际标准。某些言论可能具有自发性和更具情感性,而并非总是缜密逻辑思维的产物。此外,这一环节中文化与文化之间不同的论证方式也得以展现。

司法与刑事:这一口译类别的高文化强度是可以想象的。这是因为各国不同的法律体系要求口译员单方面做出阐释和说明。另一方面被告人的文化水平往往比较低下,这样口译员就不得不在两个语言极端之间游弋:对词汇、句法、韵律和准语言提出极高要求的法庭审判语言和被告人口语化直至低俗的语言水准。

博物馆:这一场合的口译活动被公认为与高雅文化和历史的联系最为紧密,译员对文学和艺术的了解是不可或缺的。听者同时对文化的内涵和语言的表述感兴趣,尽管他们的情感和思维不尽相同。

电影:文化和语言在这里发生了急剧的碰撞,被同声翻译的故事片和纪录片折射出一个民族真实的心理状态,它们具有鲜明的文化特色。人们在这里遇见的是语言和文化的整个跨度,即从高雅的标准语言经地区方言到口语和俚语。这些特征在戏剧翻译中更为明显。

会谈:会谈口译中也蕴含了浓郁的文化特征。采访中涉及的是一些专门话题,如文学、政治、宗教等,采访双方往往互不了解,虽事先能够猜到提问的范围,但陈述却经常极具自发性。谈话双方的受教育程度有可能千差万别。

谈判:谈判风格不可能千篇一律。虽然谈判双方最终都是为了获取经济利益和其他重要利益,但潜在的文化差异也不容忽视。拘泥于细节、热衷于规划和近乎于逻辑的论证方式明显不如旨在情感和自然大方的表现风格那样受欢迎。所有这些都要通过译者来传输,口译员不仅要表达得细腻,有时还要充当某种功利主义的先行者。

5. 口译的思维建构

作为文化之间进行交流的媒介,口译的作用在于反映出两种语言、文化的特征,将原语文化中的文本移植到陌生的目的语文化中去。不同的文化源流,不同的语言结构,以及不同的思维方式造成了语言之间的异质性和差异性。若要用一种语言文化最大限度地真实再现另一种语言文化,译者的思维建构将起着至关重要的作用。思维的建构问题最初是由德国古典唯心主义哲学家康德在《纯粹理性批判》中以"先天形式"、"图例式"、"知觉"等观点提出来的。

康德认为,建构一个概念既不能只从经验出发,因为经验不能提供普遍有效性,也不能只从单纯概念出发,因为单纯概念不能提供扩充的知识,因此建构是理性的创造物。康德的这一建构概念就是思维的建构问题。作为德国古典唯心主义的创始人,康德哲学思想的本质是唯心的,但他所提出的思维建构性无疑对口译活动有着重要的指导意义(Bell,1991:131-135),因为口译本身就是这样一个活动过程:

理解(感知、分析)→思维建构→表达

可以看出译者在对原语理解之后,必然要先进入思维建构阶段,并在这里将理解的内容加工处理后才能最终用译语来表达。换言之,口译的思维建构是整个口译思维中的一部分,同时也是承上启下的中间部分。译者的口译思维过程是译者以主体方式对原作意义的感知和领会过程,也是译者借助各种已有的辅助工具(语言知识、分析和归纳能力、社会经验和相关专业知识等)使原文向译文建构的过程。

5.1 口译中的分析综合是思维建构的基本特征

口译的理解过程实际上是分析综合的过程,它可以分为语音听辨、语法结构分析、语篇分析、文体修辞分析、历史文化分析、社会背景分析、归纳概括和总结。

人类对有声语言的理解是从对语音的听觉分辨开始的,而译者的语音听辨不是逐音进行的,更不是毫不相关的、相互独立的音节或词汇的简单拼凑,而是连续性的言语链;译者在听辨的同时运用所学的语言知识,对输入语的语法结构进行快速分析,从而揭示出各言语链之间的有机联系;译者的个人经历、社会经验、生活常识和专业知识等因素对语义和语篇意义起某种智能加工和组装作用;口译的理解离不开阐释,阐释又以两种相关语言的历史文化知识为基础,它们相互关联,相互影响、相互渗透(刘宓庆,1999:60-63)。离开了认知知识,翻译当中的编码和解码过程就成了虚无缥缈的空中楼阁,即使是单个词语的翻译,也需借助于语境和认知知识在译语中找到恰如其分的对等意义。需要指出的是,上述分析过程在口译理解中并非分阶段逐步完成的,而是在极短的时间内一气呵成的。当然口译理解不仅需要相关的知识,更需要逻辑归纳和分析综合。译者理解后的信息不是简单的语言,更不是$1+1=2$的模块堆砌,而是意义。意义的形成过程也是表述动机生成的过程,没有表述动机,表达也将无从谈起,这是语言交际的客观规律。

5.2 口译中的逻辑推理是思维建构的表现形式

神经语言学认为参与语言交际的双方或多方并非按照简单的说—听—说这一模式来机械地交谈。说话者的表述动机不一定反映在字面上,他所表达的真正含义有时隐藏在字里行间中。同样的道理,听者的言语理解也往往不会满足对字面意思的掌握,他会在记忆中的各种认知知识和经验体系的支持下,从字面意思推导出内在含义。在语音听辨、语法结构分析、语篇分析、文体修辞分析、历史文化分析、社会背景分析基础上进行的归纳概括和总结完成之后,先期意义便以内部言语的形式储存在译者的短时记忆中,成为理解更广泛意义的基础和先决条件(鲍刚,1998:94-97)。大量的口译实践表明:讲话由话语组成,但讲话的意义却并非语言单词相加之和。一般说来,理解讲话信息的根本任务就是找出其逻辑性。口译思维从主体上说属于抽象思维,因而更注重逻辑推理和信息整合,当然也离不开形象思维和灵感思维(Chestewan,1997:213)。口译是一项高智能的思维科学形式和艺术再创造活动,口译思维中语言知识固然重要,但如果忽视或缺乏逻辑分析与推理则容易使思维混乱,翻译出来的东西必然支离破碎,很难实现交际目的。事实证明,优秀的同声传译员几乎可以在讲话者结束说话的同时完成翻译,由此可见,译者的超前逻辑思维对实现同步翻译至关重要。

6. 结语

每一门学科都有可能从本学科的视角出发来考查与之休戚相关的文化问题。例如,哲学对文化的考查侧重于思想和观念的源流、演变和发展;历史学对文化的考查侧重于典章制度及经济形态的变革和更替脉络;社会学对文化的关注则是集中于多维度的人际关系及其特征、结构和功能分析等。翻译学具有明显的综合性。口译视角中的文化或多或少地涵盖翻译所涉及的各个领域,并在其中表现出鲜明的文化特色。

语言是文化的载体,更是翻译学视角中文化的主体。离开语言,翻译学将无从谈起。在翻译学看来,语言是文化的主要体现者和依据,搬开语言来谈文化,对翻译学而言无异于缘木求鱼。而文化构成了语言的深邃内涵,对语言的外在形象和内部整合起着关键性作用。可以想象,没有深厚的文化底蕴作支撑,语言的表达必然是空洞乏味和苍白无力的。口译员在极短时间内完成的思维建构不仅是对原语语言文化的深度理解过程,更是对于原语语言文化的理性加工和二度创造过程,是实现文化在语言转换中得以体现的桥梁和纽带。

【延伸阅读】

1. 鲍刚. 口译理论概述. 北京:旅游教育出版社,1998.
2. 陈慧华. 浅析口译与跨文化交际. 考试周刊. 2008(13):215-216.
3. 李春光. 口译中的文化缺省及其补偿策略. 继续教育研究. 2008(5):157-158.
4. 邱进. 论口译中的文化障碍问题. 重庆工学院学报. 2005(10):107-110.
5. 王妍,王新芳. 英语口译教学中跨文化意识的培养. 内蒙古电大学刊. 2008,106(6):108-109.
6. 赵军峰,蒋楠. 论口译者的跨文化意识. 中国科技翻译. 1998(5):29-31.

【问题与思考】

1. 口译中的"文化特征"包括哪些? 这些"文化特征"如何影响口译人员的思维建构和口译活动?
2. 试从"跨文化交际"的角度分析口译的过程。

3. 在社区口译活动中,口译人员应该"文化隐身"吗？ 如果不是,那么社区口译人员应该如何定位自己的角色?

4. 树立口译人员的"跨文化意识"对于口译实践有何指导意义?

5. 从文化学派的口译理论角度出发,举例论述口译中的"文化缺省"现象以及如何有效地进行"文化补偿"。

第六章　释意学派口译理论研究

导　论

作为世界范围内诞生的第一种、也是目前唯一一种系统的口译理论,释意学派口译理论(Interpretive Theory)出现在西方口译研究的第三个阶段,即从业人员研究阶段(Practitioners' Period),并占据着主导地位。释意学派理论又称"达意理论"(Theory of Sense),是由巴黎高等翻译学院在上世纪60年代创立的学说,其创始人是该校首任校长达妮卡·塞莱斯科维奇(Danica Seleskovitch)和继任校长玛丽亚娜·勒代雷(Marianne Lederer)。释意学派理论用语言学、逻辑学、心理学的成就来阐述翻译的理解和表达过程,比较口笔译的异同,揭示即席翻译以及同声传译的基本规律。释意学派的主要观点包括:翻译即释意,是译者通过语言符号和自己的认知补充对原文意思所作的一种解释;译者应追求的不是语言单位的对等,而是原文意思或效果的等值。释意学派的理论强调口译以意义为中心,而不是字词和语言结构的对译。持释意派观点的口译人员认为:思想在未经表达以前,并非是以语言的形式储存在人的头脑之中;而一经用语言说出和确定之后,它又会在别人的头脑中以"非语言"的形式形成某种概念。因此,口译时,译员必须能够做到抓住讲话的内容,并将其连贯地记在心里,而不是让自己陷于讲话人所使用的词句。

释意学派理论的出发点和角度与同时期的语言学派翻译理论完全不同,其理论是建立在对口译现实的观察和分析基础上,其研究对象也不再仅仅局限于语言层面,而是更深入地解剖口译的意义传递现象。

在释意理论的带动下,20世纪80年代的口译研究开始从描述性研究向规范性研究转型,在研究中更加注重翻译的过程研究。为了说明语码转换过程中语意分离的现象,塞莱斯科维奇和勒代雷提出了口译过程的"三角模型",从规范性的角度呈现了口译过程的整体理想状态。她们认为口译过程不完全是从一种语言到另一种语言的直线过程,而是要经过意义形成的非语言过程——语言含义和认知知识相融合之后再形成语言表达。并由此产生了释意学派理论所强调的"翻译的三个阶段":理解—脱离原语语言外壳—再表达。

根据释意学派翻译理论,翻译的第一个阶段"理解"包括语言因素和非语言因素(认知、知识面、对原语文化的了解等)。理解是一个调动知识和逻辑内存、由表及里的分析过程;译员在理解的基础上采用瞬间记忆、辅之以符号记录实质性信息。第二个阶段"脱离原语语言外壳"(deverbalization)并非意味完全脱离语言载体,只是意义的升华,使用更浓缩、更抽象和跳跃性的语言来把握实质信息。因为口译的现场性、即时性以及不可重复性给口译增添了很多困难,要在瞬间完成听辨、理解、分析、记忆、构思和再表达等多项任务确实有很高的难度。口译员要在这种高强度的作业中,运用释意学派理论对语言的外在形式进行感知、抽象,抛开原语的外在形式,直接接触到原语话语者内心所要表达的内在意义,然后进行大脑内部的记录。这就是"脱离原语语言外壳"的过程。释意学派理论阐述的第三个阶段——再表达,主张采取"意义对等"的原则:"释意翻译是意义对等翻译,语言翻译是字词对应翻译,"再表达则是一个由里及表的传达信息的能动过程,是口译过程的最终产品。

释意学派口译理论之所以被视为是第一种也是目前唯一一种系统的口译理论,很大程度上归功于这一学派的口译理论在其后续研究中不断得以完善和丰富。释意理论认为:成功的口译应当达到语篇意义上的对等,即对篇章进行释意,翻译的应是意义,而不是语法,不是单个的字词句。原文和译文的等值应是整体交际意义上的等值,因此应当将"交际意义"作为口译的基本单位。勒代雷认为"意义单位"的提出为释意理论进一步论证口译并非是逐字传译的问题搭建了桥梁。"意义单位"作为口译的基本单位,指的是在原语和译语篇章中建立对等的最小单位。"意义单位"类似于通常人们所称的观念,其具体的长度无法测量。语言并非是完全明晰的,在交际中充满了省略。简言之,就是要释意,不要停留在语言层面的传译上。这一点也是释意学派翻译理论有别于语言学派翻译理论的最明显标志。

在中国,释意学派理论也受到了翻译研究者的热烈关注,得到广泛的传播和认可。比如,蔡小红、鲍刚、刘和平等人在大量翻译了相关理论原著的同时,还将该理论与中国实际情况相结合,写出了诸多相关论著,为释意学派口译理论在中国的进一步发展做出了贡献。

释意理论的创立是口译理论发展的里程碑,其独特的理论视角和切入点,促成了口译研究的转型,成为目前国际口译界最有影响的口译理论,在当代国际口译教学及研究界产生了广泛而又深刻的影响。

选 文

选文一　口译中的释意与等效

常世儒

导　言

巴黎释意学派理论综合运用语言学、逻辑学和心理学的成就阐述翻译的理解和表达过程,揭示即席翻译和同声传译的基本规律,强调翻译的三阶段:"理解—脱离原语语言外壳—再表达"。释意学派认为,翻译即释意,是译者通过语言符号和自己的认知补充对原文意思所做的一种解释。释意学派注重口译者的认知能力,认为口译者应努力摆脱口译过程中原语的束缚,把握实质信息,而不是表面形式,以达到意义对等。释意学派从认知角度描述和分析口译听辨、理解、分析和记忆的过程，并在表达阶段提出了"意义对等"原则，而这一点与奈达提出的"动态对等"理论强调"接受者和译文信息之间的关系应该与原文和原文接受者之间的关系基本上相同"（Nida，1993）的观点相契合。因此，口译实践中，"释意"与"等效"理论二者可以互为补充、有机协调，共同指导口译实践。选文对如何将二者进行合理有效地结合并在口译的认知、理解、记忆和表达等各阶段中加以实践运用进行了论证和探讨。

口译是一项极为复杂的脑力劳动。翻译理论在不同时代从不同的角度和层面对这一翻译现象进行了描述、分析和解释，努力探讨其规律。本文拟初步探讨对口译实践具有重要指导意义的释意理论和等效理论。

巴黎释意派的理论从口译者的角度出发，把口译过程分为三个阶段：（1）理解；（2）脱离原语语言外壳；（3）再表达［释意派的创始人塞莱斯科维奇和勒代雷对此有很多系统的阐述，特别是在后者所著《释意学派口笔译理论》（玛利亚娜·勒代雷，2001）中］。释意派注重口译者的认知能力，努力摆脱口译过程中原语的束缚，把握实质性信息，对于口译过程的前两个阶段有重要指导意义。

在第三阶段，即再表达阶段，除了释意派提出的意义对等的原则以外，奈达的等效论具有特殊指导意义。奈达（Nida，1993：152）运用现代语言学理论，提出了形式对等、动态对等和功能对等，对翻译实践做出解释；但与结构主义语言学不同的是，他更加注重读者与听者的反应和实际效果。

笔者通过大量的口译实践、教学实践研究，深刻意识到，尽管巴黎学派的释意和奈达的动态对等是两个不同的理论体系，但在描述、解释和分析口译现象以及总结口译方略技巧时，我们可以把这两个理论体系有机地协调起来，用以共同指导口译实践。

1. 释意

释意理论是由巴黎高等翻译学院在上世纪 60 年代创立的学说，其创始人是首任校长塞莱斯科维奇和继任校长勒代雷，二者既是出色的口译大师，又是研究口译的专家。她们在口译实践、教学和研究中发现，建立在现代语言学基础上的翻译理论对于口译以及口译教学很难做出完全令人满意的解释，其与口译实践的感知有很大差异，于是便尝试建立一种完全适用于口译的理论。

释意派理论用语言学、逻辑性、心理学的成就来阐述翻译的理解和表达过程，比较口笔译的异同，揭示即席翻译及同声传译的基本规律。释意学派"认为翻译即释意，是译者通过语言符号和自己的'认知补充对原文意思所作的一种解释'；译者应追求的不是语言单位的对等，而是原文意思或效果的等值"。（参见 Nida，1993）

如上文所说，释意理论强调翻译的三个阶段：理解—脱离原语语言外壳—再表达。

——理解，包括语言因素和非语言因素（认知、知识面、对译出语文化的了解等）。

——"脱离原语语言外壳"（desverbalización），"非语言化"或"意念抽象"，并非意味完全脱离语言载体，只是意义的升华，使用更浓缩、更抽象和跳跃性的语言来把握实质信息。

——再表达，即建立在原语基础上的重新表述。

人讲话的速度非常快，每分钟可以发布120到150字词，三四分钟之内，就会出现四五百个字词。而要把这么多的单词在短短几分钟之内统统记住是根本不可能的。而且，口语信息的发布是一次性的，转瞬即逝，所以做口译的人要会听、会记、会表达，而所使用的主要方法就是释意法。

口译的现场交际功能和时限性决定了口译人员需要在极短的时间里完成听辨—理解—记忆—再表达。听辨是信息的输入和识别；理解是一个调动知识和逻辑内存、由表及里的分析过程；记忆采用瞬间记忆、辅之以符号记录实质性信息；再表达则是一个由里及表的传达信息的能动过程，是口译过程的最终产品。

勒代雷在其介绍释意理论的著作中介绍了国际会议译员如何把自己的工作经验用于教学，她告诉学生："不要着意'翻译'，应表达你们理解了的内容。若想正确理解，必须注意讲话人的表达范式和听讲人以及讲话人的环境……"（勒代雷，2001）

根据释意理论所揭示的认知过程，我们可以总结出一条很重要的口译技巧：多听少记，注意观察。口译工作中，不要只顾拼命地记录讲话人的词句，生怕漏掉丝毫。关键是要听懂、理解，要凝神细听，努力分析其思路，预测下面所要说的话，时而观看讲话人的表情和动作。同时，用简约的字符记录主要的内容。关键是脑记，而不是笔录。

按照巴黎释意派的主张，口译员需要记忆的不是词句，而是意义；换句话说，要记忆实质内容，而不是表面形式。口译员使用一种高度抽象的大脑内部语言。这不是我们通常进行表述的线性语言，而是一种高度浓缩、呈片断状、跳跃性发展、充满意象和抽象的开放式密码语言，其他人无法介入，但译员本人解读起来却十分方便。其实这种内部密码式的语言，不仅译员拥有，原语的讲话人心里也有。我们平时在某些场合的即席发言，事先只是打一个"腹稿"，只需凝神想上片刻，就可以滔滔不绝地讲上一大段话。在这瞬间里，我们不可能把要讲的话全部准备出来，而是在脑子里罗列几个要点，构筑一个用抽象意念和意象编织起来的轮廓模糊的提纲。等我们开始讲话的时候，再用线性语言阐述，选择适当的词汇和句式展开，不断地解读自己脑子里的意象，形成语言流，从而编织一张缜密的语言信息网。

在口译过程中，译员不能事先解读原语讲话人的"内部语言密码腹稿"。只有当讲话人用线性的语言，用逻辑的思维将它一一道出之后，才有可能第一次接触到。此后，译员启动"脱离原语词语外壳"程序，把听到的话压缩成自己的"内部语言记录"。由于语言、文化和个人阅历不同，原语讲话人的"腹稿"和口译员的"内部语言记录"可能会有极大的差别。但是，通过口译员的线性语言表达，译入语的受众所得到的信息应该和原语受众的感觉十分近似。（鲍刚，1998）

现场性、即时性、不可重复性给口译增添了很多困难，要在瞬间完成听辨、理解、分析、记忆、构思和再表达多项任务确实有很高的难度。口译员要在这种高强度的作业中，运用释意理论对语言的外在形式进行感知、抽象，抛开原语的外在形式，直接触到原语话语者内心所要表达的内在意义，然后进行大脑内部的记录。这就是"脱离原语语言外壳"的过程。

释意理论阐述的第三个阶段——再表达，主张采取"意义对等"的原则，"释意翻译是意义对等翻译，语言翻译是字词对应翻译"（勒代雷，2001）。释意理论虽然把意义对等作为表达的主要策略，并且进一步阐述其包括认知对等和情感对等两个方面；但遗憾的是，在这方面的叙述似乎不够详尽，给人意犹未尽的感觉。可我们发现，释意理论的对等原则与奈达的等效论堪称异曲同工。而且,等效理论方面的权威恐怕非奈达莫属。于是,在这个层面,我们完全可以尝试在奈达的动态对等理论与巴黎释意派的意义对等理论之间找到一个结合点,由此引入奈达的等效理论,以此对口译实践进行指导,这项研究颇有意义。

2. 等效

奈达(1993)提出的"动态对等"("功能对等"),简单说来,就是要使译语听众得到与原语听众相同的效果。"接受者和译文信息之间的关系,应该与原文和原文接受者之间的关系基本上相同"(Nida,1993)。"所谓翻译,是在译语中用最切近而又最自然的对等语再现原语的信息,首先是意义,其次是文体"(Nida,1993)。要达到这种"相同的效果",就要跨越语言和文化的重重障碍,根据译入语的表达特点和文化差异,使用自然流畅和接受性强的语言,让人听得懂,听得舒服。

汉语与西班牙语在表达方面存在着许多共同之处,因此,在许多情况下,可以原汁原味地再现讲话人的话语,不改变原语的句式、用词,保留原语的语言形象。这种方法在口译中广泛地运用于重大外交发言、领导人的讲话、答记者问、声明、政治交涉等。这些场合的翻译要字斟句酌、准确无误,不能随便增删、颠倒顺序、更换概念、改变语言形象,要尽量采用直译的方法。而且,不仅句式和词义,就连讲话方式也尽量不作任何变通,直接使用第一人称来翻译。这样可以让听众直接领略讲话人的口吻、用词和表达方式,翻译起来也相对容易,无需将直接引用变为间接引用。例如:

> 我们高兴地看到,自从阁下就任总统以来,贵国在维护和振兴国民经济等方面取得了显著成绩,在国际和地区事务中发挥着更加重要的作用。我们对此表示赞赏。(吴邦国在中阿企业家午餐会上的致词,2004年9月14日,北京长城饭店)
> **译文**:Hemos constatado con satisfacción que,desde que Su Excelencia llegó a la presidencia,su país ha obtenido ostensibles logros en salvaguardar y dinamizar la economía nacional,así como en otros aspectos,y desempe? a ahora un papel más importante en los asuntos internacionales y regionales,de lo que queremos manifestar nuestro aprecio.(笔者译)

各种语言都有一些非常形象的表达方式,直接克隆甚至可以"异化"出崭新的语言形象,比如汉语中的"涸泽而渔"(Agotar el estan que para pescar),"身经百战"(Ha pasado por cien batallas)、"路遥知马力,日久见人心"(Si el camino es largo se conoce la fuerza del caballo,si el tiempo es largo se conoce el corazón de la gente)等都可以原汁原味地译成西班牙语。

当然,在口译中,可以照样克隆的情形并不多见,更多的是需要作动态的调整。这是由于不同语言相去甚远,特别是不同文化之间存在着巨大的差异。口译最突出的一个特点就是跨文化交际性。由于文化的不同,会造成很大理解上的误区。语言是交流的载体,但人们沟通的是信息,因此,译员要透过语言的架构、表达方式和词汇,理解讲话人的意思。必须脱离原语表层结构,深入再现讲话人的意思。其次,译员要尽量使用译入语的表达方式,增加其可接受性。否则,译语可能只是一堆没有内在联系、结构松散的辞藻,令人不知所云。有些译文充满"翻译腔"和"欧式句",说明译者没有任何动态的转换,存在认知补充和意义对等不足的问题。在跨文化环境内,口译的对等原则离不开文化因素的解析和变通。

奈达在《翻译问题中的语言学和人类文化学》中阐述了跨文化因素是翻译的关键问题之一。他将文化分为五类:生态文化、物质文化、社会文化、宗教文化和语言文化(Nida,1945:194-208)。本文拟在这个范围内,举几例来分析口译如何跨越文化障碍,求得动态对等。先看一个笔者亲身经历的缩小社会文化差异实现对等的例子。

西班牙的一位律师,对一位前来公证的华侨问道:¿Cuál es la profesión de su cóyunge?笔者对她说:"您的配偶的职业是什么?"这位华侨妇女文化水平不高,也没有见过什么世面,不知道"配偶"是什么意思,脸上一片茫然。笔者换了一种说法:"他问你家先生是做什么工作的?""啊!明白了!他是在餐馆厨房里做二厨的,给人家打工的。"笔者翻译成:"Su marido es cocinero, de cuentas ajenas"(她的丈夫是厨师,受雇于人)。

在这里,"您的配偶的职业是什么?"和"他问你家先生是做什么工作的?"都是¿Cuál es la profesión de su cóyunge?的译文,严格说来,第一句话更加准确,与原文是完全对等的,但对方没有听懂。所以笔者作了现场调整,使用了更有针对性的语言。从字面上来说,与原文有较大的差别,但是华侨妇女却明白了,并且作了恰当的答复。这就是动态对等的一个很好的例子。而且,笔者在回答律师的时候,也没有直译(¡Ah, ya entiendo! Mi marido es segundo cocinero en un restauante. Trabaja para el jefe. 啊!明白了!他是在餐馆厨房里做二厨的,给人家打工的。)

看来,字面上有不小的差别,但是信息交流却很畅通,这就是"动态对等"的效果。雅各布森(R. Jakobson, 1967)论翻译时有一句名言:"差异之中的对等,这是语言的根本问题,也是语言学的关键课题。"林语堂(1937:78)也说过:"译者对于原文有字字了解而无字字译出之责任。"所以,"动态对等"旨在建立交际双方之间的沟通之桥。要根据交际双方的社会文化背景选择适宜的表达方式,遇到沟通的障碍,要加以变通,找出其本质的信息,用适合对方接受的语言表达出来,以便让人能够听懂,做出适宜的反应。

我们可以举另一个口译中实现动态对等的例子:

中国人宴请西班牙客人,出于礼貌和谦虚,会说:"今天的菜不太好,不知您是否喜欢?如果有招待不周的地方,请多包涵!"如果不加任何变通地翻译过去,恐怕不但达不到应有的效果,还会引起误会:(Los platos de hoy no son suficientemente buenos, no sé si le han gustado. Si no le hemos atendido bien, le pedimos muchas disculpas)。这样翻译显得很生硬,似乎没有一点殷勤备至的热情,很容易引起别人的误解,甚至国际友人会认为是对其不尊重。

贬己尊人、自谦是中国人的礼貌观之一,外国人一般没有这种客套,他们也许会说:"我拿出了最好的东西来款待您"(Le he servido lo mejor para agasajarle)。翻译如何处理这种文化碰撞?如何真实地表达主人的委婉,恐怕要在深层作一些动态的调整,向国外的表达习惯靠拢,这样才能使得外国人领略主人的本意,达到原语与译语听众同样的效果。后者进行直译,但是加上文化注解,即要解释这是我们中国的文化,贬己尊人实际上是出于对您的尊重。动态调整后的译文可以是这样的"Siento no haberle podido ofrecido algo mejor. Espero que lo hayan disfrutado y hayan pasado bien con nosotros。"(很抱歉我不能拿出更好的东西来款待您,我希望您喜欢今天的饭菜,并且与我们共同度过了美好的时光。)调整之后,达到了动态对等,可以达到预期的效果。

与国人的自谦相比,西方人不过于自谦,但对他人尊重,尊人但不贬己,很重视给对方以恰当的敬称,这一点被很多翻译忽视了。很多人遇到"尊敬的阁下,先生"一律译成 Estimado se?或者,上至总统,下至平民百姓,不加任何区分,这不符合国外的礼宾习惯。西语国家对于敬称有严格的"等级制度",对于"总统阁下"要称为 Excelentísimo Presidente,"国王陛下"称 Su Majestad,"王储殿下"称 Su Alteza,对"罗马教皇"要称 Su Santidad(教皇陛下)。如果来宾的最高级别为部长、市长或大使,要称其为 su excelencia 或 excelentísimo,其他次要级别的人称 ilustrísimo,再往下则称 ilustre、distinguido、estimado,依次递减。虽然汉语可能都是"尊敬的",但不能统统译为 estimado,因为这是对级别很低的人的敬称。

限于篇幅,我们不能一一列举,但通过以上几例,我们可以管窥动态对等在口译表达中的重要作用。通过"动态对等",译员可以在交流各方之间建立一种顺畅的沟通。译员可跨越地理和历史的空间,把两种不同文化、不同传统、不同语言、不同理念和价值观的人连接起来,使之对话、沟通和往来。口译员把本来无法表达或者十分拗口的言词,用比较通顺的语言表达出来;让本来深藏在内的含义浮出水面,摒弃无法在译入语中保留的语言形式和语言形象,使用人们熟悉的语言形式和语言形象,从而在译入语中实现原文的语用目的。这种调整后所达到的效果就是"动态对等"和"功能对等",奈达理论对于口译的理论和实践的指导意义可见一斑。

3. 结论

释意理论和等效论是指导口译的两个理论,二者相辅相成,相得益彰。许多口译的基本技巧和方法,实际上都与这两种理论相通。释意理论从认知角度描述和分析了口译听辨、理解、分析和记忆的过程,并且在表达阶段提出了意义对等的原则,与奈达的"动态对等"的理论建立了切合点,在这个层面上如出一辙。因此,奈达的等效论对口译也无疑具有权威性。释意理论和等效论珠联璧合,可以对口译的各个阶段做出全面描述、解释、分析,并提出克服认知、理解、记忆和表达等阶段的口译技巧,对指导口译实践具有重大现实意义。

选文二　巴黎释意学派口译理论成就谈

张吉良

导　言

　　作为世界范围内诞生的第一种、也是目前唯一一种系统的口译理论,释意学派理论在当代国际口译教学及研究界产生了广泛而又深刻的影响。释意学派理论可以说是理论与实践相结合的典范,它克服了同期翻译研究重"客体"轻"主体"的不足,把口译研究从语言结构的静态分析转为对意义传递过程的动态考查,开启了跨学科口译过程心理研究的先河。释意学派的研究范式和当代多种口译研究范式之间也存在着继承关系。释意学派口译理论自上世纪 70 年代末传入我国,90 年代开始在国内迅速传播,目前已成为我国口译界最为熟悉的西方口译理论。因此,系统回顾和总结释意学派理论的理论成就与历史功绩,有助于我们正确认识和理解国际口译研究的历史与现状,同时释意学派口译理论也是口译实践和教学的理论基石,为机器翻译研究也带来诸多启示。选文侧重从积极肯定的一面审视释意学派的理论成就,但不可否认的是,国际口译界对巴黎释意学派口译理论也存在着诸多质疑。比如,自上世纪 80 年代开始,有部分学者认为,如果把释意理论作为一种规定性理论,它对口译教学确实有用,但若将其视为一种解释性理论,由于其讨论的许多问题都涉及口译的认知心理过程,而这一过程又同人脑的思维活动有关,因此其研究成果中依然存在很多问题,难以获得广泛认同(参见引申阅读篇目中提供的本选文作者张吉良所著另一篇论文《国际口译界有关巴黎释意学派口译理论的争议及其意义》)。因此,对于巴黎释意学派口译理论,我们宜在充分肯定其历史地位的同时,采用更为精确的实验法对其进行进一步验证。

1. 引言

巴黎释意学派诞生于 20 世纪 60 年代末的法国,其核心人物是巴黎高等翻译学校的 Seleskovitch 和 Lederer 两位教授。在她俩的带领下,巴黎高翻院一批教师在从事口译教学与实践的同时,以认知科学理论为指导,围绕着口译过程中意义的感知、理解、记忆、提取与表达进行了坚持不懈的探索,创立了国际口译界第一套系统的、用于解释口译心理过程、指导会议口译教学与实践的理论——释意理论。巴黎释意学派便因此而得名。

释意理论诞生之后,其影响力在 20 世纪 70 年代末、80 年代初达到鼎盛。作为一个拥有共同研究路径(认知心理学)和研究范式(释意范式)的学术团体,释意学派的崛起与释意理论的诞生具有里程碑式的意义,对国际口译研究宏观格局的形成起着重要作用。但到目前为止,国内外口译界对释意理论所取得的成就还缺乏系统的分析与总结。为此,本文结合国际口译研究的历史,对释意理论的成就作一简要评述。

2. 释意学派口译理论的成就

2.1　释意理论开启了口译动态心理研究之先河

Seleskovitch 从 20 世纪 60 年代开始从事口译研究,当时结构主义语言学范式的翻译研究刚刚兴起,人们认为翻译就是一种语言符号的转换活动,翻译研究只需要进行词汇和语法结构的双语对比。但长期的口译实践却使得 Seleskovitch 相信:口译不是一个语言符号的转换过程,而是一种交际活动,一个以意义的理解与表达为核心的动态心理过程,这个过程和口译活动的主体译员有关。为此,Seleskovitch 始终把译员和译员心理置于观察研究的中心位置,并通过对口译过程各个阶段程序的分析,把口译研究从语言结构的静态分析转为对意义传递过程的动态考查。Seleskovitch 的这一大胆举措使得口译研究摆脱了笔译研究重客体轻主体的传统,走上了以译员为核心的研究道路,开启了口译动态心理研究之先河,对当代国际口译研究产生了深远影响。

2.2 释意理论对当代国际口译研究产生了深远影响

在释意学派诞生之初,口译研究主要由少数不从事口译工作的心理(语言)学家承担,他们希望通过口译研究能够对有关信息加工和语言产出的心理学认知假说进行验证,从而满足本学科发展的需要。但由于他们并不从事口译实践,再加上研究项目不多、实验次数又少、受试者还多为非职业译员,所以其研究成果并没有得到职业译员的认可,也没在口译界产生什么影响,后者对他们的研究成果也不愿提及。这一点在同期出版的几本重要口译著作中反映得很清楚(Lederer,1981)。但是,以释意学派为代表的职业译员群体性参与口译研究改变了这种局面,并使得口译研究在国际口译界开始产生广泛影响。

总体来说,20 世纪六七十年代的心理(语言)学家和释意学派一样,都十分关注口译的信息处理问题,属于认知心理学路径的口译研究。而在释意学派之后出现的各种口译研究范式也都和释意学派研究范式(IT 范式)有着许多相似之处,打下了释意学派的深刻烙印。

例如,20 世纪七八十年代之后国际口译界出现的神经语言学/神经心理学研究范式(NL/neurolinguistic paradigm)和认知处理范式(CP/cognitive processing paradigm)的口译研究也和 IT 范式一样,关注着口译过程中的信息处理问题。它们和 IT 范式的不同则主要表现在各自的研究方法和对象上。在研究方法上,NL 范式和 CP 范式的研究人员受科学主义哲学思潮的影响,倾向于采用自然科学的数学统计法,对口译过程进行量化分析;而 IT 范式则多采用人文科学的研究方法,根据个人的直觉感受对口译过程进行思辨研究(intuitive speculation),并提出假说、建立解释模型。至于研究对象,NL 范式瞄准口译员大脑不同分区的功能和作用(如人脑的偏侧性/lateralization);CP 范式关注口译过程中复杂的多任务信息处理活动,以及这些活动对人脑有限注意力资源的争夺;IT 范式则聚焦口译过程中意义的理解与表达,试图解释意义产生的前提(认知补充)与方式(同语言外壳分离)。

20 世纪 90 年代,以 Franz Pöchhacker 为代表的新一代研究人员开始登上口译研究的中心舞台。他们积极向翻译研究学习,大胆借鉴目的论(Skopos Theory)和翻译准则(Translation norms)理论,创立了口译研究的目标文本产出范式(TT/target-oriented text production paradigm,也称做通用口译学范式),重点讨论口译质量标准和译语语篇功能问题。由于 TT 范式也以意义的研究为己任,同时还关注口译员的中介作用,所以在这一点上它和 IT 范式也十分相似。因为释意学派认为:意义的理解和产生不是由语言词汇和句子结构单独决定的,而是口译员在其语言知识的基础上,借助各种非语言知识对原语讲话的语意(semantic meaning)进行认知补充的结果。这样,口译员在意义的理解与表达过程中,实际上也起着一种中介作用。

随着公共服务类口译(community interpreting)的兴起,一些研究人员把注意力投向了口译产品、口译员工作表现、口译与社会等领域,创立了口译研究的对话语篇互动范式(DI/dialogic discourse-based interaction paradigm)。互动(DI)范式视对话口译为一种交际活动,认为该活动深受译员的影响,译员的中介参与对译语的生成和交际成效有着极其重要的作用。而这也正是它与 IT 范式的共同之处。

所以说,继 IT 范式之后出现的各种当代口译研究范式与 IT 范式之间都存在着一定的继承关系。今天,释意学派及其理论虽然已经走过了它们的鼎盛时期,但其影响并没有消失,仍在以不同方式影响着当代国际口译研究。

2.3　释意理论是理论与实践相结合的典范

翻译研究可分为基础理论研究和实用理论研究两种类型,"前者主要研究翻译的一些根本问题,属纯理论探讨的范围;后者则针对翻译实践,运用理论研究的成果,解决翻译的实践问题"。口译研究也大体如此。由于口译基础理论研究的目的是要解释口译现象,为人们提供认识论指导,所以它与口译实践的距离较远,也不能直接指导它。而释意学派的研究工作既包括基础理论研究也包括应用研究,它提出的意义、意义单位、释意和认知补充等概念,以及"脱离原语语言外壳"假说和口译过程三角模型等,就是针对口译认知心理过程所作的高度抽象的纯理论性探索。而释意学派针对会议口译教学提出的职业化口译办学模式,则是把基础理论研究的成果用于指导口译教学实践的典范之作。释意学派口译办学模式今天被视为会议口译办学的标准模式,已经为世界各国所采纳。释意学派将释意理论用于指导口译教学,很好地解决了理论与实践相脱节的问题,为我们树立了光辉榜样。

2.4　释意理论是会议口译办学的理论基石

释意理论的一个突出特点是视口译为一种交际行为(过程)而非交际结果(译员表现、译语质量),为此它反复强调:口译的目的在于传递信息,其对象是意义而非语言,意义是语言知识、主题知识、百科知识和交际语境相结合的产物。这种认识为会议口译专业的招生选拔、课程设置、交同传训练与实践带来了深刻启示,构成了会议口译办学的理论基石。

2.4.1　会议口译专业的招生选拔

为了理解和传达原语讲话的意义,释意理论要求会议口译专业学生的语言能力和知识储备必须达到相当高的水准,因为只有当译员(学生)完全掌握了工作语言,并拥有较强的认知分析能力之后,跨语言的理解与表达才会变成一个内化了(internalized)的、相对轻松的职业行为,口译质量才有保障。为此,国际上知名的会议口译院系都要求考生必须拥有大学本科学历,并且在入学之前或之后在外语国学习和(或)生活 3 到 12 个月的时间。只有那些双语技能熟练、表达能力强、百科知识丰富、有培养前途的考生才被允许入学。

2.4.2　会议口译专业的课程设置

释意理论认为:口译过程中意义的理解与表达是语言知识和语言外知识共同参与的结果。这一论述对口译课程设置具有重要指导意义。在高水平的会议口译院系,由于学生入学前经过了严格的语言水平和知识能力测试,所以他们入学后不必再花费过多的时间来学习语言技能,而是一开始就接受口译技能训练。但是,对于为数众多的普通高校口译专业,其口译训练的职业化程度不如前者。对于这类训练项目,适当开设语言课程则有利于提高学生的语言水平和训练成效。同时,由于百科知识和专业知识对口译的成功起着重要作用,所以一些口译院系不仅开设了"积极阅读"课程,帮助学生掌握获取知识的方法,而且要求学生选修一两门其他专业的课程,以便毕业后成为既熟练掌握口译技能又拥有一定专业知识的人才。

2.4.3　交、同传训练与实践

释意理论认为:口译的对象是意义而非语言。这就提醒口译员和口译师生,必须专注于意义的理解与表达,而不是寻求语言形式的对等。从事交替传译时,口译员由于短时记忆力不足,需要借助笔记来暂存信息。译员不能记录讲话人的全部语词,而要调动自己的语言外知识并结合交际语境边听边分析,以便把原语讲话的关键信息与话语逻辑用简洁的字词符号记录下来。之后,口译员还要对笔记内容进行解读,忠实传达出原语讲话的意义和情感,而不是进行语言符号的代码转换。和交传相比,同声传译由于受听说时差(ear voice span/EVS)的影响,译员的理解与表达更容易受原语字词结构的干扰。为了完整、准确、迅速地传达原语讲话的意义,同传译员必须把 EVS 保持在合理的限度内,同时努力摆脱原语语言形式的干扰,迅速确定讲话人的欲说之言(vouloir dire),然后用简洁、明了的方式传达出来。

2.5　释意理论对机器翻译研究的启示

机器翻译研究源于第二次世界大战时期的情报战,当时交战双方多次成功地破译了对方的通讯密码,这使得人们相信语言也是一种编码,可以用破译电报密码的方式进行双语翻译,翻译语言就可翻译文献。起初,研究人员以为只要给电脑输入足够多的词汇和句法规则,并用目的语对应词替换原语字词,然后再按照目的语句法规则重新组句表达,就能够把文本从一种语言翻译成另一种语言。

机器翻译遵循的是形式推导的数学逻辑。数学逻辑要求符号组合严密,含义单一,但人类的语言表达和翻译活动遵循的并不是数学逻辑。机器翻译研究者主要对文本进行语义句法分析,"以为只要解决词的多义性和句子的含混不清问题,机器翻译的困难就能够消除;将语言压缩成最简单的、最接近于结构代码、最便于转换的语言结构是可能的"。可释意理论却告诉我们:翻译的对象是意义,而不是语言符号;意义的理解与表达需要译员从字、词、句多种可能的意义项中选取唯一正确的一项,而这一意义项的确定需要得到译员语言外知识的补充。此外,机器是按照句子出现的先后顺序来翻译的,而译员对文本的处理却不是线性的。译员在倾听原语讲话或阅读原语文本的过程中会思前想后,不断积累起语境知识,并试图利用刚刚获得的语境知识更好地理解新的原语信息,并增加主题与百科知识储备;同时,新的语言符号还会激活储存在译员长期记忆中的相关知识,对意义的理解进行有效的认知补充,帮助译员迅速排除原语词句与交际语境不符的含义,以确定唯一符合交际语境的意义。而翻译机器却无法通过认知补充来消除句子结构的歧义和一词多义现象,于是机器在处理复杂的句子结构时就会遇到困难。为此,Hutchins & Somers 曾经举过一个歧义句的例子:

The man saw the girl with the telescope.

孤立地看,这个句子有两种可能的含义,但在特定的语境中它只有一个意思。问题是机器无法根据语境来排除歧义,它感知到的依然是两种意思:(1)男人看见女孩带着一副望远镜;(2)男人透过望远镜看见了女孩。其原因在于:(1)机器难以像人类译员那样借助自己的认知知识来消除句子的歧义性;(2)译员用于认知补充的知识是以"脱离原语语言外壳"的意识状态储存在大脑之中的,由于这种意识是非语言的,即非形式化(formalized)和非符号化的,所以我们也不能把它输入到以形式运算方式处理信息的翻译机器,机器也就无法以"联结主义"(connectionism)神经网络模型所示的并行分布方式(parallel distributed processing)对信息进行加工处理。这就是机器翻译质量无法同人工翻译相比的一个重要原因。要提高机器翻译质量,就要把机器迅速建立起语言结构对应的能力同译员有效的认知补充能力结合起来,使译员和翻译机器在译前、译中和译后相互合作,共同完成翻译工作。

3. 结语

　　释意学派及其口译理论的诞生是 20 世纪国际口译研究史上的重大事件,作为国际口译界诞生的第一种系统的口译理论,释意理论对国际口译研究格局的形成和发展产生了深刻影响。今天,系统回顾和总结释意理论的理论成就与历史功绩,有助于我们正确认识和理解国际口译研究的历史与现状,并将激励我们在未来的口译研究工作中锐意创新,注重理论与实践的结合,为口译研究和训练事业的发展做出新的贡献。

【延伸阅读】

　　1. Lederer, Marianne(玛丽亚娜·勒代雷著). *La traduction aujourd'hui, le modèle Interprétatif*. Paris: Hachette, 1994. 刘和平译. 释意学派口笔译理论. 北京:中国对外翻译出版公司,2001.

　　2. Pöchhacker, F. *Introducing interpreting studies*. London: Routledge, 2004.

　　3. 鲍刚. 口译程序中的"思维理解". 北京第二外国语学院学报. 2009,87(1):1-12.

　　4. 黄蓓. 从释意派的视角论口译质量评估模式在会议口译中的应用——以政府领导人答中外记者问之现场口译为例. 读与写. 2009(2):21-24.

　　5. 龚龙生. 从释意理论看我国口译研究的发展. 西安外事学院学报. 2006(12):34-36.

　　6. 郭怡军. 口译释意学派在中国的译介与进展. 昆明理工大学学报. 2008,8(2):100-102.

　　7. 刘影. 释意理论与口译策略研究. 边疆经济与文化. 2008,54(6):62-63.

　　8. 许明. 口译认知过程中"deverbalization"的认知诠释. 中国翻译. 2010(3):5-11.

　　9. 杨峰. 释意理论对口译与口译教学的启示. 江西广播电视大学学报. 2008(4):99-101.

　　10. 张吉良. 国际口译界有关巴黎释意学派口译理论的争议及其意义. 外语研究. 2010,119(1):72-79.

【问题与思考】

　　1. 巴黎释意学派将释意理论引入口译研究的意义是什么?

　　2. 根据释意学派的观点,口译过程分为哪几个阶段? 分述各阶段的特点。

　　3. 释意理论与奈达的"动态对等"理论有什么共通之处? 如何将二者合理结合以更好地指导口译实践?

　　4. 释意理论从认知角度对翻译过程的描述和分析对于我国的口译研究有何指导意义?

　　5. 口译的"基本单位"在释意理论中指的是什么? 如何理解?

第七章　心理学派口译理论研究

导　论

　　当前,突破传统语言学的研究理论,超越纯经验式的研究方法,加强跨学科研究意识,积极地借鉴其他学科的研究成果,拓展口译研究范围,深化口译研究层次,已经成为中外口译研究界的共识(刘和平,2005;蔡小红,2001;Gile,1994;Pöchhacker,2004),同时也成为口译理论研究取得突破的一个新方向和新趋势。心理学派口译理论研究正是在这样一个大背景下应运而生的。心理学派口译理论研究借助于成熟的心理学研究领域的诸多研究成果,特别是心理学中的认知心理学(Cognitive Psychology)理论来系统地研究口译现象。由于口译是一种实践性很强的语言信息交际活动,更是一种心智程序非常复杂的认知加工过程,认知心理学和心理语言学(Psycholinguistics, or Psychology of Language)的引入对于深化口译研究,特别是口译深层认知加工机制,包括记忆因素在口译操作过程中的作用等,提供了科学的理论参照和论证手段。

　　认知心理学和心理语言学都是围绕"信息处理"和"认知能力"展开研究的。认知心理学的两个重要的研究对象就是"信息处理"和"认知能力",其核心是揭示认知过程的内部心理机制,即信息是如何获得、贮存、加工和使用的,其研究范围主要包括感知觉、注意、表象、学习记忆、思维和言语等心理过程或认知过程。心理语言学则正是从"信息处理"和"认知能力"的角度来考查和分析语言学习和使用的过程,并应用信息加工的观点将语言处理过程视为一个语言信息的编码、存储、解码的过程。诸多研究口译认知加工过程的相关理论正是在借鉴认知心理学和心理语言学研究成果的基础上形成的,比如口译信息加工理论(Moser-Mercer,1997,1994/2002)、口译认知资源分配理论(Gile,1995,1997)、口译认知与语用理论(Setton,1999)等,这些也构成了心理学派口译理论研究的三个主要方面。

　　口译信息加工理论突出了口译信息加工过程的两个特点,一是记忆结构(包括短期缓冲存储、长期缓冲存储、产出存储等)在口译中的作用;二是口译员对口译过程的各种控制性活动(如输入信息的筛选、译语输出的预测、输出的监控及再加工等)(张威,2010)。口译中信息接收、信息解码与编码、译语产出等各个阶段都有缓冲存储区(临时性存储),并且都在工作记忆中发挥作用,并不断从长时记忆中得到信息反馈。口译信息加工理论以直观而形象的方式呈现了口译加工过程中信息流动的全过程,既有利于清楚认识口译信息加工过程中各个环节的性质、特点和功能,也有利于明确把握各加工环节彼此间的影响与作用。

　　口译认知资源分配理论认为,口译活动中原语信息听辩、信息意义的表征与理解、信息暂时贮存、译语组织与计划、译语信息表达与监控各个处理环节都是控制性加工过程。因此,虽然表面上看,口译员,特别是专业口译员,能够非常流利、自如地在双语间进行转换,完成信息传递任务,但从内在认知加工机制来看,口译整体操作过程是一种明显的控制性过程,而成功的口译则是各种能力彼此协调、相互配合的结果(Gile,1995:161-169)。因此,Gile(1995)提出了口译操作过程的"认知负荷模型"(Effort Model),以说明认知资源的总体水平以及具体运用效率(即在各个加工环节上的分配与协调状况)如何制约着各个加工环节的处理过程,乃至对口译活动的最终效果产生重大的影响。

口译认知与语用理论则试图结合口译实际情景因素,分析口译活动中信息意义的产生、表征与转换等认知加工过程。通过研究,该理论认为在口译培训与实践中所观察到的口译效果的变化或改善,更多的是由于更有效地应用语用和知识资源,而不是由于能够更好地协调有限的认知加工资源。换言之,对口译实际效果而言,语用知识和交际策略可能要比工作记忆的作用更大。在此基础上,也有人提出口译潜能因素中 EQ 比重大于 IQ(杨焱,2011)。

总之,心理学派口译理论的诸多研究发现都紧密结合了心理学领域的相关研究成果,将其广泛深入地应用于口译研究中,这是口译理论上的很大突破,同时心理学派口译研究成果在口译实践和口译教学中也得到广泛应用。

选 文

选文一 Creativity in Interpreting

Ildikó Horváth

导 言

口译是一项高智能的思维科学形式和艺术再创造的活动。口译思维从主体上说属于心理活动,更注重逻辑推理和分析。如果说翻译是艺术,那口译更离不开形象思维、创造性思维,离不开心理感知。口译的特点包括时间上的封闭性与空间上的开放性、即席性强、压力大、独立性强、综合性强、涵盖的知识面广等,因此口译的过程和口译的最终结果无不突显和要求口译人员的心理认知素质。从心理学派口译理论的角度来看,口译人员应该在口译过程中充分发挥其创造性思维能力,在真实的交际环境下,应对"认知负荷",协调各种能力,以最终圆满地完成口译任务。选文运用心理学领域中关于"创造性思维"的研究成果对口译过程中译员如何在大脑思维过程和译文产出过程中对"创造性思维"加以运用展开了调查和论述,从口译项目、心理过程和口译员行为表现这三个层面对口译中的"创造性思维"进行了研究。

The objective of this paper is to examine how the findings of psychological research concerning creativity can be explored within the framework of interpreting studies. I will begin by reviewing the literature on the psychology of creativity, followed by the presentation and analysis of an empirical survey. Finally, I will suggest that creativity in interpreting can be examined on three levels, depending on the aspect we are focusing on: (1) the products; (2) mental processes; or (3) the behaviour of the interpreter. In the first case, the primary object is the product, while in the second and third, it is the process. What makes interpreting a special area of study in terms of creativity is not only the creative nature of the mental processes involved, but also, and perhaps even primarily, the creativity required of interpreters in terms of their professional behaviour in a communicational situation, where they are present but in which they are not natural participants.

Keywords: interpreting, creativity, convergent thinking, problem-solving, spontaneity, adaptation

1. Introduction

The present paper is based on my experiences as a former trainee in interpreting and translation, as a professional interpreter and as an interpreting teacher at the Interpreter and Translator Department of Eötvös Lóránd University, Budapest. My personal interest in the topic is also based on discussions with colleagues and with other interpreter trainers and interpreting trainees. It does not aim at any kind of theoretical exhaustiveness. Rather, its objective is to examine how the different issues related to creativity may be applied to interpreting in order to learn more about the psychological processes involved. In my opinion, creativity is one of the principal aspects of interpreting. By gaining a better understanding of creativity, we will gain a better understanding of interpreting. While there have been very few attempts to date to describe interpreting in terms of creativity, the number of publications on translational creativity is substantially higher, probably due to the inclination to relate creativity to translation, particularly to literary translation—an inclination which we see as overly restricted.

In what follows, I will strive to examine creativity in interpreting in a new light and explore its complex and manifold nature, in the hope of promoting multidisciplinary empirical research, using paradigms and methods from psychology and interpreting studies. I will then consider whether interpreting may in fact be considered a creative activity, and if so, in what respect(s).

2. The notion of creativity: Product, process, personality—a review of literature

Creativity is a multifaceted and complex construct, whose definitions are much debated. As the present article does not aim to review all aspects of this concept, my objective here is merely to discuss some of the creativity-related topics relevant to the context of interpreting.

2.1 The genius view of creativity

Perhaps the most common view is that creativity is somehow linked to genius and the main criterion is uniqueness. Indeed the study of creativity dates back to musings on such creative individuals and renowned scientists, musicians and artists as Einstein, Mozart or Picasso and aims at defining the notion of genius. According to Eysenck, "works of genius depend on the confluence of certain personality variables (intelligence, creativity, persistence, etc.) and certain social conditions" (Eysenck, 1995: 124).

Feldman studied child prodigies and found that they were the result of a rare and complex combination of individual, family, societal and cultural variables. He set up a three-phase model of creativity: First there is "the natural tendency of the mind to take liberties with what is real, mostly in nonconscious ways. [...]. The second aspect is the conscious desire to make a positive change in something real [...]. The third aspect [...] concerns the results of previous efforts by other individuals levelled at changing the world or their environments" (Feldman, 1988: 288).

2.2 Creativity as a universal human ability

Another way to study creativity is the psychometric approach, which focuses on individual differences in creativity and sees every individual as creative; creativity is seen as an inborn capacity or personality trait.

Here the product is seen as secondary, in the sense that individuals are considered creative even if they do not discover anything new, or if they are not the first to discover it but do so on their own without external help. Furthermore, the "products of creativity can include behaviours, performances, ideas, things, and other kinds of outputs, with any of all channels and types of expression" (Taylor, 1988:104).

Osborn (1998) mentions the role of creative imagination in personal relationships, such as marriage, or parent-child relations. He also stresses that creativity is beneficial in all walks of life, from doing household chores to professional life and leisure time activities. For Perkins a "creative person [...] more or less regularly produces outcomes [...] that appear both original and appropriate." These creative products may be, for example, "scientific theories, jokes, paintings, flower arrangements, advertising campaigns, parties, or most anything else" (Perkins, 1988: 378).

As a universal ability, creativity can be measured, and several attempts have been made to do so. "All have in common the aim of evaluating the unique or novel solutions to problems that might reveal the characteristic of creativity." (Wittig & Belkin, 1990: 264) (For examples of creativity tests and divergent thinking see also Barron, 1988; Eysenck 1995; Feldman, 1990; Szabó, 2002; Torrance, 1988.)

2.3　The creative personality

Although creativity is considered a basic human ability, "there are several characteristics that seem to differentiate creative people from noncreative people" (Wittig & Belkin, 1990: 263-264). Torrance enumerates the eighteen skills involved in creativity, among them flexibility; originality, unusualness, or rarity of the response; elaboration; emotional expressiveness; synthesis or combination; unusual visualisation; internal visualisation; humour etc. (Torrance, 1988: 66-67). Torrance also emphasises the importance of personal involvement and affect, and concludes that "the essence of the creative person is being in love with what one is doing [which] makes possible all the other personality characteristics of the creative person: courage, independence of thought and judgement, honesty, perseverance, curiosity, willingness to take risks" (Torrance, 1988: 68). Another classification of creativity is proposed by Sternberg and Tardiff, whereby "descriptions of the creative person fall into three general categories: cognitive characteristics, personality and motivational qualities, and special events or experiences during one's development" (Sternberg & Tardif, 1988: 433-437).

2.4　The cognitive approach

The cognitive approach to creativity studies its underlying mental processes and structures. As far back as 1950, J. P. Guilford, whose 1950 presidential address to the American Psychological Association is considered by many as the water shed in creativity research (Barron, 1988; Eysenck, 1995; Osborn, 1988), "made an important distinction between convergent thinking, in which an individual follows established rules to solve a problem, and divergent thinking, which involves generating novel or different approaches to solving a problem" (Wittig & Belkin, 1990: 243). Guilford "sees creative thinking as clearly involving what he categorizes as divergent production," which he defines as "the generation of information from given information, when the emphasis is on variety of output from the same source (innovation, originality, unusual synthesis or perspective). Included in the divergent thinking category are factors of fluency, flexibility, originality and elaboration." However, Guilford concludes that creative thinking cannot be equated with divergent thinking, and that sensitivity to problems and redefinition abilities are also important in creativity (Torrance, 1988: 46).

According to Feldman, an important ingredient of creativity is cognitive complexity, which implies "the use of and preference for elaborate, intricate and complex stimuli and thinking patterns" (Feldman, 1990: 243). According to Szabó, creative thinking implies connecting things and ideas that have not been linked before. Unlike analytical thinking, creative thinking requires creative imagination and results in several solutions. Creative thinking processes involve problem-solving in an original and useful way (Szabó, 2002: 101).

From a functional point of view, Osborn has enumerated four fundamental intellectual abilities: the ability to absorb, the ability to register through memory and to remember, reasoning, and the creative ability. Machines can accomplish the first three, but it is only humans that have the ability to produce ideas (Osborn, 1988: 1). Osborn also speaks of the universality of the creative potential, and posits that one's "mental energy" is a more decisive factor than one's innate talent (Osborn, 1988:14). The underlying premise is that creativity can be developed, taught and tested.

2.5　The adaptational view of creativity

Creativity is often seen as the capacity to adapt to new situations, environments and circumstances. Komlósi, for example, sees creativity as "a special adaptational process [which] may be found not only on the level of highly organized functions but also on the level of elementary perceptual processes" (Komlósi, 1987: 19). Schank shares this view and claims that "creativity is not mystical. It lies within the provinces of search and adaptation and is heavily dependent on reminding" (Schank, 1988: 238). Barron (1988) too sees creativity as "the ability to respond adaptively to the needs for new approaches and new products. [...] Novel adaptation is seen to be in the service of increased flexibility and increased power to grow and/or to survive" (Barron, 1988: 80).

2.6　The creative process

The most often cited characterisation of the creative process is the one proposed by Wallas, who identified "four steps of the creative process: (1) preparation, (2) incubation (3) illumination; (4) revision (Torrance, 1988: 44). This first attempt to conceptualise the creative process dates back to 1926. (For a detailed review of the different models of creativity, see Plsek, 1996 and Niska, 1998.)

Another way of looking at the creative process is to consider it as problem solving. As defined by Landau (1976: 76), a problem means that an individual wants to achieve a given goal, but does not know how to do so, i. e. s/he is unable to use well-known specific procedures or techniques and operations. Similarity between problem-solving and creative thinking ensues from the fact that both require the individual to form and apply new strategies. For Szabó (2002: 14), a problem is a deviation from the ideal situation. It arises when we set out objectives, then realise the difference between these objectives and the real situation.

2.7　Creativity and prior knowledge

An important issue in creativity research is the role of prior knowledge in coping with novelty. As Sternberg (1988: 137) puts it, "it is impossible to have novel ideas about something if one knows nothing about it." Along similar lines, Weisberg notes that "truly efficient problem solving comes about only when an individual has acquired a deep knowledge of the domain in question" (Weisberg, 1988: 155).

In Szabó's (2002) view, knowledge plays a fundamental role in creativity. Creative persons observe unusual relations and correlations and explore these actively. Their conscious effort and concentration also play an important role.

2.8 Creativity and perception

In her research on creativity, Komlósi concluded that "under suboptimal conditions in perceptual tasks creative persons are more open to stimuli [and] outperformed their non-creative mates: under difficult conditions they were able to recognize neutral stimuli with greater accuracy and speed" (1987: 19).

Kovács (1987) also suggests that "particular creative cognitive strategy can be recognized in perceptual stimulus selection, as well as in the features of processing and in response processes." She also claims that "it has been verified in several experimental studies that creative people have an open, flexible perceptual attitude and are always ready to change their viewpoint. There is some evidence for their faster information processing and their ability to use information in elementary processes" (1987: 49).

2.9 Creativity and the toleration of frustration

Finally, there seems to be a relationship between creativity and behaviour in frustrating situations. According to Kakas (1987: 79), "creative people possess such personality characteristics that can become manifest in their behaviour and serve to decrease the strain of frustration [...]. A task that demands creativity, that is, one that needs more than a mechanical application of the person's knowledge, is itself a source of frustration." The findings of her experimental research also indicate that "the control of impulses is affected by the level of creativity, as well as by intelligence, presumably as a function of expectations" (Kakas, 1987: 85).

3. Surveying practitioners: Do interpreters consider their job creative?

The survey reported below was designed to find out whether interpreters regard their work as creative; that is, to explore their attitudes, perceptions and ideals of interpreters. These essentially norm-based perceptions contribute to shaping their professional behaviour and interpreting strategies. I had hypothesized that most interpreters would regard their job as reproductive and as requiring very little creativity, if any. This presumption was based on anecdotal evidence gathered through discussions with colleagues.

3.1 Research methodology

The survey comprised a short questionnaire sent out by e-mail in May 2008 to 45 interpreters who had been practicing for at least five years, with Hungarian as an A language. The brevity of the questionnaire (consisting of only two questions—one closed, one open) was motivated by the assumption that shorter questionnaires yield higher response rates. The survey was preceded by a pilot study (also using e-mail) with five interpreters, whose recommendations were taken into consideration before finalising the survey instrument.

The two questions were the following:

1. Do you think interpreting is a creative activity?

Yes/No

2. What do you think creativity is?

Forty-one out of the 45 questionnaires were returned, one of which could not be analysed. This high return rate may be explained both by the brevity and by my being personally acquainted with most of the participants.

3.2 Analysis and evaluation

The results of the qualitative analysis appear in Table 1.

Table 1. Interpreting—a creative activity?

	Do you think interpreting is a creative activity?		
	Yes	No	Yes and no
Total number of responses	29	5	6

Two things are apparent from Table 1: (a) contrary to my expectations, whereby the interpreters would see their job as reproductive, the vast majority of those surveyed think of interpreting as a creative activity, and (b) six of them qualified their answers to this closed question by saying "more or less," "with some restrictions," etc. Their answers are displayed in the right-hand column ("Yes and No").

As for the second question, the analysis consisted of two steps. First I analysed the definitions given in the responses before grouping them into two general categories, depending on whether they referred to creativity primarily in terms of products or as something else. The results are shown in Table 2.

Table 2. Creativity defined by interpreters

	Creativity defined as	
	a product	something else
Total number of responses	35	5

Table 2 shows that all but five of those surveyed defined creativity as some sort of a product. Before going into detail about the kind of product they were referring to, it is worth citing one of the five other responses, as it is of special value in terms of our discussion of the psychological aspects of creativity.

In a psychological sense creativity means divergent thinking. It leads to novel and individual solutions in complex and open situations. It is characterised by the tolerance of contradictions and a high degree of openness and flexibility. Creativity is a force to create, and is accompanied, most of the time, by an ability to react quickly and an intense state of psychic preparedness.

This answer differs from the other 35 in that it does not focus on the product but rather refers to the process.

When it comes to the product-oriented responses, the product is characterised by its novelty, originality and unusual nature. It may be a new notion, an idea, an association, a solution, something that has not existed before, something new, quality, a work of art, a meal, a message, a new form, a joke, a saying, a structure, a perspective. Some of the respondents specified their definitions in terms of interpreting:

—"more sophisticated wording in the target language, creating new notions, new expressions, 'shaping' the language, condensing the message for lack of time;"

—"finding solutions to the "uninterpretable;"

—"making decisions by choosing among several possibilities (quickly);"

—"recreating every line of thought in the target language;"

—"interpreting is not applying pre-defined solutions in a mechanical, automatic way, but rather it means choosing to translate a given text based on our own decisions made under certain circumstances using all our knowledge;"

—"facilitating human communication by adding something to it, without which the message could not be transferred;"

—"expressing the same idea in a different linguistic form;"

—"finding a new linguistic form, translating a joke, a proverb etc. ;"

—"interpreters are not parrots, théorie du sens, the source language text is only raw material."

As can be seen from these examples, the most recurrent themes are the "process-oriented" ones, centering on how interpreters create solutions and make decisions based on their linguistic and background knowledge. This way they solve a problem, whether communicational, cultural or linguistic. In either case, the resulting products are solutions, decisions or new linguistic forms in the target language.

The assumption seems to be that only the speaker can be creative, and the interpreter only "copies" the source-language message into the target language. In this sense, interpreters' creativity could manifest itself only in the form of the target-language message, and more specifically in the interpreters' deviation from a formal equivalent of the source-language version of the text.

The responses indicating that interpreting was not a creative activity or that it was only partly creative include the following:

—"in interpreting I have to reformulate somebody else's creativity, for which I need a lot of things [...] except creativity;"

—"transferring the source language message, which is not creative;"

—"interpreting is a slavish work, you do not really need creativity."

In summary, two points seem to emerge from this survey. One is that most of the interpreters who participated in the survey consider their job creative and anything but reproductive. The other is that they have a rather limited view of creativity, since the vast majority defines it primarily in terms of a product, and only a few see it as a process. This implies that the respondents tended to focus on the solutions as something created ex nihilo rather than as a process of finding a solution to a problem. In the remainder of this paper I will therefore offer a broader discussion of creativity in interpreting with reference to both the psychological literature reviewed above and relevant contributions in the field of interpreting studies.

4. Discussion: Creativity in interpreting—products, processes and behaviour

Creativity in interpreting can be examined on three levels, depending on which aspect we are focusing on: (1) the products, (2) mental processes, or (3) the behaviour of the interpreter. The first of these focuses on the product view whereas the other two are concerned with the process view. In all events, the interpreter's personality plays a major role.

4.1 Creative products in interpreting

One of the most essential aspects of interpreting is that the original message is created by someone other than the interpreter. The interpreter's task is therefore a secondary form of creation, that is, re-creation. The term "re-creation" conveys well the idea that interpreting—and translation in general—is not simply the rendering of a source text into a target language in a mechanical and automated way, but rather the creation of a target text in a different language. Indeed, according to the advocates of the *théorie du sens*, or Paris School, interpreting means resisting the form of the original message. As Kussmaul (2000: 121) states, target-language texts therefore "can be regarded as creative because they are new in the sense that they differ from the source text." The degree of creativity, however, might vary according to the language pair in question.

For MacRae (1989), creating something new in interpreting is not restricted to the target language form of the original message; MacRae asserts that

the interpreter uses his own techniques which are in fact patterns created in the brain for problem-solving, or dealing with difficulties or situations. Examples in interpretation are the invention of a creative method of note-taking, using symbols of the interpreter's own devising; methods of remembering [...]; shortcuts; or treating very "lengthy" lists (1989:152).

Another example of creative products in interpreting is offered by Niska in his paper on interpreting neologisms. Niska distinguishes between two types of neologisms: "the source language terms and special phrases of the speaker and [...] the possible neologisms that the interpreter uses to translate either these "new" terms or other, "old" terms which lack a direct equivalence in the target language" (Niska, 1998:12). Neologisms in the source language "can be either 'accepted' neologies in the speaker's discourse community, [...] or spontaneous, idiosyncratic, created in the heat of the moment," in which case they are the products of the speaker's creativity. The interpreter, however, always works "in the heat of the moment," to use Niska's phrase, so that the target-language expression can be considered a product of the interpreter's creativity, particularly in the case of muddled or awkward source-language passages that seem "impossible" to render.

4.2 Creative processes in interpreting

As reviewed in Section 2.6, the creative process can be seen as a problem-solving process closely linked to decision-making. Walter (1988), speaking of language mediation, asserts that

a language mediator's competence comprises much more than his knowledge of languages and the relations between them. The demands made on a translator [...] are consequently extraordinarily high. They concern [among other things] his ability to recognize and solve problems of translation. [...] due to this the amount of creativeness [...] of a language mediator is extremely high (Walter, 1988:108).

An important concept here is the notion of selection. Walter distinguishes between controlled and uncontrolled activities of selection. While the former refer to automatic "one-to-one" equivalents, uncontrolled selection is less foreseeable and thus demands more creativity from the language mediator. She concludes that "controlled decisions occur most frequently in the translation of highly standardized texts under standardized communicative conditions" (Walter, 1988:108).

If Wallas's four-step psychological model of creative thinking (Section 2.6) is applied to interpreting, we need to distinguish between two kinds of processes: a macro-process including the phases of preparing for the assignment, actually doing it and evaluating it after it has ended, and the process of interpreting as such. In the former case, it seems possible to distinguish between different phases or steps during the process, but as far as the actual interpreting process is concerned, I would subscribe to the view of those scholars who assert that "the process of creative thinking is an integrated line of thought that does not lend itself to the segmentation implied by the steps of a model" (Plsek, 1996: 1). This is particularly pertinent to interpreting, where the process involves a great many factors, linguistic and extralinguistic, that come into play simultaneously under very stringent time constraints.

The unique constraints of the interpreting process are also emphasized by Riccardi (1998), who makes the case for interpreting as a creative process as follows:

> if the interpreting process is considered a problem-solving activity where the source text is the problem and the target text the solution, then it follows that it is the interpreting mode, the fact that interpreting is "on-line," that leads to a creative process. From a limited set of cues or elements continuously unfolding, with no interruption or thinking longer than a few seconds, the interpreter has to come to a correct conclusion or be able to anticipate the message in such a way that s/he can organise his language output correctly. In doing so, s/he is not simply repeating something said by somebody else, but also engaging in a creative or productive process (Riccardi, 1998:172).

An important concept here is anticipation, which implies the use of one's creative imagination relying on what has been said and done in the communicational situation where interpreting takes place. Anticipation is foreseeing, or predicting what is going to be said and what is going to happen next, and requires resourcefulness and ingenuity.

What Riccardi labels the "strategy of least commitment" is a good example of what divergent thinking in interpreting might involve, as it means envisioning a variety of possible linguistic solutions to resolve a problem while the source language message is still unfolding. This is in line with Torrance's definition of the creative thinking process, characterised as

> the process of sensing difficulties, problems, gaps in information, missing elements, something askew; making guesses and formulating hypotheses about these deficiencies; evaluating and testing these guesses and hypotheses; possibly revising and retesting them; and finally communicating the results (Torrance, 1988:47).

4.3 Creative behaviour in interpreting

Beyond the interpreting process as such, creativity plays a role also in the way an interpreter engages with the overall communicative situation. Even if a great number of cognitive processes may become automatic in the course of a professional interpreter's career, the situational characteristics (place, participants, subject matter, issues to be discussed, etc.) change with every assignment. The novel and unique features of each situation, including the peculiarities of the setting and the personalities and attitudes of the participants, require the interpreter's creativity, as "throughout the process, there is an element of responding constructively to existing and new situations, rather than merely adapting to them" (Torrance, 1988: 47). In this sense, creativity is closely related to flexibility and spontaneity.

5. Conclusion

On the basis of the psychological literature, creativity can be identified as an intrinsic element of interpreting on three levels: the level of the interpreting product, the level of the mental processes underlying cognitive strategies, and the level of the interpreter's professional behaviour in a given communicational situation. Beyond the creative nature of the mental processes involved, interpreters need to be creative, that is, adaptable, flexible and resourceful, in responding to novel and unique situations.

Practicing interpreters, while agreeing that theirs is a creative endeavour, seem to have a relatively limited view of the issue, often relating the creative nature of their work to their linguistic solutions in the form of target-language expressions. I have tried to show in this paper, however, the phenomenon of creativity in interpreting can and should be viewed more broadly.

Further research might investigate whether the level of creativity required of interpreters depends on the language pair involved or on the type of discourse to be interpreted. Moreover, the extent to which creativity is a predictor of aptitude and professional success in interpreting is a question that merits further study.

选文二　认知心理学与口译课

李明远

导　言

　　认知心理学汲取了人工智能等新兴学科的丰富理论知识,运用信息处理的观点来研究认知过程,这对于口译教学和口译实践来说是一个不容忽视的重要研究工具。选文运用认知心理学理论对口译过程以及口译课所涉及的记忆和背景知识等问题进行分析与探讨,并为如何改进口译课程学习和教学提出了诸多建议。在口译过程中,口译员要经历三个阶段的心理过程:理解阶段对于信息的循环感知、分析和使用;转换阶段;表达阶段。其中,转换过程在理解开始之后开始,要一直持续到表达完毕。在整个过程中,口译员的记忆能力起着十分重要的作用,是影响口译准确性的关键因素之一。因此,认识记忆特点,帮助学生提高记忆效果,对改进口译课教学有实际的意义。认知心理学在记忆过程研究中已经有了诸多重要的发现,提出了系统的理论,比如短期记忆特征和记忆与练习的关系、如何提高长期记忆中的信息提取速度等,这些对于口译课教学与实践都具有非常实际的启发作用。在口译课堂教学中,教师可以利用认知心理学在记忆过程研究中的发现,引导学生更有效地处理口译中的记忆问题,比如,运用"自顶而下"的信息处理方式弥补"自底而上"的不足。同时,认知心理学研究发现,已有知识能影响口译员对信息的注意和记忆,因此背景知识图式能影响学生对接收到的信息的推理,从而影响学生对信息的处理速度。认知心理学关于背景知识重要性的这一发现从心理学角度证实了"口译工作者应当有'百科全书式'的广博知识"这一观点的正确性。除此之外,认知心理学的这一发现对口译课使用的教材题材和口译考题或竞赛题的特点等都带来了重要的启发。因此,无论是对于口译课程的教师还是口译员本身来说,将认知心理学的相关理论和发现合理有效地应用到口译教学与实践中具有非常积极的现实意义。

认知心理学的发展,至今已有四十多年的历史了。当代认知心理学由于受到人工智能等新兴学科的影响和启示,吸取了高科技的营养,理论上更加丰富和充实。它运用信息处理的观点来研究人的认知过程,包括感知、认知的神经基础,记忆、信息在头脑中的表示法、专业经验知识的发展、语言结构及语言理解等,其主要的研究目标是揭示人如何认识世界,如何学习,人的大脑如何储存和检索知识,如何解决问题,做出决定等。这些内容无疑具有重要的实践意义。J. R. Anderson 在他的《认知心理学及其含意》第四版(1995)前言中对此作了扼要的说明。他认为,对所有学生说来,认知心理学的两个重要目标是使他们能对人的认知有正确的认识,使他能更有效地运用自己的智慧去思考诸种问题,如学习数学有何良方等。语言本身就是认知心理学研究的内容,外语学习者无疑能从其中获益良多。

本文旨在运用认知心理学理论对口译过程以及口译课所涉及的记忆和背景知识等问题进行分析与探讨,并为如何改进该课程学习和教学提出一些看法和建议。

一、口译过程

一般认为,口译分作三个阶段,即理解—转换—表达。按照认知心理学理论,这三个阶段分别经历如下的心理过程。

语言理解一般可分为三个互相联系的过程,即感知处理、分析和使用。这些过程具有循环性,也就是说,一个过程可以不间断地转入下一个过程,然后又可以回到前一过程。

在感知处理中,学生的注意力集中在接收到的信息上,其中某些部分可保留在短期记忆中。由于学生所关注的新信息不断替换短期记忆中的旧信息,并由于短期记忆容量的限制,特定的语言序列只能在其中保持几秒钟。在这几秒钟的时间内,语言代码初步分析开始,编码过程把话语某些部分转换成意义表示。这一过程中,注意力可有选择地集中到对理解有帮助的因素上,如语言因素(语境,包括停顿、重音;句内和句间的因果、条件、伴随关系等),非语言因素(文化、专业知识、背景知识、情绪等)以及介于二者之间的因素(双关、暗示等)。

在理解的第二个过程"分析"中,学生把单词或短语的听觉意象与储存在长期记忆中的该单词的表示相匹配,进行解码。解码的结果是词汇存取,或者说是短期记忆中的词汇与长期记忆中使我们能辨认该单词意义的某种"词典"的匹配。在长期记忆中的信息量,该信息的结构(即图式)以及在存取该信息的方式方面,学生之间存在着很大的差异。

理解的基本单位是命题,即原来的语音序列在长期记忆中以意义为基础的表示。尽管这种表示只是原来序列的抽象,它却可以用来重建原来的序列或至少是原序列所要表达的意义。我们按意义进行分析的能力至少有部分源于我们对语法结构或规则的理解,这种理解使我们能在头脑中建构命题。例如主动语态和被动语态之间的差别,用来表示过去和现在行为的时态、条件以及非条件短语等,使我们能分析并以命题形式表示语言输入、目标和意义之间的联系。口译学生听到信息,建立起一个短语的命题表示之后,其意义就与其他命题的意义结合起来,以达到对话语的更为全面的理解。

语言理解"分析"阶段的分段,或者说把语言输入划分为词组或短语音段,对确定口头语言的意思至关重要,是"分析"过程中的主要步骤。被处理的信息单位音段的大小取决于口译学生的语言知识,对涉及的题目的常识,以及信息的表示方式。在理解中划分音段的主要依据是意义。表示该意义的可以是信息的句法、语义的某种特征或特征的结合,以及语音的特征。尽管在听的过程中,语义信息似乎比句法信息能更快地引起反应,但在分段中仍有各种知识的相互作用。

第三个过程"使用",是指把话语的意思在头脑中的表示与长期记忆中的说明性知识联系起来,产生一个"精制"过程。说明性知识以命题或图式形式储存于长期记忆中。长期记忆中的"展开活动"激活与经过分析的新信息发生意义联系的节点,于是理解开始。"使用"是理解的关键,是促进理解的决定因素。

以上是口译语言理解阶段最基本的心理过程。此时,若输入语言(原语)是口译学生的母语,则理解自动化,这一过程一般能瞬时自动完成。但如果原语为外语,则需更多的有意识的认知处理。在实际口译练习中,因任务临场性很强,时间短促,不允许学生在以上理解过程全部完成后才开始口译,所以实际上理解过程常常一开始就包含有下一个阶段,即转换阶段的心理活动。具体说来,转换从听到第一个单词之后就可能开始。

Anderson(1995:383)等学者认为,语言理解具有"立即释义"(immediate interpretation)特征,也就是说,听话人在听到一个单词后,释义(或理解)就已开始进行,而不必等到听完整句话,甚至不必等到听完包含该单词的短语。这一特征,使转换有可能从第一个单词的理解完成之后立即开始。实际上,经验丰富的专家就是这样做的。在口译课教学过程中,不宜操之过急,一般要求学生在完成短语或命题的理解之后再开始转换比较适当。

转换是一个复杂的心理过程,学者们对此也进行了大量研究。B. Mclaughlin(1978)在谈到语言转换时说,与长期记忆中的意义相通的节点可以是非特定语言性质的,具有其内在特征,能送出此种或彼种语言信号。换言之,在语言理解或运用中使用何种语言,是母语还是外语,这种选择是在短期记忆中进行的。O'Malley等赞成Mclaughlin的观点,并进一步阐述说,外语学习者的母语—外语转移过程,可分为三步,即:

(1) 选用外语作为表达语言;

(2) 检索原来通过母语储存而现在作为非特定语言性质的说明性知识存在的信息;

(3) 将此信息与所需的外语形式联系起来。

其中,(1)和(3)是短期记忆的功能。同样的道理,外语学习者在进行外语口译时,也经过同样的三个步骤，只不过方向相反，即：（1）选用母语作为表达语言；（2）检索原来通过外语储存而现在作为非特定语言性质的说明性知识存在的信息；（3）将此信息与所需的母语形式联系起来。

在口译的最后一个过程表达中，学生把已经过语言转换的信息用表达语言（译语）所需的形式表达出来。在实际操作中，表达和转换间并不存在一条清晰的界线，表达的过程往往是对译语继续加工处理，进行最后润色，使之成为所需形式的过程。因此也可以说，不同程度的转换过程要持续到表达完毕。

综上所述，口译过程包括理解、转换和表达。其中，理解又分为感知、分析和使用几个阶段。转换过程在理解开始之后开始，要一直持续到表达完毕。

二、记忆

记忆在最常见的口译形式交传中起着十分重要的作用，是影响口译准确性的关键因素之一。现在有些学者认为，口译过程不只是理解—转换—表达，而是理解—记忆—转换—表达，这是很有道理的。

记忆在口译中受到重视，还在于它造成的难度，对初学口译的学生更是如此。做笔记有助于记忆，但笔记也不能保证避免信息遗失，因为动笔记录，即便寥寥数字，也可能导致其他信息的流失，而且笔记十分简单，没有记忆作基础，回忆原信息也会很困难。因此，认识记忆特点，帮助学生提高记忆效果，对改进口译课教学有实际的意义。

现在，认知心理学在记忆过程研究中已经有了许多重要的发现，提出了系统的理论，其中如短期记忆特征和记忆与练习的关系等，对口译课教学与实践都具有实际的启发作用。

认知心理学家们所揭示的记忆过程可以图示如下（Anderson：172）：

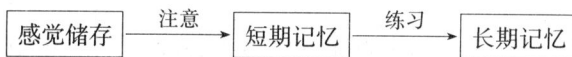

感觉储存 →注意→ 短期记忆 →练习→ 长期记忆

人的感觉器官接收到外来信息，成为"感觉储存"，这样的信息多种多样。其中，只有经过选择并加以注意的信息进入意识，即短期记忆，其余的则自行消退。进入短期记忆的信息，如果得到练习的机会，就能进入长期记忆并得到长期保留。

由上图可以看出，短期记忆在整个记忆过程中起着关键的中继站的作用。它有许多特点，其中，"容量有限"特征对口译课实践影响很大。

专家们经过大量实验后指出，短期记忆容量有限，只能储存7个左右"单位"。如果孤立地记一个个字母或数字，我们只能记7个左右字母或数字，但如果把几个数字合成一组，如1945，1998等，成为知识"块"，把字母也组成单词、短语这样的"块"，那么我们记住的就是7个左右的"块"。每块容量越大，我们记住的内容就越多。

认知心理学的语言理论为按"块"处理和记忆语言信息提供了依据。例如，前文曾提及，人们语言理解过程中的一个重要特征是"分段"（即分"块"）。如果听话人具有较丰富的语言知识和对所谈内容的知识，并又适应信息的表达方式，那么他所划分的段可以较大。Anderson在对此进行表述时所用的术语是"短语"，他认为，人们对输入信息的处理是以短语为单位的。在谈到语言理解和记忆时，他又使用了"命题"一词，即人们的语言处理是以命题为单位的。由此可见，不管表述方式有何不同，人们的语言处理不是以单词，而是以"块"进行。这样，如果学生能学会利用这一特征,他们就不但能使自己短期记忆的容量扩大若干倍,而且能有效地提高自己的口译能力。

学生要按"块"处理和记忆信息,注意力必须首先放到句子的整体结构上,抓住最主要的一"块",即主句的主、谓、宾语,然后根据句内的各种层次结构(hierarchical structure)和因果、伴随等逻辑关系再分块。如果原语是一个语段,包含若干句子,则此种处理方式更为重要。只有着眼于整体,"高屋建瓴",才能突破原语语法的黏着性,对各块作宏观的调整安排。

这样的由全体到局部的处理方式,专家们称为"自顶而下"(topdown),与注意力主要集中到单词、短语上的由局部到全体的"自底而上"(bottom up)处理方式形成对照。初学口译的学生多采用后一种形式,因此,容易对内容"记不住",也容易为局部内容所困扰,"只见树木,不见森林"。

为了改变这种状况,必须鼓励学生学习"自顶而下"的信息处理方式,如在听广播、听别人讲话时进行练习等。作为第一步,他们可以多练短语,对一些课本中提供的常用词组,要熟到能"脱口而出",达到"自动化"水平。这样,在口译时,这些已自动化的块便无需费时,而让出更多短时记忆容量给其他信息处理。

除了以上短期记忆中信息处理方式的启示之外,认知心理学还为如何提高长期记忆中的信息提取速度提供了启示。

认知心理学家对记忆中信息检索速度与练习之间的关系做过大量研究,结果显示,检索的速度和可能性取决于记忆激活程度,而激活程度又取决于记忆使用频率和使用的新近程度(recency)。换言之,练习越多,练习的时间越近,信息提取速度就越快。

Pirolli 和 Anderson 在《学习、记忆,与认知》(1985)一文中,曾记载他们在一些学生中所进行的实验的结果。这些实验显示了练习的多少与辨认练习过的句子所需要的时间之间的关系。他们用以下的幂函数来表示这种关系:

$$T = 1.4OP^{-0.24}$$

其中,T 为辨认所需时间,P 为练习的天数。由公式可以看出,练习天数 P 越大,辨认句子所需时间就越少。例如,练习 10 天,所需时间为 0.8 秒,练习 20 天,需 0.68 秒,而如果练习 50 天或 100 天,则时间分别只需 0.54 和 0.46 秒。

记忆中信息提取速度与练习新近程度的密切关系对口译课至少有两点启示作用。其一,学生应预习功课,特别是课前预习,这可以帮助他们的课堂练习取得最佳效果;其二,在进行口译练习时,可以利用讲话人词组、句子之间哪怕是极短的停顿作瞬时回忆、"复习",亦即练习一下刚听到的内容。这样,到听完后回忆原话就容易得多。

认知心理学强调练习,强调练习的"量",但更强调练习的深度,即"处理深度",也就是说,只有深入而有意义的练习才能有效地增强记忆,提高信息检索速度。"被动练习",心不在焉,无助于建立"记忆痕迹"(memory trace),口译质量也不会提高。

总的说来,记忆是口译过程中一个十分重要的环节,学生应利用记忆特征,学会"自顶而下"的信息处理方式。同时,为了提高记忆中信息检索速度,亦即提高口译速度,学生应加强练习。练习要注意深度,要当"有心人"。这样,口译课才会有所收获。

三、背景知识的作用

头脑中已有的背景知识在学习中的作用目前已得到广泛的承认。出现了不少专门术语来表达这种知识的结构，其中最有影响的是图式（schema）一词。

图式理论最早由 Bartlett 于 1932 年提出。后来，Rumelhart（1975）和 Anderson（1977）等学者进一步发展和充实了该理论。Patricia Carrell 等（1983）曾撰文讨论背景知识和图式在外语教学阅读理解中的重要作用。

根据学者们的解释，图式是"信息在长期记忆中的储存方式之一，是围绕一个共同题目或主题组织起来的大型信息结构。它的规模比命题网络大。它的典型结构是分层次的，信息子集包含于更大、更广的概念之中"（O'Malley 等，1990：232）。

背景知识和图式不仅在阅读理解，而且在外语其他技能的学习中也有重要的作用。在口译学习中，其影响主要表现在以下几个方面：

第一，已有知识能影响口译学生对信息的注意和记忆。如前文所述，感觉储存信息中只有受到注意的信息能进入记忆。具有背景知识，学生就会把听到的新信息与这些知识相联系，因而会对输入的新信息特别敏感，注意力也就能高度集中，并能从正确的角度去理解并记住信息。以文化知识为例，Carrell 等在论述背景知识在语言理解中的作用时，特别谈到文化因素。如果没有关于所学语言国家文化的背景知识，在接触到有关材料时，即使接收到的信息中全无语言障碍，学生也难以注意、理解和记忆材料中的信息。

第二，背景知识图式能影响学生对接收到的信息的推理。认知心理学家们认为，图式有助于推理。例如，如果学生听到"房子"一词，他们便会利用头脑中的图式推断，听到的房子多半用木料或砖建造，有墙壁、门、窗等。笔者曾选用 Britannica 百科全书中一段关于台湾历史的资料作为口译练习材料。其中一句，"In 1895, the island was ceded to Japan by an unequal treaty Shimonoseki."口译这段文字的学生毫不犹豫地将"Shimonoseki"正确地译成了"马关"。他说，这样做完全是根据自己的历史知识作的"猜测"。同一篇材料中的另一个字，笔者照原文拼写"Koxinga"念出，学生也能猜出是"郑成功"。

Marr 和 Gormley（1982）曾做过一个试验。他们让学生读一些熟悉或不熟悉的短文，然后要求他们复述短文，并回答问题。学生的反应如果依据短文，就被认为是"课文型"，如果包含推理，就认定为"图式型"。结果，在课文型反应方面，熟悉或不熟悉短文没有差别。但在图式型反应方面，熟悉短文就比不熟悉短文强得多。

第三，背景知识能影响学生对信息的处理速度。Anderson（p. 395）在谈到句子理解时指出，句子包含的命题数目越多，句子就越复杂，理解该句子需要的时间就越多。他举了两个长度和"其他因素"都类似的句子作例子。这里的"其他因素"无疑包括背景知识，因为他的两个例句都与古罗马历史有关。也就是说，如果"背景知识因素"不一样，对命题数多的句子的理解不一定复杂，时间也不一定多。换言之，背景知识因素可能影响句子理解的难易程度，进而影响信息处理所需的时间。

在上述关于台湾的材料中有一个描述该岛地理位置的句子：

Taiwan is an important island in the western Pacific Ocean between the southern and the eastern China seas and separated from the province of Fujian on the Chinese mainland by the

Taiwan Strait，90 miles in width at its narrowest.

此句虽包括 40 个单词，8 个命题，但信息均为学生所熟悉。结果，在笔者以中等速度念完一遍之后，一个中等学习成绩的学生就能基本上准确、通顺地将它译成汉语。另一次，学生练习中有一段关于京剧的英语介绍，包括 5 个短句，近百个单词，共有 10 个命题。笔者以中速一口气念完段落，请一位自称对京剧"很感兴趣"的女同学口译，结果该同学译得有板有眼，只遗漏了个别细节。而另一次，当笔者让学生口译一段有关美国幅员辽阔、各地风物异趣的段落时，念到这样的句子：

There are meadows with brooks and trees, and sea cliffs, and wide grassy plains, and broad spreads of grapevines, and sandy beaches.

此句二十多字，句型简单，命题数也不多。笔者特别将其中的"broad spreads of grapevines，and sandy beaches"反复念了三四遍，但学生仍反应不过来，包括几个学习成绩优秀的学生也面露犹疑之色。这显然和背景知识有关。四川学生对加利福尼亚等地的"广袤的葡萄园"和夏威夷等地的"多沙的海滩"不熟悉，难以快速地将这些信息与头脑中的已有知识相联系，进而完成语理理解和处理。

认知心理学关于背景知识重要性的理论从心理学角度证实了历来专家们的观点的正确性，即口译工作者应当有"百科全书式"的广博知识。这一点在口译课中应反复向学生宣传。背景知识的作用对口译课的另外两点启发可能是：(1) 使用的教材题材应尽量广泛，要有利于学生拓宽知识面；(2) 在准备考试题或竞赛题时，不仅应考虑各篇材料在长度、语法难度等方面的相近，而且在知识内容上也要斟酌。例如，如果有的材料是关于学生熟悉的万里长城，而有的材料是学生不熟悉的关于韩国、印尼金融危机或纽约股票交易的技术性报道，那么便难以公正地比较学生的水平和能力。

总之，背景知识在口译课中十分重要，对学生口译时的心理活动有多方面的影响。教师应鼓励学生并以选择适当的教材等形式帮助学生拓宽知识面，并在准备口译考试题、竞赛题等材料时注意背景知识因素。

【延伸阅读】

1. Bertone, Laura E. *The hidden side of Babel unveiling cognition, intelligence and sense through simultaneous interpretation*. Buenos Aires：Evolucion, 2006.

2. Cranefield, Jocelyn & Yoong, Pak . The role of the translator/interpreter in knowledge transfer environments. *Knowledge and Process Management*. 2007, 14 (2)：95-103.

3. Riccardi, A. Interpreting strategies and creativity. A. Beylard-Ozeroff, J. Kralová & B. Moser-Mercer (eds.). *Translators' strategies and creativity：Selected papers from the 9th International Conference on Translation and Interpreting, Prague, September 1995*. Amsterdam/Philadelphia：John Benjamins. 1998：171-180.

4. Timarová, Šárka & Salaets, Heidi. Learning styles, motivation and cognitive flexibility in interpreter training：Self-selection and aptitude. *Interpreting*. 2011, 13 (1)：31-52.

5. 付菁菁,付颖. 口译记忆的心理学基础及口译记忆策略. 武汉职业技术学院学报. 2009,

8(3):117-119.

6. 何瑜. 情绪因素对译员的影响. 文教资料. 2008(12):54-56.

7. 贾小妹. 口译过程中的心理负效应及其应对策略. 广东教育学院学报. 2010(4):70-74.

8. 余郑璟. 开发口译学习者的非智力因素. 成都信息工程学院学报. 2008,23(4):469-472.

9. 张蕾. 以学生为中心的口译员心理素质培养模式. 文教资料. 2006(21):20-23.

【问题与思考】

1. 简单论述心理学派口译理论研究的三个主要方面。

2. 试从口译过程和口译最终结果两个层面阐述口译人员具备良好心理素质的重要性。

3. 为什么口译人员需要具备"创造性思维"？如何理解"创造性思维"与"创造性叛逆"之间的关系？

4. 从心理学派口译理论角度出发，论述如何在口译教学中运用心理学研究成果更有效地开发口译学习者的非智力因素。

5. 认知心理学和心理语言学研究之间有何关系？它们对口译理论研究有何借鉴意义？

第八章　功能学派口译理论研究

导　论

功能学派（Functionalism）翻译理论起源于 20 世纪 70 年代的德国，其主要代表人物有凯瑟琳娜·赖斯（Katharina Reiss）、汉斯·弗米尔（Hans Vermeer）和克里斯蒂安·诺德（Christiane Nord）。

1971 年赖斯出版了《翻译批评的可能性与限制》（*Possibilities and Limitation of Translation Criticism*）一书，首次提出翻译功能论（functional approach），该书标志着翻译领域功能学派思想的诞生。作为最早提出翻译功能概念的学者，赖斯认为翻译过程中无论是分析理解原语文本（包括口译中的语言）还是构建组织译语文本都应该围绕翻译的功能来展开，这是功能学派翻译理论思想的雏形，也是"功能主义"、"功能学派"之所以得名的原因。赖斯认为，翻译应有具体的翻译要求（translation brief）和基于原语和译语功能关系的功能批评模式，有时因特殊需要，要求译文与原文具有不同的功能。理想的翻译应该是：原语文本与译语文本在内容、语言形式和交际功能等几个层面与原文建立起对等关系。值得强调的是，赖斯的这种理论观仍是建立在以原文作为中心的"等值"基础之上的，其实质指的是寻求译文与原文的功能"对等"。

另一位功能学派大师是赖斯的学生弗米尔，他的最大贡献就是打破了"等值"理论的局限，把翻译研究从原文中心论的束缚中彻底解脱开来，提出以文本目的为翻译活动的第一准则，创立了功能学派的奠基理论——"目的论"（Skopos Theory）。1978 年他在《普通翻译理论框架》一书中首次提出了翻译"目的论"的基本原则。目的论的核心概念是：翻译方法和翻译策略必须由译文预期目的或功能决定。弗米尔根据行为理论提出翻译（包括口译、笔译）是一种人类的行为活动，而任何行为都具有目的，因此翻译是一种目的性行为，具有人类行为活动的一般共性，也就是说，翻译是一种受特定背景影响的有目的的活动。因此，翻译是"在目的语情景中为某种目的及目的受众而生产的语篇"；翻译不仅仅是一种以目标文本为对象的转码过程，翻译首先是为了实现委托人与他人交流的目的，因此一切的翻译方法与手段脱离开这一目的就失去了意义。从某种程度上说，弗米尔的翻译"目的论"终结了之前学术界的很多争论，例如形式对等与动态对等、归化还是异化等等。

作为第二代"目的论"的代表人物，诺德继承和发展了第一代"目的论"者的理论。她首次用英文全面系统地整理了功能学派的各种学术思想，阐述了功能学派复杂的学术理论和术语。在 1997 年出版的《目的性行为》一书中，诺德整理归纳了功能学派的学术思想，说明了功能学派翻译理论自形成以来受到的各种批评，并对这些批评作了回答。她发现了功能学派翻译理论的两大缺陷。一是由于文化特有的翻译模式造成的。如果译文接受者所在的文化要求译文忠实再现原文而译者不能兼顾此要求时,译者应向译文接受者解释原因。另一种缺陷是由译者与原文作者之间的关系造成的。虽然翻译中有"忠实法则",但"忠实法则"要从属于"目的法则"。如果"目的法则"要求译文和原文毫无限制地背离下去的话,按照这样的关系,译者就可以无限制地脱离原文进行翻译。如果没有一个度来把握这种背离的话,翻译"目的论"也就失去了其存在的意义。针对这一不足,诺德进一步提出了"忠诚原则"作为对"目的论"的补充。"忠诚原则"要求译者在翻译行为中对翻译过程中的各方参与者负责,竭力协调好各方关系,即当发起者、目的语读者和原作者三方有利益上的冲突时,译者必须介入协调,寻求三方的共识。简言之,"忠诚原则"理论框架是为了兼顾发起人、目的语读者和原作者三方利益,避免译者随心所欲地改写。就这一点而言,诺德总结并完善了功能学派的理论思想,可称之为功能学派理论的集大成者。诺德提出,翻译要服务于目的,而翻译目的必须而且只能由委托人决定,译者对此没有任何影响的权力,只有服从的义务。诺德提出的翻译的"忠诚原则"颠覆了传统的翻译学忠诚理念,将译者的忠诚对象从文本更正为翻译的委托人或服务对象。诺德还依据布勒的研究模式将文本功能分为四种类型:指称功能、表情功能、诉求功能和寒暄功能。从诺德开始,"目的论"从译者主体这一全新视角来诠释翻译活动,为翻译理论界带来了一场新的革命。

功能学派理论是口译界乃至整个翻译学界近半个世纪以来最重要的思想流派,其思想的哲学根源可以追溯到古希腊哲学家亚里士多德的"内在目的论",其理论的核心思想主要包括了翻译的定义及实质,翻译过程参与者的角色及翻译原则。

功能学派翻译理论对翻译的定义是:"翻译是创作使其发挥某种功能的译语文本。它与其原语文本保持的联系将根据译文预期或所要求的功能得以具体化。翻译使得由于客观存在的语言文化障碍无法进行的交际行为得以顺利进行。"该定义实际强调了三层意思:一是翻译出来的译本是有一定功能的;二是译本与原文本应保持一定的联系,而保持什么样的联系则是由希望或要求译本实现的功能(即翻译的目的)所决定的;三是翻译必须化解客观存在的语言和文化障碍。这三层意思概括了功能学派对翻译实质的认识。

对于翻译过程的参与者及其角色分析,功能学派翻译理论认为,翻译不但是一种目的性的行为活动,也是一种社会性的行为。各方面的相互联系、相互影响,构成一个互动的系统。一般翻译理论认为翻译涉及三方面的参与者:原文作者、译者、译文接受者。而功能学派翻译理论将翻译过程的参与者划分为基本的五大类:翻译的发起者(initiator)和委托人(commissioner)、译者(translator)、原文生产者(source-text producer)、译文接受者(target-text receiver)、译文使用者(target-text user)。其中,译者是翻译链上最重要的一环。译者以翻译要求为指导,从特殊的翻译任务中总结出译文的交际目的(这一目的也可以是发起者直接给出的),交际目的则使译者决定如何完成翻译任务。但值得注意的是这种角色的划分并不是绝对的。一个参与者可以同时扮演几种角色。其中译文接受者是决定译文的关键因素,影响到译者的分析判断和翻译目的的最终实现,因此它也属于翻译要求的组成部分。在这一点上,诺德区分了两类不同的接受者:预设接受者(target-text addressee)和实际接受者(target-text receiver)。前者为译文所欲影响的对象,后者为译文实际影响到的对象。译文实际接受者达到译者预设范围是译文的功能得以实现的必要条件。

关于翻译原则,功能学派将其分为两类:适用于所有翻译过程的普遍原则和适用于特殊情形的特殊原则。功能学派理论认为,"目的法则"和"忠诚原则"是贯穿所有翻译过程始终的两大支柱准则，而其他法则或原则需视情况而定。根据"目的论"，所有翻译遵循的首要法则就是"目的法则"，翻译行为所要达到的目的决定整个翻译行为的过程，即结果决定方法。这个目的有三种解释：译者的目的（比如，赚钱），译文的交际目的（比如，启迪读者）和使用某种特殊翻译手段所要达到的目的（比如，为了说明某种语言中语法结构的特殊之处而采用按其结构直译的方法）。但通常"目的"是指译文的交际目的。除"目的法则"外，"目的论"还有两个法则：连贯性法则（coherence rule）和忠实性法则（fidelity rule）。前者要求译文必须符合语内连贯（intra-textual coherence）的标准，即译文必须能让接受者理解，并在目的语文化及使用译文的交际环境中有意义。而后者指原文与译文之间应该存在语际连贯一致（inter-textual coherence），即译文忠实于原文，而忠实的程度和形式则由译文目的和译者对原文的理解程度决定。其中，语际连贯次于语内连贯，这两种连贯性原则又同时从属于目的原则。由于连贯性法则和忠实性法则必须服从于"目的法则"，如果翻译的目的要求译文连贯通顺，那么译者应尽力使句子读起来顺畅、连贯，这时连贯法则是符合翻译目的的。但如果"目的法则"需要译文不必通顺，那么，连贯法则则不适用。同理，如果翻译的目的要求译文文本再现原文文本的特色与风貌，那忠实法则与"目的法则"是一致的，译者应尽最大的努力去再现原文的风格、内容及特点。但如果"目的法则"要求译文与原文的功能有某种程度的差异时，那么忠实法则就不再适用。因此，"目的法则"是普遍适用的法则，而连贯性法则和忠实性法则则是特殊法则。

功能学派翻译理论诞生之后立即获得了翻译学界的追随，也得到了学术界以外的翻译工作者和学生的追捧。如果究其原因，我们可以从时代背景中找到答案。随着不同语言人群交往的增加，翻译由少数精英的专长逐步转变为普通的工作，翻译工作的学术性渐渐被服务性所取代（这方面口译比笔译更突出）。服务的性质要求译者履行好服务的角色，以委托人的目标为自己的工作目标，这正是功能学派理论所迎合的社会和时代需求。

功能学派翻译理论与传统的翻译学理论的主要区别表现在基本理论观点和主要研究对象方面的差异。在基本理论观点方面，传统的翻译学本质上是文本翻译学，它将翻译学视为语言学的一个分支，把翻译看做是语言代码的转换。而功能学派翻译理论认为翻译学的理论基础是语用学和交际学。翻译是一种跨文化交际的特殊形式。更确切地说，翻译不是语言学意义上的代码转换，而是跨文化交际活动的语言中介和文化中介。译员应当不仅是两种语言的专家，而且是两种文化的专家。他必须乐于交际、善于交际，必须具有不断学习、理解语言和文化新领域的能力。在主要研究对象方面，传统翻译学将原语文本和目的语文本作为研究对象，试图为翻译的结果建立种种标准模式或规范，目的是获得最佳的文本结果，其理论和标准常常得不到实践中的翻译家和翻译教师的认可。而功能学派翻译理论将翻译过程作为主要研究对象，以提高这一过程的主体即翻译者本身的素质为目的。它能够帮助翻译教学从文本翻译的"死胡同"走出来，研究跨文化交际的背景要素、场合要素、语言要素以及非语言要素，研究翻译的过程，研究全过程各阶段应有的特殊能力，以及提高相关能力的方法和途径，把翻译教学变成系统提高理解能力。从这个意义上讲，功能学派翻译理论既继承了传统译论中的合理成分又突破了传统译论的束缚。它突破了结构主义"等值"翻译观，打破了传统的翻译研究视角。结构主义翻译观把翻译活动看成是静态的、简单的编码解码过程。"等值"翻译观认为，不同语言之间存在着某种程度的对等关系。而功能学派理论认为翻译不能被看做是语言间——对应的转换，开始从关注译作同原作的对等转向关注译者本身，关注译者在不同翻译策略之间进行选择的权力，认为翻译是在人为目的性参与下进行的，从而将目光转向了对翻译活动中其他相关因素的研究,拓宽了翻译研究的视野,形成了多元、多向度的翻译研究局面。

　　功能学派以"目的法则"为主导的翻译标准多元化的理论体系对中国翻译理论研究无疑具有很高的参考和借鉴价值,但该学派而引发的争议和遭受的质疑也不少。比如,纽马克(Peter Newmark)就认为功能学派理论过于简单化,强调信息而牺牲丰富的意义,损害原语文本的权威性。还有一些学者质疑其能否从根本上取代"信"、"忠实"或者"等值"作为翻译的首要标准,质疑其是否适用于文学翻译等。诸如此类的问题都有待进一步的研究和检验。但是,在口译领域,功能学派理论非常适用。虽然经典的功能学派理论没有刻意区别笔译与口译,但事实上功能学派理论对口译的指导意义比笔译大得多。相对于笔译而言,口译过程需要考虑的非语言因素更多。笔译人员不一定必须与原语文本作者交流后才能开始工作,而口译人员如果不清楚服务对象的需求和立场则肯定无法履行好自己的职责。从这个意义上说,功能学派理论对口译实践的指导意义更为突出。总的来说,功能学派理论对口译界影响至今的理念包括以下几点:

1. 口译不是对等转换的语言作业,而是一种跨文化的交际交流行为;
2. 没有绝对客观的口语翻译,所有的口译都服务于服务对象或委托人的主观愿望;
3. 口译成功与否的标准在于是否帮助委托人实现了预期的交流和交际目的。

选　文

选文一　Skopos and Beyond：A Critical Study of Functionalism

Celia Martín de León

导　言

　　德国功能学派翻译理论因其颠覆了同时期语言学派翻译理论关于"对等论"的学说而一直备受瞩目,而其引发的争议也不少。不可否认,德国功能学派理论有其自身的优势,比如,它突破了原文中心的束缚,强调译者的作用;提出了翻译发起者和委托者的概念,从而扩大了翻译过程中参与者的范围;引发了对非文学翻译的关注等。但是,因其直接理论来源是行动理论(Action Theory),因此过分强调译者的翻译行为取向也导致其存在着诸多局限性乃至自相矛盾之处。选文针对功能学派的两个著名人物汉斯·弗米尔(Hans Vermeer)和贾斯塔·赫兹·曼塔利(Justa Holz Mäntäri)分别提出的翻译目的论(Skopos Theory)和翻译行为理论(Theory of Translation Action),用一项系统性的调查对功能学派理论学说中的自相矛盾之处进行了批判和修正。

This paper deals with the main results of a systematic investigation (Martín, 2005), supported by concordance analysis, of the metaphorical expressions found in Reiß-Vermeer (1984) and Holz-Mänttäri (1984), two works that in the 1980s established the theoretical foundations of German functionalism. Based on the cognitive theory of metaphor (Lakoff & Johnson, 1980, 1999; Lakoff, 1987; Johnson, 1987; Lakoff, 1993), the analysis led to the identification of two conceptual metaphors that played a crucial role in the articulation of German functionalism: the TRANSFER metaphor and the TARGET metaphor. The paper focuses on the main implications of the use of these metaphors and on the contradictions they create. A broadening of the functionalist theoretical framework is then proposed with the goal of overcoming these contradictions.

Keywords: translation, metaphor, cognition, functionalism, theory, model

1. Introduction

The 1980s have often been described as a decade of paradigm shift in Translation Studies, e. g. Prunč (2003: 160-162). According to Prunč, the main driving forces behind this shift were German functionalism, Descriptive Translation Studies, and deconstruction. These three approaches may have contributed to the same general paradigm shift, since they share some characteristics. For example, functionalism shares a focus on culture and target-orientedness (Toury, 1995: 25) with descriptive studies, and the dethroning of the source text with post-structuralism.

One of the defining traits of functionalist translation studies is its teleological interpretation of translation. This postulate was introduced via axioms and logical deduction by Vermeer (1996a: 12-13): "Thesis 2 (Axiom 2): All acting is goaloriented ... Thesis 5: Translating is acting, i. e. a goal-oriented procedure ... ". This is one of the main theoretical foundations of German functionalism which is based on an axiomatic definition of human action. Though nowadays almost no one doubts the didactic advantage of the translation brief (which includes information about the function of a text and about the target audience), we lack empirical data about the psychological reality and the practical implications of this axiomatic principle. What does it mean to say that *translators orient themselves toward a target*? Vermeer's axiom is based on a conceptual metaphor that is part of everyday life (Johnson, 1987: 113-117), according to which actions are paths and their objectives are the physical objectives of these paths. Just as, by definition, all paths have a target (a direction and an objective), every action has a target, according to Vermeer.

Needless to say, the TARGET metaphor plays an essential role in the theoretical structure of German functionalism. It is not simply a tool for argumentation, but a fundamental concept that allows for inferences to be made about translation on the basis of physical displacement in space. The study of this metaphor may be of great help in understanding the theoretical foundations of the functionalist approach, especially of

Vermeer's Skopos Theory (Vermeer, 1978, 1989, 1996a; Reiß & Vermeer, 1984).

After briefly outlining the important role that conceptual metaphors play in scientific discourse in general (Section 2), and in Translation Studies in particular (Section 3), I will focus on the main implications of the use of two metaphors (the transfer metaphor and the target metaphor) in functionalist discourse (Sections 4 and 5), as well as the theoretical contradictions and limitations that arise. A broadening of the functionalist theoretical framework will then be proposed with the goal of overcoming these difficulties (Section 6).

2. Conceptual metaphors in scientific discourse

Today it seems generally accepted in the area of cognitive science that one of the ways in which we construct our conceptual apparatus is by metaphorically extending our basic experiences to other more complete and abstract experiences, following the patterns of the acquired language (Johnson, 1987; Lakoff, 1987). A well-known example is the metaphor that allows the understanding of time based on spatial notions. Nearly all of the languages investigated so far derive most of their vocabulary for time (including many verbal time markers) from the domain of space relations, which suggests that time is generally conceptualized in terms of space (Núñez & Sweetser, 2006).

Metaphors we use on a daily basis, usually in an unconscious manner, influence our daily reasoning. The experiments carried out by Gentner and Gentner (1983) offer a classic example of metaphors that influence how we perceive a phenomenon. The subjects of these experiments spontaneously used two different analogies to explain how an electric circuit works: one was a circuit with water running through pipes, and the second was a throng of individuals running a marathon. The experiments surprisingly showed that the subjects who applied the first analogy of water running through pipes found it easier to explain how the electric circuit works with respect to where the batteries were placed, but managed to make only a few correct inferences with respect to the resistors in the circuit. People basing their reasoning on the second model, the one of the running individuals, reached a significantly higher number of correct inferences about the resistance of the circuit, but were not as successful when it came to thinking about the batteries. The explanation offered by Gentner and Gentner (1983) is that each metaphorical model offers an adequate scheme to reach a conclusion about one of the two aspects. The water metaphor allows subjects to imagine the batteries as if they were water repositories, which leads to correct assumptions about the location of the batteries in electric circuits. However, it does not offer an adequate scheme that allows for successful reasoning about the resistors. The metaphor of the throng of runners allows subjects to see the resistors as doors or narrowings of the road, which allows them to draw correct conclusions about the effect of resistors, but does not offer an adequate model which would explain how the batteries function.

If the reasoning of our daily lives depends largely on metaphors that structure our experiences, we can assume that the same will occur with metaphors used in scientific discourse. In scientific texts, metaphors do not appear in isolation, but are pervasive elements, so we might assume that they may play an important role in scientific thinking. "It suffices to consult the most frequently used terms (electrical *current*, magnetic *field*, light *wave*, magnetic *resonance*) to be confronted with the ubiquity of metaphor and analogy [in sciences]" (Simon, 2000: 71).

Lakoff and Johnson (1980) studied the systematic character of metaphoric expressions used in daily speech in relation to different experiences, and showed how they enable subjects to construct cognitive structures based on systematic projections between two domains of experience. "Conceptual metaphors are cross-domain 'mappings' that project the inferential structure of a *source domain* onto a *target domain*" (Núñez, 2000: 135).

Conceptual metaphors occupy a central position in scientific reasoning. On the one hand, scientific discourse uses everyday language, and often also adopts conceptual metaphors that are usual in general speech. On the other hand, scientific discourse generates its own metaphors, which play an essential role in developing and articulating scientific theories [Boyd (1979) 1993: 482]. These metaphors work as scientific models [Kuhn (1979) 1993: 538], which guide the investigation and the elaboration of hypotheses, such as the analogy of the solar system used by Rutherford to explain the atom, or the magnetic iron shavings used by Faraday to explain electric force fields (Gentner & Jeziorski, 1993: 448).

The use of a metaphoric model can serve to successfully explain and predict certain aspects of a phenomenon, but it can also lead to erroneous interpretations and predictions in relation to other aspects of the same phenomenon. Each metaphor offers us one *point of view* and *shows* us one *perspective* of a realm of experience, while at the same time *hiding* other possible *perspectives*. In order to label the aspects which remain *hidden* by a metaphor, Brünner (1987) used a visual analogy and named them *blind spots* (*tote Winkel*).

One example of a scientific metaphor that has revealed its blind spots over time is the one that portrays the structure of the atom on the basis of the structure of the solar system. This analogy allows the assumption that electrons always remain in the same orbit, as planets do, but it does not lead to the prediction that they may *jump* from one orbit to another. This is an erroneous supposition, insofar as it has been deductively established that electrons *jump* between orbits (Meheus, 2000: 27).

Based on the theoretical and methodological framework offered by the cognitive metaphor approach, the study of metaphoric expressions identified in scientific discourse allows the definition of conceptual metaphors created in this discourse or imported from everyday language or other scientific disciplines, i. e. metaphors that provide scientific research with a certain perspective on its object of study (e. g. Fernández-Duque & Johnson, 2002; Johnson, 2002; Lakoff & Núñez, 2000). The description and the critical study of the conceptual metaphors reflected in scientific discourse may contribute to an increased awareness of models and paradigms used in a more or less explicit way in this discourse

(Brünner 1987: 111). This increased awareness, in addition to making the metaphorical focus obvious and, thus, showing some of its blind spots, can also increase the possibility of creatively extending and modifying the metaphorical models (Liebert, 1995).

3. Metaphors in Translation Studies

Conceptual metaphors play an essential role in structuring many approaches to translation. In Translation Studies metaphors provide a certain perspective on their object of study as well, guiding the investigation and elaboration of hypotheses, but they also leave other aspects in the dark. Pym (2004), for example, uses a cost/benefit model to elaborate his hypothesis on mediated communication. This model functions as an analogy, which projects the logical structure of the source domain (economic transactions) onto the target domain (mediated communication), which allows the elaboration of a series of interesting hypotheses in relation to the latter domain. Nevertheless, this metaphoric model also has its blind spots; namely, all those aspects of translation that cannot be accounted for in terms of economic transactions (for example, can all the translator choices during the translation process be explained as cost/benefit calculations?).

The cognitive theory of metaphor provides an adequate theoretical and methodological framework for the study of metaphors that structure translation discourse. D'hulst's project (1992) points just in this direction: it deals with the development of a meta-theoretical and historiographical analysis of Translation Studies. As an example of how he is carrying out this historiographical project, D'hulst chooses the study of translation metaphors from a cognitive perspective.

For D'hulst (1992: 37-38), metaphors play a crucial role in the development of translation theories, which, borrowing from related disciplines, have also taken from them metaphorically structured concepts. D'hulst (1992: 38) provides as examples the concepts of, among others, *equivalence*, *system*, *structure*, *function*, *communication*, and *transfer*. The existence of such concepts based on metaphorical projections seems to indicate that conceptual metaphors used in Translation Studies not only provide a heuristic orientation for the initial construction of models [Boyd 1979 (1993)], but also represent a special kind of cognitive process that cannot be replaced by literal expressions.

Hermans (1985) studied metaphors and images used in Renaissance translation discourse in France, England and the Netherlands. Though he does not explicitly adopt a cognitive perspective, Hermans considers that metaphors imply a certain way of viewing and understanding translation. His approach shows a clear cognitive point of view when he describes the basic schemes which underlie a series of metaphorical expressions:

> The underlying idea, the view of language in which form and substance, words and meaning, signifier and signified can be separated, finds expression in a series of

metaphorical oppositions revolving around the notions of 'outside' versus 'inside' or 'perceptible' versus 'imperceptible', such as body and soul, matter and spirit, garment and body, casket and jewel, husk and kernel, the vessel and the liquid contained in it, a chest and its contents. (Hermans, 1985: 120)

The implication common to all these metaphors is that, when translating, it is possible to separate form from linguistic content, which is considered to be the main element. In the terminology of cognitive theory, Hermans (1985) identified the basic scheme of the CONTAINER, defined by the inside-outside contrast (Lakoff, 1987: 272) as the structure that underlies a series of metaphorical expressions, and analyzed some of its implications for translation.

Chesterman (1997) describes some of the dominant metaphors of various translational perspectives, such as "translation is rebuilding" (p. 21), "translation is copying" (p. 23), "translation is imitating" (p. 24), "translation is sending a message to someone" (p. 33), "translation is manipulation" (p. 38), or "translating is thinking" (p. 40). Chesterman (p. 44) considers these metaphors to be translational theories to the extent that they are ways of responding to the question of what translation is, and are therefore valid conceptual tools. According to Chesterman (1997), however, these theories cannot be falsified in Popper's sense. For this reason, they cannot become the sole foundation of a modern translation theory, since this would mean accepting their blind spots without questioning them.

However, if we look through the spectacles provided by a single metaphor alone, we run the risk of missing insights that would be facilitated by some other metaphor. A modern theory of translation needs to draw on many such metaphors. (Chesterman, 1997: 20)

Like Brünner (1987), Chesterman uses a visual analogy to describe the cognitive function of the metaphors: It is not wise to limit oneself by *looking through the lenses* of a single metaphor. A first step towards looking through *different lenses* is an awareness of which lenses *are worn* (Turbayne, 1962). The more implicit the models guiding the translation, the greater our dependency on them (Risku, 1998: 141). Hence, studying the metaphors that structure Translation Studies may be an important strategy to reach this awareness, as well as an important tool for a translation historiography and meta-theory in the sense that D'hulst (1992) proposes.

4. Shifts and containers in functionalism: Remnants of earlier models?

The first conceptual metaphor found in the texts of Reiß and Vermeer [(1984) 1991] and Holz-Mänttäri (1984), the TRANSFER metaphor, is not specific to functionalism, but is found in contemporary translational discourse in general and in everyday translation language (Chesterman, 1997: 8). This metaphor permits a simplified conception of the translation process as transfer of meanings and content among texts, languages, and cultures, the latter conceived as containers (Lakoff, 1987: 272) with definite limits (see Figure 1). The main blind spots of the transfer metaphor hide the active participation of the translator in the translation process and the influence of situational factors in the construction of the meaning.

The TRANSFER metaphor may be viewed as an extension of the conduit metaphor studied by Reddy [(1979) 1993] and exemplified by more than one hundred expressions of the English language. Brunner (1987: 105) offers many examples of this metaphor in German, and Baldauf (1997: 25) identifies a total of 200 incidences of this metaphor in a corpus of German journalistic texts. According to the CONDUIT metaphor, "THE MIND IS A CONTAINER, IDEAS ARE ENTITIES, and communication involves taking ideas out of the mind, putting them into words, and sending them to other people" (Lakoff, 1987: 450).

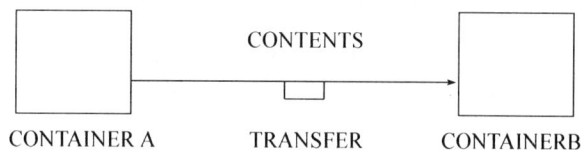

Figure 1. transfer metaphor scheme

According to the CONDUIT metaphor, we understand communication as a process in which a sender introduces his ideas in a series of signs to let them reach a receiver. By extending the analogy, we can describe translation as a special case of this process in which an intermediary, the translator, extracts the contents from a source-language text in order to introduce them into the pertinent signs of another language and, thus, transmit them to the receiver. Muñoz (1995) and Vermeer (1996b: 47-48) explicitly criticize the application of this communication model to translation.

Reiß and Vermeer [(1984) 1991: 58] and Holz-Mänttäri (1984: 11-17) criticized the approaches that define translation as a process of coding and decoding, distancing themselves from the transfer metaphorical concept. But the metaphorical instances identified in each of these works reflect the transfer metaphor, so that it can be said that it partially structures some of their key concepts, such as *Transfer* ("transfer"), *Informationsangebot* ("offer of information"), *Botschaftsträger* ("message carrier") and *Kultur* ("culture"). All of them reflect this metaphor in the logical structures of the relationships that occur in the context of the texts examined.

The concept of *message carrier* (*Botschaftsträger*), for instance, was developed by Holz-Mänttäri (1984) with the aim of broadening the traditional concept of *text* while considering as well the non verbal elements of communication, doing justice to the complexity of communicative processes. However, this concept is partially structured by the conduit metaphor: according to Holz-Mänttäri, the function of the *message carriers* consists of *transmitting* messages among interlocutors. "Der Botschaftsträger hat die Funktion, zu *einem Rezipienten eine Botschaft so zu übermitteln*, dass er sie annimmt und zu verstehen sucht" (Holz-Mänttäri, 1984: 72; italics added). "Verständigung *durch Botschaftstransfer* heisse, *Botschaften und Botschaftstrager* konzipieren, *transportieren, rezipieren*" (Holz-Mänttäri, 1984: 55; italics added). We see here a clear reproduction of the conduit metaphor's structure: the message carriers act as vehicles that allow messages to be transported and received in communication.

Nevertheless, the relation established between the *message carrier* (*Botschaftstrager*) and the *message* (*Botschaft*) is not just a relation of containment, but corresponds to a more complex process of elaboration of informative, but also appellative elements [Holz-Mänttäri, 1984: 31, 71, 122; (1996) 2001: 263]. Thus, it is an ambiguous concept that relates to the model of communication based on the conduit metaphor, and that at the same time presupposes a more complex model that would require further elaboration.

Something similar occurs with the functionalist conception of *culture*. The emphasis on the cultural aspects of translation allowed functionalist approaches to adopt a broader perspective on the translational processes than that offered by approaches focusing on linguistic aspects of translation. At the moment, there seems to be a more or less general agreement about the relevance of cultural factors in Translation Studies, but a clear consensus concerning the definition of the concept of *culture* does not exist (Koskinen, 2004).

Functionalist approaches elaborate their concept of *culture* based on the notion developed by Goodenough (1964) within the framework of first-generation cognitive anthropology, oriented towards the construction of cultural taxonomies and grammars according to the model of structural linguistics. Culture is understood as the totality of competencies needed to integrate oneself into a social group and is defined as an open structure (*Gefüge*; Holz-Mänttäri, 1984: 29) as opposed to the more rigid idea of a closed and coherent system (*System*). However, the concept of culture has to do with structures defined by an interior, an exterior and some more or less clear limits allowing for the sending and reception of discrete elements (Vermeer, 1996b: 47).

The concept of *culture* used in functionalism is partially structured by the container scheme, which is coherent with the transfer metaphor: texts, languages and cultures are understood as *individuals* [Reiß & Vermeer (1984) 1991: 104] and the process of translation takes place among them. Cultures are understood as totalities separated by *barriers* that make communication more difficult. The act of translation makes it possible to overcome these barriers (Holz-Mänttäri 1984: 82). The concept of *cultural barrier* and the division by Vermeer [1990: 229; (1989), 1992: 32; Reiß & Vermeer (1984) 1991: 97] of the concept of *culture* into the subordinate concepts of *paraculture, diaculture* and *idioculture* suggest the existence of more or less defined borders between cultures.

Nevertheless, Holz-Mänttäri (1984: 86) as well as Vermeer (1996b: 224) refer to the nature of the boundaries between cultures as blurred.

From a historical perspective, the paradoxical relationship of the TRANSFER metaphor in the structuring of concepts precisely developed to provide an alternative to the translational model of encoding and decoding can be interpreted as a gradual distancing of functionalism from previous translational approaches, when functionalism did not yet have adequate conceptual tools to develop an alternative model of communication. Most previous translational approaches (e. g. Nida, the Leipzig School, and, in general, the approaches based on the concept of *equivalence*; see Muñoz 1995: 106) were based on the mathematical model of communication [Shannon & Weaver (1949) 1963], clearly structured by the conduit metaphor [Reddy (1979) 1993]. During the 1980s, functionalist approaches developed a new model of translation as action situated among and dependent on multiple factors, which integrated the act of translation into its social context and took into account the partly unpredictable nature of the construction of meaning. These approaches denied the possibility of *transporting* meaning, i. e. of regaining it completely in the textual reception. However, to develop this new model, functionalism had to use the former conceptual schemes to a given extent, which meant that they participated in the structuring of the new concepts in a contradictory way.

5. The metaphor of functionalism: Every action is directed towards a target

The TARGET metaphor, the second conceptual metaphor identified in the texts of Reiß and Vermeer [(1984) 1991] and Holz-Mänttäri (1984), is a specific element of functionalist theory, which plays an essential role in structuring its theoretical framework. According to this metaphor (PURPOSES ARE PHYSICAL GOALS, Johnson, 1987: 114), the purposes of actions are the physical targets of a path, and actions are movements advancing toward these goals (see Figure 2). The means and the series of actions needed to achieve a goal are understood as roads or paths towards the goal (Baldauf, 1997: 140).

Lakoff and Johnson (1999: 50-54) described the structure of the target metaphor through the study of English examples. Baldauf (1997: 139-150) provides a similar study based on a corpus of German journalistic texts. In contrast to the transfer metaphor, no indications of a generalized presence of this metaphor in the translational discourse exist. As shown by Lakoff and Johnson (1999: 187-194), the TARGET metaphor allows articulation among everyday concepts such as *action*, *difficulty*, *means*, and *end* that are respectively understood as PROGRESS, OBSTACLE, PATH, and TARGET.

SUBJECT

SOURCE　　　　　　　　　　　　PATH　　　　　　　　　　　　TARGET

Figure 2. TARGET metaphor scheme

A detailed analysis of the instances of the TARGET metaphor found in Reiß and Vermeer [(1984) 1991] and Holz-Mänttäri (1984), yielded that this metaphor plays an essential role in structuring Vermeer's *Skopos Theory* and Holz-Mänttäri's *Translational Action Theory*. The application of the SOURCE-PATH-GOAL scheme to the concept of *translation* allows German functionalism to qualify the importance of the source text in the translation process and to underline the importance of the target text's function: each new action of textual production is understood as a new path directed towards a new target.

Grundsätzlich ist eine Translation eine andere Produktionshandlung als die Herstellung des Ausgangstexts. Folglich kann eine Translation anderen Zwecken dienen. Es muß ganz klar erkannt werden, das die Beibehaltung des Zwecks, wie sie Translationen oft zugeschrieben wird, eine kulturspezifische Regel, keine Grundforderung einer allgemeinen Translationstheorie ist. (Reiß & Vermeer [1984] 1991: 103)

"Translatorisches Handeln" heisst also weder Worter, noch Sätze, noch einfach Texte übersetzen, es heisst in jedem Fall: zwecks Steuerung intendierter Kooperation über Kulturbarrieren hinweg funktionsgerechte Kommunikation ermoglichen. (Holz-Mänttäri, 1984: 7-8)

This theoretical framework allowed Vermeer and Holz-Mänttäri to develop a translational approach different from the models based on comparative linguistics and on the idea of *equivalence*. It also helped them to focus on the study of the translation process in its situational and social context. Vermeer's and Holz-Mänttäri's functionalist discourse relied on the target metaphor in order to distance itself from the transfer metaphor and its implications for translation (in particular, the possibility of transferring fixed meaning or content among texts, languages and cultures). The TARGET metaphor focuses on exactly one of the blind spots of the TRANSFER metaphor, the participation of the translator in the construction of meaning. Shedding light on it underlines the intentional and subjective character of translational action.

Wir wollen hier aber herausheben, daß die Initiative zur Weiterfuhrung einer Kommunikationshandlung bei der Translation nicht aufseiten des Primarproduzenten usw. liegt, sondern daß vielmehr der Translator eine eigenstandige Position einnimmt: Er muß die Initiative sozusagen neu aufgreifen, neu in Gang setzen: Er entscheidet letzten Endes, ob, was, wie ubersetzt/gedolmetscht wird. Diese Entscheidung hängt von seiner Situationseinschatzung im Hinblick auf die Translatchancen ab. [Reiß & Vermeer (1984) 1991: 86-87]

Based on the TARGET metaphor, functionalist approaches shifted the center of attention from the *translated objects* (and, thus, from the textual comparison) to the subject that *is directed towards a goal* (and, thus, to the analysis of the factors that play a role in the process of translation as intentional action). However, the target metaphor, like any metaphorical projection, has blind spots of its own. The analysis of the metaphorical instances found in Reiß and Vermeer [(1984) 1991] and Holz-Mänttäri (1984) uncovered three aspects of the translation process that remain hidden under this metaphor:

—The greater or lesser degree of intentionality of the actions and elements of actions that play a role in the translation.

—The possibility of ascribing different purposes to a translational action. These purposes need not be subordinate to each other.

—The assessment of the aims of the translation.

5.1 Does every action have an objective?

Vermeer's action theory [Reiß and Vermeer (1984) 1991, Vermeer, 1996a] is based on a generalization that allows actions to be described as intentional. Typical human actions are intentional, but not all human actions are intended to the same degree, and it is not easy to draw a line between intentional and unintended actions, because intentions are most times declared or inferred after the action is carried out. Vermeer (1996a: 12) defines all acting as goal-oriented, and develops a homogeneous concept of *action* that does not take into account differences in terms of the degree of intentionality of those actions. He excludes from the concept of *action* any behavior that does not correspond to the scheme of a linear advancement towards a target (Vermeer, 1996a: 12). However, the examples forwarded by him in his discussion of this concept point to the vague nature of its borders.

(28) Anna betritt einen Tante-Emma-Laden und grüßt. —Es liegt Handlung vor, wenn angegeben werden kann, daß gegrüßt wurde, um keinen Unmut wegen Verstoßes "gegen die guten Sitten" zu provozieren oder um durch betonte Freundlichkeit zuvorkommend bedient zu werden. Es liegt keine Handlung in unserem Sinn vor, wenn angegeben werden kann, daß der Gruß infolge jahrelanger Gewohnheit "rein automatisch" (reflexhaft) erfolgte. (Daruber sind Anna, Ladenfraulein und anwesende Kunden u. U. unterschiedlicher Meinung.) [Vermeer (1989) 1992: 90-91]

According to Vermeer, greeting can be considered an action if we can assign it a purpose. Thus, when performed automatically, out of habit, it is a behavioral routine that does not require the subject's attention and should not be considered an action. However, routine greetings may be performed with the same purpose as when they do receive the subject's conscious attention. Hence, it does not seem very sound to ascribe intentionality exclusively in the second situation. The action of driving a car includes a series of subroutines that are more or less automatic and of which the subject is not necessarily aware, but that does not mean that a part of driving does not have a purpose and is not an action.

The intentional model of behavioral interpretation is part of the folk psychology (Suchman, 1987; Dennett, 1991; Hendriks-Jansen, 1996; Risku, 2000). Following this model, we learn to interpret our own and other people's actions as intentional, and we probably assign a high degree of prototype-likeness to those actions that most conform to this interpretation. However, Vermeer's [(1989) 1992, 1996a] contention that intentionality is a condition both necessary and sufficient in order to include a behavior within the concept of *action*, renders voluntary actions and reflex acts in a mutually exclusive opposition. This does not seem very plausible from a psychological point of view: Complex activities include minimal actions without a definite intention and automatic acts may serve the same purpose as those consciously controlled.

Honig (1995) distinguished between two *processing spaces* in translators' mental processes: a controlled workspace, and an uncontrolled workspace. The sequential (to some degree) nature of controlled processes, which require the subject's attention, allows them to be described as a series of steps, a description compatible with the metaphorical structure of advancing towards a goal. Uncontrolled processes (e. g. spontaneous associations), produced beyond the subject's control, resist verbalization and cannot be described in terms of a sequence. The metaphors used in the field of creativity studies (Kußmaul, 2000) reflect this non-linear character: the metaphors of INCUBATION and ILLUMINATION (Preiser, 1976; Ulmann, 1968) suggest a sudden and irreversible leap from one state to the other, while the metaphors of LATERAL THINKING (de Bono, 1971) and DIVERGENT THINKING (Guilford, 1975) refer to a movement towards a goal divergent from linear progress. The target metaphor does not appear adequate to describing processes such as uncontrolled spontaneous associations: In these processes, thought does not advance progressively towards a goal, but *explores the mental space* searching for new connections and associations, and conscious control can even block the process by focusing attention on advancement towards the desired object (Kußmaul, 2000).

The TARGET metaphor provides a useful frame for explaining the controlled processes that are part of translation, in particular the elaboration of macrostrategies, but it drifts away from uncontrolled processes. The translational action is thus described as a process controlled at every moment by the translator, as is the case with the verbalization of the translator's cognitive processes in think-aloud protocols, where subjects verbalize the conscious, controlled processes (Ericsson & Simon, 1984; Jääskeläinen, 2000). Furthermore, when verbalizing their mental processes, subjects tend to introduce logical-causal interpretations (Hönig, 1988: 13) based on the folk model of intentionality, which can lead to an idealized description of these processes. As part of folk psychology but also as the theoretical base of functionalism, this model of intentional action paves the way for a rationalist idealization of translation processes in both Vermeer's [Reiß and Vermeer (1984)

1991] and Holz-Mänttäri's (1984) approaches, as well as in think-aloud protocols.

Vermeer's and Holz-Mänttäri's approaches, based on the TARGET metaphor, offer an adequate framework for describing and explaining controlled processes in translational actions, and especially the elaboration of macrostrategies. On the other hand, Hönig (1995) and Kußmaul (2000) take into account the uncontrolled actions, without losing sight of the goal of the translation and the elaboration of macrostrategies.

5. 2　Assigning a single objective to each translational action

The target metaphor assigns a single goal to each path and, thus, a single objective to each translational action. Vermeer's Skopos theory [Reiß & Vermeer (1984) 1991] and Holz-Mänttäri's translational action model (1984) assign a single principal purpose to each translational action, to which all other purposes are subordinated. In the case of Holz-Mänttäri, translation is seen as a cooperative effort oriented towards a single overall purpose. This approach ignores the diversity of purposes that can be assigned to as complex an action as a translation. An action may be influenced by the interests of different stakeholders, and conflicts may arise between these purposes. Hence, this scope offers an overly simplified account of the translation process (Hönig, 1992). "Es gibt eine Menge von Zwecken (M > 1). Zwecke sind hierarchisch geordnet" [Reiß & Vermeer (1984) 1991: 101].

> Handlungen können zu Gefugen zusammengefasst auftreten und einander über-, unter-oder nebengeordnet sein. Dabei werden die gefugegebundenen intendierten Handlungszwecke am übergeordneten gemeinten Gesamtziel ausgerichtet. (Holz-Mänttäri, 1984: 30)
>
> Es wurde bereits erwähnt, daß Stücke eines Texts verschiedene Skopoi haben können (vgl. Reiß' Mischtexte). Insofern ist einem Text u. U. nicht ein Skopos zuzuschreiben. Aber jeder Text als Ganzes hat doch letzten Endes einen übergeordneten Skopos ... auch wenn seine Teile Teilskopoi haben. [Vermeer (1989) 1992: 105]

The assumption that a text has a purpose implies a metonymical displacement between the text and its author. It is the author who assigns purposes to his text. These purposes may well be inferred from most texts, but they are not "in the texts." It is the people who draft and use texts who try to achieve certain objectives by means of these texts [Vermeer (1989) 1992: 123]. When translating, the distinct goals of the participants in communication may need to be harmonized and coordinated by the translator, who decides, in the end, what the purposes of *his* translation are. For example, the client can define part of his purposes in a way that is not coherent with the needs and purposes of the envisaged recipient; in this case, the translator may have to negotiate these purposes with the client

(Vermeer, 1992: 110; Holz-Mänttäri, 1984: 97). The different purposes can be subordinate to one another (for example, a translation produced under censorship restrictions can be devised to pass censors' screening with the aim to undermine the power that supports that censorship), but they can also be of similar importance without sharing one overall goal (for example, a translator may have the purpose of reaching a wide public while at the same time intending a second meaning for some *initiated* readers). The hierarchical models of purposes offered by Vermeer and Holz-Mänttäri are simplistic to the extent that they assign a single *skopos* or overall purpose to the translation and a single main function to the target text. By doing so, they do not take into account the possibility that several purposes may coexist and that conflicts among them may arise.

5. 3　The end justifies the means

The TARGET metaphor allows an action's purpose to be considered as its determining factor, just as physical goals are elements that direct movements in space. In accordance with the notion of the pre-eminence of ends, Vermeer's Skopos theory focuses on the study of adequate ways of achieving a certain purpose. "Mit anderen Worten: Fur Translation gilt, 'Der Zweck heiligt die Mittel'" [Reiß & Vermeer (1984) 1991: 101]. "Es ist wichtiger, daß ein gegebener Translat(ions)zweck erreicht wird, als das eine Translation in bestimmter Weise durchgefuhrt wird" [Reiß & Vermeer (1984) 1991: 100].

The assessment of a translation, therefore, centers on the effectiveness in achieving a purpose, while the assessment of the purposes themselves is excluded from the field of translation and assigned to other realms beyond the scope of translation-theoretical discussion, such as the translator's personal ethics or his culture's specific values.

> Den Translator (als Translator) interessieren weder objektive Realität noch Wahrheitswerte … Wahrheitswerte interessieren den Translator bei seiner (ethischen) Entscheidung, ob er eine Translation ubernehmen will (z. B. Translation politischen Propagandamaterials) … [Reiß & Vermeer (1984) 1991: 26]

Vermeer's Skopos theory provides a criterion for evaluating the way in which a translation is carried out, i. e. the adequacy of the translation for the intended purposes, but it says nothing about the possibility of applying other criteria apart from effectiveness to evaluate the translational means, nor about the assessment of the purposes of the translation. Nord (1989; 1997) tried to solve this problem by adding an ethical principle to skopos theory, summarized in her concept of *loyalty*. For Nord (1997), a translation's end justifies the means, as long as this end does not contradict the original author's intentions. This position prompts the question of the possibility of determining these intentions, of which the author might even not be aware. On the other hand, the definitions of *loyalty* provided by Nord (1989; 1991; 1994) are contradictory, and her attempt to combine two antagonistic views of translation ("the traditional equivalent concept and the radical functionalist concept"; Nord, 1994: 100) is difficult to sustain from a theoretical point of view, without answering two questions related to the justification of means by the ends of the translation: (1) Is it possible to apply other criteria in addition to that of effectiveness in order to evaluate the translational means? (2) How can the ends of the translation be assessed?

As for the first question, the concept of *effectiveness* as the main criterion for assessing an action corresponds to the classical model of rationality of Western cultural tradition (Searle, 2000). As for the second question, Vermeer's answer (1996a) is also perfectly coherent with a model of rationality in which only the means, but not the ends themselves, are subject to rational restrictions: Skopos theory leaves the discussion about the ends of a translation to the field of ethics, since it corresponds to the translator's *private* sphere and not to his professional role. Science, in accordance with the model of instrumental rationality, is free from values and independent from ethical questions.

> I should like to distinguish role behavior from personal convictions. A theory should be value-free … , and the same applies to role descriptions, in the sense that only the range of validity or applicability can be determined, but not which application is ethically allowable or not. (*A possible misuse of atomic energy cannot stop the development of a theory of atomic fission, nor will the prohibition of a misuse be part of a general nuclear theory.*) Morality and/or ethics (whichever terminology one prefers) are phenomena concerning personal behaviour. (Vermeer, 1996a: 83)

Vermeer and Holz-Mänttäri's functionalist approach cannot be considered free of values in any strict sense. On the one hand, when translational skopos is dependent on the receivers of the target text [sociological rule, Reiß & Vermeer (1984) 1991: 101], then it is also dependent on a web of assumptions shared by these receivers, which includes ethical questions. On the other hand, translational activities, as described in Holz-Mänttäri's (1984) action framework, clearly depend on social norms and conventions (Vermeer, 1996a: 67). In this sense, Vermeer and Holz-Mänttäri's functionalist approaches do consider other criteria for assessing translational means in addition to their effectiveness. Nevertheless, following the tradition proper to scientific discourse, Vermeer excludes any explicit discussion of normative or ethical questions from his investigation.

Vermeer's [(1989) 1992: 18; 1996a: 64] assigning of certain overall purposes to a translation has clear ethical implications. According to him (1996a: 64), a translation's ultimate goal is communication and understanding among individuals from different cultures. Questions of an ethical nature cannot be excluded, therefore, from the field of theoretical study. If the concept of *communication* includes the level of interaction (Witte, 2000), i. e. , if it is not completely structured by the conduit metaphor—and, thus, is not understood as a mere mechanical transmission of content —then the responsibility for successful communication that functionalism assigns to the translator is an ethical responsibility.

5.4 The reconstruction of the transfer model

The critical study of the TARGET metaphor has not only shown the blind spots and problems that block the way to a functionalist translational framework. It has also made it clear that using this metaphor does not allow for completely overcoming the reification of meaning implicit in the TRANSFER metaphor, since both metaphors are part of a single idealized model of human action and communication. In this model, which corresponds to the ideal of instrumental rationality, communicative action follows a temporal chain of cause and effect that puts the communicative intention of the subject first, the content the subject wants to communicate second, and the form this content is going to acquire third. The division of action into discrete segments, to which a definite purpose can be assigned (according to the folk model of intentionality), allows communicative action to be explained as intentional transmission of meanings through language (Hendriks-Jansen, 1996: 274). The intention of the *sender* determines the contents he wants to transmit through his communicative action.

> In the discrete state view, a smile conveys a specific message. The message is presumed to originate within the smiler, who uses her skill in controlling facial expressions, gaze direction, and body movements to fix the precise nature of the message she is trying to put across (a smile may be joyful, encouraging, cynical, or merely polite). The smiler's intention thus shapes the nature of a discrete intentional act and determines the message it transmits. (Hendriks-Jansen, 1996: 275)

According to this idealized model of communication, the possibility of defining the purpose of a communicative action goes hand in hand with the possibility of determining the content that is to be communicated. That is, focusing on the intentional aspects of communication could also lead to emphasizing the predefined character of textual meanings. The target metaphor, as part of a communicative model, favors the reconstruction of the conduit metaphor, which is everywhere in our everyday language.

6. Broadening of the theoretical framework of functionalism

The difficulties in the use of the TRANSFER and TARGET metaphors in Vermeer and Holz-Mänttäri's functionalism suggest the need to broaden the theoretical framework of functionalist approaches, developing a more realistic model of human action and communication than that provided by folk psychology. Second generation cognitive models provide an adequate basis for it. On the one hand, Halverson (2001) points out that many of the key concepts of German functionalism, such as *objective* and *intention*, are cognitive by nature; on the other hand, functionalist approaches are based on a theory of action (Rehbein, 1977; Harras, 1978) that implies a theory of cognition to a certain degree.

There are three major paradigms in the field of cognitive science, the classical information-processing) paradigm, the connectionist framework, and situated cognition (Clark, 1997: 82, 84; Risku, 2002a). The idealized model of communication presented above is structured according to the classical paradigm of cognition (cf. Newell & Simon, 1972; v. Gardner, 1985). The brain is thought of as a computer and thinking is conceived of as the manipulation of abstract symbols with fixed contents. According to this metaphor, the activity of the brain-computer is directed towards solving predefined problems through the execution of a series of serial operations that lead to the desired solution. The information entering and leaving the processor is a predetermined and invariable entity (Lakoff & Johnson, 1999: 249, 257; Bartsch, 2002: 84; Hendriks-Jansen, 1996: 11).

In contrast, second-generation cognitive approaches—both the connectionist model as well as situated cognition—are incompatible with the model of communication as intentional action directed towards the transmission of invariable contents. In connectionism, predetermined information entering or leaving the system does not exist. Knowledge is not stored in explicit form as a memory, nor is it collected in a language of symbols with discrete meanings, but rather *emerges* from the overall activation of the system. Thus, there does not exist an unambiguous relation between a piece of information and its physical basis, which impedes the assumption of the existence of invariable contents [Hendriks-Jansen, 1996: 63; Varela, Thompson & Rosch (1991) 1993: 8]. On the other hand, the model of situated cognition defines physical interaction with the environment as an essential part of cognitive processes. Meaning does not exist as a predefined and invariable entity, but is negotiated and constructed (and hence it *emerges* in a way that is not completely predictable) during social interaction [Hendriks-Jansen, 1996: 30; Varela, Thompson & Rosch (1991) 1993: 149–150].

Now, functionalism seems to depart from the classical model of human action and cognition, and to converge with second-generation paradigms, especially with the model of situated action and cognition (Risku, 2000). Functionalist approaches take translational action as part of a broader communicative and cooperative action. The complexity of this global action seems to underscore that the individual aspects of the situation in which it occurs must be taken into account. Meaning is not a stable and transportable entity, but the result of a process of interpretation in which multiple factors play a role. It depends on the interpreter's subjectivity and on the way he perceives the situation in which it takes place. In this sense, functionalist approaches converge with second-generation cognitive frameworks and their conception of meaning as an *emerging* phenomenon (i. e. , dependent on multiple variables that are uncontrollable and not completely predictable). However, functionalism uses an idealized model of human action as a logical-causal progress towards a previously determined goal, which prevents functionalism from totally overcoming the first, information processing or classical, paradigm. [1]

The theoretical framework provided by second-generation cognitive paradigms provides for a broader epistemological base for functionalist approaches, taking into account aspects of the translation process obscured in a model structured by the TRANSFER and TARGET metaphors. Thus, the theoretical contradictions and difficulties detected in the analysis of Vermeer and Holz-Mänttäri's functionalist discourses may be solved. Below, the solutions that second-generation cognitive science offers to solve some of these difficulties are outlined.

6.1 A model of communication as construction

As we have seen (Section 4), the transfer metaphor plays a part in structuring some of the key concepts of functionalism, and it contradicts its explicit claims with regard to the impossibility of transferring invariable meanings. This contradiction becomes even clearer to the extent that some of these concepts, such as the *offer of information* and the *message carrier*, were developed precisely to offer a view of the translational processes distinct from the model of encoding and decoding. These difficulties indicate the need to explicitly and systematically develop a theoretical model of communication to serve as the basis for a functionalist translational theory.

In the models proposed within a situated cognition framework, language is understood as a basis for the social construction of meanings, and not as a vehicle for the transmission of meanings (Clark, 1997; Hendriks-Jansen, 1996). Situated cognition provides an adequate theoretical framework for a model of communication as dynamic construction of meanings, coherent with Vermeer and Holz-Mänttäri's functionalist approaches. Vermeer (1996b: 98–99) considers both the production and the interpretation of texts as constructive tasks and underlines the relative character of the construction of meaning (i. e. , it depends on the interpreter and the situation), and Holz-Mänttäri (1984) highlights the cooperative aspects of communication. Within this model of communication, translation may as well be described as a constructive task in the sense proposed by Hönig (1995): it is not about transporting a cargo of more or less invariable meanings, but about building scaffolds for new acts of meaning construction. In this way, the description of translational processes is integrated into a theoretical framework that defines meaning as a configuration emerging in each specific communicative situation, from multiple processes of negotiation and joint construction. In

---

[1] As I have tried to show elsewhere (Martín 2007), the inferential approach argued for by Gutt ([1991] 2000) explicitly distances itself from the codification-decodification model of communication. However, it still remains in the realm of the first or classical cognitive paradigm of information processing. For instance, in Gutt's model, the context functions just as a filter in order to eliminate the ambiguity of texts, but not as a dynamic environment that can produce emergent, not fully predictable results (see Lachat Leal 2003 and McElhanon 2005).

doing so, it takes into account the insights of second-generation cognitive approaches, thereby providing a functionalist theoretical framework with an empirical basis.

6.2 Cultural models instead of cultures

Situated cognition and cognitive anthropology provide for the substitution of the concept of *culture* as an integrating unit by the concepts of *scaffolding* (Clark, 1997) and *cultural model* (Quinn & Holland, 1987) as bases for socially shared action. In this way, the danger of accepting without discussion a "zero degree of divergence" (Muñoz, 1999: 169) among the receivers of a translation and of assigning stereotypical characteristics to abstract cultural groups is eliminated. Cultural knowledge and competence are not conceived of as a unit structured by rules and behavioral norms, but as a series of interpretative schemes that are not necessarily mutually coherent, and which can be applied to different settings of experience. Hence, these schemes leave room for alternative constructions, creativity, joint construction, and negotiation (Keesing, 1987: 372).

The elaboration of hypotheses about cultural models available to the receivers of a translation eliminates the need to define a given group as a cultural unit. This methodical framework allows translational hypotheses to be adapted to the characteristics of each situation and each group of receivers (Pöchhacker, 1994: 215), and the relevant factors in each case to be taken into consideration. Difficulties in communication are not understood as cultural barriers but as degrees of compatibility among different cognitive models assumed by the translator to be held or entertained by the ST and the TT readers. The relevant factor for translation is not affiliation to one culture or the other, but the possibility of making use of certain cultural scaffoldings that allow for the interpretation of a text in a given situation. This perspective allows cultural differences to be taken into account, as advocated by functionalism, without assuming cultural homogeneity at any level of abstraction proposed by Vermeer. Translation is not directed towards one culture, but towards a more or less defined group of individuals who may share some cultural models but not others.[①] The translator elaborates a series of hypotheses in this regard that may be correct or not. The empirical investigation of the reception of translations (e. g. , about the cultural models on which the receivers of a translated text base their interpretation of it, about the possible difficulties of interpretation and the degree of adequacy of the translator's hypotheses) might provide a basis for developing a realistic model of cultural phenomena, in agreement with the needs of the field of translation studies, based on the theoretical framework of recent advances in cognitive anthropology.

---

① Muñoz (2007, forthcoming) proposes defining translation as interpersonal (not interliguistic or intercultural) phenomenon.

6. 3 Situated and emerging translational action

Risku (2000; 2002b) brings together different functionalist approaches under the title of *Situated Translation*, stressing the parallelism between this trend in translatology and the paradigm of situated cognition. However, Risku (2002b: 524) points out that "the basis for this framework was not laid directly by *Situated Cognition*." Section 5 tried to show that the functionalist model of intentional action is good at explaining the controlled processes that are part of translational action (in particular, the development of macrostrategies), but it still leaves in the dark the uncontrolled processes that are also a part of this action. The adoption of a broader model of action, beyond the logical-causal schemes of instrumental rationality, allows for a coherent integration of both aspects of the translational processes.

Like functionalism, the 'situated action' model is directed towards the dynamic description of action within a situation. However, its explanatory framework does not correspond to folk psychology's concept of intentionality, which is considered to be another object of study (Suchman, 1987). Instead, the model of situated action is based on evolutionary and cultural history, and on the study of learning (Hendriks-Jansen, 1996). The concept of *situated action* provides an adequate framework for describing translational action without being constrained to the rationalist scheme of intentional action, while paying attention to the intentional models that direct action and communication (which guide, for example, the drawing of inferences about the possible intentions of communication counterparts). Furthermore, *situated action* explains both translational plans and strategies and the carrying out of subroutines or spontaneous association in terms of emerging processes, i. e. both controlled and uncontrolled processes. In this way, this model offers an integrating framework for translation didactics and for the study of the cognitive processes of translation.

Vermeer and Holz-Mänttäri's translational action does not consider the possibility that multiple objectives that are not subordinated to one another can be consciously or unconsciously assigned to a translation and cause conflicts. Connectionist and situated cognition approaches provide an adequate theoretical framework for the development of a dynamic model of translational action. This model takes into account the possibility of multiple purposes not subject to a hierarchical order being applied to a translation (and the need of resolving the possible conflicts between them). The model also considers the recursive and emerging character of this assignation of objectives. "The 'plans' used by a competent performer are not imposed from above; they are constructed, or rather they emerge in situ, through the performance of structured but flexible sequences of activity" (Hendriks-Jansen, 1996: 317).

Vermeer and Holz-Mänttäri's functionalism is integrated into a general theoretical framework according to which form is a result of a rational calculation directed towards achieving the functional suitability of the final product. The specification of the function precedes that of the form, in a *top-down* scheme. According to the concepts of *emergence* developed by the connectionist and situated cognition approaches, the processes that give rise to the emergence of the form do not necessarily correspond to a pre-established plan. The form emerges from the joint action of multiple, not entirely predictable parameters, and functional restrictions are just some of them. In textual production, the linguistic forms that are evoked or available at a given moment can co-determine the function of certain textual elements (Dennett, 1991). For example, sometimes a person is writing a text and does not know how to continue. An expression comes to his mind which he finds a good solution, but now he must rewrite his text, so as to integrate that expression in a coherent framework. The functions of the adjacent elements may change in the process. Form and function are mutually determined, since formal restrictions exist that limit the range of possible functions. Thus, in textual production, this approach considers *top-down* as well as *bottom-up* processes.

With respect to teaching, this theoretical framework offers a new perspective on the use of functionalist schemes for the explicit development of overall translational strategies. From this perspective, those schemes could serve as scaffolding to orient the first stages of translation practice, but they would be gradually set aside as the student developed and automated adequate dynamical strategies for each situation (for example, the specifications of the translation brief could be reduced as students advance, so that students would be let and led to infer or ask for the information needed in each case). This approach is coherent with Kiraly's (2000) proposal to apply insights of social constructivism to the translation education system. According to Kiraly, learning cannot be described as a *transmission* of invariable knowledge (which would be coherent with the conduit metaphor), but as a process of joint *construction* of meanings (2000: 23). According to this notion, the teacher does not play the role of transmitter of pre-fabricated truths, but rather that of a guide who advises future translators in the construction of their own meanings (ibid.). Thus, the study of translation has to be *situated*, i. e. it needs to be oriented toward the implementation of professional tasks in all their complexity.

> Rather than dissecting skills, knowledge, or instructional content for easy digestion, the constructivist perspective holds that for learning to be authentic and productive, learning tasks need to remain embedded in their larger, natural complex of human activity. (Kiraly, 2000: 43)

The completion of professional projects (based on real briefs) or simulations of professional projects can be based on translational models such as functionalism, which provides an initial orientation for the development of macrostrategies. Practice based on the framework of these models favors the emergence of habits and their identification. They, in turn, promote the creation of subroutines that lend fluency to the translation process and give rise to an expertise not restricted to the initial knowledge of the explicit scheme, imposed from top to bottom, but also encompassing knowledge which emerges in a flexible way from the sequences of activity adapted to each situation. This approach would allow for the development of didactic strategies intended to increase the confidence of future translators in their intuition, and their creative capability, as posited by Hönig (1995) and Kußmaul (2000).

6.4　Ethics and Translation Studies

Vermeer's skopos theory and Holz-Mänttäri's translational action theory focused on assessing the effectiveness with which a translation achieves the proposed objectives, i. e. the adequacy of the means to the end. The prioritization of effectiveness is characteristic of the model of instrumental rationality in Western tradition. For this reason, its axiomatic character (Vermeer, 1996a) only hides its cultural determination. In this sense, Vermeer's skopos theory was not free of values. On the other hand, the responsibility for successful communication assigned to the translator in functionalism was also an ethical responsibility insofar as communication was defined not as the mere transmission of information, that is, as a technical problem, but was situated within the domain of cooperation (Holz-Mänttäri, 1984) and social interaction (Witte, 1992, 2000).

Experientialist (cognitive) approaches (e. g., Lakoff & Johnson, 1999; Varela, Thompson & Rosch, 1991) provide an integrationist view of scientific discourse that allows the revision of theoretical viewpoints on functionalism in relation to the ethical questions included in translation theory and praxis. From this perspective, knowledge is not isolated either from its physical basis or from its social articulation, and thus it cannot be seen as separate from ethics; nor can science be considered an activity free of values. The classical cognitive model defined the *rationality* concept as the calculation of the means appropriate to achieve certain goals not subject to rational restrictions. In contrast, adopting an experientialist approach implies the use of a broader concept of rationality that also includes reflection on the purposes of an action. Within this epistemological framework, a functionalist approach to translation can undertake the theoretical discussion of the goals of translation without limiting itself to instrumental rationale as a measure of professional effectiveness. This perspective provides the opportunity of studying ethical implications and requirements of different translational discourses and different translation practices, and it does so by adopting a historical and comprehensive approach that also includes empirical investigation about the reception of translations and their effects.

6.5　Experientialism as a means of overcoming the subject/object opposition

Vermeer's functionalism opposes a relativist view to earlier objectivist approaches focused on the comparison of texts. However, this relativism leads to a view of the subject as an entity isolated from the world (Vermeer, 1996b: 35), and underlines the opposition between an external, unknowable reality and a subject to whom only representations of that reality are available. Whereas one of the basic ideas of functionalism is the situated character of a translational action, Vermeer's framework does not allow it to be carried to its logical conclusion. The translator, as a participant in a complex process of communication and cooperation, does not remain isolated from this process as a mere provider of message carriers (Holz-Mänttäri, 1984: 57 - 68). Rather, he intervenes decisively through his interaction with the other participants in the communicative process (occasionally explicitly addressing the receivers and orienting the translation towards his own objectives; Risku 1998: 83). And he can also receive feedback about the success of his work (for example, if he receives a new translation brief, he can guess his previous job was successful).

From an experientialist perspective, there is no cognitive isolation of the individual in relation to the world, since both are the product of a long evolutionary and historical chain of mutual interactions: the knower and what is known have a co-dependent origin (Varela, Thompson & Rosch, 1991), much like the colors of flowers and the sight organs of some insects are the result of a long process of co-adaptation. Experientialism attempts to overcome the dichotomy between objectivism and subjectivism, based on the physical nature of experience. It leads to adopting a translation model that also takes into account its basis in physical experience. The possibility of objective knowledge independent of all experience (of objective translation, independent from the translator's point of view) is thus rejected, as is the arbitrariness of subjective experience, which is shaped by evolutionary and cultural history, and, hence, corresponds in different degrees to socially shared patterns. In translation, and in translation teaching in particular, it suggests the need for taking into account the physical and experiential base of the capabilities brought into play in translation, e. g. analogical thinking.

The consequences of functionalism adopting the theoretical framework of second-generation cognitive frameworks point essentially in two directions. On the one hand, the theoretical assumptions based on folk psychology and on the model of instrumental rationality are called into question. On the other hand, the development of a model of translation as situated action is proposed that takes into account evolutionary, historical, and educational factors. It also integrates the different aspects of translational experience, considering physical interaction with the social environment. Empirical investigation and the search for convergent data from different fields and methods can play an essential role both in putting the theoretical principles to the test and in developing a functionalist model of *situated translation*.

选文二　论功能翻译理论

杨英明

导　言

选文针对中国传统翻译理论"只有宏观的论述,缺乏方法论,操作性不强"的缺憾,对德国功能学派翻译理论进行了具体的方法论论述和理论论证。选文首先简述了功能学派翻译理论的要点,然后详细地探讨了该理论的理论基础,选取了概念段的主题认知法、功能分类法、图式研究法、积木切分法、事件切分法、逻辑推理法、概念转换法、直译法、意译法、传统继承法等十个主要的方法论对功能学派翻译理论进行了研究,最后运用关联理论论证了功能学派翻译理论的正确性,丰富了它的内容。选文有助于翻译研究者和学习者拓宽对功能学派翻译理论的审视视角,获得对该理论的核心观点、理论基础、方法论等方面更加微观、更为全面的了解,以更有效地将该理论运用到实际翻译操作中去。

功能翻译理论强调,翻译是一种特殊的交际形式,涉及三种文本:原语文本、译者的图式文本和译语文本。对于原语文本,最重要的是抓住作者的修辞功能正确理解原语的修辞功能,是产生理想的图式文本的关键。而正确把握原文的认知图式又是正确理解原文修辞功能的基础。理想的图式文本来自原文的认知图式,来自对原文作者的修辞意图的准确把握。在这个图式文本的基础上,产生怎样的译语文本,除了修辞功能等值之外,还应该考虑翻译的目的和读者对象。

一、功能翻译理论简述

(一) 功能翻译理论的要点

根据杂志上发表的论文、学术会议上宣读的论文、学术报告和出版的专著,功能翻译理论的要点简述如下:

1. 分析概念段(conceptual paragraph,具有明确主题意义一个或多个自然段)和句子的修辞功能,使修辞功能的形式重现,从形式的等同中求得功能的等值,意义的等值,这种翻译叫做功能翻译。翻译应该是在修辞功能等值的前提下,遵守"信、达、X"规范;文体不同,翻译的目的不一样,X 不一样。[张梅岗,《中国科技翻译》,1994,(3);刘重德,《三湘译论》,湖南出版社,1995;周笃宝,《中国翻译》,2000,(2)]

2. 功能翻译理论强调修辞形式等同和功能等值的一致性,修辞是手段,是形式;功能是修辞产生的结果或达到的目的,是内容的总和。修辞包括概念段内和句内的修辞,即语言语境的修辞,也包括情景语境、文化语境、语用语境的修辞。(《科技英语修辞》,1998)换句话说,在概念段和句子中,语义、语法和语用三者合为一体表达修辞功能。

3. 功能是靠结构(structures)来体现的,任何一种语言都是由四种符号元素(词、词标志、词序和语调)构成。语言结构(constructions)的认知图式与其他认知领域的认知图式类似,由简单到复杂,由具体到抽象,构成语言因果网络。概念段贯穿了一条主题链,或称因果键。这条因果键是命题或语言事件构成的,也是它们的概念化的参考点。(《中国翻译》,1998,(5)此文已被美国 Colby Information Center of Science & Culture 收录,网上转载。)

4. 功能翻译理论强调认知图式理论对翻译实践和翻译研究的作用,各种普遍结构和特殊结构的认知图式越具体、越丰富,对翻译研究和实践的能力就越强,是译者形成图式文本的基础。

5. 功能翻译理论强调,翻译过程是个斡旋推理过程,因果链是逻辑推理的基本结构,利用已知信息,对非语言要素(如情景、文化和语用等语境)的修辞功能进行判断,产生正确的推理结论。(《英汉功能翻译》,1999)

(二) 功能翻译理论的方法论

我们用修辞功能等值的原则来看待翻译和翻译研究,自然有正确理解原文、翻译表达的一整套与此相应的方法论。这是功能翻译理论最突出的地方。由于功能翻译已经有了比较完整的体系,因此本文只能概括一些基本的、主要的方法加以研究。

1. 概念段的主题认知法

首先,把原文文本划分成概念段,研究概念段的主题思想,找出连接标志,抓住概念段的因果链(《科技英语修辞》),把握语言的功能取向和对概念段整体内容的正确理解。

2. 功能分类法

根据功能分类语言学(Functional Typological Linguistics)把英语分为五大类修辞功能:描述功能、陈述功能、定义功能、分类功能和指令功能,每大类功能又划分出若干小功能,然后与汉语进行分类功能对比研究,探索译的规律。例如,英语陈述功能(陈述部分)总是放在句首,而汉语则置于句末。(张梅岗:《中国翻译》,1999,(5);2000,(5);《中国科技翻译》,1998,(1、4))

3. 图式研究法

根据图式理论,研究和比较原语和目标语的各种结构的认知图式(cognitive schema),例如,英语的 SVO 句、SVoO 句、SVOC 句和被动句等各种句子的结构图式。与目标语的结构图式比较,研究发现它们的翻译规律和方法。[张梅岗:《中国翻译》,1994,(1、5);《英汉功能翻译》1999]值得指出的是,用认知理论去研究结构图式尤为重要。请看下面两句:

(1) The policeman caused Mary to die.

(2) The policeman forced Mary to die.

这两句的结构完全是一样,只有动词的语义不同,而第一句是符合逻辑的,是正确的,第二句不符合逻辑,因而不正确。从这种 SVOC 结构的认知图式看,主语总是表示原因的,OC 表示结果,V 主要起连接作用,使之构成符合语法的句子。Force 是"逼迫"之义;既然 policeman 已经成为"Mary to die"的原因,何需再加"逼迫"。根据认知图式理论,必须对结构的主语、谓语、宾语和补语等的内部结构和语义,加以具体分析,才能正确把握句子的功能。

4. 积木切分法

形象地说,语言是由积木块和子句构成(张梅岗,1994;William Croft,1998),运用语言就是摆弄"积木",因为子句一般而言离不开积木。积木包括名词、合成名词、名词性词组、名词化结构等。除了专有名词和具体名词,积木一般都有内部结构,而且,它们的内部结构都是句子。一个句子成分的表层,表示一个句子意义的深层内容,这对翻译来说是有重要意义的,因为翻译的基本任务就是译出事物内在要素的总和,即内在意义。

5. 事件切分法

语言是由事件构成的因果网络,根据认知的基本规律和语义原则,必须把事件从因果网络中切分出来,使之概念化。切分的基本方法是研究事件的内部结构,即时间结构和因果结构。必须分析事件的参与者以及参与者之间相互的因果作用。[《中国翻译》,1998,(5)]事件的切分非常复杂,是翻译过程理解和表达的关键。

6. 逻辑推理法

逻辑学的研究有助于译者对所译段落真正意义的确定。一切句子的存在都有其先决条件,在句子模糊不清的地方,译者不得不确定其先决条件是什么。(纽马克)

语言是个因果网络,句子之间的关系是因果关系,任何一个句子都具有背景信息(已知信息)。运用逻辑推理方法,求得未知信息,并符合逻辑地用目标语言表达。(《中国翻译》,1995,(6);1996,(1);《上海科技翻译》,1993,(1);《英汉功能翻译》1999)

7. 概念转换法

原语言表达的概念转换成目标语言表达的概念,是翻译的概念化过程,这是翻译过程的第一步,一般而言,翻译不只是概念的正确转换,还必须涉及原语的修辞环境,作者的修辞意图,即修辞功能。但是作者的意图,或语用意义是在句子意义的基础上产生的,受修辞的语言环境的影响。因此,翻译还必须考虑话语的动态意义。翻译单位的择定与所译的文本有着密切的关系。如果原语的语码的概念意义,能表达充分的语境效果,即修辞功能,"积木"则成为概念的主要载体,一般目标语言有对等语,自然成为理想的翻译转换为单位,常采用直译的方法。如果原语的语码意义不能充分表达语境效果,则必须考虑整个概念段的语言环境和修辞意图,以句子或称小句(罗选民)为翻译单位,一般用意译法。

8. 直译法

在功能等值的原则下,语码的语义意义能产生等值的语境效果时,应"直说还它直说,比喻还它比喻,在消除语言上的差异的同时,保留了言语上的差异。"(冯世刚,《翻译通讯》,1982)(2)保存原文的比喻、形象和民族特色,"不妄解原文的字句"。即用符合译语规范和习惯和对等语再现原文的全部意义。有时,归宿语言中没有的,而表达功能所必需的,即使生搬硬套出发语的词语和句型也视为正法。例如:

(1) He walked at the head of the funeral procession, and every now and then wiped away his crocodile tears with a big handkerchief.

他走在送葬队伍的前头,还不时用一条大手绢抹去他那鳄鱼泪。

这句译文把原文作者的修辞所要达到的目的,即"猫哭老鼠",体现得淋漓尽致。

(2) 你不明白,给你说也是"对牛弹琴"。

You can't comprehend it, if I explain it, that is "to play the harp to a bull."

虽然英语中"throw pearls before swine"也有"对牛弹琴"之义,但它具有较强的宗教色彩,达不到原语的修辞功能。

9. 意译法

在功能等值的前提下,消除语言上的差异的同时,没有保存言语上的特色,例如不保存原文的修辞形式和民族特色,词有增减、重复、词性和句型有转换、语序有颠倒、句子有拆、有合、正说和反说互变等译法,应该视为意译。我们把改换法(省略、借用等)、变通法(意译、意译加直译、全不译等)都归为意译。因为这些方法的本质是共同的,过细区分,实用性不大,没有必要。例如:

(1) Her mother's pride in the girl's appearance led her to step back.

她母亲看看她女儿,非常得意,所以特地倒退了几步。(张谷若译)

(2) 他又说,利用外资的重点放在农业科学研究、教育和技术推广、人才培训和智力开发。

The money in foreign currency, he added, should be used mainly for education and research in agriculture sciences and technology.

10. 传统继承法

中国的翻译历史,从有文字记载算起,有一千七百多年。第一篇论翻译的文章是三国时支谦写的《法句经序》。悠久的翻译文化传统值得继承。怎样继承,值得研究。功能翻译理论认为中国的传统翻译理论从宏观上作了比较详细的探索,归根结底是围绕"信、达、雅"做文章。对翻译的论述,大多是文艺翻译家们的实践经验的总结,不乏真知灼见。严复的"信、达、雅"翻译标准,成为后人奉为译事的楷模,视为金科玉律。随着现代语言学理论取得的巨大的成就,特别是语义学、认知语言学和功能分类语言学等对翻译理论产生根本性质的影响。功能翻译理论认为,传统翻译理论在翻译的文字表达上的论述非常精辟,而且有理论依据,即建立在对比语言学基础上。由于有明确的理论基础,传统翻译理论的许多翻译表达方法如增译、省译、重译、反译、拆句、合句等都是实用的。翻译包括两方面,"领悟为一事,用中文表达为又一事"。(傅雷)"领悟"更重要。然而传统翻译理论对于理解原语言的方法和理论没有系统地探讨。功能翻译理论强调,在继承的同时,必须对传统翻译理论加以检讨,才能建立符合翻译规律的理论体系。「张梅岗,《中国翻译》,1999,(5)周笃宝;2000,(2);《上海科技翻译》2000,(2)]

二、功能翻译理论的理论基础

近年来,笔者对功能翻译理论的基础理论进行了研究,认为:功能翻译理论建立在现代语言学(认知语言学、功能分类语言学、比较语言学)和逻辑思维学的基础上。

理论,是指系统化了的理性认识,某个知识领域里的概念、原理和方法成为体系。它是在实践的反复过程中形成,随实践而发展。功能翻译理论是以修辞功能等值为基础的方法论体系,在翻译实践上有较强的实用性和可操作性。

(一)功能翻译理论的认知

什么是功能?"功能就是意义"[胡壮麟《外国语》1998,(3)]。意义是什么呢?根据系统语义学观点和概念语义学,意义就是命题的内容。词表达最基础的概念,词构成子句,子句表示命题。命题的集合,构成了话语,成为因果链(T. Givon,1998,美国俄勒冈大学)。由此可见,功能就是命题的内容,就是意义,就是修辞产生的目的;命题是形式,是手段。换句话说,功能是命题手段所产生的结果或达到的目的。功能是由形式来体现的,"形式指事物内在要素的结构和组织"。

"内容指事物内在要素的总和","是事物内在要素的全部意义"。李奇(G. leech)教授在《语义学》(semantics)(1983年第二版)第5章论述了翻译等值的概念,认为理想的译文应该完整地表达原文的交际值(communicative value),在第2章描述了译文和原文交际值等值的七个方面的意义:概念意义(conceptual meaning)、内含意义(connotative meaning)、社会意义(social meaning)、感情意义(affective meaning)、附带意义(reflected meaning)、词的搭配意义(collocative meaning)、主题意义(thematic meaning)、其中2~6又叫联想意义(associative meaning)。

翻译,做到这七个方面的等值,就是理想的译文。意义上等值的翻译,也就是功能等值的翻译。关于这个问题,我们的前辈王宗炎教授早在1981年就有明确的论述,他指出,"在作用上最适当的译法,也就是在意义上最适当的译法","在功能上与原文不对路,从整体看来,就不见得忠实"。(王宗炎,1981)

"形式等同"、"功能等值",有个内容和形式的关系问题。"任何事物都有其内容和形式","内容总是某种形式的内容,形式总是某种内容的形式","同一种形式在不同的条件下可以体现不同的内容"。功能翻译理论强调,"形式是由修辞功能、修辞技巧、句型结构等构成的。其中决定因素是修辞功能,因为修辞功能决定修辞技巧、句型和句子结构,甚至许多语法现象也只能从修辞功能上才能得到解释。"(《论EST的功能翻译》,1994)从这些论述我们可以看出,功能翻译理论把概念段的语义、语法和修辞紧密结合,互相影响,不可分割。突出修辞功能的重要性,功能靠形式体现,靠结构体现。功能等值的翻译首先必须突出考虑概念段内的语言语境,然后从修辞功能的角度研究情景语境、文化语境和语用语境。因为修辞功能受词义、句子的语法结构和语用意义的支配。句子里每个词的义值由本句的上下文所决定。根据Van Dijk的宏观理论,情景、文化和语用等语境的意义对概念段的功能也会产生重要作用。

(二)功能翻译理论的阐释

功能等值的翻译理论,我们用关联理论也可以得到正确的阐明和解释。建立在认知理论和行为理论基础上的关联理论是一种认知语用学理论,是从语用学相关原则(Principle of Relevance)发展的。下面我们再用关联理论来论证功能翻译理论的正确性。

关联理论的定义:关联是命题(proposition)同语境(context)集合Cl…Cn之间的关系,关联是命题的基本特征,是命题对语境的关系。应该怎样理解这个定义呢?我们可以认为这个定义有两层意思:第一,"语境的集合"就是指有明确主题的概念段,关联就是这个概念段的一条意链;第二,命题本身具有关联性,是这条意链上的一小段。这一思想与功能翻译理论关于具有明确主题意义的一个或多个自然段为概念段,且有一条主题链的思想吻合。

关联理论的最佳关联原则强调,任何一个交际行为必须保证自身最佳关联。"交际行为"是什么?就是一个语言事件在时间结构上按内部时间展开,在因果结构上按因果逻辑展开。我们可以说,事件具有最佳的关联性。而且功能翻译思想阐述了"积木"理论,认为"积木"是组装了的语言单位,即"积木"的内容结构是个子句,关联性最佳。

关联理论还认为,关联性之间与语境蕴含意义(context implication)相关联,认为语境蕴含意义不是命题本身的产物,而是命题与语境集合相结合而产生的含义。我们的"修辞功能等值"认为,交际功能涉及语义和语境,两者不能截然分开。双方交际的参考事件是语义的范畴。交际双方根据语境情景调整各自的语言,符合语用意义。就书面语言而言,根据写作目的的要求,使用不同的手段和方法,描述语言事件,达到预期写作意图,实现修辞功能。翻译让原文和译文在"修辞功能"上等值,除了语言语境之外,自然还必须考虑原语言的情景语境、文化语境和语用语境。

关联理论认为,翻译是两种语言进行的特殊交际形式,只要交际一方的意图为另一方所认识和理解,这就是翻译。关联理论下的翻译的"交际效度"的权重最大,其次是"信度"等其他要素。那么,"交际效度"是什么? 就是交际功能,即修辞功能等值的权重最大。"因此,句法意义、修辞意义、句子的联想意义和语义学方面的意义都得服从修辞的功能意义。修辞功能的等值是最高的等值。"(《英汉功能翻译》,55)

关联理论认为,关联与推理(inference)有着密切的关系,指出话语理解过程主要是个推理过程,其中关联判断(judgment of relevance)对于推理结论的形式起着重要作用。功能翻译理论则更加明确地提出并论证:语言是个因果网络,概念段贯穿了一条因果主题链。阐明怎样抓住这条链,进行对原文的理解和表达。[参见《因果链的研究与翻译》,《中国翻译》1998,(5);《科技英语修辞》,1998]

【延伸阅读】

1. Colina, Sonia. Further evidence for a functionalist approach to translation quality evaluation. *Target：International Journal on Translation Studies*. 2009, 21 (2)：235-264.

2. Cranefield, Jocelyn & Yoong, Pak. The role of the translator/interpreter in knowledge transfer environments. *Knowledge and Process Management*. 2007, 14 (2)：95-103.

3. Edwards, R., Temple, B. & Alexander, C. Users' experiences of interpreters：The critical role of trust. *Interpreting*. 2005, 7 (1)：77-95.

4. Halliday, M. A. K. (2009). The gloosy ganoderm：Systemic functional linguistics and translation. *Chinese Translators Journal*. 2009(1)：17-26.

5. Vermeer, Hans J. *A Skopos Theory of translation*. TextconText Verlag, 1996.

6. 何庆机. 国内功能派翻译理论研究述评. 上海翻译. 2007(4):16-20.

7. 李玉婷. 从目的论看翻译策略的选择. 学理论. 2011(24):10-12.

8. 李越然. 论口译的社会功能——口译理论基础初探. 中国翻译. 1999(3):7-11.

9. 邱杨. 浅谈口译目的与标准. 四川教育学院学报. 2004(3):45-51.

10. 谢一铭,王斌华. 目的论连贯原则在汉英外交口译中的体现——基于现场口译的语料分析. 中国科技翻译. 2011(3):27-29.

11. 张静. 德国功能翻译学派理论对口译标准的启示. 中国电力教育. 2005(23):257-259.

12. 张泪,蔡培培. 目的论下的陪同口译策略探究. 广西青年干部学院学报. 2011(3):16-18.

【问题与思考】

1. 简述功能学派翻译理论的核心概念和翻译原则,并谈谈你对"忠诚加目的"原则的看法。

2. 相对于传统翻译理论,在功能学派翻译理论中译者的定位有何不同? 这一定位有何积极意义?

3. 功能学派翻译理论对口译实践有何指导意义?

4. 请结合实例探讨功能学派翻译理论在口译过程中的具体应用。

5. 脱离语境就无法研究语言。语境不仅包括一句话的上下文,也包括语言的社会语境。请阐述功能学派口译理论中的"语境观"。

第九章　基于语料库的口译理论研究

导　论

　　语料库早期是指按照某一规则随机抽取的书面或口头的言语总汇。语料库的萌芽可以追溯到中世纪的欧洲,当时的僧侣学者用语料库对《圣经》加以研究。现代意义上的语料库诞生于 20 世纪 50 年代末和 60 年代初,其背景是计算机技术的发展。其中值得一提的是 1962 年,美国布朗大学建成了世界上第一个可机读的语料库,研究人员为其命名为"the Brown Corpus"。"Corpus"一词源于拉丁语,原意是身体、躯体,这里被赋予引申含义——语料库,并一直沿用至今。现代科学环境下对语料库的定义是"应用计算机技术对海量自然语言材料进行处理(包括预处理、语法自动附码、自动句法分析、语义分析等)、存储,以供自动检索(retrieval)、索引(concordance)以及统计分析的大型资料库"(李文中,1999:51)。

　　从根本上说,语料库并非一种新的思想,而是随着信息产业的技术进步,人们开发出的一种语言实证研究的手段和方法。这种方法使得语言研究者不再只能进行定性研究,也可以像物理学家一样展开定量的统计分析。尽管受到以乔姆斯基为代表的理性主义学者的质疑,语料库研究还是借着信息技术飞跃进步的东风一步步地成熟起来,至今已经成为翻译研究不可或缺的子学科。

　　语料库从诞生开始就是为语言研究服务的,但语料库应用于翻译领域的历史却比语料库语言学的历史短得多。贝克(Mona Baker)是第一个提出可以运用语料库技术揭示翻译沟通的内在本质的学者。在翻译学界,语料库技术颠覆了人们的一些传统研究理念,因为它不属于很多二元对立方法(如规限研究与描述研究)中的任一方。它提供给人们的不仅仅是一种新的翻译研究方法,更是支持人们综合利用以往各种研究方法的一种整合手段。翻译研究中的平行语料库包含了两种原创语言文本及与之对应的两种翻译语言文本,在目前的使用中最为广泛和普遍。

　　爱尔兰学者奥洛汉(Maeve Olohan)认为既然语料库语言学的研究对象不是语言能力而是语言应用,那么运用该技术选择合适的文本语料为素材来验证翻译过程和现象中的各种主观推测之真伪可以是基于语料库的翻译研究的主要方向。

　　虽然语料库应用于翻译领域历史尚短,但自上世纪 90 年代中期以来,语料库翻译研究发展迅猛,逐渐发展成为全新而热门的译学研究范式。国内外学界先后建成为数众多的翻译语料库、平行语料库和可比语料库,并以这些语料库为平台,开展翻译共性、翻译语言特征、译者风格及翻译教学等领域的研究。然而,上述领域绝大多数都是以笔译语料库为研究平台。自1998 年以色列学者施莱辛格(Miriam Shlesinger)首次提出运用语料库研究口译的可能性至今已有十余年时间了,但是时至今日,全世界已经建成并投入使用的口译语料库无论从规模上还是数量上都远远比不上笔译语料库，只有日本 Nagoya 大学开发的日英同声传译语料库和意大利 Bologna 大学开发的欧洲议会口译语料库等。语料库在口译领域的运用之所以大大滞后于笔译，这其中一个重要的原因是技术层面的。笔译语料库建立所依托的计算机技术主要包括大容量高速度的数字存储器和数据库软件技术，而口译语料如果想要建立相应的语料库除了前述的技术外则还需要语音处理的软硬件技术支持。然而，我们应该认识到，虽然受到技术层面因素的限制，开展基于语料库的口译研究却依然具有非常广阔的前景，也极具紧迫性，因为更多口译语料库的建成不仅可以用来帮助验证关于翻译共性、翻译语言特征和译者风格等理论是否适用于口译，从而丰富和完善语料库翻译研究内容，而且能够帮助深入了解口译语言特征、口译策略及口译认知过程，推动口译研究由定性研究向定性和定量研究相结合的转变。

当然，近些年来，也有一些口译界学者已经开始尝试用语料库技术进行口译理论研究。由于国内的口译研究在相当长的时间里都是以规定性研究为主，口译语料库为口译的实证研究提供了一种便利的新工具。这方面目前比较常见的研究包括对现有翻译理论在口译中的检验、口译认知过程研究、口译语言特点分析、口译策略和口译技巧探究、口笔译比对研究等。但系统的、获得业内共识的、基于语料库的口译理论体系目前尚未成熟。

由于语料库强大的自动检索和统计功能，很多研究人员已经习惯于用键盘和鼠标来获得各种各样的统计数据，可是我们有必要同时认识到语料库分析的局限之处。一方面，任何语料库的容量都是有限的，抽样有时候不能代表全部，虽然计算机对库内资料的检索与统计可以十分精确，但选择哪些资料作为分析素材是由人的主观意识决定的，因此分析结果有可能不够客观和精确。另一方面，语言是会变化的，特别是口头语言，但计算机的工作程序无法自行与时俱进，因此一些创新的口译语言可能不被机器识别，进而导致分析失准。

尽管基于语料库的口译研究尚处于起步阶段，同时也存在一些局限之处，但这一新兴的研究手段无疑有助于拓宽口译研究的层面和提升口译研究的实证性特点。

选 文

选文一 基于语料库的口译研究：回顾与展望[①]

李 婧 李德超

导 言

自 20 世纪 90 年代末开始，基于语料库的翻译研究影响日增。但由于口译语料库的缺乏，基于语料库的口译研究仍不多见。选文在评价当今较具代表性的国内外三个口译语料库

① 本研究得到香港理工大学项目资助，编号为 A-P C1M。黄立波博士曾对本文初稿提出宝贵意见，特此鸣谢。

的基础上,归纳口译语料库的特点和基本的建立方法,指出基于语料库口译研究的主要问题和前景。作为 20 世纪 50 年代后期发展起来的新兴研究方法,语料库不仅可以为口译研究提供空前广泛的言语素材,而且使传统的口译研究由通过内省、自造例证或诱导询问的取样方法转变为调查取样,材料真实可靠。基于语料库的口译研究虽然起步较晚,但前景看好。口译语料库的建设可以帮助我们探寻口译译文的特点,检验现存的口译理论,考查各种口译策略对口译效果的直接影响,还可以帮助我们研究语际交流和口译的特殊性。这种基于语料库的口译研究方法将最终帮助口译研究实现从规定性研究到描写性研究的飞跃。当然口译语料库的建设也更需要相关技术支持和正确的方法引导。选文通过研究总结出口译语料库可分为类比语料库和对应语料库两种,建库过程一般应遵循以下步骤:根据研究目的决定建立口译语料库的类型(对应、类比,或者两者兼具);录音/影;录音/影资料数字化;影音资料文字转写;文本标注和对齐。选文的研究结果对未来口译语料库的建设具有很强的现实指导意义。

1. 引言

作为一种实证性研究方法,语料库翻译研究因其可以更系统、更科学地描写和归纳可见的翻译现象而在过去 15 年间得到长足的进展(参见王克非,黄立波,2008)。但迄今为止,大多数这方面的研究都限于笔译,尤其是文学翻译的研究,把语料库运用于口译的研究仍不多见。

最先提出把语料库运用于口译研究的是以色列学者 Miriam Shlesinger(1998),她认为语料库口译研究可以参照语料库笔译研究的一些课题,如研究口译中的词汇密度、类符-形符比、词汇频率、语法结构、文本样式、共生现象等,亦可以与笔译语料库相对比,来探索口译文本的独特性。Shlesinger 提出上述观点后的 12 年间,语料库口译研究取得了哪些进展? 现存的口译语料库主要有哪些? 语料库口译研究的前景如何? 本文拟对上述问题作一探讨,以促进学界对这个新领域的了解。

2. 口译语料库的类型

与笔译语料库相类,口译语料库亦可分为类比语料库和对应语料库两种(参见香港 Shlesinger,1998)。

2.1　口译类比语料库

在语料库翻译研究中,类比语料库一般指针对某一领域的同一语言中翻译文本与非翻译文本组成的语料库。若是双语类比语料库则包括两种语言的相似文本。按 Shlesinger(1998)的观点,最理想的口译类比语料库至少包括以下三个子库:口译译文文本库、在相似场合发表的与原语同类的口语文本库及与以上原语口语文本库相对应的笔译译文库。这样设计的目的主要有以下用途:第一,用于研究口语文本。口译译文作为一种特殊的口语文本,研究者可以把收集的口译译文切分成片段,与相同语言的其他自发性口语文本(spontaneous discourse)相比较。这样即使不考虑原语,亦能研究口译文本的特殊结构;第二,用于研究口译译文与笔译文本的区别。口译译文也可以与相对应的笔译译文比较,便于找出口译文本结构的其他特征。换言之,口译类比语料库可以从不同角度分别探索口译文本的独特性,亦能跨越类型、语言和口译个案特征,从而研究口译文本作为整体的共通性。这些特性和共性的研究,对某些还没有被证实的口译处理过程,如处理能力的限制等必然大有裨益(Gile,1991:15-27),同时亦更能帮助更系统地描述口译现象,如口译中的转移(shift)等(Shlesinger,1989)。

2.2　口译对应语料库

基于语料库的笔译研究,其传统研究对象是语言对的特定因素(language-pair-specific factors)和个人变量,如:性别、经历、语言背景等对翻译的影响(Laviosa,1998:474-479)。但口译语料库除了上述这些领域外,还可以拓展至研究译文的结构与形态间的相互关系,而这就可以借助于口译对应语料库。Shlesinger认为,口译对应语料库也要包括三个子库:原语文本库、相对应的口译译文文本库和相对应的笔译译文文本库。通过对相同原语和两种译文的比较(口语形式和书面语形式),研究者可以测试两种语言形式取得功能等效(functional juxtaposition)时,依赖形态(modality-dependent)的程度有多大。例如,原语"可以"一词,笔译可能为"may",而口译目标语可能除了"may"还有"can"、"shall",也即形态有了变化。而口译对应语料库的其中一个研究目的就可以用来发现和比较口译译文中形态变化的规律。这样设计的好处是不仅可以研究口译目标语的特点,还能够进一步研究非言语因素对口译的方向性(directionality)和语言特征的影响。

概括起来,口译语料库可以帮助我们探寻口译译文的特点,检验现存的口译理论,考查各种口译策略对口译效果的直接影响,还可以帮助我们撇开偏见,研究语际交流和口译的特殊性。这种基于语料库语言学的方法和技术将最终帮助口译研究实现从规定性研究到描写性研究的飞跃(Baker,1993:248)。

3. 现有口译语料库评介

迄今为止,国内外建成并完成研究的口译语料库并不多见。[①] 国外,大型的口译语料库有两个,即日本名古屋大学建立的 CIAIR 口译语料库和意大利博洛尼亚大学建立的 EPIC 欧洲议会口译语料库。国内则有中国大学生英汉汉英口笔译语料库。

3.1　名古屋大学综合语音信息研究中心同声传译语料库

日本名古屋大学的综合语音信息研究中心从 1999 年开始至 2003 年完成此语料库(简称 CIAIR)的初步建设。CIAIR 语料库收录了总时长达 182 小时的录音资料,并全部将其转写成为文字,转写后的文字总数约有 100 万词,这让 CIAIR 语料库成为目前世界最大的同传语料

---

① 已完成的语料库口译研究案例较少。以下所介绍的口译语料库均是笔者在参考网络和大量书籍的基础上所得。参考角度包括中/外,同传/交传,语料库规模(自建小型语料库/机构所建大型语料库),语料库研究类型(封闭型:针对单个研究目的/开放型:可以补充语料满足多次研究目的),语料库口语场景:真实语境/拟态(实验室)语境等。

库。语料库创建的目的在于研究语言信息处理技术，提高语言翻译技巧以及完善口译理论。数据库语料也对外出售，所得费用用于语料库维护和大学学术研究（参见 Tohyama，2006）。

从 CIAIR 语料库录音的内容来看，所用语言组合均为英语和日语，言语种类（speech type）包括对话和单独演讲。文本单位（discourse unit）同时具备时间标注（time tag）和文本识别标注（discourse ID）。单独演讲由 5 兆到 150 兆不等；对话由 2.5 兆到 110 兆不等。每一段文本都配备了讲者声音同译者声音结合在一起的波段，且均经过声道处理。当戴上耳机听时，左右耳会分别传出讲者和译者的声音。

到目前为止，CIAIR 语料库共收录了 30 位英语讲者、15 位日语讲者和 31 位口译员的录音及这些录音所转写的文本。这些录音均采自拟真场景，而非真正的口译现场。口译员在同传厢中通过麦克风发声，可以从耳机清晰地听到讲者并透过玻璃看到讲者的一举一动。讲者无法听到口译员的声音，所以可以按照自己自然的语速讲演。从录音内容来看，1999 年单独演讲录音题材主要涉及日常话题及信息科技领域，而对话录音则涉及旅游环境话题。

名古屋大学的研究者据此语料库做出的研究包括机器同声传译、同声传译中口译员的语速和翻译单位、同传译员和讲者的语言输出时间差等。

CIAIR 语料库的最大优势在于其较大的规模，且具有相对完善的建库技术，非常有利于机器翻译，包括机器口译的研制与发展。机器口译（亦称为机助口译或自助口译）是自然语音识别技术与自动翻译系统相结合而形成的一种新的翻译模式。而大规模的 CIAIR 口译语料库丰富了机器口译研究依赖的语料以及语言实践操作的基础，有助于挖掘口译中的一些自动对应的结构和规则。CIAIR 语料库的不足之处在于其收集语料的主题有限，离满足不同交际情景的机器口译需求还有相当大的的差距。另外，由于口译语料库收集语料的环境为口译训练教室，而非真实的口译工作环境，并不能客观反映实际口译操作时的情景，这在口译研究的"生态效力"（ecological validity）上亦打了个折扣（Lindquist & Giambruno，2006；Jakobsen et al.，2007：228）。

3.2　欧洲议会口译语料库

欧洲议会口译语料库（European Parliament Interpreting Corpus，简称 EPIC）由意大利博洛尼亚大学的翻译语言和文化研究小组于 2004 所建。[①] 此语料库为电子对应语料库，涉及的语种包括意大利语、英语和西班牙语。EPIC 语料库收集的录音均来自欧盟议会全体会议的口译。语料库总规模为 140 个 4 小时的录影带，包括 5 场 2004 年 2 月到 7 月的分会的口译录音（Bendazzoli & Sandrelli，2005）。这些音像资料包括全体会议中的原语演讲（标志为"Org"）以及英语，意大利语和西班牙语声道的同声传译（标识为"Int"），亦有欧洲议会的新闻发布会的传译内容。

建库时，首先是将演讲者的原语录影带数字化，形成影音文件。在此过程中，将原来以意大利、英语和西班牙语的原语录音及相对应的同传译文分离，分别存储为独立的音频和视频片段。视频信息亦保留，以利日后进一步分析。对于原语录音的转写，研究者主要参考欧盟在会议后发布的详尽的官方稿件，完成文字初稿，再经审阅而得。而口译录音的转写则较为复杂。

---

① 读者可参阅 http://dev.sslmit.unibo.it/corpora/corporaproject.php? path=E.P.I.C. 来获得关于此语料库的详细介绍。

具体而言,研究者采用同传培训中经常使用的影子跟读方法,一边听口译员的录音,一边大声重复他们的译文,同时利用语言识别软件将复述的言语自动输出文字稿。译文中的副语言特征(paralinguistic features)则由研究者补充完成。其他与译员的口译输出相关的信息,如言语的长度(长、短或中等)、发言模式(即兴、带稿或两者兼有)和平均速度(快、中等、慢)以及有关讲者的名字、国籍、性别和政治背景等,都记录在文字稿一个有着特殊设计的标头里,并可以用做检索的参数之一。在 EPIC 的网页上,如键入"发言时间"或者"译员、发言者的国籍"等,就可以搜索到整个语料库中具有所指定言语或讲者特征的语料。

EPIC 语料库采用 POS 标注,意大利语和英语的文本用的是 Treetagger 软件,西班牙语文本采用 Freeling 软件。建成之后的语料库共涵盖三个原语文本(分属意大利语、英语和西班牙语)的子语料库和六个译语文本的子语料库。换言之,每一种原语都有其他两个语言的译本,三种原语就有六个译本语料库。

EPIC 语料库最大的特点就是其语料的同质性。从译员角度看,欧盟译员全部是经过严格筛选的专业人士,专业水平相当,且口译方向均是由译者的被动语言(passive language)译为主动语言(active language),即母语。其他影响译员表现的外界因素变量,如会前的准备、工作的设备等对于所有欧盟译员而言都相似(如大家会前获得资料的途径和资料内容等都是一致的)。EPIC 语料的这些同质特点尤其适合用于研究特殊体裁同传,例如欧洲议会辩论口译的文体研究等。

由于 EPIC 语料库下共有九个不同语言构成的子库,这种结构上的复杂性为多角度地研究口译提供了可能。例如,研究者可以比较自然英文口语和口译英文在句法、修辞、词汇等方面的各种差别,进一步检验。Laviosa(2002)提出非翻译文本(non-translational)和翻译文本(translational)两者本质不同的假设。研究者亦可研究同声传译译文的方向问题,以及不同语言组合在口译中策略和结构上的特点比较等。

依笔者看来,除了研究作用外,EPIC 语料库还可以广泛应用于教学目的,包括普通外语教学和口译教学。在外语教学上,库中的原语视频片段是听力练习的好材料,而相对应的文字稿亦能帮助学生认识未知的词语和结构,以便更有效地更正错误和吸收新知识。而听力练习也可帮助学生提高外语的发音技巧。在口译教学上,博洛尼亚大学已经把语料库运用于学院的翻译和口译教学培训课程之中。其中的一些做法包括:把 EPIC 的视频片段和文稿作为口译练习材料,或者把议会译员的输出作为学生考评或者学生自我评价的标准,以增强学生对于自己优缺点的认识。另外,口译语料库还可以成为选取真实场景作业的题库,教师可以直接运用其中的某些录音或是通过软件切分加工语料,让练习语料符合学生的实际水平。

除了 EPIC 语料库,Bendazzoli(2009)等人还建立了 DIRSI 语料库和 FOOTIE 语料库。DIRSI 语料库(Directionality in Simultaneous Interpreting)主要用于研究同传的方向。在欧盟,同传通常要求译者只能从被动语言译至主动语言,而反方向则通常不被鼓励,但这却与市场的实际情况(如东欧一些国家)背道而驰。DIRSI 语料库就是为专门研究同传方向对口译质量的影响而建。它收集了三年(2005—2007)在意大利召开的国际会议中所有的同传录音,包括会议的开场白、陈述、辩论问答环节。其中辩论问答环节因为其较强的互动性而与其他独白体部分区别开来。以上录音都经过如 EPIC 语料库般的转写、对齐和标注等处理。

FOOTIE 语料库的录音均来自 2008 年欧锦赛意大利队总共 16 场比赛前后的新闻发布会口译内容,涉及意大利语、英语、法语和西班牙语。为了保证语料的同质性,文字转写的部分均为原语为意大利语和目标语为英语的录音,原语材料超过两个半小时。所有的译文都由同一位口译员提供,均从意大利语译成英语。FOOTIE 语料库为同传语料库,新闻发布会的特征体现为高互动性的对话体,因此从这个角度看,FOOTIE 的语料与通常会议中的问答环节有相似的特点,均采用一人对一人或一人对多人的交流形式。但研究时需注意的是口译听众的特殊性,即除了直接观众(如在场的记者和工作人员)外,还应当包括不在现场但关注新闻发布会的人士,如世界各地的球迷以及撰写赛况和文章的媒体从业人员等。这些都是利用FOOTIE 语料库作研究时需要注意的。

除上述两个大型的、由机构所建立的口译语料库之外,国外亦有少数为专门研究某个问题由研究者自行建立的小型口译语料库。如 Meyer(2008)创建的用于研究交传和同传中对人名的处理和研究“医疗口译”的 K6 语料库;Petite(2005)所建的专门用于研究同声传译中的纠正机制(Repair Mechanism)的语料库;Cencini(2000)建立的用于研究电视口译特点的口译语料库(Television Interpreting Corpus);Fumagalli(1999—2000)建立的研究英-意时事交传特点的类比和对应语料库等等。

以上口译语料库均属于专门用途口译语料库,针对性强,通常为解决某些专门问题而设,且库容较小,影响和应用虽不及前两者大型口语语料库,但其运用语料和实验,而不是传统口译研究中常用的思辨、内省来研究口译的方式,无疑开辟了口译研究的新天地,值得借鉴。

3.3 中国大学生英汉汉英口笔译语料库

中国大学生英汉汉英口笔译语料库(简称 PACCEL)是由我国文秋芳教授等建立的包含中国大学生口译和笔译语料的大型学习者语料库。根据文秋芳等(2008)介绍,PACCEL 语料库收集了 2003 年到 2007 年全国 18 所高校英语专业的学生在大三大四时进行英汉汉英互译测试的语料,总规模为 210 万字。PACCEL 主要分为两个子语料库:口译对应语料库(简称PACCEL-S)和笔译对应语料库(简称 PACCEL-W),规模分别为 50 万字和 160 万字。光盘里,PACCEL 语料库的结构包含三个部分:口译语料库,笔译语料库和检索工具。口译语料库又包括音频和文字转写,文字转写在句子层面实现了原语和译文的对齐,还进一步具备生文本和词性标注的文本。笔译语料库则包括文字部分,并且所有文字部分也如口译语料库的文字转写部分一样,实现了句级对齐并具备生文本和词性标注两类文本。

该语料库使用了高质量的音频设备保证较高质量的数字化转录,即把磁带与电脑连接一起,在播放磁带的同时采集语音。所有录音文件也都使用广泛兼容的 MP3 格式保存以保证文件大小适中,然后用年份、组别、序列号组成每一份音频文件的名字,为检索打下基础。

PACCEL 语料库的口译语料主要收录的是 TEM-8 测试中的口试部分,由于所选语料范围针对性强,所选群体为英语专业学生,故其同质性较高,再加上所选语料为 TEM-8 全国统一考试,其测试标准一致,所以该语料库在代表性方面具有突出的优势,它的建成可以帮助研究者了解中国学生学习英语的过程,对教学、研究、测试、培训以及教材编写、网络远程教育等都具有重要意义(文秋芳等,2008)。

以上介绍的国内外三大口译语料库可谓各具特色。日本的 CIAIR 语料库的建库技术最为完善,其基于口译语料库的机器口译研究走在世界前列,但语料库在口译生态效力上却有所欠缺。意大利的 EPIC 语料库在研究、教学以及后期可持续扩充方面都比较完善,且对语料的处理亦相当科学和严谨。我国 PACCEL 语料库检索功能齐全,具备研究和教学价值,但其本质上是一个学习者语料库,研究领域受到局限。此外,如要更好地发挥 PACCEL 语料库对学习者学习进程的研究和比照作用,宜在该语料库中增加与口译输出相比照的笔译文语料库。相对而言,外国的大型口译语料库的建立目标明确,研究对象清晰,较易根据研究目的控制变量,语料的后期处理亦更为科学,且通常兼备常规和专门用途语料库的特点。我国口译语料库的发展还处于起步阶段,建库通常用于教学目的,若要进行口译研究的话,语料涉及的变量很难控制,这是我们以后建立大型口译语料库时需要注意的。

4. 口译语料库的建库步骤

从以上对国内外主要口译语料库的回顾可以发现,如要建立口译语料库,一般要遵循以下步骤。

(1) 根据研究目的决定建立口译语料库的类型:对应、类比,还是两者兼具。

(2) 录音/影:录音分为现场录音和实验室录音。两者均要获得作为研究用途的录制许可。尤其是现场录制,应注意获得多方许可,如讲者、口译员以及会议组织方等。这是口译语料库建立的难点之一,因为口译员往往有自我防护的意识,再加上某些会议资料可能有版权保密要求,所以要取得真实口译语料往往不易。

交传录音由于是单声道,相对比较简单,使用一般的录音设备或是软件录制即可。同传由于是双声道,对于录音设备的技术要求相对较高。实验室录制时可以使用录音软件;现场录音则要使用与同传厢的输入和输出设备相兼容的录音装置。录音过程也可以转为录影过程,因为视频信息也可能是日后重要的分析材料。

(3) 录音/影资料数字化。有些通过设备获得的录音/影材料,必须通过一定的软件处理,成为音/视频文件,才能被计算机读取(Machine Readable)或分析。可以用做数字化处理的软件有 Pinnacle Studio(9.0),它是一个影音捕捉和编辑软件,影音文件的格式是 mpegl。而口译数字化使用的一般是声音编辑软件,如:Cool Edit-Pro 2.0,格式为. wav,采样速率为 32K;声道为单声道;采样分辨率达 8 Bit(Bendazzoli & Sandrelli, 2005)。好音质为研究音韵特征,如停顿、犹豫的分布等提供了良好基础。

(4) 影音资料文字转写。文字转写应该是可机读的,也应该是便于使用的,同时还要决定采用何种转写规则。国际通用的转写规则是 TEI(Text Encoding Initiative),著名的英国国家语料库(PNC)使用的即是这个转写规则(Burnard, 1994)。在技术层面上,一般借助语言识别软件效率较高,现在可用的语言识别软件有 Dragon Naturally Speaking and IBMVia Voice 等,它们可以帮助获得初稿。但现阶段的汉语语音识别软件技术很不成熟,出错率极高。所以文字转写的实质工作主要还是依靠人工完成,这也是最耗时和耗力的部分。而言语特征,例如未完成的句子,错发音,或者不合语法结构的表达,在后期还需要通过精听,于初稿基础上再进行补充。

(5) 文本标注和对齐。在实现了文字转写之后,需要对文字材料进行标注和对齐,这可为日后的分析打基础。文本标注可以根据研究目的设置搜索参数;文本的原文和译文的对齐则需要依赖对齐软件,主要用于对应语料库。此外,还可以进一步增加注解,比如增加语言学或非语言学的特征:句法、音律特征,乃至讲者的肢体语言、幽默使用等。

5. 小结

　　语料库口译研究目前仍旧是语料库笔译研究的分支,在许多方面都延续了语料库笔译研究的特点。如语料库的分类,大体分为对应语料库和类比语料库;开放型(open-ended)和非开放型语料库;研究对象多是文字文本的对比分析。但随着时间和技术的发展,语料库口译研究也开始显示出自身不同于笔译研究的特点。

　　(1)语料收集:收集难度较大。录制、分类以及声音处理都极大地依赖各种以电脑技术和软件功能为主的科技手段,收集程序比较繁复。此外,语料来源相对较少,真实场景的口译语料更是难得。

　　(2)语料库的建立:口译语料库建立的过程要比笔译语料库复杂,主要在于数据搜集、文字转写、标注以及对齐等过程。其中文字转写要根据一定转写依据进行,以及根据需要增加的笔译文本语料库。

　　(3)语音特征:口译语料库的基础在于口语资料,与笔译语料库的文本资料最大的不同是能够突显口语的特征。这对研究语音学、音韵学相关问题也能提供重要依据。

　　(4)教学价值:口译语料库能为教学提供宝贵的材料。真实场景的语料可以为学生提供实用的口译练习环境,职业译员的口译更能为学生提供参考和标准。对于外语学习者而言,不同的口译语料库对于听力以及口音训练也能起到对比,认知和改进作用。基于语料库进行的错误分析,也可为教学分析和纠正学生问题找到更有效的途径。此外,语料库还可以指导教材的编写,从而"对用法更普遍的语言事实给予更多的关注"(黄昌宁,李涓子,2002:160)。

　　最后,口译语料库建立时尤其需要注意以下的几个问题:第一,语料的代表性。正如杨惠中所言,"语料库是否具有代表性直接关系到在语料库基础上所作的研究及其结论的可靠性和普遍性"(2002:13)。但是牵制口译语料库代表性的因素繁复,除却语料库的规模,还有"语料加工层次、口译场景,口译人员实践水平(专业、学员)等也受到其他语料库所没有的限制"(张威,2009:58),所以如果单纯从代表性而言,口译语料库很难做到绝对代表性,解决办法之一可以从变量控制入手,而变量的控制取决于研究目的。第二,研究框架的科学性。口译语料库建立的目的之一要借助语料库从描写入手,归纳演绎并结合分析和诠释,以从不同角度加深对口译以及与相关现象的认识。但现在有些口译语料库设计理念不清,研究目的不明确,为建立而建立,实属浪费资源。第三,语料库的开放性。口译语料库的规模无论大小,建成后应能继续充实语料和添加标注,让先前收集的语料能"循环再用",形成语料库开放格局,并应提供给同行借鉴,以便共享和节约资源。

选文二　面向教学的口译语料库建设：理论与实践

王斌华　叶　亮

导　言

口译语料库的建设不仅对于口译研究具有实证参考价值，对于口译教学而言，也能够提供切实有效的帮助，但是口译教学界和研究界鲜有这方面的尝试。选文是对面向教学的口译语料库建设进行探讨的一次成功尝试。选文认为面向教学的口译语料库建设是实现 IT 技术与口译课程整合的一种有效形式，既能够为教师提供一个调用方便的教学资源库，也能够为学生提供一个课后自主学习的资源库。选文从口译教学的技能性、实践性和仿真性特点出发说明面向教学的口译语料库建设的作用、意义及宽广前景，并探讨口译教学语料库建设的主要环节和步骤（包括语料收集、语料整理、语料标注、技术处理等）。与其他类型语料库不同的是，口译教学语料库的建设要特别注意材料的现场性、提取的便利性、语料存储的多媒体性等特点。选文最后还结合某高级翻译学院与某省级科技公司横向合作开发计算机辅助口译教学训练系统的实际案例，总结了口译教学语料库建设的实践经验，并探讨了口译教学语料库建设的技术细节。对面向教学的口译语料库建设的研究让我们看到了口译教学语料库对于口译教学、口译研究和口译实践而言都极具切实意义，有很强的可操作性，具有广阔的开发应用前景。

导言

口译教学目前在国内方兴未艾。自 2004 年上海外国语大学高级翻译学院在外国语言文学一级学科下自主设立了翻译学二级学科——第一次确立了"翻译学"硕士点和博士点的学科地位后，2006 年广东外语外贸大学也获批了"翻译学"博士和硕士学位点。2006 年教育部批准广外大、复旦大学与河北师大三所院校招收翻译专业本科生，2008 年翻译专业本科的招生院校已扩展到 13 所。2007 年国务院学位委员会和教育部批准设立"翻译硕士专业学位"（MTI），15 所院校展开试点招生工作，其中半数以上设有口译专业。至此，在我国高等教育学科中，翻译学已经从一个从属于语言学与应用语言学的三级学科发展成为独立的二级学科，建立起拥有本科、专业硕士、学术型硕士和博士学位的完整培养体系。在此背景下，口译教学中呈现出一系列急需探讨的研究课题，如口译教学的大纲设计、课程设置、教学方法、师资培训、评估体系等。

本文尝试探讨一种口译课程与 IT 技术整合的有效形式——口译教学语料库的建设。关于 IT 技术与外语课程整合的基础性理念和基本实践方法，相关刊物（如《外语电化教学》，2006 年—2008 年多期）曾对此进行了较为系统的探讨（陈坚林，2006；曹进，王灏，2007 等）。因此，本文对此不再赘述，将直入口译教学主题。

一、口译教学的特点

口译教学是指以培养口译能力和译员为目标的教学活动。虽然目前国内的口译课程多在外语院系开设，但口译教学不同于一般外语课程的教学，它有自身的特点。与一般外语课程相比，口译课的不同之处主要体现在以下几个方面。[①]

首先，教学目的不同。就一般外语课程而言，其目的或是提升某个方面的语言技能，如听力课、口语课、阅读课、写作课等，或是提升综合语言能力，如综合英语课等。口译课的教学目的是，提升学生的口译能力以及培养学生从事口译工作的相关素质。其次，教学内容不同。一般外语课程以语言知识学习和语言技能训练为教学内容。口译课程则以口译技能培训为中心，兼顾语言、知识、心理等诸方面能力和素质的提高。最后，教学要求不同。相对于一般外语课程而言，口译课对语言能力（尤其是外语能力）的要求更高，因此它适合在外语专业本科高年级阶段及研究生阶段开设。在非外语专业本科高年级阶段开设口译课时，宜选拔培养语言能力及综合素质较好的学生，或将口译课作为选修课程。

口译教学的特点可以用三"性"来概括，即技能性、实践性、仿真性。

（1）技能性。口译是一种专业技能，无论是正规的连续传译，还是同声传译，其对口译技能的要求都很高。口译教学应以口译技能训练为中心。口译技能教学内容包括以下五个方面：口译听解技能的教学、口译记忆技能的教学（包括口译笔记技能的教学）、口译转换技能的教学、口译表达技能的教学、口译过程精力分配技能的教学（王斌华 2006:9-40）。"技能性"是口译教学的第一个特点，也是对口译教学目标定位的要求。

（2）实践性。口译是一种操作性很强的专业技能。要培养出合格的译员，除了口译技巧的系统教授，还必须以大量的口译实践练习为基础。口译学生要达到一名合格译员的水平，其口译练习量必须达到 800～1000"磁带小时"（tape hour）。因此，"实践性"是口译教学的第二个特点，也是对口译课教学形式的要求。

（3）仿真性。从口译教学的效果来看，口译课的教学语料宜采用"仿真性"材料，最好是原汁原味的口译现场录音、录像。但从目前国内教学材料情况来看，只有部分口译教材配有磁带，而且都是朗读的录音，并非口译现场的录音。此外，不少教材的选材过于陈旧，无法适应时代发展变化的新形势，使学生难以做到学以致用。这些都使口译教学的效果打了不少折扣。"仿真性"是口译教学的第三个特点，也是对口译课教学材料及教学方式的要求。

二、IT 技术与口译课程的整合：口译教学语料库

1. 口译课程的四类模块

根据笔者对国内外口译教学具有代表性大学的口译课程设置的考查，系统的口译课程设置一般包含以下四类模块的课程（王斌华，2006:72）。

（1）基于口译技巧的课程模块（skill-based interpreting course module）

---

① 需要说明的是，如果开展口译课教学的目的是为了提升语言能力，即学界讨论过的"教学翻译"（interpreting as a teaching method），那就另当别论，不在此文的讨论之列。

这一模块的口译课程以教授口译技巧为主要目标,包括连续传译(无稿传译、有原稿但无译稿传译、有原稿及译稿传译等形式),同声传译〔无稿同传、带稿视译(有讲话原稿)、同声传读(有原稿及译稿)等形式〕。

(2) 基于口译专题的课程模块(theme-based interpreting course module)

这一模块的口译课程以各类口译场合常见的口译主题来组织教学,目的是让学生掌握各种口译主题常用的表达,并熟悉相关的主题专业知识。这类课程包括专题口译、政治外交口译、商务口译、法庭口译、传媒口译等。

(3) 基于语言转换的课程模块(language transference-based interpreting course module)

这一模块的口译课程根据不同的口译语言组合来设置,目的是让学生掌握不同语言之间的转换规律,如英汉/汉英口译、法汉/汉法口译、日汉/汉日口译、俄汉/汉俄口译等。

(4) 基于模拟实践的课程模块(practice simulation-based interpreting course module)

这一模块的口译课程一般面向高年级口译学生开设,其目的是通过模拟口译现场,使学生掌握口译现场的实践要领,并为学生进入真实的口译现场作准备。这类口译课程包括口译观摩与欣赏、模拟国际会议口译、口译工作坊等。

2. IT 技术与口译课程的整合

鉴于口译教学必须具备"技能性"、"实践性"和"仿真性"的特点,以上四类模块的口译课程在教学实践中有必要与 IT 技术进行有效整合,这样才能真正从教学内容到教学形式等诸方面实现口译教学的目标。

具体而言,无论是技巧类的口译课程,还是专题类的口译课程,抑或是语言组合类的口译课程,还是模拟实践类的口译课程,其教学语料都应达到以下几点要求:首先,教学语料的内容多样,涵盖各种口译专题。其次,教学语料的形式多样,既要有即兴发言的材料,也要有准备性发言的材料;既要有配备文稿的材料(以便练习带稿口译),也要有不配备文稿的材料(以便练习即席口译)。最后,教学语料难度各异、语速及口音多样,以便不同的教学阶段安排相应的训练内容,并让学生适应如真实口译现场那样不同风格、不同语言背景的发言人的语言。

从目前口译教学现状和相关技术发展水平来看,探索 IT 技术与口译课程整合的一种有效途径是:建设口译教学语料库。

三、口译教学语料库的作用及意义

建设口译教学语料库主要有以下三方面的作用和意义。

1. 对口译教学的作用

首先,对于口译教师来说,口译教学语料库可以发挥"教学资源库"的作用。口译教学语料库的资料多样性、规模大型性、检索便利性等特点能有效解决口译教师教学语料缺乏的难题。其次,对于口译学生来说,口译教学语料库可以起到"学习资源库"的作用,便于学生的自主学习。再次,口译教学语料库还可以发挥"口译考试试题库"的作用,教师可根据多种参数来选择针对不同口译课程的试题素材。另外,教师还可使用口译教学语料库中来自口译课堂的语料进行口译教学研究。

2. 对口译研究的意义

一门科学学科的创立和发展需要一个描写(description)的基础,而在口译研究中目前尚缺乏以系统的描写性数据为基础的成果。对于口译研究来说,口译教学语料库的建立将使大规模的描写性口译研究成为可能。

　　研究结论的得出必须基于可靠的科学基础。总体来说,口译的研究路径有两类:一类是理论推演型研究,其核心是理论性抽象思维和推理;另一类是实证型研究,其核心是数据的收集和处理,方法主要有观察法和实验法。但口译研究面对的一个现实困难是口译语料收集的难度很大。与笔译不同,口译内容只以声音形式存在,而且口译中原语和目标语的呈现都是一次性的。如果不对其进行即时录音或录像,声音稍纵即逝,事后便不可能对口译现场的语料进行回溯式研究。而且,口译现场的录音/录像过程对相关技术及操作要求都比较高,往往需要专业技术人员进行相关操作。以上两个因素导致口译研究者手头往往缺乏可供研究使用的语料。因此在以往的口译研究中,研究往往是基于个人感想、经验总结、主观内省或是语料片断,缺乏系统的描写性研究。大规模口译教学语料库的建立则可望弥补口译研究这一缺陷(Cencini & Aston,2002:47-62;Shlesinger,1998)。

　　3. 对口译实践的意义

　　目前国内针对外语学习的软件开发已呈现蓬勃发展之势,并具有巨大的市场潜力。但据笔者所知,国内尚未研发出针对口译学习者和实践者的口译训练软件。[①] 以口译教学语料库为基础,可以开发出各种不同的口译训练软件,便于口译学习者的自主学习和口译实践者的实际训练。

四、口译教学语料库建设的主要环节

　　口译教学语料库建设的主要环节包括语料收集、语料整理、语料标注、技术处理等。与其他类型语料库不同的是,口译教学语料库要特别注意材料的现场性、提取的便利性、语料存储的多媒体性。下面具体分析各主要环节。

　　1. 语料收集

　　口译教学语料库的语料收集来源主要有三种。

　　(1) 口译现场,指配备了口译的会议、会谈、访谈、演讲等。收集内容包括原语发言、目标语口译以及文稿、会议日程等材料,材料形式为录音/录像和文字。收集材料时,同声传译现场要使用双轨录音,连续传译现场可使用一般的单轨录音。

　　(2) 会议、会谈、访谈、演讲现场,指未配备口译的会议、会谈、访谈、演讲等。具体来源有:会议等现场、互联网络(国际组织网站、国际会议网站、演讲网站等)、影视媒体等。材料形式为现场录音/录像、音频/视频、文字等。

　　(3) 口译课堂。使用口译实验室和语言实验室的相关设备和软件,对口译课堂的训练过程和学生的口译进行录音/录像。这类材料一方面可用于远程教学,另一方面可用于学生的课后学习,还可用做教师进行口译教学研究的素材。

　　2. 语料整理

　　与多数其他语料库不同的是,口译教学语料库的语料整理有其特殊的要求:由于原始语料多为音频/视频形式,因此需要对原始语料进行录音转写(transcription)。转写时除了写出文

---

　　① 在国外,欧盟的口译司已建立了口译远程教学和培训的网站。

字以外,还要注意副语言(paralanguage)的转写和标注。① 口译教学语料库的主体语料应至少具备音频和文字两种形式。

3．语料标注

口译教学语料库的语料标注参数主要有以下几种。

(1) 口译主题:政治、外交、国际关系,经济、贸易,金融、保险,体育、卫生,知识产权,文化、教育,管理,环保,工业、科技、农业,中国文化及中国国情,旅游等。

(2) 口译场合:技术现场口译、科技讲座口译、新闻发布会口译、法庭口译、专题论坛/研讨会口译、导游口译、商务谈判口译、技术谈判口译、外交谈判口译、招商会口译、任职演讲口译、外宾接待口译、人物访谈口译、礼仪祝辞口译等。

(3) 原语语体:叙述、说明、议论等。

(4) 专业难度:专业化、一般化、大众化三个等级。

(5) 语速:快、中、慢三个等级。

(6) 时长及字数:指每段语料的时间长度及总字数。

(7) 来源:参照上文"语料收集来源"进行标注。

4．技术处理

口译教学语料库的技术处理是一个复杂的环节,也是 IT 技术与口译课程进行有效整合的关键环节。这一环节的处理需要与相关技术人员或合作方进行紧密合作。主要合作事项包括:(1) 语料的多媒体技术处理,指语料的多媒体格式处理、噪音处理、相关软件配备等;(2) 双语语料的平行对齐处理;(3) 检索工具的开发。

口译教学语料库的整体建设程序可用下图表示。

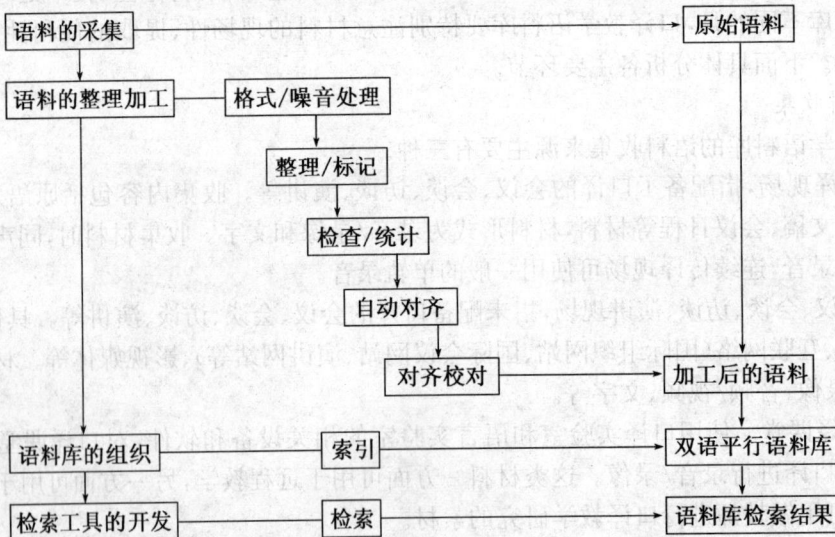

图 1　汉英双语语料库加工流程规范(北京大学计算语言所 2007)

----

① 如何对副语言进行转写和标注,是值得进一步探讨的问题。

五、实践案例:某高级翻译学院的口译教学语料库和口译教学训练系统建设

某高级翻译学院自2006年开始与某省级科技公司开展横向科研项目合作,针对口译专业教学的需要建立口译教学语料库,并在此基础上开发计算机辅助口译教学系统,其目的在于:一方面充分利用多媒体技术,为教师提供一个调用方便的教学资源库;另一方面借助互联网络,为学生提供一个课后自主学习的资源库。下面初步总结这一项目的实践经验,以资借鉴。

1. 口译教学语料库的语料整理和标注

这一项目的目标是结合口译教学的实际构建一个语料完备、功能齐全的口译教学语料库。语料库的语料分类和标注越细越好。虽然在语料的编辑和整理过程中如果分类过细会使工作量增加,但对于教学实际来说,语料分类和标注越细就越实用。比如一篇文章或一段演讲,不是单单把它录入到语料库中,还要针对它的主题、语体、专业领域、难度、来源、语速、字数等信息做出详细标注。这样就可以根据不同口译课程的需要抽取适用的语料,而且也方便不同层次的学生选择适合自己水平的语料进行自主学习。

以下为语料标注示例。

主题	语体	专业领域	难度	来源	语速	字数
环境保护	议论	环境、化学	中级	联合国会议	150 wpm	3 500 w

2. 从口译教学语料库到口译教学训练系统

(1) 设计理念和整体框架

口译教学语料库的构建以口译教学训练系统为应用平台,综合考虑课堂教学、自主学习、考试评估等多种用途,做到一库多用。在课堂教学中,教师可按照多个参数找到自己需要的教学素材进行授课。学生课后的自主学习也可按同样方式找到自己需要的材料。考试时也可以按难度或知识点等多个参数选取合适的考题考查学生的口译能力。

本项目课题组成员在对口译教学实践充分调研的基础上,设计了计算机辅助口译教学训练系统。该系统的具体设计理念如下所述。

① 口译教学理论与计算机技术结合。参考多种口译教学理念,结合 ASP、P2P 等网络技术和大型数据库,使用 Asp. net 或 Visual c# 2008 程序设计平台,使口译教学更为科学化和便捷化。

② 分级与分类训练。我们按照"译前准备→短时记忆→笔记训练→模拟训练→实战演练"的方式设计分级训练,训练材料涵盖不同的专业领域。

③ 因材施教。学生选择适合自己的训练模式和难度系数,教师通过交流版提供在线帮助。

④ 口译教学语料库即时更新。教师以管理员身份进行在线语料更新。

⑤ 动态的学习档案库。系统自动为每个学生建立学习档案,自动记录学生每项测试的结果和教师评估的相关参数。

口译教学训练系统构建的整体框架如下表所示。

系统模块	系统功能	说明
课堂教学	示范口译	模拟同声传译会场,固定设置四路口译位,其余的学生充当听众,可任意选择一路口译位收听。
	多人口译	教师根据需要随意设置口译的人数,也可以把全班都设置为译员。
	教师麦克传译	教师充当发言人,学生听到话音即时口译。
	学生传译	选择一个学生充当发言人,其余学生作为口译员。
	文本视译	发送一篇文本资料,译员根据文本内容口译成指定语言。
	视频传译	播放视频资料,译员根据要求口译成指定语言。
	同声传译	根据播放的音频资料,译员口译成指定语言。
	连续传译	根据播放的音频资料,译员口译成指定语言。与同声传译不同的是,播放的音频资料可根据教师的设置自动停顿,在停顿的间隙时间内学生口译。
	口译录音	译员口译的译语即时录入电脑。
	讲评	教师可随时把学生的译语调出来进行讲评。
自主学习	同声传译	点播音频资料,边听边口译。
	连续传译	点播音频资料,播放完一句停顿,停顿时口译。
	文本视译	打开文本,根据看到的文本内容口译。
	点播录音	对于自己刚刚口译的资料可点播收听。
考试评估	同声传译	边播资料边口译,译语自动保存在电脑中。
	连续传译	逐句播放资料,停顿的时间就是口译的时间。
	分组考试	最多分成不同的四组,分别播放不同的音频资料考试。

(2)口译教学训练系统的具体设计

① 系统功能设计

本系统的主体功能通过三个平台来实现,这三个平台分别为:课堂教学平台、自主训练平台、考试评估平台。

② 系统内容设计

口译训练分为七个阶段进行,训练者必须达到前一个阶段的标准后才能进入下一阶段的训练。

第一阶段——译前准备

译前准备板块按照各类学科知识归类,以树形结构存储各类资料,学生可以自己更新资料,作为今后口译工作的预备材料。教师管理员可随时更新数据库内容。

该板块有词汇记忆和查询子功能。系统对词汇语料进行分类,根据记忆曲线原理辅助学生记忆。电子词典方便学生查阅生词。

第二阶段——短时记忆

短时记忆训练分为跟读、复述和听写等方式。材料按五种难度系数分类,学生根据自己的情况进行无笔记训练。

跟读:系统自动记录保存训练者的跟读内容,给出训练者录音参数,并将语音资料传送给教师。

复述：学生听完材料复述，系统记录语音内容，给出参数报告，如停顿次数、声波图形，并将音频数据保存在数据库中，传送教师评估。

听写：学生设置听写起止点和间隔时间，以手写方式输入听写内容。听写结束后，学生修改经电脑识别的粗稿后提交，由电脑给出评分和听写错误的地方及正确答案。

学生完成短时记忆训练后，系统根据教师评判，给出相应的等级分。学生达到系统设置的等级后，方可进入下一阶段训练。

第三阶段——口译笔记

口译笔记训练分为关键词、数字、专有名词等特定词语、逻辑关系、符号、缩略语笔记训练。

关键词训练：学生听录音记下关键词，完成练习后提交给教师进行评估。

数字训练：学生可以设置数字范围、数字单位、数字情景（如新闻发布会、气象预报）等参数，电脑从语音库中随机提取数字让学生听写，学生将听到的内容填入规定的方框，点击提交，系统自动判断正误并评分。对于错误率较高的数字，系统提示教师进行辅导。

专有名词等特定词语训练：专有名词需要强制记忆。系统储备了各种类型的专有名词、专业词汇、人名等。学生可在数据库中添加新词汇，根据记忆曲线原理训练。

逻辑关系训练：设计关系判断选择题。学生听完材料后，系统以选择题的方式考查学生对该段材料的理解。

符号、缩略语训练：系统提供一些使用频率高的词汇，由学生自己录入常用的符号或缩略语。训练开始后，系统随机读出词汇，每个单词或短语将间隔重复多次。学生在规定时间内以手写方式录入笔记，系统将自动保存笔记记录，同时传送给教师和学生，方便点评和总结。

第四阶段——情景交际互译

对话场景根据对话内容和对话人物转化，并匹配模拟口译现场的动态背景噪音。学生可与练习伙伴扮演口译活动中的各种角色。训练开始后，系统自动录音，以分栏界面给出训练者的语音记录和参考译文。训练者相互评分，教师在线评分。系统按照设置的算法综合处理教师和学生的评分以计算学生最后的分数。

第五阶段——综合训练

本阶段口译训练材料是中英文的现场原语发言。学生可选择不同难度的材料，按照系统设定的停顿进行交替传译的训练。系统记录学生的语音数据，随机抽取片段，供不同教师评分，再计算出最后的分数。

第六阶段——模拟训练

模拟训练使用真实口译现场的视频资料。现场口译可以设置为消音，由学生模拟担当现场译员。学生综合运用口译技能完成训练。模拟训练材料分类分级，内容持续更新。训练成绩由教师评定，最后得分由系统处理后给出。

第七阶段——实战训练

实战训练使用"远程口译服务系统"。利用网络技术，我们将实现远程电视电话会议口译服务，为学生搭建实践平台。

（3）口译教学训练系统的技术实现

① 系统的开发工具

系统外层界面设计可使用网页工具 HTML 编辑器、Drcamweaver 等，素材处理选用

Flash、Photoshop、Voice2editor、"绘声绘影"等多媒体软件，底层开发运用 ASP. net、P2P 或者微软网络程序设计平台 Visual c# 2008，并调用 Sql Sever 2005 的数据库系统。

② 系统拓扑结构

在校园网络中，教师实验室是系统平台的控制中心。控制中心为大型服务器，系统管理和维护的终端可选用一台或多台普通 PC 机；Web 服务器采用 Microsoft IIS 5. 0；数据库使用 SQL Server2005。教师把教学系统安装在控制中心的服务器上，通过 PC 终端对服务器进行管理和维护，控制中心通过交换机连接到校园网络中心，学生和教师通过 Internet 与校园网络中心连接。后台数据库建立后，通过建立 ODBC 数据源可指定数据库驱动程序和数据库路径，为通过数据源建立数据库连接创造条件。ADO（ActiveX Data Object）是一项将数据库访问添加到 Web 页的技术。在 ASP 程序中利用 ADO 内置的 Connection 对象和 Recordset 对象与数据库建立连接，通过执行 SQL 命令，让用户在浏览器端对后台数据库实施添加、删除、修改、查询、更新等操作。

③ 系统模块的初步实现

系统首页采用 Dreamweaver 软件设计，部分功能模块嵌入 Java 语言，学生点击各板块进入训练系统。在该主页上，学生可以在线训练和在线交流，并能查看成绩，接受教师的点评和帮助。互动交流采用 Web 页和 ASP 技术相结合的方法将用户留言添加到数据库中，并动态生成页面供查阅和回复。运用 ASP 技术可以结合 HTML 网页、ASP 语句和 ActiveX 组件建立动态、交互且高效的 Web 服务器应用程序，运用 ADO 技术能够搜索和查找数据库，进行模糊匹配查询。

④ 口译训练板块的实现

口译训练板块采取的主要技术是数据库技术和语音识别技术。对于前者，可以使用 SQL2005 数据库语言，为用户及其属性建表，数据的存储以树形结构为主。语音识别技术目前虽然不够完善，有一定的出错率，但经过我们的试验，基本能够符合口译训练的需求。口译词库的管理在大型数据库的基础上，利用 ADO 技术实现数据库的搜索和查找。模拟训练板块则需要基于 ASP 技术进行远程链接，实现实时会议交流。

⑤ 系统资源更新维护

系统资源由系统管理员及时更新维护，音频、视频和文本材料采用二级树的存储模式。同时，系统资源根据教师和学生反馈的系统使用情况进行改进和升级。

结　语

关于翻译（笔译）及翻译教学语料库建设，翻译研究界和教学界已做出了一定的理论和实践探索，国内外均已建立了一定规模的翻译语料库。但是，口译语料库及口译教学语料库至今在国内外尚未建立，相关理论探讨亦较为鲜见。本文首次尝试探讨了口译教学语料库的作用和意义、口译教学语料库建设的主要环节以及涉及的相关问题，并以国内某高级翻译学院的口译教学语料库和口译教学训练系统建设作为实践案例，初步总结了相关经验。希望本文能为相关教学实践的研究和探讨起到抛砖引玉的作用。

【延伸阅读】

1. Baker，M. Corpus linguistics and translation studies：Implications and applications. Baker，M.，Francis，G. and Tögnini-Bonnelli，E.（eds.）*Text and technology：In honor of John Sinclair*. Amesterdam/John Benjamins，1993：233-250.

2. 陈振东,李澜.基于网络和语料库的口译教学策略探索.外语电化教学.2009(125)：9-13.

3. 胡开宝,陶庆.汉英会议口译语料库的创建与应用研究.中国翻译.2009(5):49-56.

4. 李文中.语料库、学习者语料库与外语教学.外语界.1999(1):35-41.

5. 张威.口译语料库的开发与建设:理论与实践的若干问题.中国翻译.2009(3):54-58.

【问题与思考】

1. 自以色列学者施莱辛格提出运用语料库研究口译的观点后,基于语料库的口译理论研究取得了哪些进展?

2. 口译语料库与笔译语料库有什么不同之处? 口译语料库的类型有哪些?

3. 国内外现存的口译语料库主要有哪些? 请分别给出评介。

4. 语料库口译研究的前景如何?

5. 简单论述口译语料库建立时应充分注意哪些方面的问题以及建成后对于口译教学、口译实践和口译研究的意义。

第十章　基于质量评估的口译理论研究

导　论

随着口译活动逐渐渗透到社会生活的各个层面,人们对口译质量的要求也越来越高,由此,各种口译质量评估手段也相应地得到应用。在世界范围内看,口译活动平民化、口译人员职业化是第二次世界大战后随着科技进步和全球经济一体化的进程才普及开来的。在此之前,人们对口译员及口译活动的评估基本上以个案分析为主。口译活动成为一个行业以后,如何专业地、客观地评估口译活动和译员素质就成为业内专家必须要解决的一个课题。从20世纪70年代末至今,有不少国内外的专家学者越来越多地重视从评价分析口译过程、口译成果和口译使用者的角度进行口译质量评估,力图构建口译质量评价体系(蔡小红,方凡泉,2003),分析口译质量影响因素的框架(王东志,王立弟,2007),探讨口译市场管理制度与规范(冯建中,2005)。他们的研究成果无论是对职业口译还是教学口译都产生了积极的作用。尽管如此,随着近些年来国际间的交流日趋频繁,公众对口译质量的期望越来越高,要求也越来越严格。然而,目前我们建立的评估手段却仍不能完全满足社会的需要,相关质量评估研究还相对滞后,尤其是缺乏足够的实证研究。

评价口译质量,首先应该确定口译标准。关于口译标准的研究目前主要有两个方向,一个方向侧重理论研究,探讨口译应该追求的目标和译员工作的原则;另一个方向更贴近应用,提出如何对口译活动和译员素质进行定性或定量的统计评估。

在口译标准的理论研究方面,有国内学者用"准"、"顺"、"快"作为口译质量评估的标准,相类似的还有"准确、迅速、传神","达意、准确、通顺"等。这些标准虽然符合口译的特点,但由于标准太宽泛而难以掌握,实际操作性不强。国内外还有很多学者从译员自身的口译能力角度对口译标准进行了探索。塞莱斯科维奇与勒代雷创立的"释意模式"以"释意准确"为标准,提出成功的翻译追求的是语篇意义的对等,其中囊括了认知知识的对等及情感知识的对等。而吉尔最基本的一个观点则是认为没有绝对的质量标准,因为口译活动牵涉许多不同的因素和方面,而它们都可能对口译活动,包括口译质量,产生不同程度的影响。

在口译标准的应用研究方面比较有影响力的观点有以下几个:刘和平(2001)的"口译测试评估表"分别从反应速度、理解、表达和心理素质等四个方面,采用扣分的方法对学员的口译水平进行评估;厦门大学陈菁等人则采用考核打分的模式分别从信息传递、语言使用、译文表述以及综合素质对译员的口译能力加以评定(肖晓燕,2003);台湾辅仁大学的杨承淑(2005)从忠实、表达、语言以及时间控制等四方面设定了一个"量化"和"质化"的"口译考试评分表";鲍刚(2005)的"口译竞赛评估表"从内容、隐含意义、数字、专有名词和头衔、译语表达以及沟通效果等六个方面,采用定性的方法对口译质量进行评估。

从本质上说口译是一种社会性活动,各种交际因素相互影响,共同决定口译交际效果。口译质量评估是对口译活动质量高低、优劣的衡量。研究口译质量与效果,应从口译性质、译员素质、评估定义、质量标准、口译任务、听众期待、评估操作指标等方面进行全方位的专业研究(蔡小红,2002)。刘建珠(2008:46)认为,口译评估主体多元化、评估内容多元化、评估标准多元化、评估方式和评估手段多元化,它们共同构成了一个多元化的质量评估体系。由于口译活动的好坏与成败最终还要取决于服务对象的认可和满意程度,因此,要对具体口译活动的效果做出较为客观而可信的判断,口译使用者的态度与评价是一个不可或缺的因素,也只有将口译使用者这一因素纳入口译质量评估的整体结构中,口译质量评估才有可能更真实更完整地反映口译实际活动效果(张威,2010:43)。

基于质量评估的口译理论研究无疑非常有助于促进口译质量评估市场的规范化、口译评估体系的科学化,从而有效推动口译质量的提高。总体而言,目前尽管从总量上看关于口译质量评估的研究已经不少了,有宏观、有微观,有理论、有实证,有定性的、有量化的,但其研究主要集中在规约性研究,鲜有实证性研究,发展不尽平衡。除了实证研究依然薄弱之外,在未来的发展方面,借鉴其他学科的最新成果来拓宽口译质量的评估视野进而不断完善其理论也是口译质量评估研究急需努力的一个发展方向。

选 文

选文一 Book Review of *Testing and Assessment in Translation and Interpreting Studies*

Roda P. Roberts

导 言

翻译的测试与评估实际上是针对翻译潜能认定进行的,就是用于预测一个人是否具备成为一名合格甚至优秀翻译人才的基本素质和天赋的潜在能力,翻译专业和培训机构的入学考试就属于潜能测试。与一般的语言测试研究相比较,翻译测试的研究还有待深入。测试方法的不科学、不规范、不合理严重影响了测试的有效性、准确性和可靠性。克劳迪娅·安吉莱莉参与编写的《翻译研究测试与评估》一书强调了测试与评估对翻译(包括口译)的重要性,对译员在多种工作环境下作为语言调解者的角色职能及口笔译技能评估做了研究分析,并就测试所应采取的模式和具体内涵等进行了探讨。无论对口译还是笔译研究,对译员还是对学员,该书都极具指导作用和参考价值。

While the notion of quality is central to both translation and interpreting and assessment and testing play a major role in both fields, there is a lack of empirical research on translator and interpreter competence and on assessing processes and products for different purposes. This is clearly demonstrated by Angelelli and Jacobson in their introduction to this collective volume. This work, which grew out of a two-year series of conferences on testing and assessment during the American Translators Association Research Forum, is intended to stimulate discussion, among those engaged in testing, on issues that are shaping measurement approaches in translation and interpreting. The collection of papers explores these issues across languages and settings, since one of the major challenges of testing in these fields is that it is used for different languages (not only spoken, but also signed) for vastly different purposes (ranging from formative assessment in an educational setting to professional certification and to determining the quality of localization products in industry).

The volume is divided into three parts. The first, comprising two papers by the editors, focuses on the theoretical underpinnings of translation and interpreting assessment and their relation to construct definition and rubric development. This part sets the tone for the rest of the volume.

Claudia Angelelli's article "Using a rubric to assess translation ability," which begins by listing key questions that must be considered prior to the development of translation certification tests, examines relevant theoretical literature to develop the construct of translation ability. After identifying and detailing four subcomponents of the construct—linguistic competence, textual competence, pragmatic competence and strategic competence—she presents a five-scale rubric, based on those subcomponents, which can be used to score a translation holistically. While her proposed rubric has not yet been used to assess a translation certification test, it certainly presents a more systematic approach to measuring translation competence than any that is used today.

What Angelelli has done for translation testing, Holly Jacobson— in "Measuring interactional competence in interpreting"—does for assessment of community interpreting in health-care settings. After pointing out the limitations of the conduit model of interpreting, with its narrow focus on accurate reproduction of the words of the original, Jacobson emphasizes the need for interactional (or discursive) competence on the part of interpreters. Using pertinent studies from interactional sociolinguistics and conversation analysis as well as from interpreting studies based on interactional competence, she outlines the various elements that can comprise interactional competence. Then, she focuses on two traits of interactional competence: use and transfer of contextualization cues and discourse management. After deriving the sub-competencies related to these two traits, she provides sample analytic rubrics for assessing each of them. Jacobson does not provide a comprehensive rubric for assessing interpreter performance, which, she claims, should include not only other areas of interaction, but also other areas of competence, including the lexico-semantic one. She does, however, outline step by step the process of developing rubrics, which should be of great practical use to those readers unfamiliar with this method of assessment.

Part II of the volume consists of five articles that discuss the results of empirical research implementing quasi-experimental and non-experimental methods and tools for evaluating translation (three articles), interpreting (one article) and localization (one article).

Eyckmans, Anckaert and Segers have developed a norm-referenced method of translation assessment, based on the "item" concept of language testing theory and practices. They designed an experiment that allowed them to compare their normreferenced method (called the Calibration of Dichotomous Items-method, which assesses text segments identified as having discriminatory power) with two other, more traditional methods of translation assessment: holistic (global-intuitive) and analytic (based on a taxonomy of errors). University translation students at different levels were asked to translate a non-specialized text under the same conditions. The translations were then evaluated by three teams, each using one of the three methods presented above. The results proved the researchers' three hypotheses: inter-rater reliability between the graders was the weakest in the case of the holistic evaluation method; inter-rater reliability between the graders who used the analytic method fell between that of the holistic method and that of the CDI-method; and finally, neither the holistic nor the analytic method was able to discriminate sufficiently between the participants' performances, while the CDI-method allowed sufficient discrimination. While the CDI-method is time-consuming and requires a basic understanding of psychometrics as well as constant monitoring to build up a bank of test items, the authors conclude that its discriminatory power makes it suitable for use in high-stake situations, i. e. for summative evaluation.

Formative assessment is the focus of Mira Kim's "Meaning-oriented assessment of translation." She demonstrates the application of criteria grounded in meaning analysis proposed by Systemic Functional Grammar and Skopos theory and functionalism in translation studies to the assessment of student translations in an English-Korean translation course in Australia. These criteria were devised to address the limitations of the NAATI assessment criteria as a formative tool, but remain within the framework of the NAATI criteria that are used for summative evaluation at the end of the course. In the meaning-oriented assessment criteria, translation errors are classified as minor (simple errors that have little impact on the delivery of ST meaning) or major (those that affect one or more aspects of meaning: experiential, logical, interpersonal or textual). These criteria, which allow the translation assessor to focus not only on words and grammar but also on translation as text, provide both an efficient tool for translation assessment and a formative tool designed to help students analyze their own translation problems and develop their own translation strategies. Quantitative and qualitative data used to evaluate this tool show that it is pedagogically efficient.

Like Kim, Baer and Bystrova-McIntyre are also interested in developing formative assessment tools that focus on translation as text. More specifically, on the basis of Russian and English comparable corpora, they examine the feasibility of an assessment tool that treats three features of textual cohesion: punctuation, sentencing and paragraphing. Using punctuation to illustrate their method, they show how they started with a comparative quantitative analysis of punctuation marks in English and Russian and then tried to pinpoint why the use of certain punctuation marks is statistically greater in Russian than in English. Once the analysis of statistical discrepancies was accomplished, they devised a sample assessment instrument for marking errors in the use of punctuation.

With Elisabet Tiselius's article "Revisiting Carroll's scales," we move from translation to interpreting and from new assessment tools to one previously used. John Carroll's scales of intelligibility and informativeness, originally devised to assess machine translation, have been used in the past to evaluate interpreting, although their applicability to interpreting has been questioned. Tiselius, who wanted to see if application of these scales to interpreter performance produced valid results and if the scales could be used by non-experts to assess interpreting, adapted Carroll's scales by reducing the 9-point scales to 6-point scales and by replacing references to written text and translation by references to spoken language and interpreting. She then set up a rather elaborate experiment in which she had six interpreters and six non-interpreters grade the interpretation of nine interpreters with three different levels of experience, using the adapted scales after receiving training in their use. The results demonstrated that the adapted scales were valid for measuring intelligibility and informativeness and that they could be used by non-experts. However, Tiselius herself points out that the size of this study limits the possibility of drawing general conclusions.

Keiran Dunne, in the article "Assessing software localization: for a valid approach," examines methods and tools currently used in localization quality assessment, which he considers from two perspectives: that of the vendor/practitioner and that of the customer. The former, who focuses on linguistic, cosmetic and functional testing, tends to evaluate the relative degree of formal equivalence of various characteristics of source and localized software products. The latter, on the other hand, tends to assess the quality of software localization in terms of expectations and needs, which are usually not specified at the start. In other words, in current outsourced localization projects, participants and client reviewers do not share the same operational definition of quality. This and several other problems in localization quality assessment are highlighted in this article, which proposes some solutions and lays the groundwork for a critical dialogue on this rather neglected issue.

Finally, Part III of this volume presents four case studies of broader scope, examining admissions tests for interpreter education programs, on the one hand, and professional certification tests, on the other. For each type of test, both spoken language interpreting and sign language interpreting are examined.

The first of the two articles on admissions tests, by Timarova and Ungoed-Thomas, investigates the predictive validity of admissions tests, on the basis of candidate records provided by an interpreting school. The authors want to find out whether such tests help to reliably select candidates with a high potential to successfully complete the program. By applying multiple linear and logistic regression analyses, they conclude that this particular admissions test is a poor predictor of success in the program and they call for other admissions tests to be assessed for their predictive validity. What this article highlights is the importance of identifying what elements the admissions test is intended to evaluate (linguistic skills? general knowledge? personality? motivation? correspondence between the school's teaching and the candidate's learning style?) and of choosing test exercises which, although not overtly bearing resemblance to interpreting, may be better suited to predict success in an interpreting program.

Karen Bontempo and Jemina Napier, discussing "Program admission testing of signed language interpreters," also point out the ambiguity underlying admissions tests, since such tests may assess a person's capacity for interpreting or learning interpreting, with a view to predicting their general suitability for the profession (i. e. screening for aptitude), or they may evaluate existing sub-sets of skills, knowledge and abilities required for the task of interpreting (i. e. screening for ability), or again they may incorporate a mix of both. In an attempt to avoid such ambiguity, the researchers first conducted a survey among accredited sign language interpreters in Australia, for the purpose of identifying factors that may be potential predictors of successful interpreting performance and obtaining participants' views on interpreter education programs in Australia. The survey results were used to develop a screening test, inspired to a large extent by admissions tests for spoken-language interpreting programs, which was then piloted with applicants to an Auslan interpreter education program. Finally, a comparison was made between the screening test results of those admitted on the basis of this test and their end-of-program results. The findings showed that the admissions test results from the small-scale pilot study were not predictive of final examination performance. The researchers suggest the need for greater emphasis on objectively assessing aptitude in sign language interpreter program screening via tools measuring cognitive and affective factors rather than on performance on a series of tasks that may be variants of interpreting skills per se.

Vermeiren, Van Gucht and De Bontridder present the certification exam for social interpreters (i. e. interpreters working in the areas of "public and social services and public and social care") in Flanders, Belgium. This certification exam falls under the jurisdiction of the COC (Central Support Cell for Social interpreting and translation), which was founded in 2004 to support the relatively new sector of social interpreting and was responsible for developing both a training program and a certification exam. The certification exam, which focuses on performance assessment rather than knowledge assessment, consists of the following tests: Dutch proficiency, other-language proficiency, reproduction, transfer and role play. Each of these is described and the scoring system for each is explained. This article goes beyond the certification exam proper to discuss certifying authorities, graders and the professional standard for social interpreters, as well the COC's training program—in short, all of the elements that enter into the certification procedure.

The final article of this volume, Russell and Malcolm's "Assessing ASL-English Interpreters," provides an overview of the development of a national certification system for American Sign Language-English interpreters in Canada by the Association of Visual Language Interpreters of Canada. The mission of the Canadian Evaluation System (or CES) is "to accredit interpreters who demonstrate competencies that reflect the diverse communication preferences of Deaf and hearing Canadians." While this goal has remained constant throughout the history of certifying ASL interpreters in Canada, the testing model itself has undergone some changes since its inception in 1990. What began as a two-part test (a written test of knowledge and a test of interpretation) has now evolved into a four-step process, which begins with the written test and is followed in turn by the Test of Interpretation Preparation Workshops, the Test of Interpretation, and finally, Certificate Maintenance. In other words, testing, training, and professional development are now envisioned as a whole. Not only is the Canadian testing model, including its rating processes, presented in detail, but it is also compared with those used in the United States and Australia.

A number of themes run throughout this volume: the importance of testing and assessment in translation and interpreting; the lack of theory-based empirical research in this area; the usefulness of borrowing and adapting assessment methods applied in other fields such as language learning; the need to align the assessment method with the purpose of the assessment; and the importance of assessing translation and interpreting as text/discourse rather than as a string of words/ sentences. The articles may include different approaches to testing (e. g. theoretical, empirical, descriptive), describe different test purposes (e. g. admissions or certification), and discuss different evaluation functions (e. g. formative or summative). But they all share a common purpose: that of initiating dialogue between theory and practice and improving the assessment methods currently used. And they are generally written in a style accessible to all those who should be interested in the topic of testing and assessment in translation and interpreting studies: professors of translation and interpreting, professional translators and interpreters, even students of translation and interpreting. This work is a must-read for all those interested in the professionalization of translation and interpreting.

选文二 论口译的质量与效果评估

蔡小红 方凡泉

导 言

　　口译质量评估是对口译活动质量高低、优劣的衡量。随着口译的广泛使用,对口译质量的评估研究也在不断地深入。但由于口译是一种社会性活动,各种交际因素相互制约、彼此影响,共同决定着口译质量和口译交际效果,因此,口译质量评估目前尚无一套用之四海而皆准的评估方法或标准,往往因口译活动参与者、口译使用者、口译内容、口译形式和评估目的的不同而需要采用不同标准或权重比例的评估方式与方法。选文通过对口译质量评估涉及诸如口译工作的本质、各种不同要求的任务、口译译员的主观努力、原语发言人与现场听众的客观反馈以及评估的目的等诸多因素进行定义定位,深入探讨了这些因素在口译活动中的相互关系,并由此提出影响口译质量及其评估诸因素关系的理论假设,勾画出影响口译质量诸因素关系图和影响口译质量评估诸因素关系图,为口译质量评估研究提供了全面、客观的参数。

1. 引言

　　口译的质量评估一直是困扰译界的一大难题。随着我国对外交流的迅猛发展,口译活动日益职业化。人们对口译实践、培训质量的科学界定与客观评估的要求越来越迫切。然而,无论是长期占主流地位的"准、顺、快"传统标准(1987 年由李越然在《翻译通讯》正式提出),还是近几年提倡的掌握翻译"灵活度"[详见钱伟《口译的灵活度》,1996(4):24]的新标准,围绕质量问题的讨论大都局限于从经验出发的思辨性、规约性的观点,不仅缺乏系统严谨的理论根据,更无客观的实证数据支撑。在国外,对口译质量标准的探讨由来已久。近年来不少专家学者借助跨学科的相关论述拓展了研究的领域,探索出一些新的理论模式和评估办法。可惜大都带不同程度的片面性,不是忽视译员的主观努力与口译服务对象对效果的反馈两者之间的相互关系,便是无视各种口译任务的不同要求。因此迄今为止,还没有一套完整系统的质量标准与评估方法足以提供令人信服的结果。

　　我们认为,口译质量评估涉及多方面的因素,诸如口译工作的本质、各种任务的不同要求、口译译员的主观努力、原语发言人与现场听众的客观反馈以及评估的目的等。以往的研究未能找到令人信服的质量标准,就是因为未能通盘考虑以上因素。本文拟通过对上述因素进行定义定位,以便进一步探讨它们在口译活动中的相互关系,为质量评估的研究提供尽可能全面、客观的参数。

2. 口译性质与口译评估的定义

2.1 口译性质的定义

口译作为跨文化的交际活动,其实质不是单纯地实现语际之间的语码转换,而是要忠实地转达异语双方的交际意图。因为一来语篇作为传达信息的载体,是"任何不完全受句子语法约束的,在一定语境下表示完整语义的自然语言"(胡壮麟,1994),二来语篇作为特定情景下的交际事例,附着明确的交际动机,是"交际互动过程的语言体现"(Nord,1991:12),所以"语言交际总是以语篇的形式出现"(Wilss,1982:112)。法国释意派在分析了字、词、句、话语等级的翻译后断定,前几个等级仅仅是语言转码翻译,只有充分体现讲话人的"欲言"的话语语篇才是交际翻译(Lederer,1994)。语篇分析理论则有更进一步阐述,认为既然意义是通过语言结构得以实现,那么翻译的内容、信息、概念的对等就只能建立在语篇和交际的层面上,且译员工作借助的对象不仅是语言或言内因素,还得依赖包括情景语境和文化语境在内的言外因素(张美芳、黄国文,2002)。简而言之,作为沟通跨文化交际的桥梁,口译活动只有在话语语篇这个层面展开,才能完成其本质性任务,实现其终极目标。

2.2 口译质量评估的定义

质量评估的定义:口译质量评估一般指对口译活动质量高低、优劣的衡量。然而构成翻译质量的成分很复杂,既指语产出、传输的质量,也包括现场的公众反映及由此达成的交际效果。且不同的评估目的、评估模式还会改变评估的成分比例,使"翻译质量"或专指译员的翻译能力,或倾向公众对服务的反馈,或两者兼备。

质量评估的种类:口译质量评估有成果评估与过程评估两大类型。口译成果评估包括质量评定与效果测量,前者仅指译员的译语质量,后者为口译服务对象对口译效果的客观反馈。口译过程评估主要是对译员在工作中,心理语言运用、心理因素影响、认知知识活动的了解,例如译员掌握职业技能、运用技能、发展技能、认知负荷协调等情况。当今译界不少专家学者(例如法国的丹尼尔·吉尔,美国的朱得安·霍斯)认为,要想客观评价口译成果,必须借助口译过程评估。

质量评估的标准:综合古今中外涉及口译质量评估的标准,大致可以归纳有以下几个基本指标。

(1) 可信度:主要指译文信息转达完整、准确,忠实于原文内容;

(2) 可接受度:主要指译语表达层次分明、逻辑清晰、确切到位,遣词造句贴切,发音清楚,听众容易接受;

(3) 简明度:主要指发言人的风格、说话方式能在译语中准确反映,译语简洁明了;

(4) 多样性:主要指译员适应不同口音,明悉不同题材,了解不同专题的发言,并表达自如清晰的程度;

(5) 迅捷度:主要指译员能在很短的时间内应付难题,即时转达交流双方的信息,能综合发言人的思路,概述或简译原语发言;

(6) 技术性:主要指译员必须掌握的相关技巧,诸如职业举止、交流艺术、应急策略、洞悉跨文化差异、控制交际场面等,以及译员必须熟悉的有关设备的技术,如麦克风的运用、不同语言的声道的调节、耳机的应用等。

众多的实证研究结果(如 Bühler Hildegund,1986;Kurz Ingrid,1989,1992;Lydia Meak de Trieste,1990;Gile Daniel,1990;Kopczynski A.,1992;Shlesinger M.,1992;AIIC,1992;何慧玲,1998;等)表明,在以上六个标准中,最重要的是信息的"可信度"。而最具争议的恐怕是"可接受度"。因为此标准不仅涉及译员抓住语篇整体意义结构,既能避免原语干扰,又能以译语还原原语语篇结构的能力,还关乎译员明晰不同的口译任务,针对不同的服务对象、采取不同的翻译策略,因此有专家(如 Roda P. Roberts,1984;Jean Delisle,1992;Christiane Nord,1991;Reiss et Vermeer,1984;Jean Vienne,1998)又把此项标准定为译员的翻译能力指标(traductionnelle)。如果说前一能力主要指译员的翻译水平,后一能力侧重的应该是其交际水平。"多样性"复杂之处在于,任务不同,不仅指发言题材、主题相异,更包括服务对象、服务方式、服务情景迥然。比如交际口译与会议口译就属于两类差别较大的口译任务。因此除译员的个人努力外,现场服务对象的反馈、交际效果的实现程度也应纳入测定评估之中。实践证明,翻译的成果往往只有满足听众的期待才被认可。

然而应当清楚的是,口译任务要求虽不尽相同,但可观察的变量却离不开以上六个标准,只是指标的权重会随着具体情况发生变化而已。

质量评估的目的:Moser-Mercer Barbara(1996:45)认为,倘若把口译当做艺术品来鉴赏,就得像评价参赛作品一样;如果当它为艺术工作,就得对它进行艺术批评;可要是当它为产品,就得重视在特定外部条件下它的产量与质量。如此类推,评估目的诚然是评估模式的决定因素。集大部分专家学者之所见,口译质量评估的目的可归为三类:

(1)为口译培训所用;

(2)为职业实践服务,包括雇用单位对口译任务满意度测定、译员职业晋升、竞争筛选、等级评定等;

(3)以口译研究为目的。

很显然,各类评估目的肯定有不同的侧重点,也就会借助不同的标准权重比例和评估方式。例如培训阶段应当同时重视对口译成果与过程的评估,实践中考查口译工作的满意度应主要收集服务对象的反馈,而进行专门研究时则要侧重对过程的观察与分析等。

质量评估的模式:Moser-Mercer Barbara(47)把评估模式分为评估(evaluation)、测量或衡量(measurement)、评价判断三个类型(assessment)。要想了解自然状态下(或现场口译)口译的质量,需借助评估手段;以科研为目的,分析语言实验室条件下的口译成品,需使用测量手段;而在教学培训中,要跟踪学员对口译技能的掌握情况则要依靠判断评价的手段。

迄今为止,无论哪种类型,口译质量评估模式一般都采取定性分析与量化数据互补的方式:量化旨在采集各指标的具体数据,以提供确凿的例证;定性则着重分析现象,定出质量等级。模式有自我评估与他人评估之分。在中国,较具代表性的有胡庚申(1993:101-108)探讨的口译效果评价法:现场观察法、自我鉴定法、采访征询法、记录检测法、回译对比法、模拟实验法、考核评定法和"信任"模型法;鲍刚(1998:249-263)拟订的"口译竞赛评估表";厦门大学外文系提出的考核打分模式(林郁如,Leong Ko,1996:3-4);台湾辅仁大学的杨承淑提出的"扣分法"(2000:160)等。在国外,有巴黎高等翻译学校的考核评定模式、里昂第二大学D. Gile 的公式推算模式、比利时 Maric-Haps 职业翻译学院 Hugo Marquant 以自我评估为主的"教学评估范式"模式(Modéle de la pédagogie par l' exemple),还有各国官方机构运用的标准考核模式(如英国的 NVQS,澳大利亚的 TRIST,加拿大、日本的官方标准考核等)。到目前为止,中外各大组织机构、职业翻译学校进行职业筛选、晋升等评估时,多借助以专家学者组成的评委,采取考核评定的模式。应当指出的是,较之其他职业活动,口译显得更加可能并且非常必要让译员进行自我评估。个中道理很简单,其一,译员作为异语交际的媒介,可谓唯一洞悉双方意图者,对交流过程的顺畅、阻滞及其原因应当非常敏感,话语产出时的自我监控体系、交际者的现场反馈都给译员提供了自我评估的优越条件。其二,自觉进行自我评估是译员圆满完成任务、提高口译能力的重要因素。口译现场情况复杂,任务经常随着语境、专题、听众等各种因素起变化,译员只有及时发现问题,不断调整策略,调动相关知识,才能适应现场交际的需要。一场口译任务中,总有得意的佳作和遗憾的败笔,只有译员最了解其中的缘由,如能及时进行自我评估,总结经验,定能从中得益。当然,自我评估还应当有明确的技能意识、质量标准、职业规范作指导。

3．口译任务

口译任务各异,要求自然也不尽相同,因此往往导致评估标准权重比例的改变。

3.1　交流方式的差异

例如从同声传译与交替传译的信息传送方式的差异上分析,同为会议翻译,同传的使用一则为节约时间,二则为缩短发言者与听众的时间、空间交际距离,便于交际信息及时、迅速传达。因此与交传相比,同传更注重传译的"迅捷度"。迅捷不仅指话语启动与语速,更关乎传译是否能紧跟原语意层或意段。而交传由于要不时中断发言人的讲话,明显占据交际的时间与空间,译员因要以发言人身份现身发布译语而成为听众聚焦的目标,因此"简明度"、"技术性"中的演讲艺术、个人的职业形象、举止风度更受关注。

3.2　交流程式的差异

交际翻译与会议翻译的不同之处在于,交际翻译呈双向或多向交流程式,亦即对话式交流,翻译时译员必须频繁交换使用两种工作语言,但译员可以适时控制交际场面。比如要求讲话人重复话语、解释难点、放慢语速,甚至转换话题。交际翻译中异语交流的双方可能存在着很大的背景差异、语言变体(如语音、用词等)和语域(如外交辞令、俗词俚语、日常用语等)差异。会议翻译则多为单向交流程式,或称独白演讲式交流。与其他西方语言不同,中外会议交流也经常要借助 A、B 两种工作语言,只是每种工作语言都以长篇演讲的形式发布。会议翻译时译员无法控制交际场面,只能紧紧跟随发言人的语速、思路与话题,所幸的是这样的单向交流使交际的背景差异、语言变体差异及语域差异降到最低,因为听众只能听发言人演讲,直接加入发言交流的机会很少。从交际理论分析,交传中的对话使异语交流双方频繁地转换角色,从听话人变为讲话人,再从后者还原为前者。译员不但要听懂两方的话语、揣摩其交际意图、洞悉其可分享与不可分享的背景知识,还要不时地使用两种语言适时实现适度的交际效果,否则一方的话语传输受阻或错误,交际即被打断或误导,且后果即时显现。幸好译员可以现场观察双方的表情反应,能及时采取补救的办法。而会议翻译时译员须适应的主要是演讲人一方,其语音、讲话语气、风格、语域范畴、交际意图等。译员因各种原因漏译的信息可以稍后补充，不致中断现场交际，但也可能因无法察觉两方的互动关系而失去纠错的机会。由于两种交流程式的差异，导致交际方式、交际期待等方面产生区别，致使任务要求不尽相同，由此可见一斑。

3.3 交际语境的差异

另外，交际语境的差异也会给口译任务提出不同的要求。例如日常交际应以"联谊沟通、一般交往"为典型特征，语言表达的特点主要表现为人际间的交流方式、日常性的话题内容、口语化的语体表达、及时性的沟通反馈。科技翻译则以"展示成果、研讨学术"为专业交流特征，语言特点表现为语体上口语与笔语结合、语气上论证与商榷交织、语式上宣讲与演示互补、词语上行话与术语贯通。而谈判交涉则以"据理力争、慎言善辩"为典型，语言特点表现为交涉注重攻心斗智、言语讲求策略技巧、措辞突出准确规范、行文强调合理合法（胡庚申，2000）。如果违反语境要求，交际就会产生误差。例如闲聊时长篇大论、引经据典，容易使对方反感，认为是在卖弄学识；研讨会上太多使用生活用语让人觉得非职业化；太讲求言语策略，太咬文嚼字又有故弄玄虚，治学不严之嫌；谈判桌前或学究气十足，或言语唐突、咄咄逼人，都会导致交际失败。作为译员，特别要注意的是翻译时语境经常会转换，尤其是交际翻译：对话可能从见面寒暄开始，以问候聊天拉近关系，接着展开观点性的陈述，进而进行学科探讨，得悉双方研究重点后转向合作意向谈判，经各自申述，利益分析，力争双赢，达成初步共识，最后就要遵从规范，讲究措辞，慎重地拟订会谈结果与合作决定。译员必须紧跟整个过程，且每一阶段的翻译都要准确无误，必要时还要适当调整原语中不符合语境的话语，以保证整体交流的顺利进行。

3.4 交际语篇结构的差异

语境的差异往往使交际语篇的结构发生很大的变化，而既然翻译是在语篇层面展开的，译员必须对讲话人在不同的语境中采取不同的交际策略，对不同的语篇结构反应敏捷，并能迅速决定与原语语篇对应的译语语篇。

上文口译性质定义中强调了语篇的一大重要因素便是特定语境中的交际功能，语篇主要有下列功能：叙述、描写、说明、指示、制约等，各功能借助独特的言语体以适应特定语境的交际需要。叙述、描写功能倚重叙述性言语体，说明功能突出论述性言语体，指示功能以介绍性言语体为主，如此等等。而"不同功能的语篇中，信息单元的价值取向是不同的。叙述功能语篇的信息单元总是与动作、活动有关，描写功能语篇的信息单元与性质、属性有关，指示功能语篇的信息单元常常是一个个步骤或事实，说明功能和制约功能语篇的信息单元大都是一个个的概念和事实"（李运兴，2001：85）。当然，在实际交流中，语篇常常呈现为多种交际功能的集合体，或称混合体，"因此，对语篇功能的判断的基准往往是看哪一种功能在起主导作用，哪些只体现在局部片段，只起着辅助作用，并据此认定其（讲话人）交际意图和功能并制订翻译策略和确定具体的翻译方法。"（pp. 63-64）也就是说，"作为译者，他不仅要能根据原语语篇的特征识别其功能，还必须保证译语语篇充分实现翻译目的所要求达到的功能。就是说，他必须具备根据译语语篇所处的交际环境有效地运用译语的语篇构建手段和技巧的能力。"（p. 85）比如科技类语篇侧重说明功能，以介绍性与论述性言语体为主，一般言简意赅、信息明示、重点突出、逻辑清楚、用词精确，故术语使用较多；司法翻译时常借重制约功能，译员必须遵从严格的、约定俗成的语篇格式以及专门术语;外交类语篇虽汇集各种功能,但主要还是以说明功能为主,且言语考究、表达复杂、信息时隐时现等。关于语篇结构,李运兴认为:语篇结构是某一特定文化中组句成篇的特定方式,是一种约定俗成、相对稳定的语言使用习惯,是文化因素在语言运用过程中长期积淀的结果。翻译就是"由原语语篇诱发的译语语篇生成过程"(Neubert,1992)。译文语篇的生成必须符合译语语篇的规范及译语读者的阅读习惯,不然,这个译语语篇的可接受性就会大大降低。因为话语意义的理解可以是个人现象,而语篇表达的形式则是社会现象,必须遵从各种语言约定俗成的规范。因此,在翻译过程中对语篇结构进行某些调整,是译者经常要完成的一项重要的具体工作。至于对结构调整的自由度的掌握,李运兴指出,影响译者对原语语篇结构进行调整的与其说是语篇类型,不如说是翻译目的。因此,应该从包括翻译目的在内的诸如译语相对于原语的交际影响力的大小、译者相对于作者的权威性的大小等因素来考查结构调整的幅度会更为贴近语际交际的实际。

第一,翻译的目的。翻译的学术目的性越强,对语篇结构进行变动的趋势越小;翻译的应用功能目的性越强,对语篇结构进行变动的可能性便越大。译者倾向性越强,对语篇结构进行变动的趋势越小;译文读者倾向性越强,对语篇结构进行变动的趋势越大。

第二,原语和译语影响力的大小。原语的影响力越大,翻译过程中语篇结构被变动的趋势就越小,反之亦然。

第三,权威性问题。原语语篇作者的权威越大,译者对语篇结构进行变动的余地就越小。例如,口译任务中政要的正式会晤与演讲、名人专访等;而如果译者的权威,或相对于作者的权威越大,他对原语语篇加以改动的可能性就越大,例如在社区、农村、厂矿进行的参观、采访等口译任务。

虽然李运兴以上观点主要论及的是笔译,但对口译情况也大致适用。

4. 口译质量

4.1 译员

口译的质量问题必定触及译员的定义。国际会议译员协会在其章程中为会议口译员定义如下(AIIC,1994):

A conference interpreter is a qualified specialist in bilingual or multilingual communication. He/ she makes this communication possible between delegates of different linguistic communities at conferences, meetings, negotiations or visits, where more than one working language is used by comprehending the concepts of the speaker's message and conveying them orally in another language, either in consecutive, simultaneous or whispering.

Besides carrying out a thorough preparation of the subject and terminology, a conference interpreter must possess a wide general knowledge in order to deal with all matters under discussion.

Conference interpreters are, moreover, bound to respect the code of professional ethics, including the strictest professional secrecy.

首先,国际译协的章程中要求国际会议译员成为高素质的双语或多语交际的专家,不但说明译员必须拥有高水平的母语、外语知识,还应当精通相关语言的国家的文化,才足以驾驭异语交际,成其为专家。其次,会议译员接受的任务不局限于以单向交流为特点的讲座、大会发言,还包括双向或多向交流的正式会晤、谈判、参观访问。因此,要求译员熟练掌握各类口译技巧。除此之外,还要自如地适应不同的交际语境,顺利完成不同的口译任务。再者,会议译员必须对要翻译的会议主题、讨论热点、涉及领域、专有名词、相关术语等有深入的了解,这就要求译员除译前做好充分准备之外,还要有平时的长期积累。换句话说,译员须成为知识广博的"杂家"。显而易见,会议译员代表了职业口译的最高等级,所以现如今无论是职业实践、教学培训,还是实验研究,都是以会议翻译为职业口译译员的最高标准,并以此作参照,依次为各类等级职业翻译订立标准。于是就此归纳总结出的职业意识、技能技巧形成了口译行业的专业特点,也成为教学培训追求的目标。

4.2 翻译质量:静态结果与动态操作

无论为职业晋级、职称考核设立的口译质量评估,还是教学培训中的测试考评,抑或实验科研进行的衡定测量,重点大都聚焦于译员的翻译能力上。然而,以往对口译质量的评估虽然总是针对译员的主观努力,但是多数只注重对译员翻译成果的静态分析,而忽视对翻译过程的动态观察。

实际上从国际译协对会议译员的要求分析,口译质量是由多个层面组成的,既有信息内容的层面,也有语言运用、翻译节奏的掌握、交际场面与气氛的控制、语境的适应、跨文化知识的调动等。而所有这些层面的协调组合又要依赖译员掌握的技能技巧。因为只有熟练地运用这些技能技巧才能遵循职业化口译活动的规律,因循其逻辑程序,从而保证思路畅通、思维活跃,使译员能自如地运用所拥有的知识,充分发挥自身的交际能力。概言之,口译活动具有其独特的心理模式和思维规律,译员必须遵循这些模式与规律,掌握相应的技能,培养高效的反应,才能圆满地完成口译任务。

另外,既然口译是在语篇的层面展开,那么,与之相对应的质量评估也应具有语篇意识,亦即"强调篇章在交际过程中的完整性和一体性,既要分析语篇诸层次作为语言符号系统与相应外部世界的关系,也要注意以语篇的交际功能、交际意向统辖对语篇诸层次进行观察"。(李运兴,2001:68)

显然,要评估译员的翻译能力,只着重翻译结果,不分析操作过程显然有失客观科学,何况在口译这种交换互动、充满动感的活动中只作静态评估亦颇欠均衡对等。在评估中我们就经常遇到一些看似相悖的情况,译员组织的译语虽稍显蹩脚,然交流却畅通无阻;相反,有时译语漂亮地道,交际却断续无常。对这样的现象,如只作译语分析,恐难找到真正的原因,唯有深入到操作过程才能发现其中的究竟:可能是交际策略使用的问题,可能是语调、语气或重音的问题,也可能是交际行为是否适合交际语境的问题等。

4.3 口译效果

主观努力的付出是否能得到相应的客观效果?对此,口译服务对象的反馈应是极其重要的衡量因素。鉴于口译任务的多样性,服务对象的要求也会随之变化。况且异语交际的双方对所要翻译的专题往往比译员还熟悉,因此对口译的期待带明确的方向性,一旦译员的翻译偏离了期待的方向,就容易引起服务对象的质疑,甚至不满。从交际的效度分析,讲者有意图,听者有期待,译员不仅要清楚地把握讲者的意图,还要以既符合转达此意图的言语,又是听者能接受的方式进行传译,才能满足后者的期待。换言之,抓对原语意图,并用译语体现此意图,则交际有效;明白原意,但译语差强,则交际失效;听懂原语,用错译语,交际无效;听差原话,自然错用译语,故无从交际。概言之,译员的主观努力还需达到客观的交际效果,才称得上高质量的服务。

口译服务对象在交际翻译中指异语交流的双方或多方,在会议翻译中则指发言或演讲方与听众,另外还有雇用者、组织者等。如上所述,交流者等待的是交际效果。而雇用者可能算的是经济账,希望物有所值;组织者则期望参与者都满意,活动能得到预期的、或更佳的社会效应。如此纷呈多样的要求致使口译效果的研究莫衷一是。更何况专业不同、语境差异会造成服务对象更加复杂的苛求。正是因为面临太多的困难,至今对这方面的研究可谓凤毛麟角,国外的研究数不过十(Ais & Gile, 2002),国内除了几年前台湾师范大学翻译研究所何慧玲教授及其指导的学生所作的两项研究外,则近乎空白。

4.4 影响口译质量及其评估诸因素关系的理论假设

综合本文讨论过的、有关影响口译质量及其评估的各种因素,根据它们的相互关系,我们拟建立影响口译质量及影响质量评估诸因素的关系图。

在影响口译质量诸因素关系图中,口译质量为自变量,口译任务、译员的主观努力与口译服务对象的客观反馈为因变量。换言之,口译质量受制于具体交际语境下相关任务的要求、译员重构的译语语篇及翻译操作过程中的应对努力、口译服务对象的期待满足程度。而三个因变量之间也存在着互动关系,例如译员要有判断不同的口译任务的能力,公众对各种任务会产生不同的期待等。

至于影响口译质量评估诸因素的关系图中,质量评估是自变量,其中假设拟订了通用的质量、效果标准权重比例公式,即包括主要质量指标、效果反馈在内的推算公式。其余的口译任务、评估目的与手段则是制约评估,影响评估的标准权重比例的因变量。

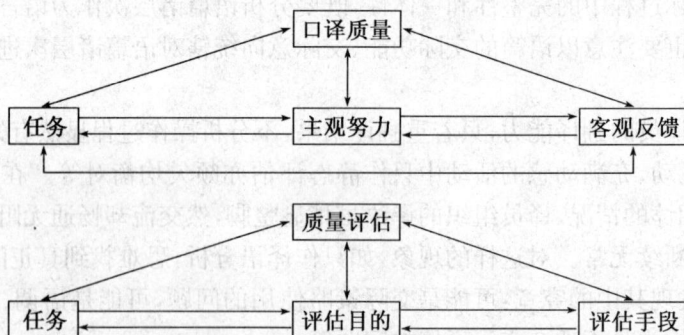

影响口译质量评估诸因素关系图

以上两个理论假设关系图旨在明示诸因素在口译活动中的相互关系,希望为口译的质量与效果评估的研究提供尽可能全面、客观的参数。

5. 结语

作为跨文化交际的口译活动要面对各种复杂的国际语境,接触各种不同文化背景的交流者,涉及各式各样的主题和专业。由此形成的各种口译任务具有各自不同的要求,口译译员的主观努力、原语发言人与现场听众的客观反馈等均与具体的任务要求密切相关。口译评估可针对不同目的,采取不同手段。因此要进行科学有效的质量评估,就必须根据具体情况设定合适的标准权重比例,使用相关的评估模式。

【延伸阅读】

1. Colina, Sonia. Further evidence for a functionalist approach to translation quality evaluation. *Target: International Journal on Translation Studies*. 2009, 21 (2): 235-264.

2. Gile, Daniel. *Basic concepts and models for interpreter and translator training*. Amsterdam/Philadelphia: John Benjamins Publishing Company, 1995.

3. 白枚. 口译的特点及标准. 大连民族学院学报. 2005(1):14-18.

4. 蔡小红. 口译评估. 北京:中国对外翻译出版公司,2007.

5. 何莉. 口译质量评估新探——并列信息忠实度的评估标准. 文学界. 2011(5):13-16.

6. 黄蓓. 从释意派的视角论口译质量评估模式在会议口译中的应用——以政府领导人答中外记者问之现场口译为例. 读与写. 2009(2):21-24.

7. 刘和平. 科技口译与质量评估. 上海科技翻译. 2002(1):33-37.

8. 钱芳. 图式理论照应下的口译忠实度评估. 顺德职业技术学院学报. 2009,7(2):62-64.

9. 张培蓓,任静生. 评估口译忠实度的策略. 中国科技翻译. 2006(3):36-38.

10. 张燕. 口译技巧——论提高同声传译的质量. 中国翻译. 2002(4):66-69.

【问题与思考】

1. 交替口译和同声传译的质量评估标准有何不同?

2. 瑞士日内瓦大学的 Moser-Mercer 提出了三种评估模式:评估、测量和判断。在她看来,由于口译质量评估的理由和目的不尽相同,因此所采取的评估方法也应该有所差别。请具体阐述评估目的对评估方法的影响。

3. 试论客观和系统地评价口译质量对规范口译服务市场的意义。

4. 口译考试也是口译质量评估的一种形式。试对目前我国各级各类口译考试的主要评估内容进行归纳,并分析其有效性及存在的问题。

5. 目前中西方口译质量评估的标准大致有哪几个基本指标? 根据众多的实证研究结果,在这些基本指标中,最重要的一个指标是什么? 最具争议的又是哪一个指标? 请简单说明原因。

第十一章 基于教学与培训的口译理论研究

导 论

在众多的口译理论研究学派中,基于教学与培训的口译理论研究可以说是独树一帜,其研究内容更加宽泛,研究的指向性更加突出,那就是:为口译教学和培训服务,提高口译教学和培训的效能。我们把这一类以研究如何解决口译教学与培训中产生的各类问题,提高口译教学与培训效能的口译理论研究,统统归为"基于教学与培训的口译理论研究"。

基于教学与培训的口译理论研究的任务和宗旨就是研究如何帮助学校或相关培训机构提高口译教学效能,加快培养符合社会需求的实用型口译人才。这也是该研究学派所有研究工作的主要出发点。

该学派研究内容十分广泛,大致包括口笔译的区别、口译教学改革、高校口译教学、口译技巧、口译训练、口译实战培训、口译教材建设、口译课程与课程群建设、口译人才培养模式以及口译师资建设等一系列口译教学与培训中广泛涉及的领域。

基于教学与培训的口译理论的研究方法和手段也更加多样化,可以说本教材前面所讲的十个学派的口译理论在这里都能够得到运用和交叉综合,比如释意学派理论在口译教学中的应用,而文化学派、语言学派、心理学派等应用于口译教学和培训,其研究理论之间也是彼此渗透和相互关联的。

基于教学与培训的口译理论研究大体遵照了口译教学和培训中最为成熟的两大过程范式。一是由巴黎高等翻译学院提出的释意"三角模型"。塞莱斯科维奇认为"释意"是"有意识的"认知努力,"意义由语言意义加认知补充(知识)构成",而且释意需要"去除原语语言外壳"(deverbalization)的干扰(1978:336)。因此,"释意"会比依靠几乎是自动化条件反射的"转码"更耗精力与时间,但达到的交际效果是生成了更加自然、地道和准确的译语,因此,"释意"是比"转码"更好的翻译策略,口译培训的要点之一就是纠正学生的"转码"倾向(Seleskovitch & Lederer,1989:75)。二是法国口译理论专家吉尔(Daniel Gile)提出的"精力分配模式",即要保证翻译的顺利进行,交传译员在第一阶段的听力与分析、笔记、短期记忆和协调以及第二阶段的回忆信息、读取笔记和译语产出方面的能力要大于或等于翻译任务的需求,而同传译员在听力与分析、记忆、产出和协调方面的能力要大于或等于翻译任务的需求(1995:162-178)。这两大过程范式对口译教学和培训的启示作用是十分巨大的。

该学派在口译教学和培训模式方面也取得了很多成功的经验,比较著名的有厦大模式、广外模式以及 3P 模式等。

厦大模式(Xiada Model)是在吉尔模式的基础上提出来的。根据厦大模式,口译是译员对原语语篇与跨文化交际成分进行分析之后,结合自己的语言和语言外的知识加以理解,应用一定的口译技巧并遵守一定的译员职业准则,用目的语对原语信息进行重组的过程。他们将技能训练作为整个口译学习的中心环节外,还把译前准备与质量控制纳入了口译训练的范畴。

广东外语外贸大学仲伟合教授总结出了一套口译教学与训练的原则、方法及方针,这便是"广外模式"(GDUFS Model)。仲伟合教授指出,口译训练应遵循机能性、实践性、理论性以及阶段性四个原则,教学安排分为基础技巧训练、口译操练、口译观摩与实践等三个渐进阶段,努力实现"八化"方针,即课程立体化、内容系统化、练习真实化、学生中心化、教材多元化、技巧全面化、教师精英化以及目标职业化。

深圳职业技术学院刘建珠将口译训练分为译前准备(Preparing)、现场表现(Performing)及译后总结(Packaging)三个阶段,并将该模式总结为 3P 模式(3P Model),分别设置了准备(Preparing)、解码(Decoding)、记忆(Memorizing)、编码(Encoding)、协调(Coordinating)、评估(Assessing)等六个模块的技能训练。他认为,口译训练不应单单局限于现场口译工作的听、记、译部分,还应包括口译工作前的准备与工作完成后的总结与评估。译前准备、现场表现及译后总结共同组成了整个口译实践活动的有机整体。该模式又进一步发展成为工学结合模式:口译训练 = 学习(技能训练+专题学习+文化构建)+ 工作(项目模拟+顶岗实习+现场实战)+ 评估(学员反馈+社会评价+教师总评)。

基于教学与培训的口译研究涵盖面极广,同时也大大促进了我国口译教学与口译人才的培养。

选 文

选文一 Learning Styles, Motivation and Cognitive Flexibility in Interpreter Training: Self-selection and Aptitude

Šárka Timarová & Heidi Salaets

导 言

口译是一种动态交际行为,真实的交际场景中有很多因素会影响到口译员的即时性发挥,从而影响口译质量。因此,口译教学和口译培训除了关注课堂教学或培训这一硬性层面之外,还要注重学生作为学习主体的一些软性条件,比如学生的口译学习动机、认知灵活度等。但以往的口译教学和口译培训研究往往关注较多的是教学和培训,而忽略了学生本身的软性条件。选文则侧重从考查学生的角度出发,以口译培训中学生的学习方式、学习动机和认知灵活度这三个因素为考查对象,以实际的口译培训效果为研究基础,通过对不同研究对象组的调查,实际论证了口译培训中可以有效帮助减少口译员心理焦虑从而提高口译质量的因素。选文的研究结果对于口译人员培训具有一定的参考价值。

Admission testing for conference interpreter training programmes traditionally focuses on skills directly related to the interpreting skills, and while soft skills, such as motivation, are recognised as important, they are not systematically tested or researched. The present study attempts to address this gap by exploring three traits and abilities, namely learning styles, motivation and cognitive flexibility, and to relate them to students' self-selection for interpreting and to their success on final exams. Three tests were used to compare a group of self-selected interpreting students and applicants (n＝32) and a subgroup of conference interpreting students (n＝14) to a control group of undergraduate students (n＝104), from among whom the majority of Lessius University College interpreting students are recruited: the Inventory of Learning Styles (Vermunt & Rijswijk 1987), the Achievement Motivation Test (Hermans 1968/2004) and the Wisconsin Card Sorting Test (Grant & Berg 1948). The results show that self-selected interpreting students are cognitively more flexible and are less negatively affected by anxiety. Compared to the control group, successful conference interpreting students, but not unsuccessful students, are cognitively more flexible and benefit more from some level of anxiety. Moreover, all conference interpreting students are less affected by stress than the control group and seem to have more clearly developed learning preferences.

Keywords: conference interpreter training, admission tests, soft skills, motivation, learning styles, anxiety, cognitive flexibility

Introduction

When asked whether anyone can be trained as an interpreter, Helge Niska, a veteran interpreter trainer at Stockholm University, replied: "In principle I would say yes, but in practice time constraints and limitations on financial resources make it advisable to select the people who need least training" (Niska, 2002). While the "born or made" debate has definitely shifted towards "made" (Mackintosh, 1999; Kalina, 2000), not everyone remains as optimistic as Niska, certainly not in the spoken language conference interpreting field. What everyone would agree with is the need for selection. Admission testing for interpreter training programmes is motivated as much by the belief that a certain aptitude for interpreting is needed in order to become an interpreter, as by practical considerations, such as time and financial constraints or demand far exceeding the number of available places. All these factors call for as efficient an admission procedure as possible, but in reality little is still known about how successful student selection is. Most admission tests are intuitive

(Lambert, 1991; Moser-Mercer, 1994; Russo & Pippa, 2004), there is currently no reliable aptitude test (AIIC Training Committee, 2006), and a number of authors have expressed scepticism about the very possibility of using an admission test to measure aptitude (Déjean Le Féal, 1998; Taylor, 1997; Alexieva, 1993). Furthermore, there is a lack of systematic research into aptitude and admission testing (Moser-Mercer, 1994) and the little research available suggests that current tests do not predict reliably whether a student will succeed or fail (Gringiani, 1990; Tapalova, 1990, cited in Sawyer, 2004; Timarová & Ungoed-Thomas, 2008, 2009). The issues involved were succinctly summed up by Kalina (2000: 13):

> There is as yet no clear evidence that the skills deemed necessary as prerequisites for successful training efforts are really the ones tested, and that it is those skills students must have before they go into interpreter training. Moreover, the tests do not as yet seem to be sufficiently objective and transparent to be used for decisions that affect the future (chances) of many students.

In effect, Kalina outlines three major tasks for research and training practice: defining the skills that need to be tested; finding a test that would appropriately assess them; and designing tests that provide reliable results. Most interpreter training admission tests focus on the so called hard skills, i. e. those directly related to language processing and interpreting, such as memory tests, summarization, short consecutives etc. (Timarová & Ungoed-Thomas, 2008). Soft skills, such as steep learning curves (Moser-Mercer, 1994), motivation (Gringiani, 1990) and stress tolerance (Moser-Mercer, 1984) have been suggested as desirable traits in students, but are rarely tested (Timarová & Ungoed-Thomas, 2008). While these skills are probably not going to be determining factors, they may contribute to the skill acquisition process (Shaw et al. , 2008) and may influence successful completion of a training programme [see also Moser-Mercer et al. (2000) for the distinction between the interpreting skill and interpreting skill acquisition]. Indeed, López Gómez et al. (2007) report on a study in which soft skills were found to be weaker predictors than hard skills but did help to predict completion of training.

It seems relevant therefore to explore the role of soft skills and their possible inclusion in admission tests. We selected three such traits and abilities: learning styles, motivation and anxiety, and cognitive flexibility. Since our main interest lies in using the tests for purposes of aptitude and admission testing, we focused on two groups: interpreting programme students and interpreting programme applicants. In the first group, our main research question was whether tests of the selected traits predict successful completion of interpreter training. In the second group, our main goal was related to self-selection; that is, to the profile of the applicants.

Psychological traits: Learning styles, motivation and cognitive flexibility

Learning styles

Learning style is a complex concept encompassing students' content processing, regulation of learning, motivation for and goals of learning and a set of beliefs about how learning works, the roles of students and teachers, etc. (Vermunt & Vermetten, 2004). A general ability to learn and acquire new skills was suggested as a factor in interpreter training (Moser-Mercer, 1994) and was addressed from the trainer's perspective in terms of creating a suitable learning environment (Moser-Mercer, 2008). Shaw et al. (2004) found that novice interpreting students transitioning from sign language learning to sign language interpreting stressed the importance of an open attitude to learning and of teacher support.

In a more general context of educational psychology, extensive studies of various student populations resulted in the specification of several basic learning styles and of their relation to a variety of factors. Vermunt (Vermunt & Vermetten, 2004) distinguishes four dimensions of a learning style: cognitive processing, metacognitive regulation of learning, overall learning conceptions and learning orientations. Cognitive processing refers to the more traditional view of learning, whereby a distinction is made between deeper and shallower processing of the content to be learned. Regulation of learning is concerned with a student's approach to learning in terms of control of learning activities using internal or external support. Learning conceptions refer to students' general beliefs about learning, how it works, how the learning environment functions, what the demands are etc. Finally, learning orientations refer to students' global attitude and motivation (Vermunt & Vermetten, 2004). Elements from each dimension combine into an overall learning style. At an even higher level, Meyer et al. (1990) suggested the term *orchestrations* for complex individual or group patterns of learning styles.

A number of studies amongst student populations in higher education supported this classification and provided evidence that enhanced our understanding of the learning styles. Personal learning orientations and strategies were found to be stable, although some adjustments were possible in response to specific course demands (Vermetten et al., 1999), perceived change in learning environment, such as during a period of study abroad (Wierstra et al., 2003) or following the acquisition of specific learning strategies (Lonka et al., 1997 cited in Vermunt & Vermetten, 2004). An important finding that emerged from such studies was the concept of *dissonance*, which refers to a conflict between individual learning orientations, the learning strategies they apply and perceptions and/or demands of the learning environment. Instances of such dissonance were shown to be related to lower study success (Lindblom-Ylänne & Lonka, 1999).

Learning styles and individual approaches to learning seem to be an important aspect of student experience. A general perception and conception of the learning process may play a contributing role in the context of an intensive one-year conference interpreting training programme, which, unlike a full university degree programme lasting three or four years, offers little room for finding one's way around. Some approaches to learning, which may work well in a traditional higher education institution at an undergraduate level, may not be suited to interpreter training. These would include reliance on extensive external support, such as textbooks, various study aids and detailed teacher guidance, or shallower forms of content processing, such as memorising or sequential progress through a piece of study text.

Motivation

Motivation is part of the highest level of performance control (Matthews et al., 2000) and together with capacity and opportunity forms the three most important determinants of work performance (Blumberg & Pringle, 1982; see Moser-Mercer, 2008 for a more detailed description of the interaction). Like learning styles, motivation too is psychologically a very complex construct which is difficult to measure objectively. Atkinson and Reitman (1958) suggested that motivation to perform a specific task is a product of two components: achievement motive and expectancy of goal attainment. Achievement motive is a general personal disposition towards applying oneself in order to achieve certain goals. Expectancy of goal attainment is related to the belief that a certain act is needed in order to achieve a goal. Motivation is the resulting state when the two components have been sufficiently aroused, and it follows that motivation differs in different situations. Hermans (1970) concluded that motivation and achievement motives are very complex and therefore it may be more appropriate to speak of measuring *an* achievement motive rather than *the* achievement motive. Nevertheless, some findings seem to be fairly robust.

Motivation, understood in more general terms as arousal, is closely related to stress and anxiety (Matthews et al., 2000: 171). Hermans (1967, 1970) developed an instrument based on Atkinson's expectancy theory, in which he incorporated three scales: achievement motive and two scales representing two separate constructs of positive (facilitating) and negative (debilitating) anxiety. All three scales seem relevant in the context of interpreter training. Motivation as a general construct and in interaction with stress appears to play an important role in successful completion of training (Gringiani, 1990; Moser-Mercer, 2008). Trainers consider it an important trait in applicants, although doubts exist about the possibility of reliably measuring it in admission tests (Timarová & Ungoed-Thomas, 2008). Shaw et al. (2004) found in interviews that interpreting students identified overcoming anxiety and taking risks as important factors in training.

Cognitive flexibility

Cognitive (mental) flexibility refers to readiness to change cognitive content and its attributes (Scott, 1962) or the ability to switch to a different action as required by the situation and to avoid stereotypical behaviour (Hill, 2004). The opposite, cognitive rigidity, refers to maintaining fixed images and their attributes and relations (Scott, 1962). Cognitive flexibility is part of cognitive executive control and under different names, such as open-mindedness or the ability to learn quickly, it has been identified as desirable in interpreting students (Timarová & Ungoed-Thomas, 2008; Moser-Mercer, 1994). As such, it is an essential component of the ability to seek innovative solutions to problems and of adaptive expertise, both of which are considered important in interpreting (Moser-Mercer, 2008).

The three constructs all seem to be highly relevant for interpreter training and empirical evidence in support of their role may provide further clues as to their potential for inclusion into admission testing procedures. Interpreter training programmes are less structured than traditional university programmes with their extensive pool of supportive learning materials and more tangible outcomes, such as correct answers to factual questions, and such lack of structure may provide an additional source of anxiety and require flexibility and self-reliance in learning. An effective approach to learning, stress tolerance and anxiety control are thus all desirable traits in interpreting students and interpreters (Timarová & Ungoed-Thomas, 2008; Moser-Mercer, 1994).

Methodology of aptitude and admission research

A methodological issue in interpreting aptitude research is related to population restriction, which is twofold. The first restriction lies in self-selection: it is quite possible that many of those who do not apply for an interpreter-training programme do possess the necessary aptitude, whereas not all of those who do apply have the aptitude to become interpreters (or at least not within the time period afforded by the training programme), which accounts for the need for admission tests. In effect, only those with an interest in interpreting (self-determined selection) and assumed aptitude (selection on the basis of admission tests) are admitted.

Aptitude and admission research typically looks at students at the beginning of their training and compares their performance on aptitude tests with their final exam performance. However, after the double selection described above, researchers have access to a very restricted population and evaluating aptitude becomes very difficult. In a nutshell, they are left with studying interpreting *students* but wish to come up with conclusions that will generalise to the population of interpreting *applicants*. These two populations, however, may be quite different and there is a danger of score range restriction. Selecting and studying only high scorers leads to lower correlations with the relevant criterion (Howell, 2001: 283), in this case the interpreting course performance. Sackett et al. (2007) demonstrated through a simulation in a known population that a true correlation between a predictor and a criterion of $r=.5$ was reduced to as low as $r=.05$ when the range was restricted.

A solution to this problem is not feasible in practice. Ideally, a group of people would be subjected to interpreter training without being preselected in any way, and their performance on aptitude tests and interpreting tests could then be compared. Other, more pragmatic solutions are therefore required, such as analyzing data from training programmes where admission tests are not legally allowed (removing the second selection based on admission tests), as is the case in Italy (Gringiani, 1990). Another valuable source of data comes from programmes where there is a compulsory interpreting component for all students in early stages of their university education and where specialisation in two or more study tracks only takes place at a later stage. Such a programme exists for example in the Czech Republic (Rejšková, 1999).

In the study reported here, we have tried to address both types of selection, using another approximation method. At Lessius University College in Belgium, most conference interpreting applicants and students are graduates of the Lessius undergraduate programme. By studying the group of third-year students towards the end of their studies, we are assuming that we will capture the unselected group as a control group. By comparing conference interpreting applicants (self-selection) and students (selection on the basis of an admission test), we expected to gain more insight into the profiles of people who tend to self-select for interpreting and into the traits of successful and unsuccessful students.

Lessius study programmes and student groups description

Lessius University College in Belgium offers a three-year bachelors programme in applied language studies. The programme includes courses in foreign languages and/or Flemish sign language, mother tongue (Dutch), history and culture, discourse and communication studies etc., and provides all-round practical and academic preparation for advanced professional language users. After completing the bachelors programme, students choose among four one-year masters programmes: multilingual business communication, journalism, translation and (liaison) interpreting. Furthermore, Lessius offers a one-year postgraduate (postmasters) course in conference interpreting, where training is offered in consecutive and simultaneous interpreting in line with the AIIC criteria (AIIC Training Committee, 2006). The training programme is designed for speakers of Dutch as a mother tongue and a knowledge of two foreign languages, with one out of English, French or German and one out of English, French, German, Spanish, Italian, Russian or Hungarian. Before the programme itself gets under way, a two-week preparatory course is offered in which applicants are taught the basic notions of interpreting, an introduction to note-taking and preparatory memory and consecutive exercises, and make a first attempt at simultaneous interpreting. The preparatory course serves both as a teaser for the applicants and as an opportunity for the trainers to meet the applicants and assess their interpreting potential over a period of two weeks. Next, applicants take an admission test that includes various aptitude exercises, a general knowledge test and a short consecutive test. Eligibility for the training programme is contingent on successful performance on this test. An alternative route exists for Lessius Master of (Liaison) Interpreting graduates, who are exempt from the preparatory course and need only take the admission test.

The majority of the conference interpreting programme applicants are Lessius graduates. Other applicants completed their master's degree elsewhere or participated in the Lessius transfer programme (an accelerated version of parts of the bachelors programme to help non-Lessius graduates meet the enrolment criteria for a given specialisation programme). Non-Lessius graduates typically completed a language-oriented programme (philology, translation) or another humanities degree. Only rarely do applicants have a substantially different background.

The third-year bachelors students therefore constitute a pool of future applicants and a population as close as possible to the selection stages (self-selection for the liaison interpreting masters programme in the fourth year and the conference interpreting postgraduate course in the fifth year). By studying the groups of third year students, it is possible to gain a better understanding of the population from which most of the interpreting students will be recruited.

Analysis 1: Self-selection

Method

Participants

Three groups of Lessius University College students participated in the study, which took place in the academic year 2007—2008. The first group were the applicants of the postgraduate conference interpreting programme (conference interpreters). The second group were students from the liaison interpreting programme (liaison interpreters). The third group consisted of students from the third year (the last year before specialisation) of an applied language studies undergraduate programme (control group). The demographic information may be found in Table 1. All participants, with the exception of one exchange student in the control group, were native speakers of Dutch. Several students reported previous training in interpreting, typically consisting of introductory interpreting classes taken during their student exchange study period abroad. The study was conducted during regular class time slots, but all participants were given the option of not participating. They received no financial remuneration for their participation.

Table 1. Participants' demographic information (2007—2008 cohort)

Group	n	Sex		Mean age (standard deviation)	Students reporting previous training in interpreting (% of total)	Completed higher education degree (bachelor, master)
		Male	Female (% of total)			
Conference interpreters	9	2	7 (78%)	23.2 (3.49)	0	Yes, all
Liaison interpreters	23	4	19 (83%)	21.4 (0.95)	6 (26%)	Yes, all
Control group	104	29	75 (72%)	21.3 (1.95)	6 (5.8%)	No

Materials

Learning styles

The Inventory of Learning Styles (ILS; Vermunt & Rijswijk, 1987) is a self-report instrument comprising 120 statements with Likert-type responses. The responses are converted into scores on 16 scales in four domains: processing strategies, regulation strategies, learning orientation and conceptions of learning. Following findings and methodology in Vermunt & Vermetten (2004) and Wierstra et al. (2003), two main learning styles were considered: the *meaning-directed learning style* and the *reproduction-directed learning style*. The former is characterised by the learner's deep processing of content matter (relating it to other knowledge, drawing one's own conclusions, abstracting from details to a whole), self-regulation of learning (one's own planning of tasks, monitoring of progress, reflecting on one's own work) and taking responsibility for one's own learning. It was calculated as the sum of scores on the following scales: deep processing, self-regulation and construction of knowledge (31 items). The reproduction-directed learning style may be seen as an opposite style, where the learner shows preference for processing the content in a more stepwise manner (going through the material step-bystep, studying each element in detail and in isolation from the whole, memorizing facts), for external regulation (learning on the basis of external support, such as study questions, assignments, teacher guidelines etc.) and for viewing learning as imposed externally. The reproduction-directed learning style was calculated as the sum of scores on the following scales: stepwise processing, external regulation and intake of knowledge (31 items). The remaining scales contribute to two other learning styles, *undirected* and *application-directed*, which are more frequently found in specific contexts (Vermunt & Vermetten, 2004) and were not considered separately in the present analysis. Further, students were classified according to one of four orchestrations (complex patterns) of learning styles (Lindblom-Ylanne & Lonka, 1999) as *both meaning high and reproduction high*, *both meaning low and reproduction low*, *high meaning/low reproduction* and *low meaning/high reproduction*, based on their above-or below-mean score for a given learning style. Selected elements of the instrument structure and sample items appear in Table 2. The description is based on the English version of ILS (Vermunt, 1994). The instrument itself was administered in Dutch, the participants' native language, and the original version of the instrument.

Table 2. Selected scales of the Inventory of Learning Styles and sample items
(Vermunt & Vermetten 2004; Vermunt 1994)

Domains (in italics) and scales	Domain description (in italics) and sample items	Number of items
Processing strategies	*Mental activities directly related to processing content, resulting in knowledge and understanding*	
Deep processing	I try to relate new subject matter to knowledge I already have about the topic concerned.	11

Domains (in italics) and scales	Domain description (in italics) and sample items	Number of items
Stepwise processing	I memorise the meaning of every concept that is unfamiliar to me.	11
Regulation strategies	*Source of direction for the learning process*	
Self-regulation	I add something to the subject matter from other sources.	11
External regulation	I study according to the instructions given in the study materials or provided by the teacher.	11
Conceptions of learning	*Internal system of beliefs and knowledge about learning*	
Construction of knowledge	I should try to think up examples with the study materials of my own accord.	9
Intake of knowledge	I like to be given precise instructions as to how to go about solving a task or doing an assignment.	9

Achievement Motivation Test

The Achievement Motivation Test (AMT; Hermans, 1968/2004) is a self-report instrument. It contains 90 statements, for each of which the participants choose the most favored response (two to four options per statement). The responses are then converted into scores measuring three scales: achievement motive, facilitating anxiety and debilitating anxiety. Individuals who score high on the achievement motive scale are considered to attach great importance to performing to the best of their ability. Low scores, on the other hand, indicate that the individual is not achievement-driven, and is typically happy with a "good-enough" performance. High scores on the facilitating anxiety scale indicate that those individuals perform better when under slight stress. Some stress such as that associated with illdefined and unstructured tasks may have a stimulating effect. Low scores indicate that the individual does not benefit from stress and unstructured tasks. Finally, the debilitating anxiety scale measures an individual's ability to withstand stress and stressful situations, such as exams. A high score indicates sensitivity to stress, which acts as an inhibitor and has a negative effect on performance. Low scores, on the other hand, indicate that such an individual's performance level is fairly stable and remains unaffected by stressful situations or a lack of structure in the task. The structure of the instrument and sample items appear in Table 3.

Table 3. Scales of the Achievement Motivation Test and sample items

(Hermans 1968/2004, 1970)

Scales	Sample items	Number of items
Achievement motive	I usually do a. much more than I resolved to do b. a bit more than I resolved to do c. as much as I resolved to do d. less than I resolved to do	44
Facilitating anxiety	I find that mild exam anxiety a. improves my performance b. has hardly any influence c. affects my performance in a negative way	19
Debilitating anxiety	If I imagine myself in a job interview then I see myself as a. calm b. slightly tense c. quite nervous	26

Cognitive flexibility

The Wisconsin Card Sorting Test (WCST; Grant & Berg, 1948) was used as a measure of cognitive flexibility. The test consists of sorting a deck of 64 cards, one by one, into one of four slots. Upon placing each card in a slot, the participant receives feedback as to the correctness/incorrectness of the categorisation, but no feedback is offered as to the reasons why the particular categorisation was incorrect. Each card may be categorised according to at least three different rules, but participants are not told which rule is being applied. Moreover, the categorization rule changes during the test, and participants must adjust to the new rule (after finding out for themselves which rule is being applied). This creates a task with a fairly "fuzzy" structure, a high incidence of errors and the necessity of integrating fairly vague feedback.

Three measures were taken: the total number of errors, the total number of perseverative errors, and a learning-to-learn index. Perseverative errors are responses that are not correct, given the present rule, but would have been correct according to the previously applied rule. For the learning-to-learn index, the percentage of errors within each segment of the test (each application of a rule constitutes a new segment) was calculated, and then compared to the previous segment. The index was high if the percentage of errors consistently decreased and low when the participant made more and more errors.

Procedure

Participants were tested in groups of up to 30 (with the exception of the Wisconsin Card Sorting Test, which was administered individually). The tests (with the exception of WCST) were administered together with a battery of language processing ability tests (to be reported separately) either in two one-hour sessions (the conference interpreting group) or in a single two-hour session (the liaison interpreting group, the control group). Individual appointments were made for the WCST. Not all students were available for individual testing and the sample size for WCST is thus lower. The two interpreting student groups were tested at the beginning of their interpreter training and the control group was tested at the beginning of the second semester in their third year of study (one semester before the end of their bachelors studies and their selection of master's specialisation). At the time of testing, participants had received no training in interpreting at Lessius. For each of the tests (ILS, AMT), participants received a booklet with test instructions, tests and space for providing responses. Before each test, the researcher went through the task instructions with the participants and gave them an opportunity to ask questions. The tests were administered in the same order for all groups. The order of tasks was the following: AMT, ILS, individual appointment for WCST. The testing session was paced by the researchers.

Results

For analyses concerned with self-selection, the two groups of interpreting students (conference interpreters, liaison interpreters) were considered as one group of students who made a decision to opt for interpreter training. The remaining group of bachelors students served as a control group from which the majority of interpreting students are recruited. Tables 4 and 5 provide descriptive statistics for each instrument and for the two groups: bachelors students as the control group, and interpreting students, consisting of conference interpreting programme applicants and liaision interpreting students. To maximise the use of available data, cases with missing values were excluded, analysis by analysis, which led to variable sample size per test. T-tests were carried out to compare the interpreting group to the control group. The results are shown in Table 4. On the WCST, there was a significant difference between the two groups on the number of perseverative errors. The mean score was 3.9 perseverative errors (s. d. 3.05) and 6.8 perseverative errors (s. d. 5.39) for the interpreting group and the control group, respectively, with a significant difference between the groups ($t(61) = -2.70$, $p < .01$, two-tailed). For the total number of errors, the interpreting group had a mean score of 15.8 errors (s. d. 7.50) and the control group a mean score of 20.1 (s. d. 10.39) with a marginally significant difference between the groups ($t(61) = -1.91$, $p = .06$, two-tailed). The learning-to-learn index did not show a significant difference. On the ILS the interpreting group and the control group scored comparably on both the meaning-directed and the reproduction-directed learning style measures. On the AMT, the mean score on the achievement motive scale was 23.1 (s. d. 8.43) for the interpreting group and 20.6 (s. d. 6.87) for the control group. The difference between the two groups was marginally significant with $t(133) = 1.69$, $p = .09$, two-tailed). The mean score on the debilitating anxiety scale was 12.8 (s. d. 5.33) for the interpreting group and 15.7 (s. d. 5.94) for the control group, with a significant difference between the two groups ($t(133) = -2.44$, $p = .02$, two-tailed). There was no significant difference between the two groups on the facilitating anxiety scale. Next, the learning style orchestrations of the two groups were compared. Frequencies of membership in the four categories appear in Table 5. A chi-square test showed no significant differences in the distribution between the two groups.

Table 4. Means and standard deviations by group and test, and differences between the groups

	Student group										
	Interpreting			Control			Total				
	n	Mean	SD	n	Mean	SD	n	Mean	SD	t	p
Wisconsin Card Sorting Test											
Errors	28	15.8	7.50	35	20.1	10.39	63	18.2	9.40	−1.91	.06
Perseverative Errors	28	3.9	3.05	35	6.8	5.39	63	5.5	4.70	−2.70	<.01
Learning-to-Learn Index	26	−5.4	11.23	28	−1.0	12.89	54	−3.2	12.21	−1.33	.19
Inventory of Learning Styles											
Meaning-directed	32	96.0	13.37	99	92.9	16.02	131	93.7	15.42	1.00	.32
Reproduction-directed	32	100.8	13.59	99	102.8	13.15	131	102.3	13.23	−.73	.47
Achievement Motivation Test											
Achievement Motive	32	23.1	8.43	103	20.6	6.87	135	21.2	7.31	1.69	.09
Debilitating Anxiety	32	12.8	5.33	103	15.7	5.94	135	15.0	5.91	−2.44	.02
Facilitating Anxiety	32	11.5	4.94	103	10.6	4.38	135	10.8	4.51	.91	.38

Table 5. Frequencies of learning styles orchestrations by group

Orchestrations	Interpreting n	Control n	Total n
Low meaning/reproduction	6	32	38
High meaning/low reproduction	11	21	32
Low meaning/high reproduction	8	15	23
High meaning/reproduction	7	31	38
Total	32	99	131

With "Student group" spanning the three data columns.

Analysis 2: Prediction of successful completion of interpreter training

Of the 32 participants who self-selected for conference or liaison interpreting, 14 continued to study in the conference interpreting training programme and sat their final exams. This cumulative sample comprised seven students from the 2007—2008 conference interpreting cohort and seven students who attended the liaison interpreting programme in 2007—2008 and progressed into the conference interpreting programme in 2008—2009. In this next section, we will explore the same tests and their ability to predict successful completion of conference interpreting training.

Method

Participants

The participants were 14 conference interpreter training programme students: 11 (79%) females and three males; the mean age was 23.1 years (s. d. 4.29). The participants were divided into two groups, pass and fail, depending on their overall final interpreting exam result.

Materials and procedure

Participants' scores from the same three tests (ILS, AMT, WCST) were included. Additionally, a measure of their interpreting performance was taken, consisting of a simple pass/fail grade for their overall final interpreting exam result.

The final exam is taken at the end of the one-year conference interpreter training programme. Students are tested in both consecutive and simultaneous interpreting for each of their two languages. The tests are administered individually by a jury of 10 to 15 members composed of (a) Lessius interpreting trainers, (b) external examiners. Jury members are professional interpreters with working languages corresponding to those of the student and Dutch language teachers (who assess the quality of the target language). Each student receives a different text, which is delivered by an invited native speaker (often an interpreter as well). Consecutive interpreting with notes is approximately six minutes long and simultaneous interpreting approximately 12 minutes long. Students are judged on the quality of content and form and are awarded a pass or fail mark for each of the four tests. The performance is reviewed by a jury, which then determines the mark. To graduate, the student must receive a pass mark on all four tests. Failed students may resit the exam once after the summer break.

For the purposes of this study, we considered only the final result, i. e. an overall pass or fail. The fail mark does not distinguish between students who failed all tests and those who failed only one. Students who had failed at the first attempt but passed on a resit (which is still considered a part of the regular academic year) were included as passing.

Results

The descriptive statistics for the two groups of students are summarised in Table 6. A total of eight students passed their final interpreting exam, and six students failed. In order to maximise the use of data, missing cases were excluded, analysis by analysis, which led to variable sample sizes for individual tests. A two-tailed t-test was carried out to test for differences between the pass and fail groups; none of the tests reached significance. Next, we compared the two groups separately to the control group of bachelors students on each test (Table 6) and on learning style orchestrations. A two-tailed t-test demonstrated that passing students made significantly fewer errors than control students on the WCST (means 13. 0 (s. d. 5. 00) and 20. 1 (s. d. 10. 39) respectively, $t(40)=2. 75$, $p=. 01$) and also fewer perseverative errors (means 2. 4 (s. d. 1. 62) and 6. 8 (s. d. 5. 39) respectively, $t(40)=3. 96$, $p<. 001$). Passing students also reported marginally significantly lower scores on the debilitating anxiety scale of AMT (means 12. 6 (s. d. 4. 41) and 15. 7 (s. d. 5. 94) respectively, $t(109)=1. 86$, $p<. 1$) and significantly higher scores on the facilitating anxiety scale of AMT (means 13. 9 (s. d. 3. 91) and 10. 6 (s. d. 4. 38) respectively, $t(109)=-2. 05$, $p=. 04$). No other test yielded significant differences between the passing and the control group. The failing students reported a marginally significantly lower score on the reproduction-directed learning style than the control group (means 92. 8 (s. d. 14. 29) and 102. 8 (s. d. 13. 15) respectively, $t(103)=1. 79$, $p=. 08$) and a significantly lower score on the debilitating anxiety scale of AMT (means 9. 2 (s. d. 4. 96) and 15. 7 (s. d. 5. 94), $t(107)=2. 64$, $p=. 01$). Due to the very small sample size of the passing and failing students, tests were not carried out on the orchestrations of learning styles and only visual representation of the results is presented in Figure 1, which shows a scatterplot of the meaning-directed and reproduction-directed learning styles plotted against each other. The vertical and horizontal lines are drawn at the means for the meaning-directed and reproduction-directed learning styles in the control group of bachelors students, dividing the space into quadrants representing the four orchestrations described in the method section: low meaning/low reproduction, high meaning/low reproduction, high meaning/high reproduction and low meaning/high reproduction. Passing students are represented in three quadrants (low meaning/low reproduction, high meaning/low reproduction and low meaning/high reproduction). Failing students are also represented in three quadrants (low meaning/low reproduction, high meaning/low reproduction and high meaning/high reproduction).

Table 6. Means and standard deviations by group and test, and differences between each group and the control group of bachelors students

	Student group										
	Pass					Fail					
	n	Mean	SD	Difference from control		n	Mean	SD	Difference from control		
				t	p				t	p	
Wisconsin Card Sorting Test											
Errors	7	13.0	5.00	2.75	.01	6	19.7	9.71	.09	.93	
Perseverative Errors	7	2.4	1.62	3.96	<.001	6	5.0	3.41	.78	.44	
Learning-to-Learn Index	7	−3.5	13.44	.4	5.65	5	−10.6	16.18	1.47	.15	
Inventory of Learning Styles											
Meaning-directed	8	95.5	10.03	−.47	.64	6	100.8	9.17	−1.22	.23	
Reproduction-directed	8	97.3	13.87	1.14	.26	6	92.8	14.29	1.79	.08	
Achievement Motivation Test											
Achievement Motive	8	23.7	4.20	−1.26	.21	6	21.0	8.29	−.13	.90	
Debilitating Anxiety	8	12.6	4.41	1.86	<.1	6	9.2	4.96	2.64	.01	
Facilitating Anxiety	8	13.9	3.91	−2.05	.04	6	12.5	5.79	−1.02	.31	

Discussion

The aim of this paper was to explore the role of the so-called soft skills, such as motivation and learning, in student interpreters' success in completing interpreter training programmes. These skills were previously hypothesised as being contributing factors (Timarová & Ungoed-Thomas, 2008; Shaw et al., 2008), but so far not systematically researched. This study focused on three such skills, namely learning styles, cognitive flexibility and motivation and anxiety, and explored them in two ways. First, we looked at their possible role in students' self-selection for interpreter training, and second, at the ability of several tests of the selected skills to predict successful completion of training.

As for self-selection, individuals opting for an interpreter training programme were found to differ from a control group of third-year applied language studies students on two tests. Self-selected interpreting students were found to show higher cognitive flexibility, as measured by a lower number of errors and perseverative errors on the Wisconsin Card Sorting Test (WCST), and to report higher achievement motive and lower debilitating anxiety on the Achievement Motivation Test (AMT). Higher cognitive flexibility would indicate that those individuals are, in general terms, more ready to cope with situations requiring innovative solutions to problems, problem solving and adaptability and to perform better in ill-defined domains with few if any fixed rules and structure. The WCST, more specifically, offers such a situation in that it requires the participant to respond to stimuli without being offered any instructions as to what constitutes a correct action. Moreover, the rules that guide decisions change throughout the task without the participant's knowledge. The errors measure reflects participants' ability to successfully navigate in such a "fuzzy" situation. The perseverative errors measure reflects the speed at which participants are able to adjust to the new rules once they find out that the old rules no longer apply. Interpreter training can be seen as an ill-defined domain, requiring students to make global (process-based) adjustments to their approach to interpreting on the basis of often very local (product-based) feedback. The two measures were found to be related to students' success in completing the training programme. Specifically, students who successfully completed conference interpreter training were found to make fewer errors and fewer perseverative errors than the control group of bachelors students. Also the failing students made fewer errors and perseverative errors than the control group, but their mean scores did not significantly differ from those of the controls.

As for motivation and anxiety, the administered test measured self-reported scores on three scales: achievement motive (general preference for achievement of goals and task completion) and two types of anxiety: debilitating and facilitating. Both are related to people's response to situations which may induce some level of stress. Debilitating anxiety has a negative effects on performance and facilitating anxiety benefits performance. Students who self-selected for interpreting had reported marginally higher scores on the achievement motive scale and a lower score on the debilitating anxiety scale. The achievement motive suggests a certain level of drive to perform and, taken together with higher cognitive flexibility, may indicate individuals who actively seek novel and challenging situations. The lower score on the debilitating anxiety scale, on the other hand, suggests greater tolerance of stress, again a trait highly desirable in interpreters (Moser-Mercer, 1994, Jiménez & Pinazo, 2001).

Turning to the AMT as a predictor of student success, both passing and failing conference interpreting students had a higher mean score on the achievement motive scale (with passing students scoring higher than failing students), but this difference did not reach significance. The debilitating anxiety scale, on the other hand, yielded a similar result in that both passing and failing students had lower scores than the control group, although the passing students only marginally so. Interestingly, the failing students were the group with the lowest scores. This finding goes against the more intuitive expectation that failing students would be more affected by debilitating anxiety than passing students and provides some intriguing food for thought. It is possible that passing students (who also scored higher on facilitating anxiety, to be discussed next) develop better coping techniques to counteract the negative effects of anxiety, or that other factors which come into play attenuate it. This explanation is consistent with the findings reported by Jiménez and Pinazo (2001, 2002), who did not find a negative effect of anxiety on student consecutive interpreting performance even though students reported medium-high to high levels of anxiety. Passing students were also the only group that differed significantly from the control group in terms of facilitating anxiety. This type of anxiety can be thought of, in layman's terms, as excitement, arousal, perhaps even adrenaline. Interpreting is stressful and so is interpreter training. The finding that successful students are those who seem to benefit from a certain level of anxiety is very much in keeping with many trainers' expectations.

Finally, we explored students' learning preferences using the Inventory of Learning Styles (ILS) test. We calculated three measures: two for learning styles and one for more complex patterns of learning. In the analysis of self-selection, we did not find any difference between students who self-select for interpreting and the control group. In the group of conference interpreting students, the failing students scored marginally lower on their preference for the reproduction-directed learning style. This would suggest they are less dependent on a structured learning environment and external teacher support. In this respect the higher scores of the successful students came as a surprise and appeared to suggest the need for further research. Taking a look at the learning style orchestrations shown in Figure 1, we note with interest that conference interpreting students are not equally represented in all quadrants. With the exception of the high meaning/low reproduction quadrant, conference interpreting students seem to cluster around the means (the intersecting axes) of the control group. This also applies to the four cases of students in the two least represented quadrants-low meaning/low representation and high meaning/high representation. Unfortunately our sample was too small to allow statistical analyses, but based on the visual inspection, we propose the following interpretation: The instrument allows for a calculation of four different styles, only two of which were calculated, as these are most representative of regular university students. It is possible that the control group students scoring low on both meaning-directed and reproduction-directed learning styles have a different dominant learning style than the two considered here. From the perspective of the two selected styles, this quadrant represents individuals with a low preference for either. In that respect, it is encouraging to see that conference interpreters have clearer preferences. Similarly, the high meaning/high reproduction quadrant represents students who scored high on two ostensibly conflicting styles (cf. Lindblom-Ylanne & Lonka, 1999 for a more detailed discussion of conflicting styles). This may indicate a certain confusion and uncertainty in approaching learning difficulties and learning itself. These implications were not explored in the present study, and are only being offered as a possible explanation. The remaining two quadrants, high meaning/low reproduction and low meaning/high reproduction, represent more clearly defined learning style preferences, and this is where we find most conference interpreting students. While we cannot support this claim with a more detailed analysis we would suggest that in comparison to the control group, conference interpreting students have fewer conflicting learning preferences and patterns than the control group, although there does not seem to be a clear difference between passing and failing students.

In conclusion, we were able to detect some patterns and differences in soft skills both in terms of self-selection and in terms of prediction of successful completion of a conference interpreter training programme. By comparing self-selected interpreting students to a control group of third-year bachelor students, we found that those who self-select for interpreting are cognitively more flexible, are more achievement-driven and suffer less from stress. Similarly, successful conference interpreting programme graduates were found to be cognitively more flexible, to suffer less from stress and to benefit more from positive anxiety than the control group. Unsuccessful conference interpreting students, on the other hand, did not show any difference in cognitive flexibility and differed from the control group only in that they too suffered less from stress. Both groups of conference interpreting students have also shown a clearer preference for a single dominant learning style. Given the very small size of our samples, these patterns and differences should be viewed as tendencies rather than facts and need to be confirmed and elaborated upon by further research. That said, the findings do seem to provide preliminary evidence that soft skills may indeed be important, if complementary, contributing factors of interpreting aptitude.

选文二　口译课程群建设的必要性及其策略

马纳琴

导　言

随着我国在政治、经济、文化等方面对外交往的日趋频繁,社会对口译的需求急剧增加,口译工作出现了前所未有的繁荣局面,国家对口译人员的专业化训练更加重视。许多高等院校纷纷设立翻译专业,开设口译课。这为培养专业口译人员提供了良好的外部环境。但是由于口译教学理论和方法的研究相对滞后,口译教学在不少方面,比如开设口译课的时间、口译教学的原则、内容与训练方法等，都存在着值得进一步探讨和改进的地方。有些口译课程或多或少地还在沿用笔译课程的教学模式，教学上主要解决的仍是语言翻译的问题。虽然口译和笔译的根本任务和性质是相同的，但口译和笔译又具有各自不同的特点和要求，因此口译教学应结合口译的特点，确立有别于笔译教学的原则和策略。作为口译教学改革方面的一次尝试，选文针对目前口译课程大多不符合口译自身特点的现状，从分析口译的特点出发，探索了口译课程群建设的相关对策，提出了强化课程群意识和体现口译技能技巧培养的阶段性这两条宏观原则，以及数条可以分年级段予以实施的具体教学措施。

随着我国对外交流的不断扩大，对口译人才的需求也进一步增长。鉴于此，很多综合性大学的英语专业都不约而同地在近几年开设了口译课，有不少院校甚至将口译作为一个专业方向来设置，但口译课的教学效果并不是十分理想，远远不能满足我国对口译人才的需求。怎样才能在本科 4 年有限的时间尽可能最大限度地提高学生的口译能力，科学合理的课程群建设应该是走出口译培训瓶颈的有效途径。

一、课程群建设的意义

课程是实现人才培养目标的重要载体，在人才培养体系中发挥着重要的作用。但单一的课程建设并不能优化课程和师资资源，提高教学效率。而科学合理地构建适应人才培养目标的课程体系，把课程体系中内在联系紧密的多门课程建设成课程群，对专业人才培养效率的提高具有重要意义。课程群是若干相关课程的集合。李慧仙将课程群的概念及本质特征归纳为以下几点：1. 课程群是将教学计划中相互影响，可构成完整的教学体系的课程的重新规划；2. 课程群是由 3 门以上性质相关或相近的课程构成的课程集合，它们之间结构合理，层次清晰，内容相互渗透并具有互补性；3. 课程群应该是指从属于某个学科、相互之间有着合理分工、能满足不同专业教学要求的系统化的课程群体。李慧仙认为课程群的建设可以跨专业、跨学科来进行。而付八军等人在文章中指出教学型的课程群是针对一定专业的同一施教对象而进行的课程捆绑。本文中涉及的课程群建设是指针对某一专业方向的学生进行的课程群建设。这样的课程群建设有利于教育者树立立体思维和整体观念，有利于提高教育效率和效益、减少课程设置间的重复、加强课程间的联系，使课程设置紧密相关，有序合理。而口译方向的课程群建设应从口译的特点入手、掌握口译课程与其他课程所教授知识间的内在联系、综合考虑课程内容、理论知识、实践内容等方面的因素，构建合理的课程群。

二、口译的特点

（一）口译的即时性

口译要求译员在特定的语境下对原语和目的语进行双向的解码与转换。口译员的思维在短时间内必须经过 3 个转换过程：从原语的语言符号到内容的转换——即理解

(Comprehension)；从内容到记忆的转换——即记忆(Memorizing)；从记忆到表达的转换——即用译语表达原语意思(Reformulation)。

这3个转换过程几乎是同时进行的。因此，口译人员需要在准备有限、口译内容无法全面预测的情况下，即刻进入双语语码切换状态。

(二) 口译的综合性

口译是一种综合运用听、说、读、写、译等各项技能的语言操作活动。交替传译要求译员在听到一段语言内容后，立即用译入语将内容准确无误地传译给对方。同声传译要求译员在听到原语的同时，用译入语传译其内容，因此，要求译员同时调动听、说、读、写、译技能，圆满地完成口译任务。

(三) 口译内容的繁杂性和不可预测性

对译员的理想要求通常是具有百科全书般的知识结构，这是因为口译内容会涉及社会、政治、经济、军事等各方面的内容，只要是世界上存在的事物或现象，在口译中都有可能会涉及。而口译内容又具有不可预测性，尽管译员在进行口译工作前有可能会了解口译主题，作充分的译前准备，但译员只能对口译主题所涉及的内容进行详细全面的了解并熟悉专业术语，仍然不能对所有的口译内容做出预测。

(四) 口译的高压力性

口译的工作强度和压力都很大。口译通常现场气氛严肃，场面正式，而发言人通常是领导或某一领域的专家学者。这一氛围会给译员造成很大的心理压力，影响译员的自信和正常发挥。

(五) 口译的跨文化交际性

口译不仅是一种即席的双语语码转换行为，也是一种跨文化交际行为，要求译员除了进行口头翻译之外，还要阐释语言之外的丰富文化内涵。因此，译员不仅要有扎实的语言基本功，还要熟悉了解两种文化背景知识，在进行语言翻译的同时，要具有跨文化交际意识，灵活应对文化障碍。

三、口译课程群建设的对策

(一) 口译课程群建设的宏观原则

1. 强化课程群意识

口译要求综合运用听、说、读、写、译等技能，即时完成口译任务。这对语言专业学生的要求是非常高的，而这一要求仅仅靠在高年级开设一至两学期口译课程是无法达到的，这需要有意识地将口译中基本技能的训练延伸至低年级。在低年级，加强听、说、读、笔译等单一技能的培训，为综合运用各项技能打下坚实的基础。因此，需要不断强化领导和授课教师的课程群意识，将教师按照不同的专业方向分成不同的课程小组，口译课程群小组的教师应定期沟通，在口语、听力、笔译、跨文化交际、公共演说等其他课程中完成口译培训的部分内容,将更多的提高和实践时间留给口译课程,提高口译课程的效率。

2. 体现口译技能技巧培养的阶段性

建构主义教学理论认为知识的学习是学习者新旧知识经验间反复双向的相互作用的结果,新知识是建立在以往习得知识的基础之上的。教学应该循序渐进,从低一级的技能向较高一级技能逐渐过渡。因此,口译教学的课程设置应当体现口译技能技巧培养的阶段性。口译从低一级到高一级的基本技能训练分别包括(1)短期记忆能力的培养:即通过听信息回答问题、听信息与复述、听信息与原语综述、听信息与概要翻译等提高学生的短期记忆能力,这一阶段的训练以无笔记训练为主,也就是说所有内容的记忆以大脑记忆为主。(2)口译笔记训练:该阶段教师介绍常用的笔记符号,要求学生运用可行的笔记符号和关键词记忆原语内容,并在听力结束后依据笔记进行复述、综述、翻译等练习。(3)主题思想识别训练:释意派理论认为口译的基本准则是意译。因此,主题思想识别训练的根本目的是训练学生在听力中理解原语的主题和中心内容,进而在译入语中重新组织语言内容。(4)目的语信息重组:这一阶段要求学生从原语复述逐渐过渡到译入语复述,并在信息重组的基础上进行有效的即时口译。除以上提到的基本技能训练外,同声传译还包括影子跟读练习、同声即席传译练习等。在语言技能培训的基础上,必要的公共演说技巧培训,跨文化交际交流意识的培养也十分重要。因此,在构建课程群过程中,应将以上语言技能及其他辅助技能和意识的培养依次从低年级到高年级贯穿于语音、口语、听力、汉语、报刊选读、笔译、跨文化交际交流、公共演讲、口译等课程中。

(二)口译课程群建设的具体措施

本人在研读其他专家学者的相关论文,并对我校英语专业四年级学生进行随机访谈后,建议将以下几门课程列入口译课程群中,它们包括语音、口语、听力、汉语、报刊选读、笔译、跨文化交际交流、公共演讲、口译。同时认为选择口译方向的学生必须选修课程群内的课程。具体课程设置和理由如下:

1. 一年级开设语音课

目前,我校在一年级开设了语音课,但时间为一学期,学生普遍认为开设时间过短,语音课内容理论性偏强,没有真正起到让学生了解基本发音规则、纠正不良语音、培养准确语音语调的目的,不能满足他们的需求。由于口译对译员语言基本功的要求很高,发音不准确意味着不能从事口译工作,而刚进入大学学习的英语专业学生往往带着不同的地方音,有很大一部分学生的语音、语调不准确,教师必须彻底纠正,使其趋于标准。因此,语音课不但应纳入口译课程群,而且应该延长学时,请有经验的教师从发音规则入手,注重课堂的实效性,针对每一位同学的弱点,提出有效的语音改进措施,培养学生良好的语音语调。

2. 一年级开设口语课

目前,我校将口语、听力课组合为视听说课,学制两年,由外籍教师授课,据笔者了解,很多综合性高校都是这样设置的。我校学生认为外籍教师授课以游戏为主,没有严格的教学计划和合理的教学进度,课堂氛围松散无序,学生学到的内容有限。结合学生的意见和本人对外籍教师授课内容的了解,本人认为口语和听力课应该分开,口语课可以由外籍教师授课,而听力课应由中国教师授课。良好的口语基础是口译的必要条件。口译要求译员不仅能听懂标准语音,还能听懂不同的方言,而外籍教师教授口语课可以给学生输入地道、准确的语言,同时,操不同方言的外籍教师授课还可以增强学生对方言的敏感度,这是中国教师无法替代的。在教学方法方面,外籍教师更注重语言的交际功能和学生自学能力的培养,会给学生创造运用语言交流的机会,会要求学生利用网络、图书馆等资源查阅资料,分组解决某一问题,并在课堂上相互交流所得信息,这对学生表达能力、公共演说能力的培养大有裨益。

3. 一、二年级开设听力课

我校学生认为听力课应由中国教师授课,最好是由上口译课的教师授课。本人认为该建议十分可取。传统的听力课主要以精听和泛听为主,精听注重的焦点是语言材料本身,要求学生在听力过程中记住细微的语言信息,在听的过程中抓住"when,where,what,why,who,how"等信息,并在掌握关键信息的基础上复述听到的内容。泛听注重听的速度、数量以及对文章的整体理解,要求学生基本了解语言信息发生的时间、地点、情节以及围绕情节出现的人物,提纲挈领并能回答简单问题。精听和泛听能力的培养在听力训练的初级阶段是十分有效的方式,但作为口译课程群中的一门基础课,听力课在基本能力训练的基础上,还应将听力训练的内容与口译技能的培养有机地结合起来。精听和泛听更注重对语言材料信息的准确把握、了解和复述。而口译要求培养学生的认知记忆。即要求学生依据"释意理论"原则,了解口译的基本要求是意义的翻译,而不是具体词语和结构的翻译,忘掉语言等值,把字词结构看做信息的传递物,掌握语言信息意思以及它们之间的逻辑关系,用译入语将语言信息的意思重新表达出来。因此,在开设听力课的第二年,应有意识地培养学生的认知记忆能力,要求学生通过听信息回答问题、原语复述、原语综述等练习形式将听到的语言信息材料梳理成主题明确、语意连贯、逻辑性强的材料。语言训练材料可以由浅入深、由易到难,从条理性强的故事到专业的科研报告,从逻辑性、连贯性的发言到次序颠倒的讲话。以此达到培养学生短期记忆、认知记忆的目的。

4. 二年级开设汉语课

口译是两种语言的交流,是两种文化的交流。只有熟练地掌握了两种语言,才能在进行口译时游刃有余。对中国的学生而言,母语应该比外语掌握得好,但是现在学生的母语水平也是很让人担忧的。在具体口译过程中,学生英汉双语转换中存在的问题层出不穷。最典型的问题是中文水平欠佳,很多英译中的即时口译语序和句型结构都采用英文结构,翻译出来的句子往往不合乎中文习惯。如"他太小了以至于不能上学","他被美丽的景色震惊了"等。因此,汉语课也应纳入口译课程群,选择口译专业方向的学生应修读现代汉语或大学语文等课程。对汉语语法、修辞等有更深刻的了解。但是,通过修读一两门课程达到根本提高汉语水平的目的是不现实的,还需要教师不断强调汉语的重要性,要求学生将汉语阅读贯穿于大学4年的学习中。

5. 二、三年级开设跨文化交际交流、报刊选读等课程

口译不仅是语言的沟通,也是文化的交流。在跨文化交际中,交际双方的文化背景不同,传统习惯以及思维和行为模式各异,这就构成了文化障碍。文化障碍给理解和沟通带来了很大的困难。口译工作者在交际交流中,应充分考虑文化个性和差异,帮助交流双方有效地沟通。因此,跨文化交际交流和报刊选读等课程在口译课程群中具有十分重要的地位。在本人进行的随机调查中,学生认为报刊选读课程对他们的口译具有很大的帮助,原因是报刊选读课程内容繁杂,涉及政治、经济、军事、社会文化等各个领域,具有一定的广度和深度。通过该课程的学习,学生对英美国家的文化背景有了一定的了解,同时也掌握了部分不同领域的专业术

语,拓宽了知识面,为高年级的口译课打下了良好的基础。学生同时反映欧洲文化、跨文化交际交流等课程提高了他们对背景文化的理解,使他们对中西方文化差异有了一定的认识,初步建立了文化批评的视角。我校开设了至少3门跨文化交际交流方面的课程,在口译课程群建设中,可以选择一门比较经典的课程,以减少课程设置间的重复,达到提高学习效率的目的,但报刊选读课应纳入口译课程群中的必修课。

6. 三年级分别开设笔译课和口译课

目前,我校在三年级第二学期同时开设笔译和口译课程,但学生认为笔译课程应当开设在口译课程之前,而且笔译课也应以实践为主,不宜过多阐释理论知识。学生的这一要求在部分研究者的论述中也得到了一定程度的论证。王晓燕在其论文中指出笔译与口译密不可分,相辅相成,其中的道理是相同的,翻译技巧也是相通的。而张捷、宋立明在文章中指出口译与笔译的标准和要求不同,笔译要求"信、达、雅"或"信、达、优"。由于笔译对译者的时间要求相对宽松,译者有时间思考、推敲、查询资料。因此对笔译准确度和严谨度的要求也高于口译。而口译要求"准确、通顺、快捷"。由于口译工作压力大,无推敲过程,口译的句子结构相对松散,严谨度较弱。鉴于以上研究结论,本人认为将笔译开设在口译之前有一定依据。由于口译与笔译道理相同,翻译技巧相通,而笔译时间要求相对宽松,学生可以在笔译课中了解翻译的基本技巧,在没有时间压力的状况下熟悉双语转换过程,提高双语转换能力,进一步推敲汉语和英语句型结构的异同,了解增词、减词、直译、意译等基本方法。在进行一段时间的笔译训练基础上,再进行口译训练可能会达到事半功倍的效果。

尽管学生建议将公共演说技巧课程纳入口译课程群,但无论从课时安排还是从师资配备角度似乎都不太可行,将公共演说技巧贯穿于口译课程群的其他课程中可能更具有操作性。口语、听力、跨文化交际交流等课程中都可以要求学生面对大家讨论观点、发表见解、演讲、做专题报告等。通过多种形式,提高学生的胆略和演讲策略。循序渐进地学习以上课程,在语音、口语、听力、笔译等课程中完成部分口译技能的培训,在其他相关课程中提高口译意识和跨文化交际意识后,再开设口译课,会让学生将更多的课堂时间用在数字口译、目的语信息重组、模拟会议口译、口译应对策略等口译技能方面,从而大大提高口译课程的效率,给学生留出更多口译实战的机会。

【延伸阅读】

1. Bromberg, Jinny & Jesionowski, Irina. Trends in court interpreter training. *Multilingual*. 2010, 21 (4): 35-39.

2. Gile, Daniel. *Basic concepts and models for interpreter and translator training*. Amsterdam/Philadelphia: John Benjamins Publishing Company, 1995.

3. van Dyk, Jeanne. Multilingual news websites as a resource for interpreter training. *Southern African Linguistics and Applied Language Studies*. 2010, 28 (3): 291-297.

4. Wang, Binhua & Mu, Lei. Interpreter training and research in mainland China: Recent developments. *Interpreting*. 2009, 11 (2): 267-283.

5. 陈菁. 口译教学应如何体现口译的特点. 中国翻译. 1997(6):25-28.

6. 陈振东,李澜. 基于网络和语料库的口译教学策略探索. 外语电化教学. 2009(125): 9-13.

7. 方健壮. 口译教学改革刍议. 中国科技翻译. 1998,11(1):38-41.

8. 郭兰英. 口译与口译人才培养研究. 北京:科学出版社,2007.

9. 刘和平. 口译理论与教学. 北京:中国对外翻译出版公司,2005.

10. 刘建珠. 基于工学结合的口译人才培养模式研究. 职业教育研究. 2009:139-140.

11. 刘靖之. 香港的翻译与口译教学. 中国翻译. 2001,22(3):36-43.

12. 刘宗和. 论翻译教学. 北京:商务印书馆,2001.

13. 马继红. 口译课堂教学策略. 解放军外国语学院学报. 2003(5):36-39.

14. 舒菲. 大课堂口译教学中分组协作与竞争机制的引入. 贵州师范大学学报. 2004(4):22-26.

15. 杨承淑. 口译教学研究:理论与实践. 北京:中国对外翻译出版公司,2005.

16. 杨峰. 释意理论对口译与口译教学的启示. 江西广播电视大学学报. 2008(4):99-101.

17. 张蕾. 以学生为中心的口译员心理素质培养模式. 文教资料. 2006(21):20-23.

【问题与思考】

1. 口译教学与培训中应如何定位学生的角色？如果以学生为中心,那么这样的口译员培养模式有何积极意义？

2. 口译课堂的教学策略主要有哪些？分别举例论述。

3. 谈一谈口译培训中应如何有效地对译员进行跨文化意识的培养。

4. 当前法庭口译培训有什么特点和趋势？

5. 在口译培训方面,比较著名的有厦大模式、广外大模式以及3P模式等。对于非英语专业的学生来说,哪一种口译培训模式更适合,为什么？

参考文献

Baker, Mona. Corpus linguistics and translation studies: Implications and applications. Baker, M., Francis, G. and Tognini-Bonnelli, E. (eds.) *Text and technology: In honor of John Sinclair*. Amesterdam/John Benjamins. 1993: 233-250.

Baker, Mona (ed.). *Routledge encyclopedia of Translation Studies*. London & NY.: Routledge, 1998.

Bertone, Laura E. *The hidden side of Babel unveiling cognition, intelligence and sense through simultaneous interpretation*. Buenos Aires: Evolucion, 2006.

Bromberg, Jinny & Jesionowski, Irina. Trends in court interpreter training. *Multilingual*. 2010, 21 (4): 35-39.

Colina, Sonia. Further evidence for a functionalist approach to translation quality evaluation. *Target: International Journal on Translation Studies*. 2009, 21 (2): 235-264.

Cranefield, Jocelyn & Yoong, Pak. The role of the translator/interpreter in knowledge transfer environments. *Knowledge and Process Management*. 2007, 14 (2): 95-103.

Timarová, Šárka & Salaets, Heidi. Learning styles, motivation and cognitive flexibility in interpreter training: Self-selection and aptitude. *Interpreting*. 2011, 13 (1): 31-52.

van Dyk, Jeanne. Multilingual news websites as a resource for interpreter training. *Southern African Linguistics and Applied Language Studies*. 2010, 28 (3): 291-297.

Wang, Binhua & Mu, Lei. Interpreter training and research in mainland China: Recent developments. *Interpreting*. 2009, 11 (2): 267-283.

de Leon, Celia Martín. Skopos and beyond: A critical study of functionalism. *Target: International Journal on Translation Studies*. 2008, 20 (1): 1-28.

Denhière, G. & Baudet S.. *Lecture, compréhension de texte et sciences cognitives*. PUF, Paris, 1992.

Edwards, R., Temple, B. & Alexander, C.. Users' experiences of interpreters: The critical role of trust. *Interpreting*. 2005, 7 (1): 77-95.

Elliott, Lawrence. Interpreters in the world. *The world of English*. 1987 (6): 106-114.

Gile, Daniel. Methodological aspects of interpretation and translation research. Lambert et al. (eds.) *Bridging the gap: Empirical research in simultaneous interpretation*. Amsterdam and Philadelphia: John Benjamins Publishing Company. 1994: 39-56.

Gile, Daniel. *Basic concepts and models for interpreter and translator training*. Amsterdam and Philadelphia: John Benjamins Publishing Company, 1995.

Halliday, M. A. K.. The gloosy ganoderm: Systemic functional linguistics and translation. *Chinese Translators Journal*. 2009(1): 17-26.

Hertog, Erik. Book review of *Multilingualism and educational interpreting: Innovation and delivery*. Marlene Verhoef and Theodorus du Plessis (eds.) (2008). Pretoria: Van Schaik Publishers. *Interpreting*. 2010, 12 (2): 263-267.

Horváth, Ildikó. Creativity in interpreting. *Interpreting*. 2010, 12 (2): 146-159.

Lederer, Marianne. *La traduction aujourd'hui, le modèle Interprétatif*. Paris: Hachette, 1994.(刘和平译. 释意学派口笔译理论. 北京:中国对外翻译出版公司,2001.)

Newmark, Peter. *A textbook of translation*. London: Prentice Hall, 1988.

Pawlak, Mirosl-aw & Bielak, Jakub. *New Perspectives in Language, Discourse and Translation Studies*. New York: Springer-Verlag Berlin Heidelberg, 2011.

Picken, Catriona (Ed.). *The translator's handbook*. (2nd ed.). London: Aslib, The Association for Information Management, 1989.

Pöchhacker, F.. *Introducing interpreting studies*. London: Routledge, 2004.

Riccardi, A.. Interpreting strategies and creativity. A. Beylard-Ozeroff, J. Kralová & B. Moser-Mercer (eds.). *Translators' strategies and creativity: Selected papers from the 9th International Conference on Translation and Interpreting, Prague, September 1995*. Amsterdam/Philadelphia: John Benjamins. 1998: 171-180.

Roberts, Roda P. Book review of *Testing and assessment in translation and interpreting studies*. Claudia V. Angelelli and Holly E. Jacobson (eds.) Amsterdam/Philadelphia: John Benjamins. *Interpreting*. 2009, 13 (1): 143-148.

·Schuster, Michal. Book review of *Crossing borders in community interpreting: Definitions and dilemmas*, 2010. Carmen Valero-Garcés and Anne Martín (eds.) Amsterdam/Philadelphia: John Benjamins. *Interpreting*. 2008, 12 (1): 115-119.

Seleskovitch, Danica. *L'interpréte dans les conférences internationales, problème de langue et de communication*. Minard, Paris: Lettres modernes, 1968.[孙慧双译. 口译技巧. 北京:北京出版社,1979.]

Seleskovitch, Danica. *Interpreting for international conferences*. trans. by Dailey, Stephanie & McMillan, Eric N. Washington, DC: Pan & Booth, 1978.

·Seleskovitch, Danica & Lederer, Marianne. *Interpréter pour traduire*. Paris: Didier Erudition, 1984.(汪家荣等译. 口译理论实践与教学. 北京:旅游教育出版社,1990.)

Seleskovitch, Danica & Lederer, M. *A systematic approach to teaching interpretation*. trans. by J. Harmer. Luxembourg and Diere. Erudition: The Office for Official Publications of the European Communities, 1989.

Setton, R. *Simultaneous interpretation: A cognitive-pragmatic analysis*. Amsterdam: Benjamins, 1999.

Setton. Deconstructing SI: A contribution to the debate on component processes. *The interpreter's newsletter*. 2002(11): 1-26.

Shuttleworth, Mark & Cowie, M. *Dictionary of Translation Studies*. Michigan: St.

Jerome. Pub，1997.

Thomas，Alexander. *Kultur-und sprachenvielfalt in Europa*. Münster，New York：
Waxmann. 1991：192.

Vandeweghe，Willy，Vandepitte，Sonia & Velde，Marc van de（eds.）. The study of
language and translation. *Belgian Journal of Linguistics*. 2007(21)：1-200.

Vermeer，Hans J. *A Skopos Theory of translation*. TextconText Verlag，1996.

白枚. 口译的特点及标准. 大连民族学院学报. 2005(1)：14-18.

鲍刚. 口译理论概述. 北京：旅游教育出版社，1998.

鲍刚. 口译程序中的"思维理解". 北京第二外国语学院学报. 1999，87(1)：1-12.

蔡小红. 口译评估. 北京：中国对外翻译出版公司，2007.

蔡小红，方凡泉. 论口译的质量与效果评估. 外语与外语教学. 2003(3)：41-45.

常世儒. 口译中的释意与等效. 外语与外语教学. 2008，229(4)：61-63.

陈慧华. 浅析口译与跨文化交际. 考试周刊. 2008，(13)：215-216.

陈菁. 口译教学应如何体现口译的特点. 中国翻译. 1997(6)：25-28.

陈菁. 弗里斯的语言学理论与口译原则. 厦门大学学报. 2005，167(1)：125-128.

陈振东，李澜. 基于网络和语料库的口译教学策略探索. 外语电化教学. 2009(125)：9-13.

方健壮. 口译教学改革刍议. 中国科技翻译. 1998，11(1)：38-41.

付菁菁，付颖. 口译记忆的心理学基础及口译记忆策略. 武汉职业技术学院学报. 2009，8(3)：
117-119.

付天海，刘颖. 口译中的文化特征与思维建构. 外语与外语教学. 2006(2)：55-57.

龚龙生. 从释意理论看我国口译研究的发展. 西安外事学院学报. 2006(12)：34-36.

郭兰英. 口译与口译人才培养研究. 北京：科学出版社，2007.

郭怡军. 口译释意学派在中国的译介与进展. 昆明理工大学学报. 2008，8(2)：100-102.

何莉. 口译质量评估新探——并列信息忠实度的评估标准. 文学界. 2011(5)：13-16.

何庆机. 国内功能派翻译理论研究述评. 上海翻译. 2007(4)：16-20.

何瑜. 情绪因素对译员的影响. 文教资料. 2008(12)：54-56.

胡庚申，盛茜. 中国口译研究又十年. 中国科技翻译. 2000(2)：39-43.

胡开宝，郭鸿杰主编. 英汉语言对比与口译. 大连：大连理工大学出版社，2007.

胡开宝，陶庆. 汉英会议口译语料库的创建与应用研究. 中国翻译. 2009(5)：49-56.

黄蓓. 从释意派的视角论口译质量评估模式在会议口译中的应用——以政府领导人答中外记
者问之现场口译为例. 读与写. 2009(2)：21-24.

贾小妹. 口译过程中的心理负效应及其应对策略. 广东教育学院学报. 2010(4)：70-74.

蒋凤霞，吴湛. 口译的跨学科理论概述. 外国语文. 2011(27)2：79-84.

李春光. 口译中的文化缺省及其补偿策略. 继续教育研究. 2008(5)：157-158.

李金泽. 国内口译研究的历史与现状. 边疆经济与文化. 2010，74(2)：101-102.

李婧，李德超. 基于语料库的口译研究：回顾与展望. 中国外语. 2010(37)：100-105.

李明远. 认知心理学与口译课. 四川外语学院学报. 1998，70(4)：79-83.

李文中. 语料库、学习者语料库与外语教学. 外语界. 1999(1)：35-41.

李玉婷. 从目的论看翻译策略的选择. 学理论. 2011(24)：10-12.

李越然. 论口译的社会功能——口译理论基础初探. 中国翻译. 1999(3):7-11.

林煌天主编. 中国翻译词典. 武汉:湖北教育出版社,1997.

刘和平. 科技口译与质量评估. 上海科技翻译. 2002(1):33-37.

刘和平. 口译理论与教学. 北京:中国对外翻译出版公司,2005.

刘建珠. 基于工学结合的口译人才培养模式研究. 职业教育研究. 2009:139-140.

刘靖之. 香港的翻译与口译教学. 中国翻译. 2001,22(3):36-43.

刘宓庆. 口笔译理论研究. 北京:中国对外翻译出版公司,2006.

刘绍龙,王柳琪. 对近十年中国口译研究现状的调查与分析. 广东外语外贸大学学报. 2007(1):
37-40.

刘绍龙,夏忠燕. 中国翻译认知研究:问题、反思与展望. 外语研究. 2008,110(4):59-66.

刘影. 释意理论与口译策略研究. 边疆经济与文化. 2008,54(6):62-63.

刘宗和. 论翻译教学. 北京:商务印书馆,2001.

罗选民主编. 语言认知与翻译研究. 北京:外文出版社,2005.

马继红. 口译课堂教学策略. 解放军外国语学院学报. 2003(5):36-39.

马纳琴. 口译课程群建设的必要性及其策略. 西北民族大学学报. 2009(2):136-140.

梅德明. 英语高级口译资格证书考试口译教程. 上海:上海外语教育出版社,1996.

钱芳. 图式理论照应下的口译忠实度评估. 顺德职业技术学院学报. 2009,7(2):62-64.

邱进. 论口译中的文化障碍问题. 重庆工学院学报. 2005(10):107-110.

邱杨. 浅谈口译目的与标准. 四川教育学院学报. 2004(3):45-51.

舒菲. 大课堂口译教学中分组协作与竞争机制的引入. 贵州师范大学学报. 2004(4):22-26.

帅林. 跨学科口译理论研究在中国. 中国科技翻译. 2007(3):50-52.

唐姿. 语言·文本·翻译——论翻译研究的语言学派与独立的翻译学科的建立. 山东外语教
学. 2003(5):109-112.

王斌华,叶亮. 面向教学的口译语料库建设:理论与实践. 外语界. 2009,131(2):23-32.

王东风. 中国译学研究:世纪末的思考. 中国翻译. 1999(2):7-11.

王东志. 我国口译研究的现状和发展趋势——第六届口译大会综述. 广东外语外贸大学学报.
2007,18(3):109-111.

王妍,王新芳. 英语口译教学中跨文化意识的培养. 内蒙古电大学刊. 2008,106(6):108-109.

王永秋. 论口译的特点. 长春大学学报. 1996(1):47-49.

伍铁平. 语言与思维关系新探. 上海:上海外语教育出版社,1990.

吴莹. 认知心理学在口译记忆中的应用研究. 辽宁教育行政学院学报. 2010,27(4):104-105.

夏伟兰,文军. 打开口译理论的大门——评介刘宓庆的《口笔译理论研究》. 外国语言文学研究.
2006,6(1):66-69.

肖晓燕. 西方口译研究:历史与现状. 外国语. 2002(4):71-76.

谢一铭,王斌华. 目的论连贯原则在汉英外交口译中的体现——基于现场口译的语料分析. 中
国科技翻译. 2011(3):27-29.

熊毅. 口译认知过程的符号学阐释. 罗选民主编. 语言认知与翻译研究. 北京:外文出版社,
2005:340-351.

许明. 口译认知过程中"deverbalization"的认知诠释. 中国翻译. 2010(3):5-11.

许钧,袁筱一编著. 当代法国翻译理论. 南京:南京大学出版社,1998.

杨承淑. 口译教学研究:理论与实践. 北京:中国对外翻译出版公司,2005.

杨峰. 释意理论对口译与口译教学的启示. 江西广播电视大学学报. 2008(4):99-101.

杨英明. 论功能翻译理论. 中国翻译. 2001(6):39-42.

余郑璟. 开发口译学习者的非智力因素. 成都信息工程学院学报. 2008,23(4):469-472.

张柏然,许钧. 面向21世纪的译学研究. 北京:商务印书馆,2002.

张吉良. 巴黎释意学派口译理论成就谈. 中国科技翻译. 2009,22(4):16-19.

张吉良. 国际口译界有关巴黎释意学派口译理论的争议及其意义. 外语研究. 2010,119(1):72-79.

张静. 德国功能翻译学派理论对口译标准的启示. 中国电力教育. 2005(23):257-259.

张蕾. 以学生为中心的口译员心理素质培养模式. 文教资料. 2006(21):20-23.

张泪,蔡培培. 目的论下的陪同口译策略探究. 广西青年干部学院学报. 2011(3):16-18.

张培蓓,任静生. 评估口译忠实度的策略. 中国科技翻译. 2006(3):36-38.

张威. 口译语料库的开发与建设:理论与实践的若干问题. 中国翻译. 2009(3):54-58.

张燕. 口译技巧——论提高同声传译的质量. 中国翻译. 2002(4):66-69.

赵军峰,蒋楠. 论口译者的跨文化意识. 中国科技翻译. 1998(5):29-31.

赵彦春. 认知词典学探索. 上海:上海外语教育出版社,2003.

钟述孔. 实用口译手册. 北京:中国对外翻译出版公司,1999.

仲伟合. 巴比塔隐蔽的一面——通过同声传译揭开认知、智力和感知的面纱. 中国翻译. 2009(3):36-40.